JUST WORK

JUST WORK

Get Sh*t Done, Fast & Fair

KIM SCOTT

St. Martin's Press
New York

First published in the United States by St. Martin's Press, an imprint of
St. Martin's Publishing Group

JUST WORK. Copyright © 2021 by Kim Scott. All rights reserved. Printed in the
United States of America. For information, address St. Martin's
Publishing Group, 120 Broadway, New York, NY 10271.

www.stmartins.com

Library of Congress Cataloging-in-Publication Data

Names: Scott, Kim (Kim Malone), author.
Title: Just work : get sh*t done, fast & fair / Kim Scott.
Description: First edition. | New York : St. Martin's Press, 2021. |
    Includes bibliographical references and index.
Identifiers: LCCN 2020045306 | ISBN 9781250203489 (hardcover) |
    ISBN 9781250275707 (international) | ISBN 9781250277718 |
    ISBN 9781250270740 (ebook)
Subjects: LCSH: Discrimination in employment. | Sex discrimination in
    employment. | Diversity in the workplace. | Organizational change. |
    Organizational behavior.
Classification: LCC HD4903 .S25 2021 | DDC 658.3008--dc23
LC record available at https://lccn.loc.gov/2020045306

Our books may be purchased in bulk for promotional, educational, or business
use. Please contact your local bookseller or the Macmillan Corporate and
Premium Sales Department at 1-800-221-7945, extension 5442,
or by email at MacmillanSpecialMarkets@macmillan.com.

First Edition: 2021
First International Edition: 2021

10 9 8 7 6 5 4 3 2 1

For my soul mate, love, and partner in all things, Andy Scott. You shouldered all the Zoomschool and cooking so I could retreat to the shed in the backyard during the Covid-19 quarantine and Just Work. Now that this book is finished, it's my turn to make the meals and help with homework and do more of the million other things that make love joyful and livable.

And for our children, Battle and Margaret. You are inheriting a broken world. Your father and I have worked to mend it, but we have much further to go. I hope this book will give you some of the tools you'll need to continue our work.

Difference must be not merely tolerated, but seen as a fund of necessary polarities between which our creativity can spark ... Only then does the necessity for interdependency become unthreatening.

—Audre Lorde

Contents

Introduction

We Can't Fix Problems We Refuse to Notice

I never wanted to think of myself as a victim, a person harmed by injustice at work. Even less did I want to think of myself as a perpetrator, a person who causes harm or contributes to injustice. And so I didn't think about it. I marched through my career ignoring the unfair disadvantages and advantages I had, the ways I was automatically underestimated and overestimated.

If you'd asked me five years ago whether being a white woman had an impact on my work, I would've shrugged and said, "Not really."

It's hard for the author of *Radical Candor* to admit, but I was in denial. I worked in Memphis, Boston, New York, Silicon Valley, Paris, Moscow, Jerusalem, Pristina, and elsewhere. I have managed teams that spanned the globe, from Japan to China to Australia to India to Ireland to Brazil to Mexico. But wherever you go, there you are. I was always a woman and there was always gender injustice, everywhere. I also had a host of privileges[1] that made my life easier, usually in ways I didn't like to think about. I was always white, and there was always racial injustice, everywhere. I was never poor, and there is always economic injustice, everywhere. I was always straight, and there is always homophobia, everywhere.

To expose the depths of my refusal to recognize reality, let me tell you about my first job after college. This happened in 1991. I was 23 years old and I'd taken a job working for a private equity firm.

It all started with an anecdote. Robert (not his real name),[2] the CEO of the firm, had a story he loved to tell about going to the Bolshoi

Ballet with some of our company's Soviet partners. The first time (but certainly not the last) I heard the story was at the end of a strategy meeting. Here's how Robert told it:

"So, the ballet is finally over, and Vladimir leans over and whispers, 'Robert, do you like ballerinas?'"

Robert mimicked how he felt taken aback by the question and said, "Sure."

"But, Robert," the Russian factory director hissed, "*which* ballerina?"

Robert looked around at his audience—three young men and me—with raised eyebrows. "He was offering to deliver the ballerina of my choice to my hotel room!"

The men laughed, half in admiration and half in disbelief, but I felt sick to my stomach. How could they possibly think this was funny?

"Did you take him up on his offer?" one of the young men asked. "Do you think he could really deliver?"

Here Robert glanced in my direction and then turned the full force of his self-righteous glare on the young man. "No, of course not. I am not that sort of person. But, yes, I think he could have delivered."

The young men were impressed. I was horrified.

Robert seemed to think he'd done enough by not availing himself of the offer. Robert is no hero in this story, but I do know he and the other men on my team shared my belief that human trafficking was immoral. Yet when we were working with a partner who claimed it was his right to procure for Robert any dancer he wanted, nobody said a damn word—including me. Robert turned the whole thing into a "funny" anecdote, as if laughing at the situation made the whole thing not quite real. Denial.

Not long afterward, I learned that I was being paid significantly less than the market salary for my role. A friend of mine in a similar job told me she was being paid *four* times more than me. My friend explained her salary was the market rate, what the guys got paid. When I told my boss, Thomas, this, he exclaimed, "She must be sleeping with her boss!" That was BS, and I said so. When I asked Thomas for a raise, he acted as though I were putting him in an unreasonably difficult position with Robert, the CEO. A legend in our business, Robert was known equally for his success as a contrarian investor and his explosive personality. I suspected that Thomas didn't think I'd talk to Robert myself.

At the first opportunity I asked Robert for a meeting and soon found myself facing him in a conference room. He was seated comfortably in an armchair. Something about his big belly and unruly white hair gave him a benevolent appearance, like Santa Claus. He motioned toward a small wooden chair opposite him. At first he was genial, if patronizing. "You know that our Russian partners call you my secret weapon." He laughed uproariously, and I tried to laugh along, not quite sure what was so funny. When I raised the issue of my salary, the shift was immediate: Santa Claus was gone. Now he resembled a bird of prey. His piercing glare and furrowed gray eyebrows made it clear that he wasn't used to being challenged, especially not by the likes of me. He stared at me unblinkingly for what seemed like several minutes.

"I don't know what makes you think you're underpaid, but I can assure you it wouldn't be fair to the others to pay you more," he said with a note of finality, and put his hands on the arms of the chair as if he was about to get up. But I had come prepared with data about my peers and average salaries in the industry, and I forced myself to put my evidence forward. My data pissed him off.

"If I paid you that much, you'd make more than my daughter makes. I know you don't want to come between me and my daughter." This non sequitur was so egregious that I didn't even bother pointing out that his daughter was a teacher, or that the solution to not paying teachers enough wasn't to lower the salaries of women but not men in finance. I didn't dare say that because Robert was *really* angry, almost unhinged. The conversation ended abruptly.

Today, 30 years later, I know that Robert's response was classic gaslighting.[3] At age 23, though, his irrational rejection of my reasonable argument made me wonder if I'd done something wrong. What had I failed to understand? Unfortunately, gaslighting works, unless you know how to confront it—which I did not. Instead, I tried not to think about the issue of unfair pay anymore.

Our team spent most of our time in Moscow collaborating with our Soviet partners. While in Moscow, we lived and worked together in a big house provided to the project by the Soviet Ministry of Defense.

My boss, Thomas, and I were frequently traveling together all over Russia and Ukraine all the time, eating most of our meals together. When he confided to me that he had a serious and chronic medical condition and feared that he might not live much past 40, I started to worry about him. One night after we'd been up late working on some financial projections, he kissed me—and promptly burst into tears. He told me he was a virgin and deeply afraid that he would die that way. I made sure that he didn't. Friends later told me I'd been played. Maybe I had been. Either way, I'm glad Thomas is alive and well today. I don't wish him ill, but I do wish he'd been held accountable.

Sleeping with my boss was a big mistake. I own it. Well, half of it. Problem was, I paid for *all* of it. When Robert heard about our relationship, he told Thomas to inform me that I had to move out of the group house in Moscow. Thomas complied. Knowing that Thomas was not a good advocate for me, I talked to Robert myself. "Russia is a sexist society," Robert told me. "I am worried the Soviet government will think we are not using the house appropriately if there are young women living in it."

I was speechless with anger. Robert was putting me in harm's way by making me rent an apartment. Not only did I now have to find an illegal sublet on my own in Soviet Moscow, but the U.S. Embassy had recently issued an alert that the metro was considered unsafe for Americans. Since Moscow had no reliable taxi service, I would have to hail down random cars to get to and from work; a friend of mine had recently been forced to jump from a speeding car when the driver she'd hailed decided to make a detour through a deserted park.

I found an illegal sublet, took my chances with transport, and tried not to think about how unfair and dangerous the situation was. I even continued to date Thomas for a couple more months until he told me—again weeping—that the woman he really loved didn't return his feelings. He seemed to expect me to hug him and tell him it didn't matter because *I* loved him so much. He'd finally hit the wall between my himpathy[4] and my dignity. I broke up with him. Unfortunately, he was still my boss.

Consensual relationships in which one person has positional power over another (e.g., one person is the boss of the other) often become psychologically abusive, especially after they end. Ours was no exception. One evening I was sitting in the lobby of a hotel where we were staying on a business trip, reading the newspaper. Thomas walked by and snatched the paper from my hands, announcing, "Directors read before analysts." He'd taken to doing this sort of thing all the time.

Fred, Thomas's boss, who was with us on this business trip, observed the incident and followed me to the elevator. Fred knew about the relationship and was working to get me transferred to another manager. We had also talked about my salary, and he'd gotten me a small bump up. He'd become a trusted mentor.

"He was really nasty back there," Fred said, with just enough sympathy to make my tears of anger well up.

I nodded as the elevator ascended to the floor where my room was. I was counting by prime numbers in my head to control my emotions, a trick that I had learned from a high school math teacher. Fred held out his arms for a hug. Partly because I trusted him and partly because a hug would prevent him from seeing me cry, I walked into his arms. Next thing I knew, he was grinding his erect penis into me. Mercifully the elevator door opened; I ducked under his arm and darted out. I've rarely felt so alone or under siege. But I put the whole thing out of my mind.[5] I'd like to think a young woman today, post #MeToo, would feel emboldened to respond differently if the same thing happened to her. I don't think that's something we can take for granted, though. These things still happen and they are still hard to respond to.

A few weeks after this Robert came to Moscow with Peter, his chief of staff, and Emmett, who was a partner at the firm. I noticed that Emmett was reading a worn copy of *Pride and Prejudice*. Seeing him reading one of my favorite novels made me decide to open up and try to have a conversation with him. We started with books and moved on to reality. Emmett agreed with me that my salary, which was half what it should've been even after my recent bump up, was unfair. He also told me he was horrified that I had been thrown out of the company housing. "Seems like Thomas should've been the one to go," he muttered. He told me he'd already brought it up with Robert, but to no avail. Even though his intervention didn't improve my pay or my housing, it meant a lot. He'd validated my sense of injustice. Emmett was a real lifeline. I'd routinely been awakened at 3:00 A.M.

by all the thoughts and anger I'd repressed all day long: Was *I* the one being irrational, or were these men I was working with the irrational ones? Knowing that someone saw things the way I did helped me sleep through the night.

Emmett suggested I talk to Peter, who had a lot of influence. I went to Peter, who responded sympathetically and suggested we discuss it over dinner. I agreed and felt a flicker of hope: perhaps things might work out after all. A few hours later, he told me that he'd been unable to get a reservation at the restaurant he had in mind, so he'd just bring the food over to my apartment. This felt off to me, but I didn't know how to say no.

He arrived with the food, and as we sat down across from each other at the dining table, he once again expressed sympathy for my position. This was a stressful industry, he said. Stress was hard for women. He wouldn't want his sister to find herself in my situation. I said I didn't feel stressed, but I *was* angry about being underpaid. Peter nodded, but his tone began to change as he told me that he'd grown up in a country where virtually everyone was underpaid, in ways I couldn't even imagine as an American. I saw what he was doing— trying to make me feel guilty about asking for more money when so many people in the world were so much worse off than me. I also knew he was being hypocritical, since he was making probably 20 times my salary. My peers who were men were making twice my salary, but he would never have given them a guilt trip. Even though I knew all this, his ploy worked. I found myself feeling pushy, greedy.

Before I knew what was happening, he had come over to my side of the table and started massaging my shoulders from behind. I just sat there: tense, paralyzed, and creeped out.

People often criticize women for not immediately leaving situations such as this. But this was one of the top guys in the company. He had what seemed like unlimited power over me. He was also in my apartment. Where was I going to go?

It only took Peter about 30 seconds—an extremely long and uncomfortable 30 seconds—to reach over my shoulder and touch my breast. *That* spurred me into action. I jumped up, opened the door to my apartment, and ran down the stairs out into the street. I looked over my shoulder to make sure he wasn't following. As I strode along in the cold Moscow night air, I laughed to myself, thinking how foolish he must feel all by himself in my apartment. I wondered how I'd had the sudden insight to realize that I was safer alone at night on the streets of Moscow than in my own home with an executive at the company where I worked.

Needless to say, the raise didn't happen.

Did I tell HR about any of these incidents? I did not. There were many reasons, but a big one is that I feared that the situation with Thomas would come back to bite me. People would say that Fred and Peter knew about Thomas and would speculate that if I'd dated Thomas, I must be open to dating other co-workers. I knew this was BS. Just because I'd dated Thomas did not give Fred the right to frot[6] me without my consent in the elevator or Peter the right to grab my breast. Yet I also knew these absurd insinuations would somehow work, like Robert's gaslighting me about my salary. It was a fight I was unlikely to win.

Not only would my character be questioned, so would my competence. One of the first things that people say to women reporting sexual misconduct is "Make sure your performance is beyond reproach." Despite how I was being treated, I had done good work. But, let's face it, *none of us* can do our best work when being treated that way. In my next job I was able to do my best work. I created a business that was on a $100 million/year run rate within two years. I believe that better working conditions were critical to that success. If Robert had paid me fairly, had put in place the kinds of checks and balances that would have discouraged Peter and Fred's predatory behavior, it might have been one of the best investments he ever made. This is a universe-through-a-grain-of-sand way of explaining why diverse, well-functioning teams are good for business.

Back to why I didn't report Robert to HR. I was 23 years old and just starting out in my career. Robert was the firm's founder, CEO, and majority shareholder. There were no checks on his power. I decided my best option was to get the hell out of there and find a new job. Emmett, the same partner who had intervened with Robert about my salary, introduced me to a different firm. They offered me a job—at a market salary.

To my surprise, Robert wanted to talk to me when he heard I was quitting. Once again, he reacted angrily, calling me disloyal. And once again, I found myself speechless. What I wanted to say was, "What in the *&^% did you give me to be loyal to? You treat human trafficking as though it's a joke, you underpay me, you yell at me when I ask for a raise, and you create an environment in which it's safe for your executives to grab my boob and grind their dicks into me on the elevator and not safe for me to report it!"

Unfortunately, I didn't say any of that—in part because I would've been forced to describe exactly what happened. And I suspected that if I used the words that accurately described what had happened, I would be shamed, but Fred and Peter would not be held accountable.

So I simply said, "Robert, they are paying me twice what you paid me."

"So it's all about the money for you, is it?" Robert replied. As if his own career in finance hadn't been motivated by the desire to make money. As if a woman were suspect for expecting to earn a fair salary.

This was my very first job out of college, and I left it more than a little broken. All these experiences felt of a piece and yet also separate and different from one another. I couldn't make sense of them. It was so much easier for me to notice what was wrong with the Soviet Union than it was to admit that something was not right in my own environment. The injustices and inefficiencies of the Soviet system were easier for me to recognize because they had nothing to do with me. I could observe clearly that injustice—the imprisonment of dissenters and the trafficking of ballerinas—was part of what brought that system down. And the fact that the system just didn't work—toilet paper and bread were hard to come by in Moscow—also brought it down. Communism (like fascism) was as ineffective as it was unjust.

I was both fascinated and puzzled by how such a corrupt and dysfunctional regime had perpetuated itself for so long. This curiosity was part of what propelled me to attend business school. And yet for years I failed to recognize that my lifelong interest in building the kinds of environments that allowed people to do the best work of their lives and to enjoy doing it was also rooted in my own personal experience at that private equity firm (which fell apart along with the Soviet regime).

That first job was so deeply disorienting, in fact, that it took me 30 years to come up with a theory that united my intellectual questions about how to build just working environments with my personal experiences of being mistreated at work. This book is the result of that effort.

I can now parse the problem I experienced in that job, break it down into its component parts, and begin to identify effective responses to each. The workplace injustice I experienced felt monolithic, but, with the benefit of 20/20 hindsight, I can now understand that it wasn't. Workplace injustice is actually six different problems: bias, prejudice, bullying, discrimination, verbal harassment, and physical violations. This book will go deep on each of these attitudes and behaviors to identify how leaders, observers, people harmed, and even people who cause harm can respond in a way that moves us toward Just Work—an environment in which everyone can collaborate and respect one another's individuality. It will also explore the dynamics between these attitudes and behaviors and the systems leaders create that either reinforce or interrupt these bad dynamics.

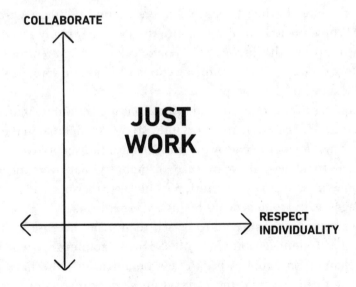

Gender injustice doesn't exist in a vacuum. It's affected by and affects other forms of injustice in the workplace and beyond. Bias, prejudice, bullying, discrimination, harassment, and physical violations combine differently for me than they do for other people. The only way we can combat workplace injustice is if we move forward together. It wouldn't simplify the issue for me to consider only the problems encountered by straight white women with Ivy League degrees and more than their fair share of economic resources; rather, that approach would make the problem impossible to solve.[7]

While writing this book, I found that I learned the most about how to address workplace injustice at what Kimberlé Crenshaw calls the intersections[8] where gender injustice meets racial injustice, where gender injustice meets economic injustice, where the fight for women's rights meets the fight for gay rights, where the recognition of how language creates a bias against people who are disabled meets the recognition of how language creates a bias against women.[9]

These intersections were distressing places for me to find myself because at each one I was both the victim and the perpetrator. I didn't want to be either. But we can't fix problems we refuse to notice. Only when I recognize the way my privilege harms others can I lay it down. The intersections may have felt uncomfortable, but they were also where the most healing happened, where I found the most wisdom, where I could breathe freely and notice things as they really are. When I pushed through the discomfort, I could feel an ancient tension melting in my shoulders. In these intersections I found both practical and moral lessons for the workplace.

Inequities in corporations and institutions are not only unfair; they are ineffective. According to a McKinsey study, "companies in the bottom quartile for both gender and ethnic/cultural diversity were 29% less likely to achieve above-average profitability than were all other companies in our data set. In short, not only were they not leading, they were lagging."[10] Homogeneous teams underperform.

Homogeneous teams tend to be self-reinforcing because so many people have homogeneous networks. Hiring committees will take more chances on people who are less qualified but who have connections. It can be very difficult to get in the door if you don't have a connection, no matter how good your skills are.[11]

And the underrepresented people who do get hired can't possibly achieve their potential if the environment isn't inclusive. I could not do my best work after being frotted. This reinforces the bias that people who are underrepresented are not good at the job, and that bias plays out in hiring decisions. The firm then winds up with homogeneous teams, which on average underperform diverse teams. Innovation and productivity suffer.[12] It's hard to miss what you don't have, but when the competition has it, the problems show up in the bottom line.

For both moral and practical reasons we *all* have a role to play in creating Just Work. I will offer strategies for people harmed by injustice, acknowledging that we can't expect victims to take on the full burden. I will also offer strategies for people who *observe* workplace injustice, so they can become upstanders, not bystanders; for people who *cause* harm to learn to recognize how their behaviors poison a team's ability to collaborate; and for *leaders,* so they can learn not only to react effectively when such issues arise but also to prevent injustice from occurring in the first place.

This book is about the things we can do, now, to create just, effective work environments. I don't have the answer to all the world's problems. But the fact that we can't fix everything is not a good reason to do nothing. If we don't intervene, we reinforce vicious cycles in which injustice compounds over time. Unjust dynamics are all too common but not inevitable. We *can* learn to notice the connection between unexamined attitudes and behaviors that cause real harm. We *can* recognize how the systems we have created perpetuate injustice, and we *can* change those systems. And when we take proactive measures to create the kinds of working environments where we respect one another's individuality and collaborate more effectively, we all enjoy our jobs and our colleagues more, make better decisions, and become more successful.[13]

I will explore how we can Just Work by telling stories from my own career about times I got things right and other times when I failed to respond as I wish I had. This book is an effort to make sense of my personal experiences in a way that I hope helps others make sense of theirs—and helps us all build more equitable working environments. As author and designer Kat Holmes wrote, "Solve for one, extend to many."[14]

Since you'll be hearing so many of my stories, I'll tell you a little bit about myself. Despite the inauspicious professional start described above, I've been blessed with a happy and successful career.

Much of that was made possible not only by hard work but also because I have automatically been included and overestimated on a number of dimensions. That I was born a white, straight American citizen in good health and comfortable economic circumstances does not make me automatically guilty; but a refusal to recognize—let alone address—the injustices suffered by people who don't have these privileges would be wrong. Likewise, being a woman doesn't make me automatically a victim; but denying the harm that has been done to me as a woman in the workplace leaves me and others more vulnerable to being harmed, not less. This book is my effort to begin the long process of coming to grips with my denial, and righting that wrong.

I grew up in Memphis, Tennessee, the daughter of a lawyer and a homemaker. Everyone in my family went to college, as far back on both sides as I know about. Everyone in my family is white, hailing from England or Ireland originally. Raised as a Christian Scientist, I went to a private Episcopalian girls' school from kindergarten through graduation from high school. From the time I was five, I was groomed for all the things it takes to get into college. With a lot of encouragement from dedicated teachers, many, *many* SAT prep classes, and tons of hard work since my IQ is nothing special, I got into Princeton, where I studied Russian literature. My parents and grandparents paid for my college, so I graduated debt-free, which gave me the freedom to take risks. Those risks paid off. Privilege compounds.

I lived and worked in Moscow from 1990 to 1994. This is where I got my first management experience, starting up a diamond-cutting factory, and where my lifelong obsession with good management began. Some working environments created misery and suboptimal results, whereas others created joy and got sh*t done. Why? My road to find out took me from Harvard Business School to serving as CEO of two tech start-ups, to being an executive at Google and Apple, to coaching the CEOs of Dropbox, Qualtrics, and Twitter. Eventually I wrote a book about what I'd learned, *Radical Candor: Be a Kick-Ass Boss Without Losing Your Humanity.*

When I published *Radical Candor,* I joked that it was a guerrilla feminist text—even if all the feminism was buried in the subtext. Embarrassingly, I failed to notice the irony here: that I had encoded a clandestine message about equitable work environments in a book about candor. I was not living in accordance with my personal philosophy.

Radical Candor did a great job painting a picture of how things ought to be at work: we get more done and we like each other better when we care personally and challenge directly. But I couldn't create BS-free zones at work if I was in denial about the nature of the BS. And here was the thing I didn't want to admit, even to myself. Radical Candor worked. But it didn't work equally well for everyone.

Many women told me that Radical Candor felt risky. One woman at a large multinational oil company raised her hand and said she came by Radical Candor naturally, and she believed it had cost her a promotion. I acknowledged that this was probably true. When a woman is radically candid, she often gets called bitchy, abrasive, bossy, and so on. Furthermore, the competence/likability bias is real. Radical Candor helps you be more competent at your job. But for women there is a rub: the more competent she is, the less people, including her boss, like her. And when the boss doesn't like you, it's hard to get promoted. Is this a reason to be less competent? No, of course not. But it puts women in an unfair catch-22. The relief and gratitude on her face when I acknowledged this reality in a way that simultaneously educated the men in the audience was unforgettable.

This kind of bias impacted the ability of different people to employ Radical Candor in different ways. James, a participant in a seminar I led, pointed out how differently people respond to him than to me when each of us is radically candid. He was correct. I am a short white woman. He is a tall Black man. We share a problem: people often have incorrect preconceptions about who we are based on our height, gender, and race; as a result, people are apt to misinterpret or underestimate us. Both of us have experienced bias, prejudice, bullying, harassment, discrimination, and physical violence—but in very different ways. It would have been ignorant of me to say that the way I dealt with my version of the problem was the way he should deal with his version. At the same time, I did learn some new approaches by listening to his experiences, and I hope my stories helped him, too.

Black women told me that they felt Radical Candor was a riskier strategy for them than for white women. When I did a training at a company led by Michelle, a CEO who is Black, she told me she had to be exceedingly careful when she offered Radical Candor. "If I seem even a tiny bit annoyed, people accuse me of being an angry Black woman," she explained.[15] "It is an age-old stereotype." Only at that moment did I realize that I'd known her for the better part of a decade and had never once seen her appear stressed or angry. What did that repression cost her? Why had I never noticed this extra tax she had to pay?

Radical Candor worked, but it was easier for straight white men to put it into practice than for anyone else. That was a problem. And even these men reported feeling unsafe. After talks and workshops, men often told me that practicing Radical Candor with their women colleagues also felt risky. Some straight men were afraid that "caring personally" would be misinterpreted as somehow romantic or sexual. Other men said they were concerned that their attempts to be candid would be viewed as "mansplaining." Of course, mansplaining is rarely used as an excuse for denying a man a promotion, whereas "abrasiveness" is frequently given as a reason not to promote a woman. Nevertheless, these concerns are real, and they must be addressed if we are to solve the problem of workplace injustice.

One man, John, told me about a meeting in which a marketing executive, Susan, named the launch of her team's major marketing program Rolling Thunder. The name felt catchy for a massive and wide-ranging media campaign, but John was worried that Susan didn't realize that it had also been the name of a disastrous bombing campaign during the Vietnam War that led to tens of thousands of civilian casualties. He kept this fact to himself, however, for fear of being accused of mansplaining.

I knew Susan well enough to feel certain she would have been grateful for the information. I also knew that John cared deeply about creating opportunities for all the people who worked with him, regardless of their gender. He wasn't trying to punish Susan with his silence; he was genuinely reluctant to speak up. This kind of fear and distrust erodes collaboration on a team. It's bad for results, it's bad for relationships, and it's bad for morale.

This book is equally for John and for Susan, for James and for Michelle, for my son and my daughter. And while many of my stories will center on gender and race, I hope the solutions will extend to workplace injustice in all its manifestations. Once we learn how to interrupt one kind of bias, it's easier to change the often unconscious thought patterns that can lead to other kinds of bias, or worse. When we clean up these misconceptions and the behaviors that go with them, we build happier, more productive workplaces.

TRYING TO JUST WORK IN 2020

I started this book in the summer of 2017. As I wrote, world events kept exposing the injustices that corrupt not only the workplace but society more broadly. Denial was becoming more and more impossible. #MeToo highlighted gender injustice as never before. Then Covid-19 made economic and racial injustice all too evident. The murders of Breonna Taylor and George Floyd sparked a movement that made it impossible to ignore violence against Black people in the U.S.

While my husband cared for our children as they Zoomed into school from their bedrooms, I retreated to a shed in the backyard—the trifecta of quarantine privileges: a husband willing to take on the lion's share of domestic responsibilities, a backyard, a shed already built in the backyard—and edited this book. Unemployment hit Great Depression levels and Congress went on recess without providing unemployment benefits for those in need. Next, California caught fire and the smoke drove me from the shed back into the house, where it was much harder to Just Work.

In this context, I came across a sentence I'd written just six months previously: "Organizations, because of their scale and ability to enforce norms of conduct, have the potential to change the culture in the place where most of us spend most of our time: at work." It had seemed like a reasonable assertion when I first wrote it. But now, that sentence seemed like a prime example of what I'll call in this book "oblivious exclusion." With so many people out of work, and those who do have jobs wondering how to do them in the current realities, is Just Work just another privilege, inaccessible to most?

No, Just Work is more urgent than ever. Why? High ethical standards are important in good times and bad, but creating more just workplaces at a time when jobs are scarce is especially important, because employees are especially vulnerable. And we as a society have a lot to attend to: an economic crisis, a social crisis, an environmental crisis. We can't afford to screw around. Just Work is fair *and* effective. Injustice is both immoral and inefficient.

It's impossible to know as I finish this book what kind of world it will be launched into. Will the economy come roaring back as it did after the Great Depression, forcing leaders to create better working environments or risk losing the war for talent? Or will mass unemployment make it risky for employees to raise issues of injustice? Will more people work from home, and if they do, will men step up on the domestic front, or will we return to a 1950s division of labor that makes it impossible for women to Just Work? I hope it's the former not the latter, but early indicators show it's probably the latter. The Women in the Workplace 2020 report[16] indicates that due to Covid-19, one in four women are considering downshifting their careers or leaving the workforce. However, it's too soon to say what the impact will be.

What I do know is this. These times are filled with grief, but also with optimism. Black Lives Matter, still going strong and by many measures already the largest protest movement in American history with 15 million to 26 million protesters,[17] has reminded people around the world that we have the opportunity to unite and remake our institutions, including our workplaces. The injustices and inequalities in our society are not new, but they do seem much more pronounced and evident now. And when we notice and name problems, we are more likely to fix them.[18] The year 2020 laid injustice so bare that we can no longer refuse to notice it. We now have an opportunity to unite and learn to live up to our ideals.

Workplace injustice is a human problem we must solve together, not an issue that pits any one group of people against another. To the extent that there's a culture war in the workplace, the struggle is between the people who are committed to taking action to create just working environments versus those who are not. Whoever we are, whatever our role, wherever we are, it is about consciously choosing to join this struggle. There is room for all of us. We are all needed.

So many millions of people are more aware now than ever that we—*all* of us—tend to underestimate some people and overestimate others. We undervalue and therefore underutilize some people and promote others beyond their level of competence. This tendency is ineffective and unjust. The goal is to give everyone the opportunity to do work they love and to enjoy collaborating with their colleagues, free from the inefficiency and resentment that unjust treatment breeds. This is a lofty goal; the best way I know to make progress is to set lofty goals, continually measure the gap between the goals and the realities, and to work day by day to close that gap.

The fundamental premise of this book is that there are things each of us can do to eliminate injustice from the workplace. A dozen different catalysts could have brought you to this book. Perhaps you've been hired to create a more diverse and inclusive work culture. You may be concerned about the treatment of the only transgender person on your team. Or maybe you looked around and realized that everyone on your team is a white man, and this struck you for the first time as a problem you need to solve for everyone. Whatever reason you began this book, my goal is that you will finish it with an ability to parse problems you are confronting and with several strategies for how to address them so that you and the people around you can Just Work. *Today.*

Bias, Prejudice, and Bullying

How to Confront Each Effectively

What gets in the way of basic fairness[1] at work? In my experience, there are three root causes of workplace injustice: bias, prejudice, and bullying. Each is different and must be considered separately if we are to come up with the most effective ways to combat each. When a power imbalance is present, things get much worse quickly—discrimination, harassment, and physical violations occur. We'll consider these problems in Part Two. Let's start by examining how to root out the root causes.

PROBLEMS

Before we begin, let me offer some supershort definitions and a simple framework to help keep us oriented in a problem that can be very disorienting.

Bias[2] is "not meaning it." Bias, often called unconscious bias, comes from the part of our mind that jumps to conclusions, usually without our even being aware of it.[3] These conclusions and assumptions aren't *always* wrong, but they often are, especially when they reflect stereotypes. We do not have to be the helpless victims of our brains. We can learn to slow down and question our biases.

Prejudice is "meaning it." Unfortunately, when we stop to think, we don't always come up with the best answer, either. Sometimes we rationalize our biases and they harden into prejudices.[4] In other words, we justify our biases rather than challenging their flawed assumptions and stereotypes.

Bullying is "being mean": the intentional, repeated use of in-group status or power to harm or humiliate others.[5] Sometimes bullying comes with prejudice, but often it's a more instinctive behavior. There may be no thought or ideology at all behind it. It can be a plan or just an animal instinct to dominate, to coerce.

RESPONSES

The most effective responses match the problem we're trying to solve. To root out bias, prejudice, and bullying we must respond to each differently.

In my experience, when people's biases are pointed out to them clearly and compassionately, they usually correct them and apologize.

Prejudice, however, is a conscious and ingrained belief. People don't change their prejudices simply because someone points them out. Holding up a mirror doesn't help—people like what they see. What's important is to draw a clear boundary between people's right to believe whatever they want and their freedom to impose their prejudices on others.

Bullying has to incur real consequences to be stopped. If bullies were swayed by being aware of the harm they are doing to the people they are bullying, they wouldn't be treating other people badly in the first place. Usually they are *trying* to hurt someone. Pointing out the pain they are inflicting doesn't make them stop and may even encourage them to double down.

Your degrees of freedom and responsibility when confronting bias, prejudice, and bullying depend on your role. Chapter 1 describes the different roles we all play, and chapters 2–5 describe specific things you can do to confront these attitudes and behaviors, depending on what role you play. No matter what role you play, though, it's important to understand the perspective of the people in the other roles if you want your attempts to combat the problem to be effective. Also, the better you understand each role, the more skilled you will be if you later find yourself intentionally or accidentally *in* that role. The shared goal is to create an environment in which everyone can do better work and be happier while they are doing it.

PROBLEM	RESPONSE

BIAS
NOT MEANING IT

Unaware of stereotypes

**BIAS
INTERRUPTER**

Make the person aware

PREJUDICE
MEANING IT

Aware of / rationalizing
stereotypes

**CODE OF
CONDUCT**

Do not allow one person to
impose prejudices on others

BULLYING
BEING MEAN

Intentional use of
stereotypes to harm

**CLEAR
CONSEQUENCES**

Demonstrate that
bullying won't work

1

Roles and Responsibilities

Who Is Responsible for Fixing These Problems? Everyone.

I n any instance of injustice you encounter at work, *you will play at least one of four different roles:* person harmed, upstander, person who caused harm, or leader. Each of these roles has its own responsibilities.

As you consider these roles, recognize that they are not fixed identities. Instead they are temporary parts you play. You may at different moments play *all* the roles. And sometimes, confusingly, you may even find yourself in two or more roles at once.

Our active awareness that we are playing one or more roles in certain moments reminds us that these roles are neither static nor conclusive. When we understand the perspectives of people playing the other roles, we can come up with better strategies for responding in a way that creates real change. We can take a broader view of ourselves and others as people who can always learn and improve. This distinction is of the utmost importance because it allows us to grow and change after harmful incidents rather than feel we will forever be defined by them.

In the stories I'll tell, sometimes I am the person harmed; sometimes I am the person who causes harm; sometimes I observe harm being done; and sometimes I am the leader whose job it is to prevent harm from being done. In some of these stories, I respond badly or not at all. In others, it seems impossible for me to do my job. Occasionally I feel good about my response.

A key goal of this book is to build compassion for ourselves in all the roles and to develop strategies for responding more effectively to workplace injustice, no matter what role we find ourselves in.

ROLE: PERSON HARMED

CHOOSE YOUR RESPONSE

If you're on the receiving end of workplace injustice, your responsibility is first and foremost to yourself. This means remembering that you get to choose your response, even when your choices are hard or limited. Recognizing those choices, evaluating their costs and benefits, and choosing one of them can help to restore your sense of agency. Even when you have been victimized, you have a choice in how you respond. When you make that choice, put yourself first. You have a right to act in self-defense.

In my experience, no one who has suffered injustice *wants* to keep quiet about it. One's initial instinct is to speak out. Yet that instinct then gets repressed in a thousand different ways. In fact, psychologist Jennifer Freyd's research shows that when you're in a dependent state (e.g., you need a paycheck), it becomes harder for your brain to encode the injustice in memory, let alone speak out about it.[1] And that repression, that loss of ability to speak out, is debilitating—sometimes even more harmful than the original experience. How can we learn to recognize the injustice so that we can respond in a way that restores our sense of freedom and agency?

While this book will offer a number of suggestions, I am all about choices, not additional pressure. In some instances of workplace abuse, there may be considerable pressure on a victim to come forward—even when the risks are both obvious and considerable. I do not want to encourage people harmed to make any choices that will harm them further.

I offer this observation. Confrontation has obvious costs and hidden benefits; silence has hidden costs and obvious benefits. The more aware you are of both the obvious costs and the hidden benefits, the better your decision will be. If you weigh the consequences and decide to confront the injustice, this book will offer specific suggestions for how to do so in a way that doesn't destroy your career; I also acknowledge there's wisdom in choosing your battles. Choosing not to respond is a legitimate choice, and nobody, least of all me, should judge you for making it. Either way, making a conscious choice enables you to reclaim your sense of agency.

Finally, if you later regret whatever decision you *did* make, cut yourself some slack. Beating yourself up for not responding the "right" way just adds insult to injury; don't forget that you were the wronged party in the first place! Self-forgiveness doesn't mean ignoring our regrets. It means acknowledging how hard it is to confront workplace injustice, forgiving ourselves for missed opportunities, and doing our best to learn and do better next time.

ROLE: ~~OBSERVER~~ UPSTANDER

INTERVENE. DON'T JUST WATCH

The word "observer" suggests passivity. If you witness injustice and want to help fight it, you need to be an upstander who proactively finds a way to support people harmed, not a passive bystander who simply watches harm being done, perhaps feeling bad about it but not doing anything about it.

When you notice injustice, whether it's small or large, you have a responsibility to take action. And you have an obligation to notice it: being unaware does not give you absolution. Admittedly, you can't always solve the problem. But you can always show solidarity with the person who is being harmed, and that acknowledgment—that "something is wrong here"—is invaluable.

ROLE: PERSON CAUSING HARM

LISTEN AND ADDRESS

Maybe you didn't mean to cause harm, maybe you were unaware of how what you said or did affected the person. Or maybe you actually *meant* to inflict harm, but you didn't expect anyone to notice. Maybe you were just angry on that particular day or felt threatened. Maybe you later regretted what you had done.

The fact remains, you harmed another person, and now someone's pointing it out to you. How are you going to react? Are you going to explode in a defensive/aggressive rage? Are you going to be coldly dismissive? Or are you going to take the complaint to heart?

It doesn't feel good when someone tells you you've harmed them, particularly when that wasn't your intention. But as with critical feedback of any kind, consider it a gift. Feedback can help you learn to be more considerate, to avoid harming other people, and (at minimum) to correct your behavior before it escalates and causes greater harm and/or gets you into serious trouble. Listen to what you're being told and address it.

ROLE: LEADER

PREVENT AND REPAIR

One of the great joys of leadership is the opportunity to create a collaborative, respectful working environment. A healthy organization is not merely an absence of unpleasant symptoms. Creating a just working environment is about eliminating bad behavior *and* reinforcing collaborative, respectful behavior. That means teaching people not to allow bias to cloud judgment, not to allow people to impose their prejudices on others; it means creating consequences for bullying and preventing discrimination, harassment, and physical violations from occurring on your team. Workplace injustice is not inevitable. There are specific actions you can take so that you and your team can love the work and working together, so that you can all get sh*t done, fast and fair. And once you start taking these actions, you set in place a virtuous cycle.

ROLES	RESPONSIBILITIES
PEOPLE HARMED	Choose a response
UPSTANDER	Intervene
PEOPLE CAUSING HARM	Listen and address
LEADER	Prevent and repair

What It Looks Like When Everyone Plays Their Role

Emelia Holden, a waitress at a pizzeria in Savannah, Georgia, felt someone grab her butt as she was printing the check. She turned, grabbed the man's shirt, and threw him to the ground, saying, "You don't touch me!"[2] Her manager, having observed the customer grope Emelia, called the police. Other waiters and cooks came out and surrounded the man so he couldn't leave. The police arrested the man on charges of sexual battery, a misdemeanor.

Let's look at the circumstances that allowed Emelia to safely defend herself:

First, Emelia had both the will and the physical strength to respond as she did. But her ability to stand up for herself was not the only reason this story ended in justice being served.

It's not hard to imagine a workplace where the boss would have accused Emelia of overreacting and fired her; or one where her manager might not have witnessed the incident or come to her defense. Her co-workers, instead of surrounding the accused, might have feared for their own jobs and looked the other way. And the police could have taken Emelia, rather than the man who grabbed her, away in handcuffs.

Happily, almost everyone had a good response in this case. Emilia had the agency and strength to defend herself. Her manager was committed to protecting his employees from predatory patrons and had installed a camera. Her co-workers defended her. The police upheld Emelia's right to self-defense. *And* they treated the man who grabbed her fairly. They looked for evidence before arresting him and did not use undue force. As we all know now, things very well may have ended tragically in this story if Emelia or the man who pinched her were Black. We all must commit to creating a more just police and legal system.

Just Work requires that each of us is clear about our role and our responsibility.

Navigation Bar

I've written that workplace injustice is not a monolithic problem. Its component parts are bias, prejudice, bullying, discrimination, harassment, and physical violations. The people who can address these problems are leaders, upstanders, people who cause harm, and people who are harmed. That's a lot to keep in mind. This book will consider what we can do about each problematic attitude or behavior depending on what role we are playing. But to keep you oriented throughout, I'll introduce a navigation bar at the bottom of odd-numbered pages. It will name the role being considered and circle the particular attitude or behavior that is being addressed. For example, when a section is explaining what leaders can do about bullying, you'll see this:

LEADERS &
BIAS   PREJUDICE   [BULLYING]   ⚡   DISCRIMINATION   HARASSMENT   PHYSICAL VIOLATIONS

When a section is explaining what people harmed can do to distinguish between bias, prejudice, and bullying you'll see this:

PEOPLE HARMED &
[BIAS   PREJUDICE   BULLYING]   ⚡   DISCRIMINATION   HARASSMENT   PHYSICAL VIOLATIONS

2

For People Harmed

What to Say When You Don't Know What to Say

Your silence will not protect you.

—Audre Lorde

The poet Claudia Rankine expresses the disorientation and discomfort of realizing that someone is incorrectly assuming things about you based on a stereotype:

> What did he just say? Did she really just say that? Did I hear what I think I heard? Did that just come out of my mouth, his mouth, your mouth? The moment stinks . . . Then the voice in your head silently tells you to take your foot off your throat because just getting along shouldn't be an ambition.[1]

Part of what makes it hard to respond in such moments is one's uncertainty about where the person is coming from. Is this unconscious bias talking? Or does the person mean what they said? Or is the remark a power play of some kind, intended to intimidate?

In the spirit of "show, don't tell," here are three stories that illustrate just how complex even the briefest of interactions can be. In one sense, these were trivial encounters, each lasting less than 60 seconds. In another, they speak volumes.

Mr. Safety Pin

I was just about to give a Radical Candor talk to the founders and executives of some of Silicon Valley's hottest start-ups. A couple hundred men were at the conference. I was one of only a handful of women. Just as I was about to go onstage, one of the participants approached me, his lips pursed in frustration.

"I need a safety pin!" he hissed at me. He was clutching at his shirtfront—a button had popped off. Evidently, he assumed I was on the event-staff team. To prevent this situation, the conference organizers had given the event staff bright yellow T-shirts. But all he could notice was his need and my gender.

I didn't know what to say. He was being rude and seemed almost panicked about his exposed belly. More striking than his rudeness was his utter certainty that it was my job to solve his problem. I was about to give my presentation, so I was a little agitated myself. Let's slow the moment way down and explore why it was hard to know what to say.

I wanted to believe that Mr. Safety Pin was manifesting garden-variety unconscious gender *bias* when he assumed I was staffing the event. Not a federal offense. Most of us have made an incorrect assumption about another person's role based on some personal attribute, and these moments are as painful as they are common. In these situations, often the best tactic for someone in my position is to lightly correct the error and move on: the classic "Sorry, I don't work here" moment.

But maybe his comment had sprung not from unconscious bias but rather from conscious *prejudice*. Maybe he believed women should have support roles and not write books about leadership. Perhaps if I explained, "I need to prepare for my talk right now, so I can't help you out," he'd reply, "Oh. You must be the Radical Candor lady. I don't believe in that soft, feminine leadership bullshit." Unlikely, but certainly not impossible: That kind of thing has happened to me, more than once. If my attempt at a courteous response prompted him to reveal a conscious *prejudice* against women, it would piss me off, and that would make it harder for me to focus on my talk. I didn't want to risk that.

Plus, there was a third possibility: *bullying*. What if I corrected him and he escalated, saying something like "Hey, lady, no need to get your panties all in a wad"? I wasn't sure I would be able to resist the temptation to respond to that sort of obnoxious remark with something equally obnoxious: *"I am here to teach you to be a kick-ass boss, not to fetch your safety pins!"* And then I'd go onstage roiling mad at him, and at myself for losing my temper. I'd be knocked off my game.

There was another confounding factor here beyond gender: power and privilege. The man assumed he had a right to be rude to the people staffing the event. Perhaps when he realized I was a speaker, not a staffer, that I had the same economic and network privileges he did, he would apologize and snap into polite mode. But talking to *anyone* the way he'd talked to me was objectionable.

All this felt like too much for me to deal with in the five minutes before I walked onstage. So I said nothing, and the man stomped off, evidently wondering why I was refusing to do my job, muttering something about complaining to the event organizers about the unhelpful staff.

In hindsight, I was hamstrung by two sorts of confusion. The first, as outlined above, was my uncertainty about the attitude behind his behavior. Was it bias, prejudice, or bullying? The second confusion was about my role in the exchange. Was I the person harmed, the leader, or an upstander? And if I failed to live up to my responsibility in one of these roles, did that cast me as a person who caused harm?

In one sense, I was the person harmed. He was treating me rudely and I was worried about being distracted before an important talk. Correcting his misapprehensions in that moment shouldn't have been my job. In another sense, though, I was a potential upstander: my failure to correct him meant that he might complain about the event staff—people who were more vulnerable than I was. But perhaps most important, as a speaker I was there in a leadership capacity, so I had an obligation to speak up.

In retrospect, my silence was bad for everyone: bad for the staff; bad for me, because I hadn't lived in accordance with my own beliefs; and even bad for Mr. Safety Pin. Because by not pointing out his bias (if that's what was behind his request), I was making it more likely that he'd repeat his mistake.

PEOPLE HARMED &
BIAS   PREJUDICE   BULLYING   ⚡ DISCRIMINATION   HARASSMENT   PHYSICAL VIOLATIONS

Fist-Bump

My colleague of many years Derek shared a story with me about his experience at a conference focused on building more inclusive workplaces for women, where attendees were ~90 percent women. Here's what happened.

Derek is not the biggest fan of tactile greetings—hugs, handshakes, and the like—primarily because of the germ transfer inherent in such physical contact. So, when Derek goes to conferences, he prefers to fist-bump rather than to shake hands.[2] In the Covid-19 world his reluctance feels understandable, but it was a little more unusual then.

Derek was having a great time at the conference, was learning a lot, and was fully engaged. He approached the keynote speaker, a major thinker/scholar on diversity and inclusion, to ask a clarifying question. When he introduced himself, she said, "Oh, yeah, the fist-bump guy." When he questioned her, he learned that other participants at the conference had been gossiping about his preference for fist-bumping, attributing it to a "bro" attitude. Nobody had mentioned this to him directly. They were all talking behind his back—at a conference about inclusion.

Derek's initial reaction was that he'd been unjustly accused; it was unfair for people to jump to the conclusion that he was a "tech bro." That was certainly not how he saw himself, or how people who knew him well thought of him. Once he blew past his initial hurt at having been stereotyped, however, Derek's curiosity took over. Was this assumption a form of bias, belief, or bullying? Probably bias. But maybe these women consciously believed all men in tech exhibited stereotypical tech-bro behavior. Or maybe it *was* bullying. Maybe these women were just doing to him what had been done to them all too often—singling him out because he was of the underrepresented gender.

This exploration led him to the insight that *any* majority group, irrespective of its composition, is capable of creating an exclusive environment. If *this* group of people—thought leaders around diversity and inclusion—were capable of creating an exclusive environment, any group could. Any majority group, especially a supermajority, is likely to create the conditions for bias, prejudice, and bullying. Usually accidentally, sometimes on purpose. And that, in turn, creates an environment that excludes or even feels hostile to those who are underrepresented.

Finally, Derek felt grateful for this clarifying moment of empathy. For years he had known intellectually that it was unfair that, on a team that was ~90 percent men, the smallest gesture of a woman might become a source of unkind gossip and unreasonable conclusions about her character. He had known it, but now he *felt* it.

It's important to point out the difference between the safety-pin moment for me and the fist-bump moment for Derek. The "safety-pin" moments happen to me all the time, and the "fist-bump" moment was for Derek a unique experience. I am often one of very few women in a group because of systemic injustice that has caused women to be underrepresented in tech. I've been on too many teams that are all white because of systemic injustice that has caused white people to be over-represented in tech. More on systemic injustice in chapters 9 and 10.

The Haircut

A colleague who is gay had been hired to give a big presentation to a client. Unbeknownst to her, the client had found an old picture of her with long hair and sent it out to all the partners. They were expecting that hair. As it happened, she had since gotten a short haircut. Upon meeting her, the client complained that her short hair was "unprofessional." Since all the men in the room had short hair, there was nothing inherently unprofessional about short hair. If she'd been wearing a more traditionally feminine business attire with makeup and heels rather than a pantsuit, it's unlikely the short hair alone would have bothered the client. But she was not conforming to their expectations of the way a woman "should" look. It is strange that one person would think they get to tell another what haircut to get or what clothes to wear, but it happens all the time.

The unfairness of the complaint was obvious, but its source was not. Was it at the intersection of gender bias and heteronormative bias? Or did it reflect real prejudice? If so, was the prejudice against women in business or against gay people? Or was the client trying to bully my colleague? If so why? Because she was a woman? Because she was gay? Because she was both?

PEOPLE HARMED & ⸺
| BIAS PREJUDICE BULLYING | ⚡ DISCRIMINATION HARASSMENT PHYSICAL VIOLATIONS

This confusion about the offender's intentions can be a big obstacle to sticking up for oneself, so focusing on that confusion and thinking consciously about how to get some clarity is important.

RECOGNIZING BIAS

The vast majority of us exhibit bias.[3] This by itself doesn't make us bad people—and it also doesn't make bias inevitable. The moral failure comes when we refuse to notice or address the bias, the harm it does, and the ways in which bias often leads to prejudice, discrimination, harassment, abuse, and violence. Sometimes, recognizing your own bias can help you to confront the bias of others with more compassion.

You don't have to have done tons of research or nailed down a perfect definition of bias in order to recognize it and respond to it when you feel it somehow working against you at your job. To help you get started, here are some examples of how bias commonly plays out in the workplace:

- **Making incorrect role assumptions.** A Latino CEO I know once had an employee hand him her car keys on the way into a meeting, assuming he was the valet. Luckily for the employee, the CEO had a sense of humor about the mistake. A white American man who is married to a well-known African woman got an education about racial bias the first time he traveled with his wife. When the couple arrived at their hotel, not one, not two, but *three* people assumed she was a hotel clerk. This despite the fact she was in line with them and not behind the desk.
- **Making incorrect "task" assumptions.** A team at a big tech company decided they wanted to go out for Mexican food. A white man who worked on the team asked a Puerto Rican colleague to find the best Mexican restaurant in town. Perhaps he didn't know the difference between Puerto Rico and Mexico; perhaps

he simply thought women should be in charge of the restaurant choices; perhaps both nationality and gender came into play. Perhaps he thought her heritage was Mexican, but even if it were, his request struck her as odd. Why would he assume she therefore should make the reservation? Given his last name, she assumed his heritage was Italian, but it would never have occurred to her to ask him to pick an Italian restaurant. People often expect people who are underrepresented to do what legal scholar Joan Williams calls "the office housework"—taking the notes, planning the off-site, clearing the coffee cups.[4]

- **Making incorrect assumptions about intelligence/skills.** In his memoir, civil rights attorney and presidential adviser Vernon Jordan tells of a searing incident that occurred during his summer job driving a retired white banker around Atlanta. While his employer napped after lunch, Jordan used the free time to read. "Vernon can read!" he later heard the man exclaim in astonishment to his relatives.[5]
- **Making incorrect assumptions about expertise.** An anecdote told by Rebecca Solnit illustrates how bias plays out as "mansplaining." When a man at a party asked her what she wrote about, she replied that she'd written a biography of the nineteenth-century photographer Eadweard Muybridge. Had she heard, he wanted to know, about the "very important" new book on Muybridge that had come out that very year? Solnit writes, "So caught up was I in my assigned role as ingénue that I was perfectly willing to entertain the possibility that another book on the same subject had come out simultaneously, and I'd somehow missed it . . . Mr. Very Important was going on smugly about this book I should have known when [my friend] Sallie interrupted him, to say, 'That's her book.' Or tried to interrupt him, anyway."[6] Even after Sallie had succeeded in making it clear to Mr. Very Important that Solnit was, in fact, the biography's author, he continued to lecture her about it as if he knew more about the book than she, the woman who had written it, did.

PEOPLE HARMED &

[BIAS] PREJUDICE BULLYING ⚡ DISCRIMINATION HARASSMENT PHYSICAL VIOLATIONS

- **Using names or gender pronouns incorrectly.** Admittedly, relearning a person's name and gender pronouns can take a concerted effort, but it is fair to hold others to the commitment of respecting their colleagues. When colleagues persist in using incorrect pronouns, or use a trans person's "dead name" (the name the person was assigned at birth), we are imposing our assumptions about gender and who the person is. Nobody has the right to tell others who they are.

- **Ignoring one person's idea, then celebrating the exact same idea from a different person moments later.** Sometimes, a woman offers a good idea at a meeting and everyone seems puzzled. It's as though a piece of furniture has just spoken up. There's an awkward silence, and then the meeting proceeds. About 90 seconds later a man says exactly the same thing and is hailed as a genius. This experience is so common that there's a name for it: "he-peating." Since Covid-19, many women have noted that they are even more likely to get talked over or "he-peated" on a video call than in an in-person meeting.

"That's an excellent suggestion, Miss Triggs. Perhaps one of the men here would like to make it."

- **Confusing people of the same race, gender, or other attribute.**
  Claudia Rankine describes the pain she experienced when a close
  friend would accidentally call Rankine by the name of her Black
  housekeeper. It's hurtful to be conflated with another person
  because of some shared physical attribute—especially when the
  person making the mistake has a very different relationship with
  you than with the person you're being conflated with.[7]
- **Belittling/insulting word choices.** For example, when men are
  "men" but women are "girls." Using the feminine as a derogatory
  term: "throw like a girl" or "lose to a girl" or saying, "Hello,
  ladies," to a group of men as an insult.[8]
- **Unexamined expectations based on stereotypes.** A woman is
  expected to be "nurturing" or "quiet" and so is punished if she
  has strong opinions; a man to "act like a man" or "grow a pair."
  This disparity explains why men are admired for being tough
  negotiators while women are often punished for the same behavior.
  These stereotypes have become even more problematic in an
  era in which trans and nonbinary people in the workplace may
  find such gender- or body-related stereotypes particularly insulting.

RESPONDING TO BIAS

USE AN "I" STATEMENT TO INVITE THE PERSON TO SEE THINGS FROM YOUR PERSPECTIVE

If it is bias you're confronting, you may choose to help the person notice the mistake. It's not your job to educate the person who just
harmed you. But you may choose to do the work because saying something may cost you less emotionally than remaining silent. If that's the
case, you're not calling the person out; you're inviting the person in to

PEOPLE HARMED &
| BIAS | PREJUDICE BULLYING ⚡ DISCRIMINATION HARASSMENT PHYSICAL VIOLATIONS

understand your perspective. Easier said than done. Quick rule of thumb: even if you don't know what to say, start with the word "I." Starting with the word "I" invites the person to consider things from your point of view—why what they said or did seemed biased to you.

The easiest "I" statement is the simple factual correction. For example, in the safety-pin story above, I could've said, "I'm about to go onstage and give a talk; I think one of the staffers in the yellow T-shirts can help you find a safety pin." Or the executive who was handed the car keys could have said, "I think you've confused me with the valet. I am your CEO, not your valet, here to serve, but in a different capacity." I spent some time, time you won't have in the moment, editing those two suggestions. An "I" statement doesn't need to be perfect; doesn't have to be clever or witty. It can even be clumsy. The point is to say something if you decide you want to respond. My great-grandmother needlepointed pillows for her four daughters with the words "Say something. You can always take it back." I find this a useful mantra for such moments when I want to respond but don't know what to say.

An "I" statement can also let a colleague know you have been harmed without being antagonistic or judgmental. For example, "I don't think you meant to imply what I heard; I'd like to tell you how it sounded to me . . ." An "I" statement can be clear about the harm done while also inviting your colleague to perceive things the way you do or to realize that an incorrect assumption was made.

An "I" statement is a generous response to someone else's unconscious bias. It may be more emotionally satisfying to say, "Don't you realize what a pig you're being when you say that?" But shaming is an ineffective strategy. When a person feels attacked or labeled (e.g., "They're calling me a sexist/racist/homophobe/other label"), it's much harder for the person to be open to your feedback.

Another benefit of an "I" statement is that it's a good way to figure out where the other person is coming from. If people respond politely or apologetically, it will confirm your diagnosis of unconscious bias. If they double down or go on the attack, then you'll know you're dealing with prejudice or bullying.

What if you're not sure it's bias? It's OK. You don't have to be 100 percent sure to speak up. Whether you're right or wrong, your feedback is a gift. When you speak up, remain open to the possibility that you're wrong about which attitude is behind the behavior, yet also confident in your own perception—this *is* how it struck you. If you're right and it was bias, you've given the person an opportunity to learn; if you're wrong, you've given the person an opportunity to explain what was meant. Either way, if a colleague's comment feels "off," it's often worth exploring further. Though I want to acknowledge there *are* times when the risks clearly outweigh the rewards. I am not saying you "should" speak up. I am offering you a way to think about how to speak up if you want to.

Below are more examples of the sorts of "I" statements you can use when confronting common experiences of bias. Note that these are not meant to be used verbatim, like scripts. They will be more effective if delivered in language that seems like it's you talking, not me.

Incorrect role assumption. You, a woman, are negotiating a deal with Wilson, and you have brought along your summer intern, Jack, to take notes. But Wilson directs his comments to Jack.

> **What you might be thinking:**
> *You're assuming Jack is the boss because he has a dick. Typical.*
> **"I" Statement:**
> *Wilson, I am the person you are negotiating with. This is Jack, my summer intern.*

Incorrect "task" assumptions. You get asked to take the notes in every meeting.

> **What you might be thinking:**
> *Because I'm a woman, you assholes always ask me to take notes.*
> **"I" Statement:**
> *I can't contribute substantively to the conversation if I always have to take notes. Can someone else take notes this week?*[9]

Ignoring one person's idea, then celebrating the exact same idea from a different person moments later. Every time you offer a recommendation you get ignored, but when a man says the same thing five minutes later, it's a "great idea."

What you might be thinking:
Why are you hailing him as a genius when he is simply re-peating what I just said two minutes ago?
"I" Statement:
Yes, I STILL think that's a great idea. (N.B.: You don't have to do this for yourself; you can ask upstanders on your team to notice when an underrepresented person makes a key point but someone from the majority later repeats it and gets credit for it; ask the upstanders not only to notice but to chime in and say, "Great idea, it sounds a lot like what X said a few minutes ago.")[10]

Conflating people of the same race or gender when they are the minority in a group. You are one of two people of your ethnicity and/or gender on your team of thirty people. Multiple people keep confusing the two of you.

What you might be thinking:
We don't all look alike, you asshole.
"I" Statement:
I am Alex, not Sam.

It can be useful to be more explicit about what just happened. "I think you confused me with someone who looks like me to you." If you have the kind of relationship and humor that makes it comfortable, you can make a small joke. "Sam is the other woman/person of color on the team. I am Alex" or "It's not a mystery why you put me into the same bucket as Sam. It's bias." Growing up in Memphis, I was friends with a Korean American. When I once called her by the name of another Korean American, she said to me, "When my father moved here, he thought all white people looked alike, just like you think all Koreans look alike." Her remark gave us an opportunity to have a real con-versation about this sort of biased conflation. It was embarrassing to talk about but would have been more embarrassing *not* to talk about.

Responding to bias with an "I" statement has a number of benefits. I am not trying to "should" all over you. I'm not saying you "should" speak up. But many of us are more acutely aware of the downsides than the upsides of responding. It can be helpful to think through the pros since we feel the cons in our gut.

First, by speaking up, you are affirming yourself. Every time someone says something that bothers you and you ignore it, a tiny feeling of helplessness creeps in. Every time you respond, your sense of agency is strengthened.

Second, you are interrupting the bias that is harming you, and you may even persuade the offender to change behavior, which will improve things not only for you but for others.

Third, by speaking up clearly and kindly, you will be supporting the notion that doing so is acceptable behavior, encouraging others to do the same. Doing this often establishes that having one's bias confronted does not make one irredeemably bad, thus making others more comfortable pointing out bias when they notice it. This is how norms—standards of social behavior—are established. When we ignore bias, we allow it to be repeated and reinforced.

Fourth, your relationship with your colleague may improve thanks to your intervention. It is easier to get along with someone who isn't doing something that pisses you off over and over.

Fifth, you are doing the person who is saying the biased thing a favor. If they don't consciously mean what they are saying, when you point it out, you give them an opportunity to stop making that mistake.

Often corporate feedback training will advise you to respond by saying, "When you do X, it makes me feel Y." But I don't recommend this approach when confronting bias at work. In these situations, you don't want to give anyone else the power to "make" you feel anything. Furthermore, you don't want to fuel the "She's overly sensitive" or "He's always angry" flames of bias. You want to correct the bias, get the facts on the table, and show the harm done.

THOUGHTS ON BIAS AND EMOTION

In his Instagram curbside ministries, entrepreneur and brand guru Jason Mayden advises people who are overrepresented, "Stop saying that us being emotional is somehow regarded as a negative thing in corporate America."[11] And he offers this advice to people who are

PEOPLE HARMED &
BIAS | PREJUDICE BULLYING ⚡ DISCRIMINATION HARASSMENT PHYSICAL VIOLATIONS

underrepresented: "What's wrong with being emotional? It means I'm human, it means I care, it means I'm actually present, I'm available to understand with an EQ not just an IQ how to treat people."[12]

Anger in particular is an emotion that bias makes it dangerous for underrepresented people to show. This harms people's health and careers. Being constantly on guard against saying what you really think and showing how you really feel can disrupt sleep patterns and diminish one's ability to contribute at work. Research has only recently begun to measure this toll on the health of BIPOC in the workplace.[13]

"By effectively severing anger from 'good womanhood,' we choose to sever girls and women from the emotion that best protects us against danger and injustice," writes Soraya Chemaly in *Rage Becomes Her*. Rebecca Traister's book *Good and Mad* explores how our society tries to repress anger in women, but how important anger has been to galvanizing women to push for change. Anger has created a sense of solidarity among women of all classes and races since the 2016 election.[14]

I once dated a white man who was an investment banker. I watched in fascination one evening as he started screaming profanities at his colleagues on a work call. I was afraid he might lose his job. When he hung up and I expressed concern, he looked puzzled. "Oh, it's no big deal." And it wasn't, I realized—not for him. But if I had expressed even a tenth of the rage he had, I'm sure I would have been fired instantly.

Those of us who are committed to a just workplace must strive to strike an equitable balance. There is a difference between expressing legitimate anger/annoyance/disappointment/impatience and being abusive. For example, I thought the investment bank where my boyfriend felt free to scream profanities at his colleagues had an abusive culture. One problem was that underrepresented people wouldn't have been allowed to behave that way while white men were. But the more fundamental cultural problem there from my perspective was that *nobody* should've been allowed to behave so disrespectfully and obnoxiously.

The incessant fear of letting one's feelings be known even as one attempts to process them is exhausting and debilitating. It is important to make sure that the standards of expressiveness or restraint expected are reinforced equally across the board.

RESPONDING TO PREJUDICE

USE AN "IT" STATEMENT

What do you say when people consciously *believe* that the stereotypes they are spouting off about are true—when you are confronting active prejudice rather than unconscious bias?

It's hard to respond to bias, but it's much harder to respond when people believe that your gender, race, religion, sexual orientation, gender identity, socioeconomic background, or any other personal attribute makes you incapable or inferior in some way.

One, if you're like me, prejudice makes you madder than bias. I am *way* more pissed off when someone asserts that it's been scientifically proven that women are biologically programmed to be this or that than I am when someone makes a remark that reveals some unconscious bias. Anger can make it harder to respond—especially for people who are not "allowed" to show anger as a result of bias. It's bias piled on top of prejudice.

Two, you're probably less optimistic that a confrontation will result in change when it's prejudice rather than bias that you're dealing with. People won't apologize for their prejudiced beliefs just because you point them out; they *know* what they think. So why bother discussing it? The reason to confront prejudice is to draw a bright line between that person's right to believe whatever they want and your right not to have that belief imposed upon you.

Using an "It" statement is an effective way to demarcate this boundary. One type of "It" statement appeals to human decency: "It is disrespectful/cruel/et cetera to . . ." For example, "It is disrespectful to call a grown woman a girl." Another references the policies or a code of conduct at your company: For example, "It is a violation of our

PEOPLE HARMED &
BIAS | PREJUDICE | BULLYING ⚡ DISCRIMINATION   HARASSMENT   PHYSICAL VIOLATIONS

company policy to hang a Confederate flag above your desk. It invokes slavery and will harm our team's ability to collaborate." The third invokes the law: For example, "It is illegal to refuse to hire women."

BEYOND THE BOUNDARY:
AN INVITATION TO CONSIDER

Once you've established that boundary, you can decide whether you want to engage with the person further. Is this a "Good fences make good neighbors" situation or a "Let's sit down and break bread together" situation? If you decide it's the latter, your "It" statement has already made it clear that it's not OK for the person to impose the belief on you. At the same time, you must realize that the odds are against your changing the person's mind or convincing the person to abandon the prejudice. What, then, should be your goal? Why engage? Here are some possible reasons.

- **To offer another perspective:** You want to express who you are and what you believe, not necessarily to change the person but rather to express yourself, to avoid feeling silenced. *Rising Out of Hatred,* a book about how Derek Black left white nationalism, illustrates this. Matthew Stevenson invited his classmate Derek to a Shabbat dinner to share with him a very different worldview. Matthew put it well: "It's our job to push the rock, not necessarily to move the rock."[15]
- **To hone your argument:** You aren't only challenging the prejudice; you're also allowing the person to challenge your point of view. That can help you deepen and improve your opinions. If your goal is to clarify and improve your own thinking and arguments rather than to change the other person's, the conversation will be far less frustrating.
- **To find common ground:** A prejudiced belief, no matter how profoundly you disagree with it, does not constitute the whole person. Sometimes, if you manage to find something you agree on—music or hiking or the importance of family, or even the job itself—you may find it easier to work with the person. Take the friendship between Justices Ruth Bader Ginsburg and Antonin Scalia as inspiration here.[16]

"PROOF" AND PREJUDICE

Sometimes a person's belief is so blatantly prejudiced that it leaves you feeling gobsmacked. You hardly know what to say. Toni described a fellow employee, Don, who loved to talk about the Big Five personality test, a taxonomy for personality traits often used to explain success at work or academic performance.[17] He claimed it "proved" that women were biologically more neurotic than men, and that this explained why his company's employee-engagement data showed that women were less happy than men. The company's leaders, however, had concluded that the reason for the discrepancy was the disrespectful way that women were treated on teams that were over 70 percent men, and so the leaders required all their employees to go through unconscious bias training. Don refused, arguing that he had "proof" that the problem was women's neuroticism, not men's bias and the resulting microaggressions in meetings and macroaggressions in promotion committees.

If you were Toni and Don said this to you, how would you respond? The easiest thing would be to shut down the debate: "It is a requirement of your continued employment here that you attend the training. If you don't want to go, talk to your boss, not to me" or "It is a giant distraction from our work to assert unfounded interpretations of Big Five research. I will not discuss this with you."

If you want to, you could also say something that acknowledges, then disputes, his stance: "The Big Five personality test is a tool. It does not produce irrefutable facts. So it is inaccurate to assert things like 'women are biologically more neurotic than men' as though this is a proven fact. If you dig deeper, you'll find that in countries where women and men face equal economic insecurity, men and women are equally neurotic. Furthermore, it contributes to a hostile work environment for women when you say women are more neurotic than men. And if management doesn't take action when one person contributes to a hostile work environment, the company is legally liable, and so is the individual manager. Continuing to assert that women are unhappy

PEOPLE HARMED &
BIAS [PREJUDICE] BULLYING ⚡ DISCRIMINATION HARASSMENT PHYSICAL VIOLATIONS

because they are neurotic and not because of the way they are being treated is therefore likely to get you fired."

Prejudiced Beliefs About Child-Rearing

I once had a colleague, Alexander, who believed that women with children should not work outside the home. We were chatting amiably about our kids one day when, out of the blue, he said it:

"My wife stays home because it's better for the children."

At first, I thought he meant it was better for his own children. It was inconceivable to me that he was implying that I was a bad parent because I chose to have a career. So I made a little joke to give him a chance to clarify: "Oh. I decided to show up at work today because I thought it was better to neglect my children."

He didn't let it go. "But, Kim, studies show it really is better for the children if the mother doesn't work."

That's when I reached for my "It" statement: "It is an HR violation to tell me I am harming my kids by showing up at work. It creates a hostile working environment for women when you tell them they are bad mothers. Plus, it's disrespectful and downright mean. I love my kids as much as you love yours."

As I intended, the simple words "hostile work environment" shut him down. But I still had to work with him. His idea that I was harming my children could play out in all kinds of subtle ways that would hurt me. For one, how could I expect him to respect me if he thought I was neglecting my children by having a full-time job? I worried that he wouldn't want to work with me on projects that required travel because he'd feel uncomfortable about my being away from home. (It was strange that he'd worry about my time away from my family but not his time away from his family.) So I decided to engage with him.

"Look, Alexander, I'm not going to make a thing of this with HR. But you should know that it is a gut punch to tell a woman she is neglecting her kids. It will hurt your ability to collaborate with women if you go around saying that sort of thing. And it will probably get you into trouble."

"I see," he said.

"But since you brought it up, let me tell you why I think you are wrong. That OK?"

"Sure. I'd like to hear how you think about it. I mean, you don't *seem* like a bad person."

I felt more, not less, annoyed after this backhanded remark, but I took a deep breath and kept going. "I could give you studies that show that the children of mothers who work are better off, not worse off. But I won't give you those studies because I don't want to leave you with the impression that I don't respect the choices you and your wife have made, and also because they are irrelevant to the choices you've made. There's not just one right way to live, one right way to raise your children. What is best on average may have nothing at all to do with what is best for your family or for my family."

Now, to my surprise, *he* was offended, even though I felt I was bending over backward to be respectful. "Are you saying," he asked indignantly, "that my wife is wasting her time staying home with our kids—or even hurting them? Now who's creating a hostile work environment?"

"No, that wasn't at all what I was saying." I was frustrated but willing to keep going. "I was trying to say—and I am sorry if I wasn't clear enough—that I am sure that you and your wife are making the right decisions for your family. *And* I am equally sure that my husband and I are making the right decisions for our family. You and I have different studies about what is best on average. But there's no point arguing about them because what's best on average may have nothing to do with a specific situation—yours or mine."

"Well, I still believe it's better if the mother stays home."

We were back where we'd started.

"Do you believe I would do something that harmed my kids?" I asked.

"Not knowingly" was as far as he'd concede. "I just don't think you have all the data I have."

"And I don't think you have all the data I have. I'll read your studies if you will you read mine."

At this Alexander laughed, acknowledging that he didn't want to commit to taking the time to read my studies any more than I wanted to read his. Neither of us wanted to spend more time talking about this: we were ready to get back to work. But it seemed to me that we'd arrived at a truce and were on friendly ground again. Still, I wanted to make it explicit.

"How about this?" I proposed, going back to another "It" statement. "Can we agree on these two things? It is my decision, with my husband, how we raise our kids. And it is your decision, with your wife, how you raise yours. And that you and I respect one another enough not to judge each other's decisions harshly?"

"Of course." He smiled and stuck out his hand. I shook it. I didn't change his belief, and he didn't change mine, but he never again accused me of neglecting my kids. Engaging took a little time and some emotional energy, but not engaging would've taken more out of both of us in the long run. And would probably have harmed me more than him.

That is why we do any kind of work. We get more out of it than we put into it.

"F*^k That Noise" Is Not an "It" Statement, but It May Be the Opening Salvo You Need

In business school, I took a class called Economic Strategies of Nations. One evening my friend Terrence and I were studying together, reading an article our professor had assigned by the sociologist Charles Murray that offered the following, er, wisdom: "Young males are essentially barbarians for whom marriage—meaning . . . the act of taking responsibility for a wife and children—is an indispensable civilizing force."[18] This was not unconscious bias; this was a conscious prejudice.

When I read that, I jumped up, read it again out loud, threw the article on the table, and exploded, "I'm supposed to make myself economically and physically vulnerable to a barbarian so that I can civilize him? F*^k that noise! He can figure out how to civilize his own damn self. And, Terrence, why aren't you more offended than I am?"

Perhaps the professor had deliberately assigned a provocative reading, knowing that we would encounter such prejudiced beliefs in our careers and needed to be ready to confront them. Or perhaps he believed that crap. Either way, I dreaded class the next day.

When I got to class, nobody voiced an objection to the illogic of what we'd read. I sat there mutely. I wasn't sure I could make my feelings known about Murray's argument without dropping an f-bomb. And I wasn't sure I could get away with that. Of course, men dropped f-bombs all the time at business school. There it was. Bias repressing my emotion, making it harder for me to confront prejudice.

Terrence kept shooting me meaningful looks, silently urging me to say what I'd said the night before. The longer the minutes ticked by and nobody else called BS, the more alone I felt in my outrage. Had nobody else found the article offensive? If not, why not? Was I wrong?

Finally, Terrence, in an upstander moment, raised his hand. "I was talking to Kim about the article last night, and she made some really good points."

"Yes, Kim?" the professor asked.

"Well . . ." I pulled out the text about civilizing barbarians and read it out loud. "Here's what I told Terrence I think about this paragraph. *F*^k that noise.*" Before I could say more, the whole class, including the professor, burst out laughing. It turned out I *could* get angry and I *could* curse and it was OK—more than OK. It was an important revelation.

"I can certainly understand your point of view," the professor said, and waited for me to expound on what I meant. I was so offended by what I'd read, though, that I didn't know where to start. While I tried to gather my thoughts, someone else jumped in and moved the conversation in a different direction.

Twenty-five years later, I still think about that moment. At the core of so much prejudice against women is the pernicious belief Murray articulated in that essay: that men can't be held accountable for their own executive function and, implicitly, that it's women's responsibility to keep them in line. It's not just Charles Murray. It's an old and persistent myth that women *should* not only remain subordinate to men but also be responsible for managing their behavior. The Beast is a beast until Belle comes to save him from himself.[19] *Walk the Line* does the same thing: Johnny Cash is an alcoholic and a drug addict until

PEOPLE HARMED &
BIAS [PREJUDICE] BULLYING ⚡ DISCRIMINATION HARASSMENT PHYSICAL VIOLATIONS

June comes to the rescue.[20] Pundits such as Jordan Peterson assert that because these myths are so prevalent in ancient mythology and popular culture, they must be true.[21] I say it's time to call BS.

Also, it astounded me that the men in the class didn't object to the notion that they should cede their executive function to women. They were all planning to become executives, after all! Yet they often seemed to feel they "couldn't" control themselves. This wasn't just an abstract intellectual prejudice. Some of my classmates tried to impose this idea on me in the classroom.

For example, the guy who sat above and behind me in the class's stadium seating complained to me that when I stretched or even just sat up straight, my breasts distracted him. He suggested that I sit hunched over to hide my chest or wear baggier clothing. His friend backed him up, doing an exaggerated imitation of me, arching his back and sticking his chest out. "How can he possibly concentrate with you sitting there like that?" I was infuriated—but also suddenly self-conscious.

I slouched a little the next couple of days. My confidence started to wane. After one class the professor, who had noticed that I hadn't been participating as much as usual, even asked me if I was OK.

To understand why this was a big deal, I need to give you a little context about business school. Participation was the biggest part of our grade, and a normal class was more like a performance. People had little warm-up routines they'd do before class started. The guy sitting next to me would sit up straight, puff his chest out, and roll his head around, cracking all the bones in his neck. A guy a couple rows behind me always brought in a large empty cup in case he needed to pee during class because he feared that missing even a few minutes might harm his participation grade. A couple of times, to the horror of those sitting around him, he actually used it. The atmosphere was intense, and to deal with it I had my own routine: to sit up straight and stretch before class. It made me feel more ready for action. When I stopped stretching, I stopped talking, and that was going to hurt my grade.

I decided to confront the guy who couldn't keep his eyes off my chest. Although I didn't know it at the time, it may have been my first "It" statement: "It's not my job to control where your eyes or your mind go. It's not reasonable to ask me to slouch or wear different clothes because you can't manage your own brain."

"But you don't understand how hard it is to be a man!" he exclaimed.

"I'm sure I don't," I replied. "Enlighten me!" I may have sounded sarcastic, but though I felt skeptical, I was also genuinely curious. I wanted to know if he could possibly believe what he was saying.

"Everywhere I look, every ad is telling me to stare at women's breasts. It's like there's this constant music everywhere, and it's really hard to tune it out!"

I'd never thought about sexual objectification from a man's perspective before.[22] He seemed sincere, so I decided to give him the benefit of the doubt and listen.

"OK. I can understand how society has conditioned you," I said. "But again, only you can control your mind. I cannot control it. Asking me to make myself invisible is not reasonable for me, and it won't work for you. Even if no women are in the room, your mind is going to wander unless you learn to manage it."

He conceded the point. More important, he quit giving me crap about the way I sat in class. If I saw him glancing at my chest, I'd raise my eyebrows and he'd look away. Pretty soon he managed to stop staring at my chest. My "It" statement—"It's not reasonable"—explained my position much better than "F*^k that noise," as satisfying and important as it was to say that, too.

This ancient prejudice that it's a woman's fault if a man stares at her—or rapes her—runs deep and still causes a lot of harm. Years later, I coached a woman who was having a hard time being taken seriously in meetings at a male-dominated company. As I watched, I noticed her slouch and I knew exactly what she was doing and why. I played her psychologist Amy Cuddy's famous TED Talk where she talks about "postural feedback," the idea that sitting up and standing up straight can make you feel more confident. I had her practice Cuddy's Wonder Woman Pose, which I'd come to understand was what I was doing at business school before class started. The woman I was coaching still slouched during the meetings.[23]

Finally I just said it bluntly. "Look, I may be wrong, but I think I

PEOPLE HARMED &

BIAS [PREJUDICE] BULLYING ⚡ DISCRIMINATION HARASSMENT PHYSICAL VIOLATIONS

know why you slouch like that. You are trying to hide the fact that you have breasts. I did that in my business school class, and it was bad for my performance. You will look and feel more confident if you sit up straight with your shoulders back."

I knew I was giving her good advice, but even I was astounded to notice how well it worked. At the next meeting, the difference in her performance was remarkable. Her boss, a woman, called to thank me and asked me what in the world I had recommended to get such a dramatic improvement in such a short time. I told her, and we had a good laugh: we'd both been there.

It would have been easy simply to dismiss the guy at business school who gave me a hard time for sitting up straight. But I was glad I took the time to identify the core prejudice he was giving voice to and argue with him about it. I don't know if I persuaded him to think differently, but the conversation proved helpful to *me*—and, later, to the women I coached.

RESPONDING TO BULLYING

USE A "YOU" STATEMENT TO CREATE CONSEQUENCES

What is the difference between bullying and conflict? Here's a simple way to think about it, adapted from the work of PACER, a nonprofit that leads a bullying prevention center.[24]

CONFLICT	BULLYING
Disagreement in which both sides express their views	One person aims to hurt, harm, or humiliate another
No status difference between those involved	Person bullying has more in-group status
Person causing harm generally stops and changes their behavior when they realize it is hurting someone	Person causing harm continues their behavior when they realize it is hurting someone

A bully is often emboldened by some sort of illegitimate status. I use the words "in-group status" (e.g., being white when the majority of leaders are white, or having a degree from a university that is particularly respected at the company), not "power," deliberately here. When I talk about bullying, I'm talking about behavior between people who don't have positional power over one another. Once positional power enters the equation, bullying becomes harassment. (See Part Two.)

When someone is bullying you, the person's *goal* is to harm you. Telling the person you are being harmed is just going to result in more bad behavior. Ignoring bullies doesn't work, either. The only way to stop bullying is to create negative consequences for the person doing the bullying. Only when bullying stops being practical or enjoyable will bullies alter their behavior. When you're the victim of bullying, though, you often feel powerless to stop it.

One way to push back is to confront the person with a "You" statement, as in "What's going on for you here?" or "You need to stop talking to me that way." A "You" statement is a decisive action, and it can be surprisingly effective in changing the dynamic. That's because the bully is trying to put you in a submissive role, to demand that you answer the questions to shine a scrutinizing spotlight on you. When you reply with a "You" statement, you are now taking a more active role, asking them to answer the questions, shining a scrutinizing spotlight on them.

An "I" statement invites the person to consider your perspective; an "It" statement establishes a clear boundary beyond which the other person should not go. With a "You" statement, you are talking about the bully, not yourself. People can let your statement lie or defend themselves against it, but they are playing defense rather than offense in either case.

I don't relish conflict, so "You" statements don't come naturally. My impulse, when someone harms me, is to let that person know how the behavior made me feel. It was my daughter who first pointed out to me that showing that kind of vulnerability when you are being bullied is counterproductive.

PEOPLE HARMED &
BIAS   PREJUDICE   [BULLYING]   ⚡ DISCRIMINATION   HARASSMENT   PHYSICAL VIOLATIONS

She had come home one day from school upset that a kid whom I'll call Austin was giving her a hard time on the playground. I advised her to give Austin the benefit of the doubt, to say something along the lines of "When you knock my lunch off the table, I get really hungry, and it hurts my feelings." That got me a big eye roll. Her teacher had made a recommendation along the same lines. "What is wrong with adults?" my daughter wanted to know. "Why don't you get it? Austin is *trying* to hurt my feelings! If I say, 'What you did hurt my feelings,' it's like saying, 'Good job, Austin, mission accomplished, you did what you wanted to do.' It's like giving Austin a *cookie* for being mean to me!"

My daughter was absolutely correct.

IF POSSIBLE, FOLLOW UP THE "YOU" STATEMENT WITH IMMEDIATE CONSEQUENCES

One rainy morning in New York, I was running late for work in Manhattan and decided to take a cab. After what seemed like an interminable wait, I finally hailed one. Sopping wet, I had just slid the door open and was about to get in when a man ran out of his building, put his hand on top of my taxi as if he owned it, and said, "*My* cab, little lady." He was using his size and gender to intimidate and bully me.

I said, "You can't just steal my cab!" I followed up my "You" statement with action. I caught the cabdriver's eye to establish solidarity, slid under the big man's arm into the car, pushed him out of the way with my feet, slammed the door shut, and locked it. The driver, an excellent upstander, locked the rest of the doors, and then slapped his leg, laughing as he pulled away from the curb. We laughed all the way downtown.

You won't always be able to offer immediate consequences. And don't take unnecessary risks. But the closer the consequence is to the behavior, the faster the person will learn that bullying doesn't work.

"If You Think That Little Old Thing Is Going to Intimidate Me, You're Wrong"

Here's another rare moment in my career when I was ready with a "you" statement. Most of the time I bungled these moments; I'm telling these stories because they were as gratifying as they were rare. In 1999 I worked for a nonprofit in Pristina, the capital of Kosovo. I was managing a pediatric clinic for Albanian refugees. Shortly after I arrived, two of the Albanian staff came to me in tears. William, the man who headed up logistics for the nonprofit, had said racist, threatening things to them. This wasn't the first time he'd behaved this way.

I called the head office in Munich, and they agreed he needed to return home to Germany, after which they would figure out next steps. However, William refused to come into the office to have a conversation with me, so I told him I was coming to his apartment and brought along a colleague for backup. When we arrived, he didn't answer the front door, so we walked around to the back, where we saw him through a sliding glass door, standing with his back to us in a red bathrobe drinking beer. I knocked. William whirled around, and when he saw me, he took a step forward, looked me in the eye defiantly, opened his bathrobe, and exposed himself.

"If you think that little old thing is going to intimidate me, you're wrong," I said.

At my words, he wrapped his bathrobe back around himself. My colleague and I persuaded him to get on the next plane to Munich.

It's hard to think of the right thing to say when confronted with that kind of bullying, and most of the time I am left gobsmacked, and not in a good way. One thing that helps is simply to start by saying "You" even if you don't know what you'll say next. Then notice what comes out of your mouth. Maybe it will be "You are behaving like a bully" or "You are not funny" or "You are being unprofessional" or "You . . . Why do you say that?" or "You . . . What is going on for you here?" Sometimes you might just say "You . . . are wearing a white shirt." Whatever you say, though, you've shifted the attention to the other person, they have to respond, and you are no longer on your back foot—even if you determine it is too risky to point out the bad behavior explicitly.

PEOPLE HARMED &
BIAS   PREJUDICE   [BULLYING]   ⚡ DISCRIMINATION   HARASSMENT   PHYSICAL VIOLATIONS

Unaffiliated or Unattached?

Not long after I returned from Kosovo, I joined a very formal institution dedicated to increasing knowledge about foreign policy. Members convened regularly in the group's stately Manhattan headquarters for a luncheon and an address by an academic expert or a government official. One such meeting concerned U.S. policy toward Kosovo. After the speaker finished his talk, he offered to answer questions from the audience. Even though I knew more about the situation there than most of the other people in the room, I was reluctant to ask a question myself. The protocol required standing up, introducing yourself, and saying where you worked. The room was full of high-powered people, most of them older men, and I was a young woman, unemployed at the moment.

As I was gathering up my nerve, a well-known investor and philanthropist rose to ask a question. When he stated his name and affiliation, everyone smiled because they already knew who he was. The idea of standing up and saying "I'm Kim and I'm unemployed" felt even harder.

The next question came from a well-known, recently retired investment banker. He stood up, stated his name, and said he was "unaffiliated." Oh! So that was the word the club members used for "unemployed." I put my hand back up. When the speaker called on me, I rose to my feet and said my name and that I was "unaffiliated."

A man in the back of the room shouted out, "Unaffiliated or unattached?" The room burst into laughter. I wish I could say that I took this in my stride. But the threat of hot, humiliated tears stung my eyes. I took a deep breath, pretended not to notice the remark, and asked my question.

Before I write what I wish I'd said, it's important to point out that if even one person had stood up, turned to Mr. Unaffiliated-or-Unattached, and said, "Why are you being so rude?" or "You can't talk to other members so disrespectfully," it would have changed the tone in the room 180 degrees. He would have felt embarrassed instead of me. If even one person had come up to me afterward and said this behavior was bullying and unkind, that *also* would have made a world of difference to me. But nobody did.

I never felt comfortable there again and I wound up resigning, even though that meant giving up an extraordinary network. Worse, my failure to respond was terrible for my self-esteem. Speaking up would have restored my sense of dignity—and it would more than likely have helped my reputation and hurt his.

If I were advising my younger self, I'd tell her to trust the "You" statement, to open her mouth, say the word "You," and trust what comes out next:

- "Why would you ask me such an inappropriate question?"
- "Are you uncomfortable having more women join this organization?"
- "Do you make it a habit to bully younger women members?"
- "Are you trying to haze me? This isn't a fraternity."

People often want me to give them a script, but it's much better if you choose language that works for you; my words won't necessarily feel right in your mouth. Even a script I write for myself in advance may not feel right in the moment. Choose a few "you" statements or "you" questions that you can imagine actually saying when you feel bullied. And then practice saying them. Practice in the mirror, practice with other people. Break them in, like a new pair of hiking boots, so they will feel just right when you need to use them.

DON'T GO NUMB OR REPLICATE BULLYING

Comedian and author Lindy West describes the best response to bullying: "Do a good job. Be vulnerable. Make things. Choose to be kind."[25]

As my daughter pointed out, you don't want to expose your vulnerability to the bully, whom you cannot trust. But that doesn't mean you can't show your vulnerability to anyone. Vulnerability is necessary to form relationships. As Brené Brown writes, "We need to trust to be vulnerable. And we need to be vulnerable to trust."[26] You don't want a bad experience with bullying to stop you from sharing with colleagues what happened and how it made you feel. Telling your story, showing

PEOPLE HARMED &

BIAS   PREJUDICE   [BULLYING]   ⚡   DISCRIMINATION   HARASSMENT   PHYSICAL VIOLATIONS vulnerability, rather than hiding from the world the harm that bullying caused, can be a much more powerful challenge to bullying behavior than the common response of ignoring it. If you ignore bullying, it's likely to escalate. But that doesn't mean you have to fight bullying with bullying. Don't allow the bullying to turn you into a bully.

HOW DO YOU KNOW IF YOU'RE FACING BIAS, PREJUDICE, OR BULLYING?

TRUST YOUR INSTINCTS

As noted, when I'm not sure whether it's bias, prejudice, or bullying I'm confronting, I usually start by responding as though it's bias. If I'm right, this puts me in the best position to point out the bias without eliciting a defensive response. I can always escalate from an "I" statement to an "It" or "You" statement if the person's initial response indicates that I'm dealing with prejudice or bullying.

My freedom to default to bias may be an example of privilege. The Black Lives Matter protests have highlighted what mainstream white America has long refused to notice: how frequently what we call bias is not unconscious bias, but rather conscious prejudice; and how both bias and prejudice turn violent in the blink of an eye. Treating racism as though it were simply unconscious bias puts people in harm's way. A painful illustration of this: during the Black Lives Matter protests in summer 2020, a San Jose police officer shot rubber bullets at and seriously injured a Black man who'd provided unconscious bias training to the same police department.[27]

I do not want to put anyone in harm's way by giving advice that is not relevant to the situation the person is in.

My advice to you is this: *trust your instincts*. If you respond to a remark as if it's evidence of prejudice or bullying when it was in fact bias, that's OK. It's still useful feedback. It communicates that what they've said suggested to you that they hold prejudiced beliefs, or that their goal was to be intentionally hurtful. That's good for people to know so that they are in a better position to understand the harm and correct themselves in the future. It's not your job to dance around other people's defensiveness or denial.

Remember, we have not yet talked about discrimination or harassment or physical violations. Discrimination is what happens when people have enough power to put their bias or prejudice into action—for example, to refuse you a job or a promotion. Harassment is what happens when people have enough power to put their bullying into action. Physical violations are what happen when people have the power to touch you in a way you don't want to be touched. Often, though not always, discrimination, harassment, and physical violations cross a line from inappropriate to illegal. You'll want to deal with these behaviors differently from the way you deal with bias, prejudice, and bullying. We'll cover how to deal with them in Part Two.

DECIDING WHETHER TO RESPOND: DO NOT DEFAULT TO SILENCE

You're in the flow of a meeting and out of nowhere it happens. Someone drops a comment that leaves you gasping. Maybe it's what Dr. A. Breeze Harper, co-founder of Critical Diversity Solutions, calls "racist compliment syndrome," where she gets complimented by a white person for something basic. For example, "You dress so professionally!" or "You are so articulate" or, in an extreme case discussed earlier, "Vernon can read!" But it also could be something like "We'd better send Bill in your place since we are up against a really tough negotiator." Or "Remember, don't get emotional/angry/weepy." Or maybe it's a comment like "You plan the party; I'm not good at that kind of thing." Or "Can you get us a reservation at the restaurant?"

In these moments I know that if I speak up, odds are high I'll be told I'm overreacting—and then I'll *really* be pissed. So pissed I might react in a way I later regret. How can I break free of this catch-22?

The default response for me and many others is to stay silent. I'd

PEOPLE HARMED & ⎯⎯⎯⎯
⎡ BIAS   PREJUDICE   BULLYING ⎤ ⚡ DISCRIMINATION   HARASSMENT   PHYSICAL VIOLATIONS

like to change that default. Which is not to say silence is never the correct response. It just doesn't need to be the *default* response.

I had a mentor who I always assumed was skeptical about gender bias, so I didn't generally talk much with him about my experiences of it. One day I posted on LinkedIn about something biased someone had said to me and asked people how they would have responded. To my surprise, my mentor read the post and said to me privately: "Thank you for posting that. I'm sure I've said things like that to women. I hate to think I've done it, but I'm sure I have. Now that I understand, I'll do better." I wished I'd said more sooner. If I'd given myself permission to speak up, it might have protected someone else from being the target of his unthinking bias. And he was genuinely grateful to me for telling my story.

SOME COMMON RATIONALIZATIONS FOR SILENCE

The pressure to be silent comes in a dizzying array of disguises, internal and external.[28] Here are some common excuses or rationalizations I've used for remaining silent when it would have been better for me to speak up.

RATIONALIZATION: "I'M A NICE PERSON. I DON'T GET IN PEOPLE'S FACES."[29]

One of the reasons I wrote *Radical Candor* was to confront my deeply ingrained tendency to remain silent when it would be better for everyone if I spoke up. That instinct is hardwired into my brain, probably a result of all the times as a child I was told, "If you don't have anything nice to say, don't say anything at all."

But I've learned that I'm not doing *anyone* a favor by ignoring problematic behavior. It's bad for the other person, whom I'm ostensibly trying to protect because the person is "nice." If someone says something that is biased and I don't point it out, that person is going to keep saying it until one day it gets them in real trouble. It's also bad for the other people on my team. The bias that is bothering me probably bothers others as well. And it's bad for me. If I hear the bias enough, I'm likely to internalize it, so my failure to confront it becomes a form of self-harm.

With *Radical Candor* I also wanted to change the way we define "nice." It's not actually nice to withhold critical feedback simply to avoid making someone feel bad. When we deliver critical feedback kindly and clearly, we help colleagues improve—and, in some cases, avoid being fired. Now *that's* nice. In truth, silence in such situations, far from being nice, is little more than a selfish and ultimately unkind attempt to avoid conflict.

When I explained this idea in *Radical Candor,* I used examples such as pointing out to people that they had spinach in their teeth or their fly was open. Most people would agree that it's uncaring not to point those things out. But if someone makes a casually sexist or racially biased remark or uses "gay" as a pejorative or refers to someone using the wrong pronouns, our instinct is often to let it slide rather than confront it. And yet these are the moments that truly call for Radical Candor. If you care about your colleague who said the problematic thing, you don't want them to keep saying it. And if you care about the other people on your team, you don't want them exposed to harmful comments and attitudes.

This is not as difficult when the problem is bias. Prejudice and bullying can be less comfortable to confront. But if what a person is saying or doing violates a norm or a rule or a law, I am doing them a kindness when I say "It is degrading to . . ." or "It is a policy violation to . . ." or "It is illegal to . . ." And in most cases I am protecting myself and the others on my team by speaking up. Same with bullying. Bullying that runs unopposed escalates until the bully does real harm to me and others, and eventually such bullying gets the bully into real trouble, but not before it has caused huge problems for everyone else. The world would truly be a better place if everyone confronted bullying early and often.

If I clam up in these moments out of concern for my friend's or colleague's feelings, I actually put the person at risk of greater harm. People rely on others to point out their mistakes. My failure to confront them prevents them from addressing a fixable problem. Not so nice of me after all.

PEOPLE HARMED &
| BIAS   PREJUDICE   BULLYING | ⚡ DISCRIMINATION   HARASSMENT   PHYSICAL VIOLATIONS

RATIONALIZATION: "THEY ARE 'A GOOD PERSON'" OR "THEY 'DIDN'T MEAN ANY HARM.'"[30]

Let's say someone I like makes a comment that is off. Because the person is one of my favorite colleagues, I start to rationalize why the person said it. The person is older or younger, or from a different part of the country, or maybe the remark reflects religious beliefs. I don't want to come down hard, hurt feelings, or expose the person to criticism or worse from colleagues and management. So I don't say anything.

In *Radical Candor,* I called this Ruinous Empathy—a failure to deliver feedback for fear of hurting someone's feelings. When gender is added to the equation, there's another dynamic as well: the tendency of many of us to feel the pain of men and dismiss the pain of women. In other words, I might feel that I have to tiptoe around the "fragile male ego," even though such a thing is just a figment of my imagination. Moral philosopher Kate Manne calls this himpathy.[31] So perhaps the "I don't want to hurt his feelings" argument is best characterized as Ruinous Himpathy.

Ruinous Himpathy is bad for me, bad for my colleagues, and even bad for the "him" in question. That's why I've tried to eliminate the phrase "He's a good guy" from my vocabulary. We all do good things and bad things. People who are committed to being good people want to know about the bad things they do so they can make amends and avoid doing them again.

RATIONALIZATION: "IT'S NO BIG DEAL."[32]

Minimizing is a really common rationalization for keeping silent. But if it's no big deal, why am I still thinking about it? And if it's no big deal, then it's also no big deal for me to correct it. Furthermore, if bias, prejudice, and bullying were rare, they *wouldn't* be that big a deal. And yet I experience all three all the time—bias most often.

To combat the rationalization that such moments are no big deal, I think about the *cumulative* impact that experiencing these attitudes and behaviors and then ignoring them will have on me. The one thing may be not a big deal, but when it happens over and over, ignoring it becomes like a repetitive stress injury on my sense of agency. Then I compare that to the cumulative impact on me of experiencing it and then responding. Sometimes people are mad, but often they are grateful. Responding has deepened more relationships than it has strained. This calculation leaves me more likely to respond.

RATIONALIZATION: "I DON'T WANT TO HURT MY WORKING RELATIONSHIP."[33]

I once worked with a man who tended to refer to the women in the office using derogatory words. I didn't know him well, so I kept silent and told myself I'd talk to him about this once I got to know him better. These things were irritating, but he was a creative, interesting person and I wanted to learn from him. But my annoyance was building. Meanwhile, he was pushing the boundaries. When he got away with "girls," he moved on to "babycakes" and "puddums." I just rolled my eyes, but I was getting madder and madder, and he was getting worse and worse. Then one day he walked by me and said, "Hey, toots." I went absolutely apeshit. The damage wasn't irreparable, but it took some time for us to feel comfortable around each other again, and some more time for us to be able to laugh about the incident. It would've been so much better for our relationship if I had responded the first time. When I express my anger early, it's usually a small thing. When I repress my anger, it usually blows up into a big thing.

RATIONALIZATION: "IT WILL ONLY MAKE THINGS WORSE."[34]

A common technique of bullies is to punish anyone who calls them on their behavior. So the fear of retribution is not irrational.

At the same time, I have had a big negativity bias when it comes to confronting injustice. I have consistently overestimated the risks and underestimated the benefits. As a result, I've feared challenging injustice more than I needed to.

PEOPLE HARMED &
| BIAS   PREJUDICE   BULLYING | ⚡ DISCRIMINATION   HARASSMENT   PHYSICAL VIOLATIONS

Over time I've found the cost of *not* speaking up is also real—for me and for my colleagues. When I've stopped to ask myself how likely retribution really is, the answer is often not that likely. Your answer may be different. But ask yourself the question.

RATIONALIZATION: "IT'S NOT WORTH PUTTING MY REPUTATION AT RISK."[35]

I get questions like this from young women all the time:

- "The literature shows that when women are funny, they don't get taken seriously. Is humor dangerous for me in the office? Will being funny hurt my reputation?"
- "This study shows that when women negotiate hard, they are punished. Will being a good negotiator hurt my reputation? Should I quit negotiating so hard?"
- "When I am as aggressive as I must be to get the job done, I get a reputation for being 'abrasive' or 'not likable' and dinged in my performance review. Should I just quit? I can't succeed in this catch-22."

All these questions make me want to scream, "*Nooooo!* Do what you have to do to combat bias; don't conform to it. Don't allow it to make you less than you are."

The worst thing you can do for your career *and* your reputation in the long term is to hide your talents or suppress your voice or not do your best work. But that is exactly what bias, especially the "likability" bias, pressures us to do.

My advice? If you're funny, be as funny as you can be, even if you read an article that says that when a woman is funny, she's taken less seriously; if you're a good negotiator, negotiate, and if you are punished for it, use those negotiation skills to go get a new job; if you must be aggressive to get the job done, be aggressive and confront the "she's abrasive" barbs by taking a few moments to show you care; if you know what you're talking about, don't pretend you don't just because the people in the room might prefer the experts to be men.

As Target's chief diversity officer Caroline Wanga explains eloquently, you can't be great at your job if you can't be who you are at your job, *and* you are well served to focus first on earning credibility at the basics of your job in order to accomplish everything you want to accomplish.[36] Focus on being great at your job, staying true to yourself, and building real relationships; if you do that, a good reputation will follow. A good reputation is the result of being your best self, not something you can achieve by trying to be what you think others want you to be.

One thing that will help you get better at your job, build better relationships on the job, and be yourself at work is feedback. Ask for criticism, don't tune it out. But when what I got was *biased feedback*, I wish I'd challenged it rather than ignoring it. The rap that most bedeviled me, especially early in my career when I felt most vulnerable, was being called "not likable" or "abrasive." In my first job out of college, it was whispered that the CEO of the company called me a "pushy broad." This was name-calling, not feedback. Being told I was "not likable" made it tempting to back off. But when I did, I didn't do as well at my job, and, surprise, surprise, people didn't like me any better. I liked myself best when I was doing my best. And it turns out when I liked myself, other people liked me better, too. I have found that when I confront the bias and hold my ground, I do better work, build better relationships, and wind up with a better reputation. Paradoxically it was learning not to care about my "likability" that made me feel more "likable."

I'll never forget a management offsite with one of my peers. We had to go around and describe one another with a word that began with the first sound of our first name. I braced myself for what he might say because we'd just worked on a project together and I'd been, well, intense about it. "Kim cares," he said. "Some days you might wish she cared a little less. But she really cares. About the people and the work." At another company, I worked with a man who made the usual "Kim is abrasive" or "Kim is a pain in the ass" comments. But after about a year of working closely together, he explained my style to a

PEOPLE HARMED & ⎯⎯⎯⎯⎯
| BIAS   PREJUDICE   BULLYING | ⚡ DISCRIMINATION   HARASSMENT   PHYSICAL VIOLATIONS

new team member: "Kim really loves to debate. At first, you might think she's doing it to drive you nuts. But she's just trying to help you do great work."

Don't get pushed around by bias; push back on it!

SILENCE AND RAGE

I referred to the relationship between silence and rage above, and it's worth emphasizing how debilitating silence-and-rage syndrome can be. The more silent I am, the more angry I am, and the more angry I am, the more likely I am to be silent. In the words of Simon and Garfunkel, "silence like a cancer grows." And it hurts me more than it hurts anyone else.

It works like this.

Silence in the face of bias, prejudice, or bullying is rarely a peaceful silence. I hash and rehash the event, usually at 3:00 A.M., when I should be sleeping, and finally I come up with the snappy comeback I wish I'd said. And then it happens again, but again I'm not ready with my response. The more these problems repeat themselves, the more they bother me. The more often I ignore them, the more likely they are to happen again. Since I haven't confronted the person, the person is either unaware of the offense or thinks the behavior is acceptable to me. I feel even madder the next time it happens, until I become really and truly furious. And when I am furious, I'm even more likely to remain silent, not trusting myself to speak, fearing that if I do, I'll get angry and then get told women aren't allowed to express anger, which will make me even madder.

A vicious cycle of silence and rage forms. Chances are, I'm so angry that I worry *any* response at this point is going to feel disproportionate to whatever straw finally breaks my back. More silence, more rage. Following are some strategies for breaking free from the cycle of silence and rage.

NAME-CALLING IS NOT HELPFUL FEEDBACK

People almost never change their attitudes or behavior because someone called them an asshole. A frontal attack will likely only make them double down on their bad behavior.

In the moment, it can feel as if turnabout is fair play. Maybe it feels fair, but it's not effective. It's hurtful and destructive in a workplace that depends on teamwork and collaboration. And it's not just bad for the team, it's bad for you. It causes you to close your mind to your own flaws and inhibits growth and improvement. "You're bad, I'm good, so I am entitled to treat you terribly." Thus, hypocrisy is born.

The best way to fight bias, prejudice, and bullying is to confront them but *not* mimic them. Listen to what the other people are saying, point out the problems they are causing with their attitude or behavior. Use an "I," "It," or "You" statement.

LOOK FOR ALLIES, NOT ENEMIES

I've found that if I look for people who can be supportive, I'll definitely find them. I am always more successful when I spend my energy cultivating supporters, even imperfect ones, than when I go looking for enemies. I've also found that people who say things that might seem off-putting at first are usually not my enemies. If I can engage with them, I may learn that someone I was tempted to dismiss as an asshole can become an ally.

For example, I once worked at a company where I was the only parent. One of the young engineers was curious about what it was like to juggle work and family, and he asked me how I managed it. I talked about blocking time with family over breakfast and dinner, and the bedtime routine. "Oh!" he exclaimed. "It's kind of like baseball season." At first I was a little offended. My family was sacred to me. Baseball, to put it mildly, was not. But I decided it would be better to get curious, so I asked him what he meant. "Well, I played baseball in college. Before the season started, I always wondered how in the world I was going to get all my schoolwork done when practice started. But I always found it was kind of like you just described—there were long chunks of baseball time, but I somehow still had time to get my work done." Once I understood what he meant, I saw that "baseball season" was a good metaphor for parenting—albeit an extremely long season.

PEOPLE HARMED & ———
| BIAS PREJUDICE BULLYING | ⚡ DISCRIMINATION HARASSMENT PHYSICAL VIOLATIONS

ALLOW FOR CLUMSY CURIOSITY

I had a conversation with someone from a company located in a part of the United States that is overwhelmingly white. Many of its employees had never traveled abroad. So when a woman from India joined the team, it was the first time that many of her new colleagues had met a person from another country. Shortly after she started, one of her colleagues asked her, "So back in India, did you ride an elephant to work?"

Understandably, she was offended and retorted curtly. But later she came to understand that he was an ally, albeit a woefully uneducated one. She developed an approach she called "allow for clumsy curiosity." Her colleague's question stemmed from the kind of bias that forms an incorrect impression of an entire country from a single scene in a single movie. But he wasn't prejudiced; he genuinely wanted to know more. That was why he'd asked the question. She learned to allow for that kind of clumsy curiosity and to reply to those sorts of questions in a way that left room for the person to become a supporter. She knew that she couldn't educate every single person at the company about her culture. That would have been too exhausting. But it was also exhausting to mistake clumsy curiosity for hostility. She didn't need to educate him, nor did she need to "cancel" him. Rather, she answered his question factually and recommended a couple of books and movies that might give him a more accurate picture of India.

PICK YOUR BATTLES

It is exhausting for underrepresented folks to educate overrepresented folks. I try to carefully pick whom I invest my energy in educating. It's reasonable to expect people who are in the majority to learn on their own, too.

Toni Morrison explained how racial bias, prejudice, and bullying can get in the way of Just Work: "The very serious function of racism . . . is distraction. *It keeps you from doing your work*. It keeps you explaining, over and over again, your reason for being . . . None of that is necessary."[37]

Toni Morrison is right. None of this is necessary. Do the work you want to do, not the work that others are imposing on you with their problematic attitudes and beliefs.

Changing the default to silence is not the same thing as *always* confronting people or becoming totally consumed with the fight. My "algorithm" for picking my battles may not be right for you. But I share it in the hope it may be helpful. My approach has been to develop an active process for evaluating what happened and to then make a conscious decision about how I will respond. If I decide to be silent or to do nothing in the name of picking my battles, I try to make my silence a proactive, mindful forbearance, not a passive avoidance. When I decide not to respond, I try to do so because I have something more important to work on, not because I am afraid. I try, but I don't always succeed. Sometimes, like all of us, I am afraid.

USE HUMOR

You don't have to be funny to respond. Indeed, humor can backfire because a common misuse of humor is to minimize what just happened to you.[38] However, if you're comfortable, humor can be a great asset. (Note to those causing harm: Making a joke of having caused harm will almost certainly backfire.)

In her forthcoming book *Funnier,* professor of comedy at Columbia College in Chicago Anne Libera offers evidence that the evolutionary purpose of humor is insight. One person can use humor to help other people notice their mistake, without pissing them off or making them defensive. This is what Libera calls "Ha-ha Ah-ha!"[39] Or, as Lindy West says, "The world is full of terrible things . . . and it is okay to joke about them. But the best comics use their art to call bullshit on those terrible parts of life and make them better, not worse."[40] This kind of humor can be an effective way to communicate with well-meaning but clueless people who are oblivious to the mistakes, moral and practical, that they are making.

For example, Amy Cuddy, whose work on the power pose I mentioned

PEOPLE HARMED &
| BIAS   PREJUDICE   BULLYING | ⚡ DISCRIMINATION   HARASSMENT   PHYSICAL VIOLATIONS

above, developed an excellent response to a frequent experience. She would be on a flight and the person sitting next to her would strike up a conversation, asking, "What do you do?" When she responded, "I'm a professor at the Harvard Business School," the response would often be something along the lines of "Really?! You don't look like someone who would teach there. What class do you teach?" Amy would reply, "Typing."

Author and executive Nataly Kogan once walked into a board meeting carrying a purse, a laptop bag, and a black backpack. Another board member, a prominent VC, laughed and said, "Why are women so obsessed with carrying so many bags?" As everyone looked at her, Nataly unzipped the backpack slowly, revealing . . . a breast pump.

The Cost of the "Baby Shower Moments"

A manager, Todd, walked into his staff meeting one morning complaining because he had to attend unconscious bias training that afternoon, declaring, "I don't believe that unconscious bias is a real thing." Adriana, the only woman on his team, was annoyed but kept her mouth shut. She wasn't even sure what she was confronting. He was dismissing the very notion of bias. Did he really believe what he was saying? If so, here was a prejudiced belief. But maybe he was just trying to bully her a little bit, to see how she'd react. Whatever he was up to, it felt hostile.

Later in the meeting, a man named Ty offered to buy a baby gift for another colleague who was going out on paternity leave. "Nah, Adriana will do it," Todd replied. "Women are better at that sort of thing."

Adriana was in the middle of a critical project on a tight schedule. She didn't have time to collect money from 30 people, select a gift, buy it, and wrap it. But she did it anyway because it seemed less burdensome than dealing with Todd. As a result her schedule slipped a bit, which slowed down the work of four other people as well. Meanwhile, her colleague Ty had just wrapped up a big project and had a little slack in his schedule—that was why he had offered to buy the gift in the first place. These moments can cause real harm to a woman's career and sabotage an organization that's running smoothly. When "office housework" tasks default to women, their productivity takes a hit, their careers take a hit, justice takes a hit. And when women's productivity takes a hit, whole teams suffer.

Every woman I know has hundreds of these moments. If it's not helping with a baby shower, it's being asked to take the notes or get the coffee or make the reservation or get the birthday cake or plan the offsite.

It can be tempting to just let these moments go. Why expend the energy needed to confront them? In a TED Talk, the Reverend Paula Stone Williams, a transgender woman, describes what she learned about bias and the dismissive assumptions men make about women: "The more you're treated as if you don't know what you're talking about, the more you begin to question whether or not you do, in fact, know what you're talking about."[41] This is workplace injustice in a nutshell. It is corrosive. It makes you start to doubt yourself. Challenging injustice is so important—if we don't challenge it, we often start to internalize it.

PEOPLE HARMED &
BIAS   PREJUDICE   BULLYING   ⚡ DISCRIMINATION   HARASSMENT   PHYSICAL VIOLATIONS

CHEAT SHEET

PROBLEM	RESPONSE

BIAS
NOT MEANING IT

**BIAS
INTERRUPTER**

"I" Statement

PREJUDICE
MEANING IT

**CODE OF
CONDUCT**

"It" Statement

BULLYING
BEING MEAN

**CLEAR
CONSEQUENCES**

"You" Statement

PEOPLE HARMED &
BIAS PREJUDICE BULLYING ⚡ DISCRIMINATION HARASSMENT PHYSICAL VIOLATIONS

3

For Observers

How to Be an Upstander

What hurts the victim the most is not the cruelty of the oppressor, but the silence of the bystander.

—Elie Wiesel

When you see something that is not right, not fair, not just, you have to speak up. You have to say something; you have to do something.

—John Lewis

A big part of why I wrote this book is to recognize and express gratitude for the essential role of people who stand up for their co-workers. For every bad experience I've had as a woman in the workplace, I've had multiple good experiences with people who were there to help me navigate these moments and support me afterward. I am so grateful to these friends, colleagues, employees, bosses, and even strangers. They are upstanders, and they far outnumber the people who cause harm. Upstanders fuel my optimism that we can solve the problem of workplace injustice.

Upstanders are essential to a culture of Just Work. Not only do they help the targets of workplace injustice feel less alone and less gaslighted; they also provide clear feedback to the person who caused

UPSTANDERS & ⎯⎯
| BIAS PREJUDICE BULLYING | ⚡ DISCRIMINATION HARASSMENT PHYSICAL VIOLATIONS

harm in a way that minimizes defensiveness and maximizes the odds that the offender will make amends: everyone feels better about the workplace as a result. Upstanders also show other potential upstanders how to make things a little bit more fair. They demonstrate that standing up for justice can be done without as much risk as many fear.

In homogeneous environments, being an upstander is especially important because people who are underrepresented are so small in number that confronting bias, prejudice, and bullying is likely to be both especially intimidating and so frequent as to be exhausting.

USE AN "I" STATEMENT TO HOLD A MIRROR UP TO BIAS

An upstander's job is to hold up a mirror, inviting others to notice what the upstander notices. Something as simple and direct as "I think what you said sounds biased" can be surprisingly effective. Upstanders can use a version of the "I" statements described in chapter 2.

When you're offering critical feedback on any topic, but especially one as sensitive as bias, it's not effective to attack someone's personality, morality, or character, or to imply disgust. If you say or even imply something like "You're a sexist/racist/homophobic turd ball," it may feel warranted and cathartic, but it's not likely to motivate a person to examine their thinking. Can you imagine anyone who would respond sincerely, "Oh, thanks so much for letting me know. Now that I understand what the problem is, I will change my ways"?

Though many fear that confronting bias will harm their relationship with the person they're confronting, there are simple and productive approaches you can take that will *improve* your working relationships—and your team's culture. This is not about giving in to someone's idea of PC orthodoxy. Effectively standing up to bias when you notice it, as the story below illustrates, will help you and your team work better together to achieve your goals.

A Seat at the Table

When Aileen Lee was a partner at the venture capital firm Kleiner Perkins, she and two other partners, Steve Anderson and Matt Murphy, attended a meeting with three senior executives at a Fortune 500 company. Steve, Matt, and Aileen arrived before the others and sat down in the middle of the table.

The executives they were meeting with, all older white men, took their seats opposite the Kleiner team. But they chose seats at the end of the table closest to Steve, leaving Aileen with nobody sitting across from her, subtly but unmistakably excluding her from the conversation.

The meeting proceeded. The three men made eye contact with Aileen's colleagues and addressed their comments to the men, further marginalizing Aileen. She suspected that they weren't even aware they were excluding her.

If Aileen called the men on their behavior, she risked being labeled "abrasive" or "too sensitive." Or, if they felt too embarrassed by their behavior, rather than apologizing they might decide not to proceed with the nascent relationship. This is the kind of catch-22 situation that underrepresented people being "invisibilized" face all the time. But not confronting the bias in the room was an even worse option.

Fortunately, one of Aileen's partners picked up on what was going on in the room and came up with a simple, effective solution: "Aileen," he asked, "would you mind changing seats with me?"

By putting her in the seat directly across from the people they were meeting with, and seating himself in the chair facing nobody, Aileen's colleague reset the dynamic. For the rest of the meeting, everyone present naturally included Aileen in the conversation. This intervention took all of 30 seconds and greatly increased the chance that this important meeting would be successful. That is how and why to be an antiracist, an antisexist. It's not so difficult.

UPSTANDERS &
BIAS | PREJUDICE BULLYING ⚡ DISCRIMINATION HARASSMENT PHYSICAL VIOLATIONS

USE AN "IT" STATEMENT
TO STAND UP TO PREJUDICE

Let's go back to that baby shower moment and imagine a different ending, an ending in which an upstander intervened. When Todd said he didn't believe gender bias was a real thing, six other men and Adriana were present, all of whom were aware of—and made uncomfortable by—Todd's behavior, but nobody said a word.

What if, when Ty volunteered to buy the baby gift and Todd told him to let Adriana do it, one of those six other guys in the room had pushed back? It wouldn't have taken much. Just one person joking, "Oh, so there's no such thing as gender bias? It sure sounds like gender bias when you say Adriana should buy the gift because she's a woman. Or do you really believe she should do it because she is a woman? If that's the case, then you're right. It's not bias. It's prejudice." That sounds pretty aggressive. But men on that team gave each other shit like that all the time in a kind of jocular way. Or one of them could have taken a more serious approach and pointed out to Todd that he wasn't only harming Adriana but also slowing down the whole team by giving her a time-consuming task when she was already on a tight deadline and Ty had some extra time on his hands. They might not have persuaded Todd that gender bias was a real thing, but they could have prevented him from making Adriana find the time to buy the gift when it was more logical for Ty to do it.

It Is Degrading to Be Asked to Pee in a Bucket

Once a colleague, David, and I flew halfway around the world to negotiate a partnership with a company that had never had women employees; their religion prohibited women from working outside the home. I think they viewed me as an American, not really a woman at all—which worked OK until, after many cups of tea, I needed to use the bathroom. They didn't have a ladies' room. I suggested that, if nobody was in the men's room, perhaps I could use it. They explained that would violate their religious beliefs. One of the men motioned for me to follow him, led me to a mop closet, and pointed at a bucket. I started to laugh, but one glance told me he wasn't joking.

"It is degrading to ask me to pee in a bucket!" I said, and headed toward the men's room: I really needed to pee. But another man cut in front of me and blocked the door. Suddenly, what had seemed like a benign conflict had become quite tense.

I looked to David for help. An important note here: there is nothing wrong with looking to your colleagues for help. Asking for help is a sign of strength, not weakness.

Happily, David was an upstander. He reiterated what I'd said: "It is degrading to ask Kim to pee in a bucket when there's a bathroom right here." Then he proposed, "If Kim agrees, I suggest either she uses the facilities here, or Kim and I will drive back to the hotel and use the bathroom there." I am an efficiency freak: the idea of wasting a whole hour to go to the bathroom was something that would never have occurred to me. But, to my surprise, the men chose to wait while we drove to the hotel and back.

David was telling our hosts that it wasn't acceptable for them to impose their belief on me. He came up with a solution that inconvenienced not only us but them as well. It felt important to me that they bear some of the cost of their prejudice. It wasn't a perfect solution, but I could live with it. I certainly didn't have any better ideas, so I was grateful to David for his.

WHEN YOU MAY WANT TO HAVE A REAL CONVERSATION

There will be moments when you, as an upstander, want to go beyond preventing people from imposing their prejudices on others and invite them to consider how their stereotyping beliefs are harming your team's efforts. This would typically be when a colleague's prejudice is making it difficult for your team to work together productively and for whatever reason you are stuck working with this colleague. Or perhaps when you care enough about the colleague to try to offer another point of view.

UPSTANDERS &
BIAS [PREJUDICE] BULLYING ⚡ DISCRIMINATION HARASSMENT PHYSICAL VIOLATIONS

In my experience, this approach is likely to work only if you have an underlying respect for the person. You don't have to respect the prejudiced belief to respect the person; a prejudiced belief does not define the whole person. If you can notice the whole person, who is bigger than that belief, you'll be having what Martin Buber called an "I-Thou" relationship, not an "I-It" relationship with the person.[1] If you're looking at a tree, you can either experience the whole tree or you can home in on that one broken branch.

If you can approach the whole person instead of this one prejudiced part of the person's thinking, you'll be better able to view the conversation as an act of compassion and bridge building rather than one of judgment and punishment. And when you can do that, you'll maximize the chances of the conversation's being productive.

USE A "YOU" STATEMENT TO STAND UP TO BULLYING

On a practical level, upstanders are in the best position to intervene because the nature of bullying is to isolate the target and separate the individual from the pack. The minute an upstander stands up to bullies, they know that they're facing two people, not one.

Sometimes it may be your fear of the person doing the bullying that gets in your way; other times, you may wonder if it's appropriate to insert yourself into this situation. Might it be seen as patronizing to act on behalf of the bullied? Hollaback!, a nonprofit that develops training for upstanders, offers an effective "5D" approach to be aware of the different things you can do to shine a spotlight on bullying.[2]

DIRECT

Challenge the person doing the bullying in the moment. Often a "you" statement will work for the upstander as well as for the person harmed. Here are some other things upstanders can say directly to a person who's bullying another person.

> "What's going on for you here?"
> "Do you realize how you sound?"
> "You're being inappropriate, disrespectful, etc."
> "Yo, not cool/OK."
> "You need to leave them alone now."
> "What you're saying is biased, prejudiced, offensive, etc."

Remember: Bullying doesn't always look like a big kid on a playground pushing around a smaller one. Sometimes a bully can just be a person who's in an overwhelming majority making assumptions about someone who is underrepresented. At one company where I worked, liberals outnumbered conservatives by about the same margin that men outnumbered women (80–20). One day, when the conversation turned to the election, Ted joked that Republicans were all immoral assholes. I felt terrible for Calvin, the only person in the room who—I happened to know—was a Republican. Having been a minority of one in a room full of men making offensive assumptions about women, I had an idea of how difficult it was for Calvin to speak up at that moment.

"Hey, you're making a bunch of assumptions here, Ted," I said. "We do have Republicans on our team and they are neither immoral nor assholes."

"Yeah, now who's the asshole, Ted?" another person joked.

"Sorry, sorry, you're right." Ted held his hands up in mock surrender, and we got back to work. If I hadn't said anything it probably would have been difficult for Calvin to focus for the rest of the day. It's hard to get back to work productively after you've been bullied.

DISTRACT

While it may be more satisfying to confront bullying directly—*Hey, why are you talking so rudely?*—sometimes the direct approach makes things worse for the person being bullied. Other times, it's just not going to be effective. We've all been in meetings where someone is behaving horribly and it feels more effective to try to change the dynamic and deal with the bullying later.

When I was in high school interning at a bank, I was asked to answer the phones. I was sitting at the front of a large, quiet floor, and I accidentally hung up on a caller I was trying to transfer to one of the people silently executing trades at terminals.

"Jesus *Christ,* girl! Can't you even work a goddamned telephone?" the trader bellowed.

Seeing this, one of the other traders stood up and threw a squishy ball he had on his desk at the man who'd yelled at me. The bellower missed it, and it bounced off his head. "Jesus Christ, boy, can't you catch a goddamned ball?" said an upstander, and I'm still grateful to that person 30 years later.

DELEGATE

By delegate, I don't mean ask someone below you in a hierarchy to do the work; I mean get help from another colleague who is in a better position to intervene. You can delegate up, down, or sideways.

Janet observed her colleague Rachel being bullied by an IT administrator, Bert. Bert insisted that Rachel give him her log-on credentials for a software program she was using. Rachel was working on a tight deadline; if she didn't make it, the project would fail. Bert seemed to enjoy having her in a vulnerable position. When she asked him why he needed her username and password for the tool, all he would tell her was "It would make me happy." He kept bugging her, and tired of arguing, she relented. Then, when he got her information, Bert locked Rachel out of the program, putting the project at risk.

Standing up for Rachel, Janet first tried the direct approach: she asked Bert to reinstate Rachel. He replied that he didn't understand why Rachel needed the software in the first place and wouldn't let her have access to it until Janet provided an answer that "satisfied" him. But it wasn't Bert's job to decide who needed which tools to do their jobs; it was his job to make sure the tools they used stayed up and running.

After it became clear that the direct approach wasn't working, Janet decided to delegate. She went to Bert's boss and got Rachel the access she needed. She also asked Bert's boss to address Bert's bullying. Once tempers had cooled, Bert's boss called Bert into his office and explained to him there would be consequences if he behaved this way in the future. Bert's behavior did not improve and he was eventually fired.

DELAY

Sometimes uncertainty about the risk of retribution may make you reluctant to intervene on the spot. But you can still check in later.

Once, at a sales conference, a woman I worked with commented in front of thousands of people about the "rock-star thighs" of a man on the team. She probably thought that kind of language was acceptable because her boss, a man, regularly made inappropriate comments about the looks of women on the team. Nevertheless, her remark bothered me. Harassment is still harassment, whether it's aimed at a man or a woman.

The problem here was that the woman worked in HR! Ordinarily, she would be the very person I'd report the incident to. I didn't feel it would be safe or productive to confront her directly. She supported a leader at the company who was known to be a bully and who was also known to dislike me specifically. I decided this was not a battle I wanted to fight. (Today, I would choose to fight it. But I am less vulnerable today than I was then.)

Even so, fear of retribution didn't mean I had to ignore what had happened, either. After the conference I made sure to find the man who'd been singled out and tell him that I'd felt her remark was out of line. He expressed gratitude, saying that her comment had, indeed, pissed him off.

DOCUMENT

Your ability to act as an observer of situations, and to document them, can be an invaluable service to victims of bullying—whether because they want to report an episode (and third-party evidence helps) or simply because it is comforting to get a reality check that what happened to them was wrong. An upstander can take notes on what is happening during an incident in a way that the person harmed can't.

When you see something that seems wrong, you have several options for how to respond. If you're not sure what to do, run through the 5 Ds and choose to do *something*. Direct. Distract. Delegate. Delay. Document.

BEWARE OF THE HERO COMPLEX

It can be tempting to put yourself at the center of the drama—to make the situation about you and your virtue and fearlessness in confronting bad behavior. This will cause you to lose focus on the person harmed and can even lead you to make things worse for the person you're trying to help. An effective upstander remains attuned to what the victim of injustice wants or needs.

Several "hero" behaviors can be particularly dangerous to your efforts to be an effective upstander: moral grandstanding, the Incredible Hulk, the knight in shining armor, and the opportunistic hypocrite.

MORAL GRANDSTANDING

Few things will kill good communication on a team faster than moral grandstanding: when people talk about sensitive topics in a way that shames others and puts themselves on a pedestal of virtue.[3] Moral grandstanding usually results in deeper misunderstanding, and it rarely fixes the problem. Three minutes on any social media platform will leave you flooded with examples of this kind of behavior.

Online communications, in particular social networks, speed up the process by which we exaggerate both our own virtue and the perfidy of others. In the real world our friends tend to get annoyed by self-righteousness, so there's a natural slow-down mechanism. Also, we are confronted with the humanity of others when we are face-to-face—we may get angry, but we aren't so fast to dismiss them as worthless human beings. Of course, mobs do attack real people in real life, as well. It's just that extreme sentiments seem to spread more quickly online. If you jump on your soapbox at a dinner party subtle eyerolls will warn you to get off. But online likes pump you up. There are no subtle eyerolls online. Moral grandstanding gets rewarded with likes and shares, creating more of it and a more extremist, toxic environment.[4] Which explains a lot about the state of our current political discourse. This snowball effect also explains why it's even *more* important for leaders to confront bias, prejudice, and bullying when managing teams working remotely than when everyone is working together in person.

Moral grandstanding tends to be used more by people on the extremes of *both* sides of any issue. Moderates do less moral grandstanding than extremists do. But in an environment with a lot of self-righteous finger-pointing, people tend to move to the extremes.[5]

There are many unattractive aspects of moral grandstanding, but perhaps the most important one is that it makes things worse, not better. Research shows that most of us tend to believe that we are better than others along any number of dimensions, especially our moral judgment. Which, conversely, makes us unaware of our own moral failings.[6] Denial. Shaming other people rarely causes them to look carefully at their own behavior. Rather, it causes them to retreat deeper into their sense of moral superiority.[7]

That's because it's *very* hard to hear criticism from someone who clearly feels morally superior to you. Almost everyone in such situations reacts angrily and defensively, and that produces more anger and defensiveness, and so on. The sad thing is that later, replaying such moments in our heads, we can sometimes acknowledge that the colleague's original criticism had some merit. But by that time, it feels impossible to go back and unsay everything that was said, particularly when subjects such as gender or race or sexual orientation or religion are involved.

THE INCREDIBLE HULK

My team and I were pushing hard on a project late one Friday night when Amy, a woman who'd recently joined the company right out of college, came into my office in tears. Charles, a guy on another team, had taken one look at some analysis she'd done and said, "There you go doing sales math again. I am an engineer, and so I get the final say

UPSTANDERS &
BIAS   PREJUDICE   BULLYING   ⚡ DISCRIMINATION   HARASSMENT   PHYSICAL VIOLATIONS

on this." She'd tried to ignore this asshole comment and walk him through her analysis: in fact, Charles was about to make a big mistake that would set our project back at least a week. But he didn't want to hear it and completely shut her down.

I was tired and hungry and dying to go home. Instead, thanks to Charles, I was now facing a Friday night that would turn into Saturday morning before I got to leave the office. I wanted to strangle him. "That little sh*thead pip-squeak!" I exclaimed. "Watch this."

I picked up the phone, and when Charles answered, I started shouting. And I didn't stop for about ten minutes. I was behaving like an asshole and enjoying myself way more than I should have.

Years later, as my sister and I were watching *The Avengers* with our kids, a scene reminded me of this pip-squeak episode. Loki, the bad guy, says to the Hulk, "Enough! You, all of you, are beneath me. I am a god, you dull creature. And I will not be bullied by you."

The Hulk looks at him for a moment, then picks Loki up by the feet and smashes his head on the ground. *Bam bam*. Pause. *Bam bam bam*. Pause. *Bam bam* to the left, to the right, to the center a few times, back to the left. Loki is left humiliated and unable to get up.

"Puny god," Hulk says, stomping off in disgust. My sister and I roared with laughter. Who doesn't have these Incredible Hulk fantasies?

The way I treated Charles was a Hulk moment for me. But did it make the situation better for Amy? No! I had deprived her of the ability to confront Charles directly. And in doing so, I had engaged in bullying myself. About five years later, my husband was working on a project with Charles. When Andy mentioned I was his wife, Charles's eyes grew wide. "You are married to *Kim Scott*? She got really, really, really mad at me once."

"What in the hell did you do to that guy?" my husband asked with a concerned laugh over dinner. I'd given in to my Incredible Hulk fantasy and acted like an asshole.

THE KNIGHT-IN-SHINING-ARMOR / WHITE-SAVIOR COMPLEX

The desire to help others is good. But when it becomes about you, not them, your help may not be so welcome. If you cast the person being harmed in the role of damsel in distress, for example, you reinforce the problem that you're supposed to be interrupting. This may sound unlikely, but it happens all the time. One of my colleagues at work repeatedly told me he wanted to "save" me from a man I was dating. He was right in one respect: I was in a bad romance and I needed to get out of it. But I did not want or need to be "saved."

A related but different complex happens when white people arrogantly decide they are going to speak for Black people against racism rather than listen to their Black colleagues about their experiences of racism. This approach can feel self-aggrandizing and often demonstrates the white colleagues are in fact unaware of their own racism.[8] Teju Cole has written about "The White Savior Industrial Complex." He explains it "is not about justice. It is about having a big emotional experience that validates privilege."[9]

THE OPPORTUNISTIC HYPOCRITE

Not long ago, a prominent Silicon Valley academic, a man, decided to take up the cause of women in tech. Alicia, who was leading a diversity, equity, and inclusion initiative for her company reached out to him to find out what ideas he had about creating more enlightened workplaces. He responded that he would only meet with her if the CEO of her company attended. When she said that it might be tough to get on the CEO's calendar, this self-important academic threatened to tweet about how little the CEO cared about workplace gender issues.

Eventually, Alicia set up the meeting. But what could have been a productive session turned into an opportunity for the academic to sound off. Alicia spent a lot of time prepping, thinking she'd be asked to offer her perspective. She couldn't get a word in edgewise. She shifted into listening mode, hoping to get some interesting ideas to improve things. But his only idea was to offer a referral bounty to anyone who referred a woman who got hired, which is illegal. Someone from his department was there, and corrected him. Alicia concluded he was just a cynical hack at that point. Yet the meeting went on. He

UPSTANDERS &
BIAS PREJUDICE BULLYING ⚡ DISCRIMINATION HARASSMENT PHYSICAL VIOLATIONS

spent 30 minutes lecturing the CEO about the lack of women on his company's board. The academic said he was going to write an article about it. He then suggested that the CEO make a donation to the academic's nonprofit, saying he didn't write about major donors. This was made more galling because the academic expounding on respecting women never once looked at or talked to Alicia, the only woman in the room. Several other women she knew also reported feeling ignored and disrespected by him.

BAD FAITH COMMUNICATION

Sometimes a person who doesn't care about an issue will weaponize it to hurt another person. When dozens of cases of sexual misconduct at Uber came to light, the company hired former attorney general Eric Holder to investigate and recommend solutions. In a discussion at the company about Holder's report, board member David Bonderman made a sexist comment about having more women on the board: "Actually, what it shows is that it's much more likely to be more talking."[10]

CEO Travis Kalanick immediately started treating the incident as an excuse to push for Bonderman's removal from the board.[11] It was remarkable that Kalanick took this approach because much of his formal authority had already been stripped from him as a result of the company's mistreatment of women. Under Kalanick's leadership the company had consistently ignored or actively buried reports of egregious sexual harassment, as outlined in Susan Fowler's famous blog post; in an interview with GQ Kalanick joked about a service that would supply women on demand, which he nicknamed "Boob-er." Travis himself had attended company events at strip clubs.

You would think that the chair of the board would've pulled Travis aside and said something about not casting the first stone or getting the beam out of his own eye. (The Bible is not often quoted in tech company boardrooms, but this was as good an opportunity as any.) If Bonderman's resignation was warranted, certainly so was Kalanick's. Unfortunately, a lot was going on that obfuscated this fundamental fact. To the astonishment of many outside observers, Kalanick's hypocritical gambit succeeded and Bonderman was pushed out.

THE UPSTANDER'S ADVANTAGES

The upstander's voice is crucial because upstanders may have advantages that none of the other players possess:

There is strength in numbers. In a meeting of ten people, there may be one person causing harm, one person harmed, and one or no leaders. If just one or two of the other seven or eight become upstanders, the whole tenor of the meeting changes—and imagine what it would be like if four or five did. Too often, though, everyone waits for someone else to step up, so no one does: the number of people present ends up diffusing responsibility. Much has been written about this—the so-called bystander effect—and whether the number of witnesses increases or decreases the likelihood of someone intervening. There's one clear lesson: don't wait for someone else to speak up!

The opinion of a neutral third party is hard to dismiss. It's usually much easier for people to acknowledge that they have made a mistake when it is pointed out by a third party—both because the person challenged usually feels less threatened and because the challenger is usually perceived as more objective. For example, American designer John Maeda refers to himself as a "type O minority," as in type O blood, which can be used by anyone in need. Because he can connect with many different kinds of people, he can help heterogeneous teams work together successfully. He has dedicated much of his career to elevate the voice of underrepresented people. As a neutral third party in most situations, he has dedicated his career to improving diversity, equity, and inclusion in tech.[12]

We all learn from the diverse experiences of others. Often upstanders have different but related experience they can bring to bear on a situation. I have learned a lot about how to confront my own experiences from the way that trans people stand up for women. Upstanders who have lived part of their life as a man and part of their life as a woman will have unique insight when confronting gender injustice, having experienced gender firsthand from both points of view.

UPSTANDERS &
[BIAS PREJUDICE BULLYING] ⚡ DISCRIMINATION HARASSMENT PHYSICAL VIOLATIONS

A personal connection makes it easier to communicate. If the person whose unconscious biases are causing problems is someone you get along with, you can use that access/trust to bring up an uncomfortable issue. If you are overrepresented along the same dimensions as the person causing harm, it may be much easier for you to be heard by that person.

Many hands make light work. People who have to confront bias, prejudice, or bullying week after week, month after month, are sick of it. They appreciate knowing that others notice what they notice and are willing to speak out. Upstanding also reminds everyone in the workplace that making it compassionate and fair is *everyone's* job.

CHEAT SHEET

If employees took their roles as upstanders seriously, they could transform the workplace everywhere on the planet. But it can be difficult in the moment to know what to say. You can borrow this cheat sheet for the people harmed:

PROBLEM	RESPONSE

BIAS
NOT MEANING IT

**BIAS
INTERRUPTER**

"I" Statement

Hold up a mirror

PREJUDICE
MEANING IT

**CODE OF
CONDUCT**

"It" Statement

Hold up a shield

BULLYING
BEING MEAN

**CLEAR
CONSEQUENCES**

"You" Statement

5 Ds: Direct, Distract,
Delegate, Delay, Document

UPSTANDERS &
BIAS PREJUDICE BULLYING ⚡ DISCRIMINATION HARASSMENT PHYSICAL VIOLATIONS

4

For People Who Cause Harm

Be Part of the Solution, Not Part of the Problem

We *all* harm others from time to time, often unintentionally. Exhibiting bias, prejudice, or bullying does not make us evil people incapable of redemption. These are attitudes and behaviors we *all* exhibit—and things we can all do less of if we make a conscious effort. Still, like it or not, we all need someone to hold up a mirror for us, to point out when we are not behaving in a way that reflects who we really want to be. Of course, some people want to be evil. This chapter isn't going to fix that problem. It's written for you, and I assume that if you bought this book and have read this far, you want to be part of the solution, not part of the problem.

You may be wondering what offenses can be solved by apologizing and changing behavior, and what offenses have legal consequences or will get you fired. I wish I could respond with something more reassuring than "It depends." Here is what I will say: by and large, if you are working to become more aware of when your biases, prejudices, and bullying harm others, and you are making real, visible efforts to change, you're doing the most important thing you can to stay out of trouble. If you deny wrongdoing, you may feel safer, but you're actually maximizing the odds that you'll repeat your wrongdoing and put yourself and others in harm's way.

This chapter will offer techniques that can help us all become more aware of our damaging behaviors so that we can become the colleagues we want to be—and achieve the kinds of results we want to achieve.

INTERRUPTING YOUR OWN BIAS

I hope to enrich the vocabulary that people use when they talk about the judgements and choices of others, the company's new policies, or a colleague's investment decisions. Why be concerned with gossip? Because it is much easier, as well as far more enjoyable, to identify and label the mistakes of others than to recognize our own. Questioning what we believe and want is difficult at the best of times, and especially difficult when we most need to do it, but we can benefit from the informed opinions of others.

—Daniel Kahneman

There are a number of paths to becoming more aware of your thought patterns and unconscious biases: meditation, religion, therapy, novels, the arts, travel. But I have known few colleagues who have been able to interrupt their biases alone. Most of us need someone else to hold up a mirror.

Every generation grows up using certain words and expressions carelessly, never stopping to think about what they are actually saying and how such use of language might hurt others and reflect badly on the speaker. For example, as a kid I used "retard" as a common insult. I would never use this word that way now, but, unfortunately, I did growing up. If you were born before 1970, you probably did the same. If you were born after 1990, you probably find this horrifying.

I might never have realized that I was reflecting and reinforcing a prejudice against people whom I cared about, not to mention an incorrect belief about intelligence, had someone not pointed this out to me in a way that was as clear as it was kind. It's tempting for me to write that it should have been obvious to me. But the words "should" and "obvious" are dangerous, especially when paired: the thing was, like many in my generation, I didn't get it. Once someone explained it to me, I wanted to quit using the r-word, but it took a little time and conscious effort—old habits are hard to break.

FIND YOUR BIAS BUSTERS

If you don't want to unintentionally harm or anger your colleagues, if you don't want to contribute to making your workplace an unfair or unreasonable environment, the first and perhaps most difficult part of your job is to become aware of your biases. As Nobel Prize–winning psychologist Daniel Kahneman points out, "acquisition of skills requires a . . . rapid and unequivocal feedback about the correctness of thoughts and actions."[1]

How can you get this feedback? We've already considered the many reasons why people who are harmed by bias are reluctant to bring it up. And if you're the one doing the harming, it hardly seems reasonable to ask people harmed to get over their natural reluctance to point out your mistakes to you. In *Radical Candor* I write about an order of operations for feedback. It starts with *asking* for feedback.

I recommend explicitly asking people to be your "bias busters," people who will be on the lookout for the things you say or do that reflect your unconscious biases. I'll bust your first bias: don't go out and ask people who are underrepresented to be your bias buster with no understanding of the fatigue they may already feel from having to confront daily the biases of the folks around them. People who are overrepresented often expect the people in their lives who are underrepresented to educate them and do not recognize or compensate in any way for this work or even show any appreciation for what a burden it is. If you have a team of ten with only one Latina, you don't want to put the burden on her to correct every biased thing the other nine people say.

There are a number of different ways to compensate people for doing this work. Saying "thank you" and recognizing them publicly for their service is a good start, but probably insufficient. I am a CEO coach, but I enjoy coaching all sorts of different people. So I can offer some free coaching. An editor might offer to edit people's work in return for bias-busting services.

PEOPLE CAUSING HARM &
┌─────────────────────────────┐
│ BIAS PREJUDICE BULLYING │ ⚡ DISCRIMINATION HARASSMENT PHYSICAL VIOLATIONS
└─────────────────────────────┘

If you are in a position to pay, pay. There are a number of DEI (diversity, equity, and inclusion) strategists you can hire. Some people I know who do this work have been criticized for charging. This criticism is total BS. You wouldn't expect a lawyer or a plumber or an accountant or a doctor to share their expertise without compensation. Why would you expect a person who has spent years building their DEI expertise to educate you for free?

When I was editing this book, I hired bias busters, and several other people volunteered to share their perspectives. Thanks to all these people's work, I learned and grew enormously. Chris Bartlett, director of William Way LGBT Community Center; Laura Eldridge, PhD, a feminist scholar; Jennifer Gomez, PhD, a professor of psychology at Wayne State University; A. Breeze Harper, PhD, founder of Critical Diversity Solutions; Annie Jean-Baptiste, head of product inclusion at Google; Zach Shore, a historian at the Naval Postgraduate School; and Danae Sterental, a lecturer at Stanford University, all provided invaluable insight. I am so grateful to each of them for pointing out my biases to me.

Ideally, you'll also identify someone in your everyday life who can play this role. There's nobody quite like the people who observe you regularly to tell you how your unconscious biases may be surfacing in your daily life. As we worked on this book together, my editor and I frequently said to each other, "Yo! Bias!"

The most important thing is to choose a person who is thoughtful, someone whose judgment you trust and whom you can count on to act in good faith. If you're a man worried about your gender bias, you may feel you must ask a woman, but what do you do if there's only one woman on your team and all the men want her to be their bias buster? This woman has things to do other than coach you. Ditto regarding a liberal bias, a heteronormative bias, a racial bias, and so on.[2] Look for other upstanders on your team you can ask. Look for people like John Maeda, type O upstanders, who understand a wide range of perspectives. Don't choose one person, choose a few. You want a diverse set of people helping you to identify your biases.

And if someone is generous enough to go through this process with you, you have a responsibility to engage in it with good faith. If your goal is to "prove" you didn't do anything wrong, you are wasting the other person's time.

Finally, don't do this only once and assume you've attained self-knowledge: it's a continuous process.

GROWTH MINDSET

No matter what your role is, confronting workplace injustice is difficult. Success requires that we adopt and foster what psychologist Carol Dweck calls a growth mindset. People with a growth mindset view failure and criticism in any context as an opportunity to learn and improve themselves. The opposite of a growth mindset is a fixed mindset, which views failure and criticism as signs of a fixed/negative trait.[3]

Let's imagine someone tells a joke and is told it's racist. The response of the person with a growth mindset would be "I'd like to understand why so I don't repeat that mistake." The fixed-mindset person, on the other hand, would reject the feedback by asserting their fixed attributes: "I am not a racist, so therefore what I said could not possibly be racist." And so the person continues telling the joke.

We must also avoid a fixed mindset in evaluating the actions of others. When we notice evidence of bias, prejudice, or bullying in others, we often judge them reflexively and harshly, condemning them as evil people. This fixed mindset—if someone *does* something bad, it means the person *is* bad and there's no hope of growth or redemption—makes it risky to give or acknowledge feedback about attitudes and behaviors that could use improvement. A fixed mindset incentivizes denial and disincentivizes self-awareness.

Developing a growth mindset in our approach to changing our own attitudes and behaviors, and confronting attitudes and behaviors in others, is essential to Just Work and a core goal of this book.

For example, a colleague, Bart, started working with a new employee, Avery. Avery used she/her to refer to herself, but Bart often referred to Avery as he/him because of his incorrect assumptions about Avery's gender. The first time this happened, Avery corrected Bart. He

PEOPLE CAUSING HARM &
BIAS | PREJUDICE   BULLYING   ⚡ DISCRIMINATION   HARASSMENT   PHYSICAL VIOLATIONS

apologized but repeated the mistake. Now Avery was angry. Bart did respect Avery's individuality, but Bart knew that overcoming years of assumptions would take time. He asked for the whole team's support in changing his behavior. This meant that everyone would be willing to step up and interrupt Bart's mistakes when he made them, so that the whole burden of correction wouldn't fall on Avery.

This was bias, not prejudice. At a conscious level, Bart really did believe that Avery was the only person who got to say who she was; he knew it wasn't his right to tell Avery who she was, or what gender she was. At the same time, it was hard for Bart to change habitual, biased assumptions about gender. And so he asked his colleagues to correct him. But Bart went further: he also worked with the management team to develop training to help everyone respect the individuality of colleagues.

They developed a saying, "As our trans colleagues transition, we transition with them," meaning that good managers will do their own work to be supportive of colleagues' stepping more firmly into their own true self. This saying broadened from trans people on the team to everyone. As a woman on the team was learning to embrace a more confident stance, her colleagues worked to eliminate the biases they held (e.g., calling her abrasive when she spoke up) that were making it harder for her to change her behavior.

Bart's efforts to acknowledge his mistakes and take Avery's complaints seriously by addressing them with action improved his relationship with her. This was important to their ability to enjoy working together and also important to the team's success. Avery has proven to be a great asset to the department. And the work Bart did to support Avery's transition helped *everyone* on the team have the freedom to bring their best, most whole selves to work.

I can't impose this kind of growth mindset on you or anyone else. Nor can your boss. It's up to you.

BE AWARE OF HOW "SMALL" THINGS ADD UP TO BIG THINGS

Sometimes the things you're called on to do to make amends feel disproportionate to the thing you did wrong. Be aware that your biased comment or action may be the straw that broke the camel's back. Even though it's not your fault that this person has experienced the same biased remark you just made 5,000 times before you said it, you still need to attend to the harm done by what amounts to a repetitive stress injury. This may be a simple acknowledgment about why what you said was problematic. One of the big problems of bias is that people start to internalize it. So your acknowledgment of the problem can be important. And if you're in a position to do so, offer to educate others on your team about the biased thing you just said or did so that this person doesn't face the same old sh*t day after day.

Don't focus on whose fault it is that the bias you just expressed is so common. And whatever you do, don't tell people they are "overreacting." Do what you can to address the harm the bias does.

MANAGE YOUR DEFENSIVENESS

When you mess up, as we all are bound to do, it's natural to feel defensive. There's no denying that it can be hard to accept being told the things you do or say are biased. You might feel as if the zipper to your soul has come undone, revealing a shameful flaw. Or maybe you're not so deeply ashamed, but you fear that the consequences will be unpredictable and disproportionate.

This defensiveness is natural and may not be unfounded. But remaining unaware of your biases is even riskier. Don't hide from your mistakes. And don't double down on them, for example bellowing at a woman who points out that you keep interrupting her. Acknowledge them. Apologize. Make amends.

AAA: ACKNOWLEDGE YOUR MISTAKE, APOLOGIZE, MAKE AMENDS

Recently, at my son's Little League game, one of two Indian American kids on the team got hurt. A couple innings later, I asked an Indian American man sitting next to me if his son was feeling better. He

PEOPLE CAUSING HARM &
| BIAS | PREJUDICE BULLYING ⚡ DISCRIMINATION HARASSMENT PHYSICAL VIOLATIONS

looked at me quizzically, then replied, "Oh. That wasn't my son." It was tempting not to acknowledge what I'd done wrong and wander off to chat with someone else. But if I didn't acknowledge what I'd done wrong, I would be compounding my error. Not only would I have said a racially thoughtless thing, I would now be avoiding a person of another race—*doing* a racist thing.

So I acknowledged my mistake. "Gosh, I feel like a jerk. So sorry," I said, giving in to the temptation to keep my error vague rather than name precisely what I'd done. I wish I'd said, "I hate it when my mind jumps to biased conclusions. I am sorry I assumed." When it comes time to discuss the moment of bias, it's crucial to be clear. When pointing out someone's bias, it's tempting to use euphemisms or vague language ("Gosh, I feel like a jerk") instead of clear language that shows you really do know what you did wrong ("I hate it when my mind jumps to biased conclusions. I am sorry I assumed").

Even though I didn't say exactly the right thing, it was OK. It was better than saying nothing. My fellow Little League parent laughed and answered, "It's OK. It happens all the time." This is an important lesson. Saying something, even if it's not exactly right, is better than saying nothing.

I didn't have this idea in the moment, but since then I've learned to follow up my apology with a question to better educate myself, something like "I'm sorry it happens all the time. Does it piss you off?" or "When else has something like that happened?"

People have so many stories about having experienced bias. Giving them an opportunity to share those stories can be a service because it's a relief to do so. And it can be a service to you because you might learn about a bias someone else exhibited that you've also been exhibiting but were unaware of.

When it becomes routine for us to notice our biases, they feel less threatening. Before I started writing this book, I would have found it damn near impossible to say something like, "I am really sorry that I assumed that Indian boy was your son. That was biased of me." I feared that for me to acknowledge the bias would have been tantamount to labeling myself a racist. And even now, after considerable practice, I still don't relish calling out my own biases. And yet it's not nearly as difficult as it used to be because I know that it's precisely by recognizing them that I become more the person I want to become, that I do the antiracist thing.

CORRECT THE BIAS

The best way to make amends is to correct your bias. Changing biased behavior can be hard if that behavior has been your default. It may be that you've come to agree that referring to women as "guys" or "dudes" is not inclusive or accurate, but if you've been doing it your entire life, you may slip up or freeze at first as you attempt to change your default.

YOU MAY FEEL WORSE BEFORE YOU GET BETTER

Recently I got some feedback that I tend to use language that assumes everyone identifies as either a man or a woman, an assumption that

PEOPLE CAUSING HARM &
[BIAS] PREJUDICE BULLYING ⚡ DISCRIMINATION HARASSMENT PHYSICAL VIOLATIONS

is obviously both incorrect and harmful. Shortly thereafter, I went on a live podcast and found myself saying, "Whether you are a man or a woman," and I suddenly became aware I was doing it again, so I added, "Or whether you are . . . ," and somehow I couldn't retrieve the word "nonbinary." Luckily the host knew what I meant, filled in the word I'd forgotten, and we continued our conversation. It was embarrassing to find myself at a loss for words so publicly, but that was still better than not attempting to make a change. Change is often messy and embarrassing, even when it's change for the better. But that's not a good reason to resist it.

There are two important lessons here: you will have to make yourself vulnerable if you're going to tackle your biases. You will also have to forgive yourself for the mistakes you'll surely make.

The key thing is not to give up.

HOW TO MANAGE POTENTIAL BURNOUT

It is easy to feel utterly paralyzed by the newfound awareness of the sheer volume of your newly discovered biases. In these moments, it can be helpful to do three things.

RUN THE NUMBERS

Dr. A. Breeze Harper, one of my bias busters, suggested I would benefit from thinking more deeply about the following words: lame, colorblind, blind, see, moron, psychopath, male, female. What was my response? "Oh my God, every word in the English language is going to offend someone. There are no words I can use!" When I stopped to count, I realized that there are over 170,000 words in the English language. Breeze had suggested I rethink my sloppy use of *eight* words. This math helped me gain some perspective.

THINK OF A PERSON YOU CARE ABOUT

Abstract "shoulds" can become exhausting. Thinking instead about specific people you care about who will benefit from your efforts—people you want to support, not harm—can reenergize you.

Zach Shore, a historian who helped me edit this book, is blind. My first motivator to quit using sloppy sight metaphors was a desire to honor Zach, whom I admire. He has never mentioned my use of ableist language. And as the person harmed, he shouldn't have to. He chooses to focus his energy on making a dent in the stubbornly high 70 percent unemployment rate among people who are blind and getting more of these folks interacting with people who can see. If my changing my language might help him achieve those important goals, it was the least I could do. I'd been unaware of the problems with my language and was glad Breeze, my bias buster, had educated me. I thought I was aware and addressing the problem with my sloppy sight metaphors. But when I finished this book, I did a search on the word "see." Guess how many times I'd used this word thoughtlessly? Ninety-nine times! When another bias buster read this, she pointed out another sloppy metaphor that is all too common and that I wasn't aware of: blinders. We all have a lot to learn.

THINK ABOUT HOW BIAS BUSTING HELPS YOU DO BETTER WORK

Once I started making changes, I realized how sloppy sight metaphors were misleading or imprecise. For example, when I wrote "see," I often meant "notice" or "understand," and the sentences flowed better when I substituted the more accurate word.

You may not be a writer, but you may find that you make better promotion decisions, for example, when you are aware of not using language that is ableist or reflects gender or racial bias. You may find you sell more of your products when you eliminate biases about your customers, when you hire a team whose demographics mirror those of your customers. Becoming more aware of the language we use pushes us to think more precisely. It's work, but we get more out of it than we put into it. A refusal to keep learning is like a child who says, "I know my multiplication tables, I can quit math now."

PEOPLE CAUSING HARM &
BIAS PREJUDICE BULLYING ⚡ DISCRIMINATION HARASSMENT PHYSICAL VIOLATIONS

LETTING GO OF YOUR PREJUDICES

Be sure you choose what you believe and know why you believe it, because if you don't choose your beliefs, you may be certain that some belief, and probably not a very credible one, will choose you.

—Robertson Davies

It is never too late to give up our prejudices. No way of thinking or doing, however ancient, can be trusted without proof.

—Henry David Thoreau

A Prejudiced Belief

Until I was about 18, I believed that women were superior to men, and I did not yet understand there were alternative gender designations. I didn't believe it fervently or talk about it much. I just assumed it was a fact of life that everyone understood.

My family belonged to the Christian Science Church, a religion founded by a woman, Mary Baker Eddy. She wrote, "The Mind or intelligence of production names the female gender last in the ascending order of creation. The intelligent individual idea, be it male or female, rising from the lesser to the greater, unfolds the infinitude of Love."[4] My understanding of her words was that women were more godlike than men. This interpretation was reinforced for me by the fact my grandmother and her sisters dominated the church where my family worshipped. Both at home and at church, these strong women were in control. I thought this was just the way things were.

The message about women's superiority was also reinforced at the all-girls school I attended in Memphis, Tennessee. Students at St. Mary's did better on standardized tests and got into better colleges than the students at the elite all-boys schools in the city. We were reminded of this fact constantly: we weren't equal to the boys, we were *superior* to them—smarter, nicer, and more likely to be guided by our ideals. Today I think these were not so much firmly held convictions on the part of our teachers but rather an effort to counterbalance the messages about women in the wider culture.

When my father read this story, he was bewildered. First, he disagrees with my interpretation of Mary Baker Eddy's words. Second, how could I possibly believe that my grandfather was inferior to my grandmother just because of a couple of sentences Mary Baker Eddy had written? You'd think my love and admiration for my grandfather—and my father—would've made me question those prejudiced beliefs, but, somehow, it didn't. Just as there are many millions of men who love and admire their mothers, wives, and daughters but who still unconsciously assume or actively believe that women are inferior.

I was a junior in high school before I questioned my prejudice about men's intellectual and emotional inferiority. For some reason, it was reading William Wordsworth that did it. His words moved me, and then it dawned on me: a *man* had written this poem.

Once I had questioned my prejudice, it was a huge relief. My happiness and my ability to live the life I imagined depended upon men *not* being brainless and heartless. I knew at least half and probably three-quarters of the people I'd work with would be men. I knew enough about my own sexuality to be certain my life partner would be a man. I wanted to have two kids. Odds were, one would be a boy.

That life was going to challenge my prejudiced belief was pretty much inevitable. Unfortunately, it's far, far less inevitable that life will challenge a young man's assumption that men are superior to women. The number of women writers he'll read will be dwarfed by the number of men writers he'll read, the overwhelming number of world historical figures he'll study will be men, and so on.

Either way, though, if you do have such essentializing beliefs about men or women lurking in your mind, you may find it a relief to let go of them, as I did. As Simone de Beauvoir wrote, "What people have endlessly sought to prove is that woman is superior, inferior, or equal to man . . . To see clearly, one needs to get out of these ruts; these vague notions of superiority, inferiority, and equality that have distorted all

PEOPLE CAUSING HARM &
BIAS | PREJUDICE | BULLYING ⚡ DISCRIMINATION HARASSMENT PHYSICAL VIOLATIONS

discussions must be discarded in order to start anew."[5] Let's all just try to become our best, truest selves and break free of these prejudices!

How can you do it? How can we make sure our biases don't harden into damaging prejudices? Here are some of the things that helped me.

QUESTION FALSE COHERENCE

Our brains love to sort the chaos of life into various boxes and buckets and patterns. That's what the brain does—automatically but not necessarily wisely. Daniel Kahneman teaches us to challenge the kind of false coherence our brain serves up by reminding ourselves and one another, "The world makes much less sense than you think. The coherence comes from the way your mind works." Kahneman's book *Thinking, Fast and Slow* describes how our brains process information along two tracks, which he defines as System 1, fast thinking, and System 2, slow thinking. "System 1 operates automatically and quickly, with little or no effort and no sense of voluntary control. System 2 allocates attention to the effortful mental activities that demand it, including complex computations. The operations of System 2 are often associated with the subjective experience of agency, choice, and concentration."[6] System 1 tends to look for "coherence" where there is none.

A green light means go; this information is managed by System 1. You put your foot on the gas without "thinking." Someone presents you with a crossword puzzle. System 2 takes over. You begin testing out possible answers, making choices, recalling half-remembered facts. Yet System 2 is far less objective than we would like to believe. Kahneman explains, "The defining feature of System 2 . . . is that its operations are effortful, and one of its main characteristics is laziness, a reluctance to invest more effort than is strictly necessary. As a consequence, the thoughts and actions that System 2 believes it has chosen are often guided by . . . System 1."[7]

In short, our prejudices are often a result of System 2 lazily justifying the biases that System 1 energetically serves up. It takes discipline, effort, and self-awareness to question these assumptions and to understand that the categories we construct are often arbitrary. In other words, if we don't want to get duped by our own brains, we must become conscious of our biases, note the way they tend to harden into beliefs, and question them energetically.

BEWARE OF STEREOTYPING/ESSENTIALIZING

People who hold prejudiced beliefs often open a conversation by saying, "Men/white people/straight people are this" and "Women/Black people/gay people are that," then degrading what they consider to be feminine/Black/gay. It's "dichotomize and degrade" prejudice.[8] For example, Pythagoras wrote, "There is a good principle that created order, light, and man, and a bad principle that created chaos, darkness, and woman."[9] Yes, this single sentence, which pretends to explain the entire universe, has a certain balance and symmetry; unfortunately, it is wildly illogical and even malevolent. I'm not saying we have to reject the Pythagorean theorem. Pythagoras' ideas about triangles have stood the test of time. His ideas about women have not.

Anytime you hear yourself or anyone else making sweeping generalizations such as "Men are X" or "Millennials are Y" or "Chinese Americans are more likely to Z," no matter how clever or ostensibly well informed the statement may be, stop and ask, Is this a stereotype? Is it an essentializing belief? An essentializing belief attributes particular characteristics to everyone in a particular category, as in "All women are ___" or "All millennials are ___."

First, ask if this generalization rests on a solid factual framework. Then, question those facts. Question whether the justification for the generalization is science or pseudoscience. In the nineteenth century, the "science" of phrenology was used to rationalize mistreatment of non-European people and to justify slavery. While that prejudiced practice seems like an unfortunate relic of a bygone era, the effort to justify gross overgeneralizations with science continues today. On the internet the line between legitimate science and crackpot theories gets blurred with exhausting frequency. Be alert for moments when you consciously misuse data or studies to justify your unexamined biases

PEOPLE CAUSING HARM &
BIAS | PREJUDICE | BULLYING ϟ DISCRIMINATION HARASSMENT PHYSICAL VIOLATIONS

because that seems easier than questioning your biases. Often "confirmation bias" reinforces gender, racial, or other biases.

Essentializing is especially dangerous because it can cause you to ignore new information or overlook a person's capabilities. It might be comforting to live in a world circumscribed by limiting beliefs, but in the end, you are doing yourself and your workplace a disservice.

Challenge your beliefs rigorously.

FUNDAMENTAL ATTRIBUTION ERROR

The fundamental attribution error, a flawed thinking pattern described by Stanford psychologist Lee Ross, fuels prejudice. This happens when we use perceived personality attributes—"You're an idiot"—to explain someone else's behavior rather than considering our own behavior and/or the situational factors that may at least in part have been the cause of the other person's behavior. It's a problem because (1) it's generally inaccurate and (2) it renders an otherwise solvable problem hard to solve because it invokes a fixed mindset.

DON'T EXPECT EVERYTHING TO CONFORM TO AVERAGE

Ask yourself, Even if it is true on average, does it apply to the specific situation at hand? It is true that, for example, men are on average taller than women, but what does this have to do with the heterosexual couple you just met in which the woman is taller? After all, while men are on average taller than women, in *some* couples the man is shorter. Yet this happens less frequently than statistics would predict.[10] In other words, our biased expectation that we and others will conform to average (in heterosexual couples, the man is taller than the woman) creates a world with a number of unnecessarily lonely short men and tall women.

As Todd Rose describes in his book *The End of Average,* when the U.S. Air Force designed a cockpit for the "average" pilot, they designed a cockpit for no one.[11] This is why, if we want Just Work, we must always be defeating the tyranny of the average and instead respecting each person's individuality and adjusting to it.

If you find yourself questioning or mocking people who don't conform to some arbitrary average, stop and think. Why are you doing
this? Is this your biases hardening into prejudices? Are you misusing
the data to insist that people conform to what is on average true but
not always true?

HOW TO REALIZE WHEN YOU ARE BULLYING OTHERS—AND STOP IT

Here's my story of bullying a colleague. I tell it not to shame or to
justify myself but because I believe the only way to do better is to acknowledge mistakes. I can't do better if I am in willful denial about
what I'm doing wrong.

I Am Not an Asshole. But, Like All of Us, I Do Sometimes Behave Like One

I was working on a podcast with Russ Laraway, a colleague of many
years with whom I'd recently co-founded a company. One of the pro-
ducers suggested we discuss Amy Cuddy, the Harvard social psychologist famous for a TED Talk on postural feedback effect. As mentioned
in chapter 2, Cuddy's research has shown how and why adopting a
physical posture that projects confidence—standing up straight with
your shoulders back—can make you *feel* more confident, and it has
helped me a great deal. As the podcast began, I brought up a much-
quoted finding from her research. "It's remarkable," I said, "how a
two-minute Wonder Woman Pose, standing with your legs apart and
your chest puffed out, can increase testosterone and decrease cortisol!"

I didn't know it at the time, but the evidence that good posture affects testosterone and cortisol levels is mixed—something Cuddy her-

self had acknowledged. I also didn't know that Russ had learned this after doing some research when the producer suggested we discuss it. So he knew that Cuddy had called into question the link between the Wonder Woman Pose and testosterone/cortisol levels.[12] Her research about how good posture makes a person feel, however, was borne out.

Russ brought this up during the podcast and tried to give me a chance to correct myself. Instead of listening to what he was trying to tell me, I shut him down, hard:

"With all due respect," I began (helpful hint: any time you start a sentence with the phrase "With all due respect," you're probably not being respectful), "what you don't understand is that you, Mr. White Man, were *born* doing the power pose." All the women in the room let loose with great whoops of laughter, and Russ clammed up. He was the only man in the room.

It's important to note that in the vast, vast majority of similar situations in my career the shoe has been on the other foot—I was the only woman in the room, being excluded and mocked in some way. But turnaround is *not* fair play. It's simply a repetition of injustice. My attitude was also highly problematic. *Because you are a man, you have no right to speak on this topic.* I was pretty actively excluding Russ from the debate. And mocking him for his gender.

When I later realized what I'd done, I apologized. Russ admitted that he'd felt that I'd shut him down harshly and that he'd been powerless to fight back. But he forgave me—probably more easily and quickly than I deserved.

By bullying Russ I betrayed my own beliefs about how to treat people. A listener wrote in to point out that I was guilty of the same gender stereotyping I theoretically decried—which was absolutely correct. Russ was understandably angry about the way I'd behaved, so it took some back-and-forth to assure him that I regretted what I had done and agreed with his criticism. Bullying Russ was as inefficient as it was unjust. It put a strain on our relationship. It harmed the message we were trying to get out into the world. It wasted a lot of time.

ANGER + BEING IN THE IN-GROUP = HIGH POTENTIAL FOR BULLYING

A good way to prevent yourself from bullying people in the future is to examine times when you've bullied others in the past. Be as honest as you can with yourself about why you did it and its impact on the other person, on you, and on witnesses. What were the circumstances? How did you feel just before you bullied the person? Were you angry? What does your body do when you are angry? If you're not sure, ask the people closest to you. My daughter recently pointed out a hand gesture I make when I'm about to have a bad parenting moment (i.e., to bully her). Often your body will warn you when you're about to act like a bully.

When I'm about to behave horribly, there are usually two warning signs. One, I'm in the in-group. Two, I am mad as hell. In this case, I wasn't mad at Russ, but I was angry with the world for the way it was treating Amy Cuddy. When I made fun of Russ during the podcast, he was my peer and my business partner. I didn't have "power" over him. But an in-group dynamic came simply from his being the only man in the room. As a woman, I was in the majority. Being in the majority was all it took for me to bully someone I like and respect.

SOME USEFUL TIPS FOR RESPONDING TO FEEDBACK

If you're getting feedback that you've been biased, that one of your beliefs is prejudiced, or that you've bullied someone, first take a deep breath. This is hard to hear. A few things are always helpful to keep in mind:

- Focus on impact, not intention
- Telling other people they are too sensitive is a refusal to listen

BIAS PREJUDICE **PEOPLE CAUSING HARM &** [BULLYING] ⚡ DISCRIMINATION HARASSMENT PHYSICAL VIOLATIONS

- Respect the individuality of others
- Learn how to apologize

FOCUS ON IMPACT, NOT INTENTION

When someone points out that you've been biased, or that a belief you hold is prejudiced, or that you've behaved like a bully, denial is a normal human response to this feedback. It can be tempting to tell people, "Don't be so sensitive" or "I was only joking." After all, you didn't mean any harm.

Rather than focusing on your intention, take a moment to look for the actual harm your attitude or behavior may have done. If someone is upset, what is the reason? Try to understand why rather than reject the person's emotions.

This sometimes turns out to be an exercise in enlightened self-interest. You may find that you have harmed yourself more than you've harmed the person. When you make a biased assumption that the man in a meeting is the decision maker—and not the woman sitting next to him—the problem isn't that you've hurt the woman's feelings. The problem is that you don't know who the decision maker is—which harms your chances of accomplishing your team's mission.

ASSUME GOOD INTENT OF OTHERS, BUT DON'T DEMAND THEY ASSUME IT OF YOU

Be careful when insisting that others "assume good intent" of you when you've said something biased. It can sound as if you think the person who is harmed should not be angry.

Code-of-conduct consultant Annalee Flower Horne suggests thinking about moments of bias in a more neutral way.[13] If you were stepping on someone's toe and the person said, "Get off my toe" or "Get off my damned toe" or even "Get off my f—g toe!," you wouldn't stand there still stepping on the toe while you delivered a lecture about assuming good intent. You'd first get off the toe. Then you'd apologize for the pain you had caused. Your intentions are beside the point: you still caused hurt. Results matter more than intentions. People respond with some heat when we've hurt them. That's to be expected, not rejected.

Also, telling people to "assume good intent" often ignores the cumulative pain and anger that builds up in people when they experience bias many times a day, every day of their lives, and when they feel, or are, powerless to respond to it. This is a moment to step back and realize that while you are involved in this problem, it goes well beyond you—you are one tiny piece of this person's justified anger. Perhaps on the flip side, you have an opportunity to be one tiny part of making it better by changing your behavior.

When *you* assume good intent, rather than ordering other people to do so, several good things happen. You feel more optimistic about human nature. You're probably correct—most people are well intentioned most of the time.

When you trust people, your good faith is often rewarded. From an economic standpoint, trust is key for free markets to work efficiently and with the lowest possible transaction costs.

But it's usually not effective to insist that others assume good intent about you. If you feel someone is assuming bad intent in a way that is not fair to you, it's fine to assert your good intentions. But remember the stepping-on-the-toe analogy. If you're stepping on someone's toe, the first thing to do is to get off it. Show first that you heard what people told you and understand it—or, if you *don't* understand it, that you want to understand it and are willing and eager to put forth the effort to do so. Then, show some concern for how people are feeling. You want to demonstrate that you notice the impact you've had and are committed to changing it. Expressing your commitment to not repeating the mistake in the future is a lot more important than talking about your past intentions, which, though good, did not help you avoid harming that person. "I can understand why you are angry, and I am sorry. I never intended to make you angry, but that didn't help here. I want to make this right. I'm not going to do X again."

PEOPLE CAUSING HARM &
BIAS   PREJUDICE   BULLYING   ⚡ DISCRIMINATION   HARASSMENT   PHYSICAL VIOLATIONS

SAYING "YOU'RE TOO SENSITIVE" IS A REFUSAL TO LISTEN

Communication is measured at the listener's ear, not at the speaker's mouth. Maybe something you said upset someone, but you don't quite understand why. You didn't mean any harm. You simply used a word you've used your whole life, a word that has always been in common usage.

By refusing to understand why what you said causes harm, you are demanding that the other person conform to your expectations of "normal." Furthermore, telling other people how they "should" feel is an exercise in futility. People feel how they feel, and the best you can do is to try to understand why. Ordering someone, "Don't be sad," is not going to make the person less sad. You can't manage or control another person's feelings, and efforts to do so are futile, arrogant, manipulative, and rarely sincere. Caring about another person's feelings is productive.

Once I worked with a couple of people who objected to what they called the "word police" on the theory that they didn't mean any harm and people should just quit being so sensitive. My boss explained to them that he did not consider himself to be the word police but that he was responsible for making sure his team worked well together. He pointed out that we all have words that make us see red when we hear them. If we are going to communicate well with one another, we must know to avoid each other's red words. We do this because we need to be understood to collaborate effectively and because we care about and respect one another. If you're trying to communicate with someone, why use a word that will make it almost impossible for the person to focus on the next 50 words you say? Why would you insist on using that word when it would be so much more efficient to choose another one?

Admittedly, habits of speech are hard to break. Even when your team knows one another's red words, people will still say the wrong thing from time to time. Asking for forgiveness in the service of changing a habit is reasonable; insisting that you get to use whatever word you want to no matter what is not.

I once worked with a man who referred to women as "dudes." He thought "dude" was a gender-neutral term. I don't think of myself as a dude. I explained that being called dude was, if not quite a red word, jarring. From then on, whenever he called me "dude," I would simply say, "Yo," or if I had an extra second, "Yo, I'm not a dude." He would apologize, and we'd move on. Enough said. No big deal. Pretty soon the "dude" habit was broken. I wasn't the word police. And I wasn't a dude.

Recently, in a post on social media, I thoughtlessly misused the word "crazy." A couple of people pointed out (with greatly appreciated kindness) how my imprecise use of language harmed people with mental illness. I posted an apology and linked to an article explaining in more detail why what I'd said was inaccurate and harmful.[14] A bunch of people replied to the post thanking me for saving them from making the same mistake. But many others only wanted to "reassure" me that what I'd said in the first place was OK, that we as a society have gotten "oversensitive."

It can be tricky for a woman to respond to a charge of oversensitivity, so I was happy to have my former colleague Russ Laraway weigh in on this point:

> For the "we've become too sensitive" crowd . . . Please consider trying to evaluate this with a simple Return on Investment calculation.
>
> What does it cost me to change / not change and what do we get if I change / not change?
>
> The Investment: Adapting my language costs what? Some cognitive difficulty for like two weeks?
>
> My search for an answer on this topic and many others tells me that it costs effectively nothing.
>
> Then, I ask myself what I get in return. If I keep using insensitive aphorisms—especially as a white man—I will create ranging inclusion issues—big for some, small for some, nonexistent for others. If I change my language, though, I take a small step toward a more universally inclusive environment. I think that the "we've become too sensitive" take implicitly invalidates the perspective of those offended or hurt, and I'm just not sure we should be doing that.

Well said.

PEOPLE CAUSING HARM &
BIAS   PREJUDICE   BULLYING   ⚡ DISCRIMINATION   HARASSMENT   PHYSICAL VIOLATIONS

RESPECT INDIVIDUALITY

It seems that it goes without saying that I get to decide who I am, and you get to decide who you are. Yet all too often we try to tell other people who they are, what they "should" wear, how they "should" feel, whether their hair "should" be long or short, whether they "should" have kids, how many kids, whether they "should" be in a relationship, and on and on. And all too often we let other people define us without even realizing what is happening.

Employees frequently fail to respect the individuality of their nonbinary colleagues by refusing to honor their preferred pronouns. It's exhausting to correct co-workers about this, day after day, week after week.

I was a tomboy when I was young; once, someone yelled at me for being in the women's room. It was such a jarring experience, this stranger yelling at me, insisting she knew my gender better than I did. It gave me just a tiny glimpse of what it must feel like to be told by others which bathroom to use.[15]

Each of us gets to decide who we are. Nobody else gets to tell us who we are, or who we "should" be. I get to decide who I am. You don't get to tell me who I am. This is pretty basic.

HOW TO APOLOGIZE

In *Art of the Apology,* Lauren M. Bloom explains that an effective apology has the following important steps:

- Say you're sorry . . . sincerely
- Explain what went wrong
- Take responsibility
- Make amends
- Express appreciation
- Listen to the person's pain with patience
- Offer repair

- Request forgiveness
- Promise it won't happen again

These principles are featured in an apology to Lindy West, who was targeted by a troll after her father died. The troll opened a Twitter and Gmail account in Lindy's deceased father's name and started sending her cruel messages. Rather than ignoring the troll, West wrote about the experience on the website Jezebel and got this response:

> Hey Lindy,
> I don't know why or even when I started trolling you. It wasn't because of your stance on rape jokes. I don't find them funny either.
> I think my anger towards you stems from your happiness with your own being. It offended me because it served to highlight my unhappiness with my own self.
> I have e-mailed you through 2 other gmail accounts just to send you idiotic insults.
> I apologize for that.
> I created the **PawWestDonezo@gmail.com** account & Twitter account. (I have deleted both.)
> I can't say sorry enough.
> It was the lowest thing I had ever done. When you included it in your latest Jezebel article it finally hit me. There is a living, breathing human being who is reading this shit. I am attacking someone who never harmed me in any way. And for no reason whatsoever.
> I'm done being a troll.
> Again I apologize.
> I made a donation in memory to your dad.
> I wish you the best.[16]

PEOPLE CAUSING HARM &
BIAS PREJUDICE BULLYING ⚡ DISCRIMINATION HARASSMENT PHYSICAL VIOLATIONS

HOW NOT TO APOLOGIZE

The best way to make an apology is this. Go to the person in private and say, "I am sorry." *Then, shut up and listen.* When you apologize to people, make sure to focus on them and understand the harm done to them, not just their feelings. Don't make it about yourself.

Here are few common "apologies" that really are not apologies at all:

- *"I am an asshole."*
  Saying this focuses on you, not the person you harmed.
  Moreover, it implies that no change will be forthcoming.
- *"I was just kidding."*
  If your joke harmed someone, then it was a bad joke, and you're better off apologizing for it than trying to use humor to cover up what you did wrong. Good humor reveals hidden attitudes and behaviors in a way that creates change. Bad humor reinforces harmful attitudes and behaviors.
- *"This has been really hard for me."*
  Once again, it focuses on you. In this case, you are not apologizing, you are looking for sympathy, or himpathy. A VC who was accused of sexual misconduct began his apology with "The past twenty-four hours have been the darkest of my life." An upstander, another man in tech, responded, "Are you kidding me? This is how you start? *No one gives a shit about you.* The only acceptable way to start this statement is with the words 'I'm so sorry.'"[17] Another common manifestation of this is "white women's tears," a phenomenon in which white women, when called out for having said a racist or racially unmindful thing, burst into tears as a strategy for avoiding accountability.[18] As a white woman prone to tears, my advice here is that if you can't help crying, make sure you remain focused on the person harmed and that everyone else does, too. Don't let it become about you.

- *"I'm sorry if I've made you feel uncomfortable"* or *"I'm sorry you feel that way."*

    This misses the point. It shows you still don't get that you caused any harm beyond hurting someone's feelings. Sometimes this is a communication in bad faith, not an apology at all, as in "I'm sorry you feel I was harassing you." What the person in this case is really saying is "I wasn't harassing you, and if you feel I was, there's nothing I can do about it."

- *"I was having a bad day."*

    Nobody is interested in why you did what you did. People are interested in what you're going to do to make it right, and they want to make sure you don't repeat the mistake.

- *"Let me explain."*

    Now you are justifying, not apologizing.

- *"Can you forgive me?"*

    People often ask for forgiveness or demand forgiveness before they've taken a single step to make amends or to ensure they won't repeat the mistake. Don't say "Will you please forgive me?" while literally blocking the person's path to an exit.

DON'T USE AN APOLOGY TO DISTANCE YOURSELF FROM A DIFFICULT SITUATION

Sometimes we offer a quick apology in an effort to avoid feelings of discomfort or shame. When we do that, we fail to hold ourselves accountable for our mistakes and lose an opportunity to learn and grow. Once I gave a talk and I told the anecdote about being asked to pee in a bucket (see chapter 3). In the talk, I named where this had happened. One of the participants raised her hand and told me that I had just erased her. I knew I'd done something wrong, but I didn't understand in the moment *what* exactly.

I felt deeply ashamed. The physical sensation of shame is the same

PEOPLE CAUSING HARM &
BIAS   PREJUDICE   BULLYING   ⚡ DISCRIMINATION   HARASSMENT   PHYSICAL VIOLATIONS

as that of fear. I felt the same way I feel when one of my children walks too close to the edge of a cliff: my stomach drops and the back of my legs, the area behind my knees, burns and tingles. I was ashamed of two things at once. One, I had hurt someone. Two, I didn't know why. Had I been culturally insensitive? Was I expressing religious intolerance?

Rather than seeking to understand, I simply apologized and moved on to my next question. I was reluctant to expose my own ignorance and ask why what I'd said was offensive. That was a mistake. It looked to the whole audience as though I didn't get it and, much worse, didn't care. And it was a missed opportunity for education.

In retrospect, the right thing to have done would have been to open the room up for a conversation rather than to shut it down with a perfunctory apology. Instead of just saying, "I am sorry," I wish I'd said, "I can tell I have said something that caused harm. Even worse, I don't know why what I said caused harm. But I would like to know. If someone is willing to tell me now, I would be grateful. If it's more comfortable after, that would be fine, too."

After the talk, once I had managed to move out of shame brain, I did talk to the woman who had been brave enough to give me this feedback during the Q&A. What I'd done wrong was to say that "no women worked there." It sounded as if I'd said that no women worked in the whole country, which was incorrect, rather than that no women worked at the company where I was having the negotiation. She was a woman, and she worked in that country!

I wish I'd given her the chance to explain more during the Q&A because it was a missed opportunity to educate everyone in the audience. Several other participants I bumped into later asked me what the question was all about. It was a women's conference, and the participants were predominantly white American women. Sensing my shame and empathizing, many participants were too quick to dismiss the question and "side" with me, in the tendency often called white women's tears. I didn't cry, but the dynamic still played out. I wanted to be an ally, but I had alienated this woman. Many of the other white American women in the audience were likely to make the same mistake I'd made. Because I wasn't willing to learn publicly, they didn't learn. This was a lost opportunity for all of us.

CHEAT SHEET

There are things you can do today to move from being the person causing harm to being a real ally in the struggle for Just Work.

I wish becoming aware of our own negative or harmful behaviors were as easy as looking in the mirror. But often we remain unaware of our mistakes unless we want to know. And the only way you'll want to know is if you can forgive yourself for your mistakes and if you have some confidence that those around you will forgive you, too. But it all starts with what's going on inside your own head: if you can't forgive yourself for mistakes, then you will refuse to notice them, and you won't be able to fix them.

PEOPLE CAUSING HARM &
| BIAS   PREJUDICE   BULLYING | ⚡ DISCRIMINATION   HARASSMENT   PHYSICAL VIOLATIONS

PROBLEM	RESPONSE

BIAS
NOT MEANING IT

**BIAS
INTERRUPTER**

Find Your Bias Buster

PREJUDICE
MEANING IT

**CODE OF
CONDUCT**

Do Not Essentialize

BULLYING
BEING MEAN

**CLEAR
CONSEQUENCES**

Beware of Power and Anger

PEOPLE CAUSING HARM &
BIAS   PREJUDICE   BULLYING   ⚡ DISCRIMINATION   HARASSMENT   PHYSICAL VIOLATIONS

5

For Leaders

Create Bias Interruptions, a Code of Conduct, and Consequences for Bullying

For me, the chief joy in being a leader is creating an environment in which people on a team love their job and love working together. Leaders can create the conditions for each person to do the best work of their lives and to build the best relationships of their careers. Just Work enriches our personal lives, too, because everything gets better when we bring home joy instead of angst and when we are energized rather than depleted by our work. We start to take a step in the direction of our dreams. Just Work allows a team to achieve remarkable results collectively to be happy individually.

Too many leaders act as though creating a fair and equitable working environment is somehow separate and apart from their core job as a leader, as if their "real" job is achieving a particular metric. But more and more leaders are beginning to understand that they will have trouble getting sh*t done unless they first create a just working environment.

As Bill Walsh, the former head coach of the San Francisco 49ers, put it in the title of his book *The Score Takes Care of Itself.*[1] Yes, his job was to win football games. But he couldn't win games by focusing too much on the score. The score was a lagging indicator of what he was doing well or badly as a coach. He needed to back up and understand the leading indicators: behaving ethically, demanding high standards, holding people accountable, and teaching the players the right way to play.

The good news is that there are specific things you can do to stamp out bias, prejudice, and bullying on your team, and by doing them you can create a virtuous cycle, making them less likely to occur in the future. The bad news is that it's only a virtuous cycle, not a perpetual motion machine: you have to tend to it daily.

If you think bias, prejudice, and bullying don't exist on your team, you're kidding yourself. No, it's not your fault that these attitudes and behaviors are so common in every society on the planet. But you're the boss and so it *is* your problem if you ignore them. To make things more challenging, you can't take them on alone. You're going to need your team's help. And getting that will require you to make it safe for them to help you, because they are even more reluctant to address these issues than you are.

Get started! Don't wait for reports of incidents and problems to come to you.

LEADERS AND BIAS

BIAS HARMS INDIVIDUALS & COLLECTIVE RESULTS

The range of what we think and do is limited by what we fail to notice. And because we fail to notice that we fail to notice, there is little we can do to change; until we notice how failing to notice shapes our thoughts and deeds.

—R. D. Laing

It *Is* a Big Deal

I once had a new employee, Mitch, who called the women on his team "girls." I hoped one of the men from my team with whom I'd already had this conversation would give my new employee a heads-up. I was sick to death of having this conversation. But I didn't explicitly hold anyone on my team accountable for doing so.

About a month into his tenure on my team, Mitch went to a meeting with my boss, a woman. I was meeting in my office with a couple of other teammates at the same time. When Mitch knocked on the door, he was pale. Unlike me, my boss had told him exactly what she thought of his use of the word "girls." I immediately felt guilty for having put him in that situation.

Instead of apologizing to Mitch for not giving him the feedback that it was my job as his boss to give him, though, I tried to make a joke of the whole thing. I turned to the other people on my team and said, "You can thank me now. You all thought I was a pain in the ass, but aren't you glad that you know to call women 'women'?"

Now Mitch looked mad. "Why didn't you tell *me*?"

I didn't have a good answer. "Oh, it's no big deal."

"When you meet with your boss's boss for the first time and all you talk about is how you are an asshole for using the word 'girl,' I'd say it *is* a big deal."

He was right. It was my job as his leader to have said something. Part of the reason I failed was that I treated his use of the word "girl" as though I were the person harmed by it. And, to be fair, for years I had been. As the person harmed, I had every right to pick my battles. But I learned something important that day. You may feel like the victim, but if you are the leader, you'd better act like one. It was my job to give Mitch that feedback, both for his sake and for the sake of the women on his team. I failed to do my job.

STEREOTYPE THREAT AND FEEDBACK

One's awareness of a negative stereotype about a group to which one belongs can actually harm one's performance: fear of confirming the stereotype raises that person's level of anxiety and makes it harder to perform at one's best. This can occur in people at all levels of organizations, including at the top, so leaders must manage it in others and be aware of it in themselves.

In *Whistling Vivaldi*, Stanford psychologist Claude Steele describes how negative stereotypes inhibit people's ability to do work they are more than capable of doing.[2] He described a Princeton study in which students were asked to play golf. A group of white students were divided into two groups; the first was told the task was part of an athletic aptitude test, while the second was told nothing. The white students who were told the task measured natural ability tried just as hard as the other students. But it took them an average of three strokes longer to get through the course. They performed worse. The hypothesis was that stereotype threat (white people have inferior athletic ability) had hurt the performance. The experiment was then repeated with Black students, and both groups performed equally. The difference, Steele explained, was that the Black students didn't suffer a stereotype threat when it came to athletic ability.

Steele ran a similar experiment at Stanford, only this time looking at stereotype threat related to intellectual ability. He brought together a group of Black and white undergraduates and asked them to complete a section of the Advanced GRE test. This test was beyond what they had learned, and Steele hypothesized that the frustration at not knowing some of the answers would trigger a stereotype threat related to intellectual ability in the Black students and cause them to underperform. Indeed, the Black students did do worse than the white students on the test. To test his hypothesis that this was a result of stereotype threat and not intellectual ability or educational achievement, Steele repeated the test with a different group of Black and white students. This time, he lifted the stereotype threat by telling the students that the test was not a test but rather a "task" for studying general problem-solving. He emphasized that it did not measure intellectual ability. This time, the Black students performed at the same level as white test takers and significantly better than the Black test takers who believed the test was measuring their intellectual ability.

Steele and other researchers have tested the impact of stereotypes on a wide variety of different biases. In another experiment, researchers gave girls five to seven years old an age-appropriate math test. Just before taking the test, some of the girls were asked to color a picture of a girl their age holding a doll, while others were asked to color a landscape. The theory was that reminding the girls they were girls would be enough to trigger a stereotype threat: girls aren't good at math. And in fact the girls who colored a landscape did better on the math test than those who colored a girl holding a doll.

Another group of researchers asked white men with good academic track records to take a difficult math test. In the control condition, the test was taken normally. In the experimental condition, the researchers told the test takers that one of their reasons for doing the research was to understand why Asian men seemed to perform better on these tests than white men. The theory was that the stereotype threat that white people aren't as good at math as Asian people would harm the performance of the white men on the test, and this happened.

Part of your job as a leader is to recognize and eliminate the pernicious effects of stereotype threats for the people on your team. Regardless of the stereotype in question, good, candid performance feedback can go a long way toward eliminating stereotype threat people may be experiencing. The key is to explain clearly what the standards are and reassure the person you're giving feedback to that you have confidence in their abilities.

Steele describes the role of good feedback in helping people who are underrepresented overcome their stereotype threats. Straightforward critical feedback from Tom Ostrom, Steele's PhD faculty adviser, helped Steele overcome the struggles he experienced as one of the few Black students in his program. He also references research that demonstrates this was true for Black students at other universities around the country. (Note that the feedback was about the *work*—not about their clothing or affect or something else that might reveal bias and trigger stereotype threat.) Similarly, Stanford sociologist Shelley Correll's research has shown that career success requires candid criticism—and that many women don't get that kind of candor from their bosses who are men.[3]

There is considerable evidence—both anecdotal and research-based—that good feedback, a clear explanation of expectations, reassurances that an employee can meet those expectations, and guidance when a candidate falls short are *crucial* in helping people who are underrepresented succeed in the workplace. Important note: Feedback about how other people perceive a person because of bias is *not* helpful feedback. The feedback should be based on performance or behaviors that can be changed, not personal attributes. You'll read later about a boss who told me I was suffering from the competence likability bias (or

LEADERS &
BIAS | PREJUDICE   BULLYING   ⚡ DISCRIMINATION   HARASSMENT   PHYSICAL VIOLATIONS

perhaps I was objectively unlikable) and that I should try to be more likable. This was not helpful feedback, to put it mildly.

Yet, the very people who would most benefit from good feedback get it least. Overrepresented managers are most comfortable giving feedback to employees who are "like" them. White managers are often more reluctant to give straightforward feedback to Black employees than they are to white employees; men are more reluctant to give this kind of feedback to employees who are women, and so on.

Why? Sometimes this happens because the manager is a bully or actively prejudiced. But more often it happens because *another* stereotype threat is at play: fear of being seen as biased, sexist, or racist. A desire not to be seen as biased paradoxically leads to discriminatory behavior, a failure to give candid, helpful feedback to women or BIPOC employees. Therefore, the "fear of being seen as biased" stereotype threat can inhibit bosses from giving the feedback it's their job to give.

Stereotype threat might prevent an overrepresented boss from giving critical feedback to an underrepresented person on the team. This is *really* unfortunate because it's precisely that kind of feedback that will most help underrepresented people overcome their *own* stereotype threats and do great work.

If you're a leader, get proactive. Make sure that you are aware of and managing your own stereotype threat and that you are giving *everyone* on your team feedback.

REMEMBER THAT UNCONSCIOUS BIAS TRAINING IS ONLY A START

Bias awareness training can be helpful in rooting out unconscious bias when it's done well by people who understand the issues deeply and who are excellent communicators. But in practice it often feels like a sort of "check the box, CYA, protect the company from legal liability, but don't actually try to address the underlying problem" exercise. The best unconscious bias training includes both an educator/facilitator and participation from leaders to show real commitment to change. However, simply requiring everyone to go to unconscious bias training, even a great one, won't be enough.[4] No training can possibly change deeply ingrained patterns of thought. Practice is key. Education without follow-through breeds cynicism and even reinforces stereotypes.[5] Therefore, as a leader, it's your job to figure out how you and your team can *interrupt* bias when you notice it.

Interrupting bias is not something leaders can simply outsource. Leaders must be personally involved with both helping to educate the team during the training and, crucially, figuring out how they and their teams will interrupt bias when it shows up afterward in conversation, in meetings, in business processes. If you don't take action to interrupt bias once you recognize it, your employees will notice and think, "If the boss still refuses to do anything, I'm powerless to do anything, so I guess I'll just accept the way things are."

An important first step is to get to a place of shared commitment. When it comes to interrupting bias, these are your goals:

1. Make sure that the interruption is clear enough—don't use euphemisms that belittle the problem.
2. Make sure that the interruption does not re-harm the person at whom the bias was directed.
3. Make sure that the interruption does not humiliate or attack the person who said the biased thing.
4. Make it safe for the interruption to be public when appropriate so that everyone can learn. Usually I advise people to "criticize in private." So it's important that a bias interruption feel more like a correction of a typo than personal criticism. The reason interrupting bias in public is important is that you get more educational leverage that way. Often multiple people in the room will share the bias that was spoken and will therefore benefit from the intervention. Bias that isn't interrupted is reinforced.
5. Make sure the interruption is quick enough not to derail the whole meeting. At times something said may be so harmful that

LEADERS &
BIAS   PREJUDICE   BULLYING   ⚡ DISCRIMINATION   HARASSMENT   PHYSICAL VIOLATIONS

the meeting *should* be derailed. But if you want bias interrupting to become a norm, it usually has to happen quickly, in the flow of business.

6. Make it safe to ask for clarification. Often a person will not understand the problem with what they said. It needs to be safe to say, "I don't understand why that was biased. Can we talk after the meeting?" Make sure there's a commitment to come to resolution if there's disagreement about whether what was said was biased. Ideally this would happen after the meeting. And if the person harmed is the person who interrupted the bias, an upstander should be present as well as the person who caused harm.

CREATE A SHARED VOCABULARY TO INTERRUPT BIAS

Simple bias interruptions—words or phrases that everyone uses to point out bias—can help a great deal. If everyone's speaking the same language to interrupt bias at work, people will more quickly understand what it means and also find it much easier to speak up. A leader's job is not to choose the words but to get the whole team on the same page about what words they will use to flag bias during conversations and meetings.

Bias interruptions won't work if they feel like some kind of boss-mandated or HR-imposed initiative.

If your team comes up with their own words or phrases, rather than having you dictate them, they're more likely to use them. However, you do need to offer some guidance. Bias interruption will backfire if the phrases chosen are themselves unconsciously biased. Words matter. Take some time with them. You can encourage "I" statements that invite everyone to consider the situation the way the speaker does. But the interruption doesn't have to be an "I" statement. Here are ideas that have been proposed in talks and workshops I've led:

- "I don't think you meant that the way it sounded to me."
- "Bias interruption."
- "I'm throwing a flag on the field."
- "Yo, bias!"
- "Bias alert."

Some teams like a sentence, not a phrase. Many have found it helpful to adopt Daniel Kahneman's phraseology from the book *Thinking, Fast and Slow*. If you've read the book and if your team is interested in reading it, they might adopt his suggestions and say things like "I'd like to invite your System 2 to interrupt your System 1. Slow down and let your System 2 take control."[6]

The nice thing about the language around System 1 and System 2 is that it offers an explanation for the bias and how to change it rather than a judgment of the person who said the biased thing. It also demonstrates an understanding of the energy and effort it takes to interrupt bias. I love that language. But for some it might sound annoyingly wonky. Let your team choose words that work for them.

It's not always easy to talk about bias interruption with your team, and the conversation may be difficult. Some may feel that phrases like "bias alert" or "yo" trivialize the harm that bias does. Others may be irritated that you are "wasting so much time on this." And you may feel stuck in the middle. Remind everyone that you have a goal: to come up with a shorthand phrase that allows for a quick intervention. The quicker the intervention, the more often it is likely to be used; and the more often biases get interrupted, the more the team learns. It's a little bit like reminding your kids to brush their teeth every night. If you delivered a long lecture on dental hygiene and how plaque builds up and will give them cavities if they don't brush, pretty soon you'd hate saying it as much as they'd hate hearing it. Just saying "Teeth!" is more effective.

If your team hates the idea of bias interruptions, ask them for other suggestions for accomplishing the same thing. Be open to their ideas. But if they come up with an alternative, hold them accountable for following through with it. And be open to the possibility that there may simply not be enough trust on your team to make this work. Then you're going to have to do more digging to find out why and figure out how to fix it. Not only can you not interrupt bias if there's not trust—you can't collaborate effectively, either.

Entrepreneur Jason Mayden explains why it's important that

LEADERS &
[BIAS] PREJUDICE BULLYING ⚡ DISCRIMINATION HARASSMENT PHYSICAL VIOLATIONS

teammates are safe to both make mistakes and point them out. He encourages people to "get beyond the fear of saying the wrong thing because you can't get to the right thing without first making some mistakes in between." At the same time, Mayden points out, "I should not hide my truth to make you feel comfortable in your bias."[7]

MAKING BIAS INTERRUPTIONS WORK

People will only speak up if they feel safe doing so. And I promise you, there are people on your team who do not feel safe. As a leader, it's your job to create a safe environment, not to feel impatient that people don't feel safe. Telling people to feel safe or, worse, that they "should" feel safe just won't make it so. Make it clear that changing bias is an organizational priority and that all of you must be fully invested in it. Here are some things you can do.

Protect people harmed: If people attack or ridicule, vocally or through body language, the first person who flags a bias, your efforts will fail. If someone flags bias and a couple of other people in the room roll their eyes, ask the eye-rollers to talk to you right after the meeting and let them know there will be consequences if that kind of behavior continues. *And* give them the opportunity to tell you why they rolled their eyes. In this case, you have got to be the emotional shock absorber for your team. If you let them vent their negative emotions about bias interrupters to you, two good things happen: you get the opportunity to try to persuade them why interrupting bias is worth doing; and they are less likely to vent their anger on underrepresented people. Be alert and speak up if this happens.

Share the work: The whole weight can't fall on your shoulders or on the shoulders of the people who are harmed by the bias. If they are the only ones speaking up, they'll get tired of talking and it will be harder for the team to listen. Hold folks accountable for upstanding. If you are consistently the only person who interrupts bias, point that out. Let everyone in the room know you expect them to do the same.

Make it easy: Once a catchphrase is agreed upon, make sure everyone practices using it until the whole team knows how to deploy it quickly and without drama.

Take the shame out of the game: Everyone's bias will be corrected from time to time, and people will become more open to it when they know it's not the end of the world.

Minimize disruption/maximize learning: Work out a norm for responding. If the person understands and agrees, they can say "You're right, I'm sorry, thank you for pointing it out." As suggested above, if the person doesn't understand or disagrees, they should know to say something like "Thanks for pointing it out, but I don't understand why what I said was biased. Can we talk after the meeting?" The person harmed by the statement should be invited but not required to join. That person probably has more of these conversations than the upstander and the person who said the biased thing. Let the upstanders do some of the heavy lifting. Of course, at times the meeting *should* be disrupted. If someone on a promotion committee, for example, is objecting to a woman's promotion for reasons that feel gendered, then the promotion decision shouldn't be made without resolving the basis of the objection. If you don't do this, bias gives way to discrimination.

Reward upstanding: When you witness examples of good upstanding, praise the upstanders publicly. Note it in performance reviews.

Hold yourself accountable: Early on encourage others to correct your bias publicly and respond with gratitude and confidence when they do. When others correct your bias and you respond well, it feels safer for them to correct one another and to be corrected.

Hold upstanders accountable: If you notice someone said something obviously biased, and nobody speaks up, interrupt the bias yourself. But pull the people who failed to be upstanders aside immediately after the meeting and ask them if they noticed the bias and, if so, why they didn't speak up. If *you* realize you said something that reflected your own unconscious bias, hold the others who were present accountable for not interrupting.

Remember, it's OK to be funny as long as you are the butt of all jokes: If you're the leader or the most senior person in the room, the only person who should be laughed at is you. Humor that speaks truth to power has a prominent and useful place in history. Part of a leader's

LEADERS &
BIAS   PREJUDICE   BULLYING   ⚡   DISCRIMINATION   HARASSMENT   PHYSICAL VIOLATIONS

job is to solicit feedback, and one way to do that is to be strong enough to laugh at yourself and to encourage others to poke fun at you as a way of giving feedback.

Once you've established a norm, you'll find that people learn pretty quickly and increasingly catch themselves *before* making a biased comment. But that only happens when you establish language and norms that recognize and correct bias and ensure that everyone is doing their part. None of that will happen without conscious leadership and proactive intervention from you.

BUILD BIAS-INTERRUPTING NORMS

How can you teach your team to interrupt their own biases so that they can treat one another with respect; make more rational, impartial decisions; and collaborate in a way that makes the whole greater than the sum of its parts?

STORYTELLING

One company I know started an initiative called "Yes, this really happened here." People who experienced bias, and sometimes bias that had given way to discrimination or harassment, wrote their stories down and submitted them to a group of employees committed to stamping out these attitudes and behaviors. These employees selected several stories each week and shared them via email to a list of people who'd signed up to receive them—thousands of people each week. Telling and reading these stories built awareness at the company about the ways in which bias played out there. After reading these stories, it was impossible to deny that bias gives way to discrimination and bullying and worse—and not "elsewhere" but right there, in a company where most employees did not expect these sorts of things to happen. Many who read these stories reported realizing that they had been biased in ways they were not aware of and became committed to changing. Many who told the stories reported feeling acknowledged and respected in ways they hadn't previously felt.

Reading through these stories to distinguish which ones reflected bias and which ones required action took time on the part of a group of dedicated people. It would have been unfair if this work had been deemed purely "extracurricular." Their managers considered it part of the people's jobs and made time accommodations for this work.

In the past, the legal department's warnings about the risks of soliciting such stories would have carried the day. But the leadership at that company realized that they couldn't fix problems they didn't know about, and they were committed to addressing those problems once they did. Rather than avoiding knowledge of workplace injustice, they went looking for it. They actively resisted the default of exclusion.

IMPROV

Improvisational theater has its roots in a program that Viola Spolin developed under the Works Progress Administration (WPA) during the Depression. The goal of Spolin's Improv Games was to transcend the cultural and ethnic barriers of the immigrant children with whom she worked and to unlock the individual's self-expression. Her Improv Games helped people overcome what she called Approval/Disapproval Syndrome and unblock their creativity by letting go of the instinct to please teachers, peers, or anyone else. Her techniques became the basis of many modern improv techniques.

You can use these improv techniques to help your team cross cultural and ethnic barriers to challenge bias. For example, to help build empathy for how deeply disorienting he-peating (see chapter 2) is, Second City Works has developed an exercise called "yes, and, exclude."[8] People break into groups of six and are asked to plan a party. Going around the circle, everyone offers ideas and builds on other people's ideas, but the group is to exclude one person. If people like an idea offered by that person, they can repeat it, but they cannot under any circumstances acknowledge that it came from the excluded person. Even though everyone knows that they are simply playing a role, this exercise is deeply unnerving. Participants and leaders alike have reported feeling astounded by how good it feels to address these weighty issues with laughter and how helpful it is to practice.

LEADERS &
BIAS | PREJUDICE BULLYING ⚡ DISCRIMINATION HARASSMENT PHYSICAL VIOLATIONS

To keep the laughter productive, having rules of engagement and trained facilitators is key. The goal is to structure the exercise in a way that keeps it safe for everyone. The laughter must come from recognition of a truth that we often try to ignore rather than from ridicule of anyone in the room.

FIFTY WAYS TO FIGHT

The Lean In Foundation created an effective free online course to help eliminate bias in the workplace. The genius of this course is that it offers real anecdotes about things people say and do every day at work that reveal bias. It doesn't just leave people feeling discouraged about this, though, because it also offers specific suggestions for confronting these situations and helping people change their behavior.

GENDER BIAS BINGO

Invented by legal scholar Joan Williams, this game categorizes the kinds of biases women deal with all the time in the workplace and forces participants to confront their own similar behaviors. The great thing about it is that it prompts people to tell stories in a way that explains exactly what happened to them. The game does not offer specific strategies for how to respond to these incidents, so you'll need to push people to think about the best ways to combat the problems they're bringing up. It's cathartic for people harmed and educational for upstanders.

LEADERS AND PREJUDICE

Remember, bias is your brain serving up stereotypes you are not aware of and wouldn't agree with if you stopped to think or became aware. Prejudice is, at some level, your conscious brain rationalizing stereotypes and biases.

In cases of both bias and prejudice, you have to intervene. In the case of bias, you hold up a mirror, and usually the person self-corrects. But in the case of prejudice, if you hold up a mirror, the person is likely to say, "Yeah, that's me, aren't I good-looking?" Pointing out the prejudice probably isn't going to change it. In the case of prejudice, your job is to prevent that person from imposing it on others.

As a leader, you're overstepping to try to control what people believe. People are free to *believe* whatever they want. But they are not free to DO whatever they want. At the same time, it is your job to prevent people from imposing their beliefs on others. Everyone is free *to* believe whatever they want, and everyone should be free *from* other people's prejudices. This is really seriously tricky. If you don't want to deal with it, don't become a leader.

CODE OF CONDUCT: A RULE BOOK FOR RESPECT

Leaders are responsible for setting and communicating clear expectations about the boundaries of acceptable behavior. A code of conduct is one of the best tools for ensuring expectations are clear and fair. A code of conduct does not tell people what to *believe* but instead what they can and cannot *do*. Most people will respect boundaries—if they know where they are.

In general, for performance issues of any kind, employees should (1) understand clearly what is expected and (2) be given some warning when they are failing to do what is expected. There are of course grounds for immediate termination: violence or theft, for example. But where is the line for your organization? As a leader, it's your job to articulate it. And then you'll have to interpret it case by case.

Writing a code of conduct takes time, but it will push you as a leader to think as clearly about behavior as you do about performance. It forces you to articulate what is OK and not OK to say and do in your workplace, and to decide what the consequences ought to be for violating the standards you are setting forth. When do people get a warning, and what are grounds for immediate dismissal?

One of the most memorable classes I took at Harvard Business

School was about James Burke's tenure as CEO of Johnson & Johnson. When he became CEO in 1976, the first thing he did was visit every Johnson & Johnson office globally in three years and work with the leadership in each office to rewrite the credo—the company's code of conduct. At the end of this, there was a summit in New York City with the company's top leadership. Burke himself then spent 40 hours working through everyone's edits to the document.

I was astounded. Was this really how CEOs spent their time? Burke visited our class and explained that this collective effort to unify the corporation's identity would later pull it through a crisis that threatened Johnson & Johnson's very existence, because everyone had a shared set of values that guided their actions. Of course, Burke was exceptional: many CEOs have no idea what is written in the code of conduct they inherited; even worse, they are often the ones in their companies most likely to violate it.

IF YOU DON'T HAVE A CODE OF CONDUCT, WRITE ONE

If you don't already have a code of conduct, how do you go about writing one? I recommend that you offer your services as the writer and ask your team to be the editors. The editors in this case are not just making sure your writing is clear, or that words are spelled correctly; they are evaluating whether the document reflects the reality they observe in the office.

Once you and your team have a draft you are happy with, you can get each person on your team to repeat the process with *their* team. You then come back together with comments and make changes. Each of your direct reports must report back to their direct reports about why edits were or were not accepted. This is crucial—you must share your logic and make sure people understand the decisions that were made, even if they don't fully agree with them.

Then you want to share what is still a draft with the whole organization. If you have a big organization, you'll want to task someone with being the comment czar. The comment czar should be in charge of categorizing comments/suggestions so that you can more quickly understand the response of the broader organization to the draft. The comment czar should also get back to every person who wrote a comment or suggestion and explain why it was or was not accepted.

Below is my *first draft* for the team at Radical Candor, the executive-education company I co-founded.

1. **Act with integrity.** Honesty and ethical behavior are the bedrock of productivity. If we cannot trust one another, we cannot collaborate or innovate. Lying, cheating, stealing, acts of violence, and other ethical violations are grounds for dismissal.
2. **Show common human decency.** Remember, even if your relationships at work are not friendships, they are still real human relationships. *Everyone* you interact with deserves to be treated with respect. This is especially important when you have a disagreement. When you treat people with disrespect, you hurt both your long-term work and our collective efforts. Collaboration is more effective than domination for you as an individual and for our company as a whole. Bullying behavior is grounds for dismissal.

    Seek to understand when there are differences. Do not merely tolerate differences; seek to understand the other person's logic *and* emotions. Do not rush to condemn people wholesale.

    Do not impose your beliefs on others. You have a right to believe whatever you want, but you do not have a right to do whatever you want. When your words hurt your team's ability to get things done, you don't have the right to say whatever you want, either.

    Care. You are more likely to do great work and to help your team do great work when you care about the people you work with not just on a professional level but on a human level.

    Be aware of the impact you have on others. If you hurt someone, saying "I wasn't aware" or "I didn't mean to" is

BIAS **LEADERS &**
PREJUDICE BULLYING ⚡ DISCRIMINATION HARASSMENT PHYSICAL VIOLATIONS

not good enough. It is your responsibility to be aware of the impact you have on others and to make amends when you've hurt them.

3. **Challenge directly.** If you disagree with people, say something directly to them rather than talking behind their backs. Gossiping, backstabbing, and political behavior will have a negative impact on your performance evaluation and on your career.

   Correct bias. If people say or do something that seems biased to you, correct them without attacking them, in the spirit of helping them learn, not punishing them. We are all biased in our own ways, and we will move in the right direction only when we correct one another's biases.

4. **Respect consent.** It is the responsibility of the toucher to be aware of how the other person feels about being touched. If the other person doesn't want to be touched, don't touch. If you're not sure, don't touch. Unwanted touching is grounds for dismissal. Dating in your chain of command, even when consensual, is also grounds for dismissal. The power dynamic can make it hard to express consent.

5. **Honor checks and balances.** Unchecked power corrupts, and we have put in place a structure that ensures none of us are corrupted by it. Nobody here has unilateral authority, and nobody is above the rules. If you notice a problem, you have multiple escalation options. Click *here* to read what they are. Behaving as though the rules don't apply to you or seeking to avoid the checks that have been put upon your authority is grounds for dismissal.

Note the length here. I was proud of myself for keeping it under 600 words. As a rule of thumb, I'd suggest not going over 600—if you want people to read and internalize it, that is. By the time they have gotten through multiple levels of approval, many codes of conduct—even the good ones—are way too long. I would guess few employees have read these documents in their entirety. For example, Google's is excellent and worth reading, but it's 6,322 words—22 pages. Think of all of the documents you've clicked your way through without really taking much in.

It's worth noting the team didn't like my first draft. Your team probably won't love yours either, and that is OK. As of this writing they are still editing it. The most important feedback came from Candor Coach Melissa Andrada. She pointed out that this code was not aspirational. It didn't articulate values as much as establish a floor of behavior. The team at Radical Candor came up with something much shorter, but we suspect it's too short:

Power is bad.
Inclusion is good.
Stay open to new perspectives.
Care personally.
Challenge directly.

I don't recommend that you adopt either of the versions above for several reasons. First, they are still drafts. But even if either were final, polished documents, you don't want to take another leader's code of conduct as your starting place. You are better off starting fresh with your own. You are much more likely to get buy-in from your team if (1) it reflects things you truly believe rather than things you copy-pasted from someone else, (2) it reflects things *your team* truly believes (that's why they must be involved in drafting it), and (3) its language and principles clearly reflect your team's culture.

FAIR PROCESS AND CONSEQUENCES FOR VIOLATING THE CODE OF CONDUCT

A code of conduct makes the rules of engagement clear. It can help you create a culture in which problems are less likely to arise in the first place. Job candidates who disagree with the code can decide not to work at your company. Employees who disagree with the code can quit. And if those employees refuse to abide by the code and don't quit, you are within your rights to fire them if you've made the rules clear.

However, no matter how clear and reasonable your code is, one thing is sure: it will be violated—often in ways you couldn't possibly anticipate. Human behavior is endlessly surprising, sometimes in ways

LEADERS &
BIAS   **PREJUDICE**   BULLYING ⚡ DISCRIMINATION   HARASSMENT   PHYSICAL VIOLATIONS

that inspire, other times in ways that horrify, bewilder, and disgust. There must be consequences for violating the code of conduct. And coming up with fair and reasonable consequences in response to the kinds of difficult situations that inevitably arise is *much* easier if you have thought through the principles and communicated them to employees *before* you try to figure out what to do about someone's unexpectedly awful behavior.

People can be fired for violating the code of conduct. But they can't be fired for simply being *accused* of violating the code of conduct. As a boss, it's your job to make sure any complaints are handled fairly.

In addition to a code of conduct, therefore, you also need to design a fair system for deciding what violates the code and what doesn't. As a leader, you'll have to come up with a system for making judgments case by case, and it's important that everyone understand the process for making these judgments. Helpful hint: Don't decide unilaterally or abdicate entirely. Your process can't be "Trust me, I'm a good leader" or "I don't know, HR will figure it out."

It's vital that the people who work for you have confidence in the process. One common cause of mistrust is the belief that HR reports to the CEO—who is all too often one of the biggest violators of the code, as are the senior executives the CEO protects. Though HR gets the blame, the real culprits here are the boards of directors who fail to hold the CEOs and their teams accountable. When HR reports to the CEO, we're asking the employee to hold their boss accountable. That's not reasonable. More on ways that organizational design can solve this problem is discussed in chapter 6.

What Would You Do?

You manage an IT department at a big company. One of your employees, Paul, goes to a meeting in which recruiters are asking employees to refer more women. Paul hates going to meetings in general, and he is particularly grumpy about this one.

"I'll tell you why there aren't more women in our department!" Paul explodes. "It's because with very few exceptions women just aren't good with computers! It starts early, when kids are like ten, and it compounds over time. I'm sick of everyone trying to deny the basic facts of biology here."

Paul may as well have thrown a grenade into the room. Everything blows up and the meeting ends.

You talk to Paul. You explain to him that he has violated the code of conduct. You point to the part that says, "Employees must treat each other respectfully. We do not permit intimidation, discrimination, or harassment in the workplace."

"I was not being disrespectful, it was just the truth!" says Paul. "I can't help it if the PC crowd doesn't like hearing the facts."

"It is not a fact that women are not good with computers. That is your opinion, many would say it's prejudiced, and you do not have the right to impose it on others."

"Oh, great, so now you are taking away my First Amendment rights?"

"Your First Amendment rights are political rights, not workplace rights. If you say things that create a hostile work environment, you can be fired for the following reasons. One, creating a hostile work environment violates the code of conduct, which you signed and read before you took the job. Two, it creates a legal liability for the company. Three, it makes it impossible to get sh*t done. It hurts our team's ability to collaborate when you don't respect each team member as an individual. Four, I can be held *personally* liable if I don't take action, and that's not a risk I am prepared to take."

"So are you firing me?"

"No. I *am*, however, warning you that if you continue to impose your prejudices about women and computer skills on your colleagues, you will be fired."

Paul leaves your office in a huff. The next thing you know, he has posted articles about women and IQ on the company intranet. A virtual riot has erupted, involving not just Paul's IT department but also the sales team and the marketing department. Pretty soon, HR is wading in, trying to calm things down. Now not only is Paul wasting his team's time, he's wasting the time of dozens of teams.

You know that if you fire Paul, which seems increasingly likely, he will claim that he was a victim of PC culture. This wouldn't be accurate. If you decide to fire Paul it won't be because of his beliefs.

LEADERS &
BIAS [PREJUDICE] BULLYING ⚡ DISCRIMINATION HARASSMENT PHYSICAL VIOLATIONS

You would be firing him for trying to impose those beliefs on others through the company intranet in a way that was disruptive and harmful to the team's productivity. If employees were nudists, they wouldn't be fired for their beliefs. But they would be fired if they insisted on coming to work naked or posting naked pictures on the intranet.

Armed with this analogy, you go to talk to Paul.

LEADERS AND BULLYING: ENFORCE CONSEQUENCES

It would be nice to think you can avoid hiring bullies. Unfortunately, bullying is a behavior, not a personality type; while some people are more prone to it, we all engage in it from time to time for the simple reason that it can be an effective way to establish or maintain status or to coerce others. And bullying will continue until you, as a leader, make it clear that it simply won't work in your organization.

Bullying creates an atmosphere of fear that undermines a team's success. If you don't create consequences for coercive, dominating, retaliatory, and intimidating behavior, *you,* as the one responsible for your team's results, will be the one facing the consequences. Bullying often confers status, but it rarely improves performance. Bullying often covers up ignorance, incompetence, insecurity, or just plain laziness. You owe it to your team to put a stop to it.

The Workplace Bullying Institute's 2017 survey reports that an average of 19 percent of Americans are bullied at work, and another 19 percent witness the bullying. In total, workplace bullying affects 60 million people. Seventy percent of bullies are men (with 61 percent being bosses), and 60 percent of those bullied are women. And 45 percent of people reported an increase in workplace bullying in recent years.[9]

One of the things that makes dealing with bullying so difficult is that almost no one thinks that they've ever bullied someone at work—1 in 200, according to a Workplace Bullying Institute survey.[10]

But, according to the same survey, nearly half of those questioned answered that they had been bullied or witnessed bullying. How can this be? Maybe people who bully are incredibly energetic and bully all the time. Or, more likely, maybe we all do it sometimes and are unaware of how our behavior impacts others. It's easy to recognize when other people bully, and hard to be aware of our own bullying. And *both* may be true. It may be that much of the bullying is committed by "repeat offenders," people who consistently bully. But at least *some* bullying happens when people who do not see themselves as bullies behave in a bullying way—as I did with Russ in the story above.

If you're a leader, and someone's behavior strikes you as unduly coercive, it's your job to confront the situation. You may end up learning you've misunderstood the dynamic—there can be a fine line between conflict and bullying. But the only way to know is to talk to both parties. Even if you're wrong, you've sent a signal that (1) you're actively seeking to counter bullying and (2) it's safe for people to approach you if they feel they have been bullied.

If you don't keep a keen eye out for bullying behavior, you probably won't notice it; people who bully often "kiss up and kick down." That is why it is all the more important for your intolerance of bullying to be widely understood throughout your team. If you don't remark on it when you are present for it, that won't reflect well on your leadership—or on your understanding of your team and its dynamics. If you want victims and/or upstanders to inform you that bullying is taking place behind your back, you need to show them you care about it. If you ignore it when you see it, people are less likely to come to you when they need your help.

CREATING CONSEQUENCES FOR BULLYING: CONVERSATION, COMPENSATION, CAREER

It's a leader's job to create an environment in which coercive and intimidating behavior backfires. It backfires only when leaders create real consequences for bullying. At a minimum, when people engage in

BIAS   PREJUDICE   ⌐LEADERS &⌐ $\lightning$ DISCRIMINATION   HARASSMENT   PHYSICAL VIOLATIONS
⌊BULLYING⌋

bullying behavior, their behavior must have a negative impact on them, not the people they are bullying. As a leader, you have three levers at your disposal: conversation, compensation, and career advancement.

Conversation: Create consequences without becoming a bully yourself

As a leader, your first response to bullying should be to pull the bully aside and give clear feedback. People who bully will be defensive. They might say they were unaware they were crossing a line or simply deny it. Or they may argue some version of "I'm doing what I have to do to get results. If others can't take it, they should find a new place to work."

Don't let them off the hook. Reiterate what you noticed and how it negatively affects the team. Then explain that if the behavior continues, it will be noted in their performance review and may affect compensation and even their future at your company.

It's equally important to follow up with the people who were bullied to understand how they experienced the situation and to let them know you have their back. If the person who engaged in bullying does it again, you must follow through with the consequence you outlined.

Compensation: Don't give raises, bonuses, or high performance ratings to people who bully

Compensation shows what a leader values. Behavior uncorrected is behavior accepted. Behavior rewarded is behavior requested. Never, ever give a raise or bonus to people who bully their peers or employees.

In many companies, people who browbeat and demean colleagues and employees are allowed to continue doing so as long as they get results. They might be given feedback about the damage they're doing, but if their performance review and bonus are based on their numbers, not their behavior, their behavior won't change. Eventually, no one wants to work with these bullies; valued employees quit. Over time, as the best people refuse to work with them, the bullies' performance suffers. But the process is so gradual that the bullies, and also their managers, don't make the connection between the bullying behavior and performance. After years of getting rewarded for their behavior, they may be punished for it and they don't get that big bonus one year. But they behaved exactly the same way that year as they did the year before: the punishment seems arbitrary to the person doing the bully-ing. Either way, the victims of the bullying are driven away, the person doing the bullying doesn't learn in time to change, and the results of the team suffer.

It's easy to say that people who mistreat their co-workers and em-ployees shouldn't get raises or bonuses. But it's even better to create a system that explicitly discourages bullying. I once spent some time working on the performance review system at a company I admire. Their whole process of evaluating employee performance was impres-sive, but what really struck me was its commitment to putting team-work on par with results. Even if you hit all your performance goals, you'd still get a bad performance rating if you weren't a good team player, as measured by your peer reviews in a 360 review process. A poor teamwork rating came with a heavy cost—no bonus, no raise. If the employee didn't push that number up in subsequent reviews, the employee would be fired. And the boss couldn't determine unilaterally who was bullying and who wasn't; peer assessment was key.

This was important for the whole company. It was good for leaders because it gave some "teeth" to their feedback about bullying. It was good for the people who would have been bullied if that kind of be-havior had not been discouraged. In many cases it was even good for the people doing the bullying. Pushing them to develop knowledge and competence instead of trying to dominate or coerce their colleagues in-creased their self-assurance. And it was good for the company because it helped stamp out bullying and improved results.

Atlassian, an Australian enterprise software company, provides an-other great example of a performance management system that actively punishes bullying. The company explicitly designed their performance review system to eliminate the "brilliant jerk," the bane of so many tech companies. Atlassian's global head of talent, Bek Chee, explained that managers rate employees along three different dimensions: how they dem-onstrate company values, how they deliver on expectations of their role, and the contribution they make to the team. Employees get a separate rating for each of those areas, not just an average rating.[11]

BIAS   PREJUDICE   [LEADERS & BULLYING]   ⚡ DISCRIMINATION   HARASSMENT   PHYSICAL VIOLATIONS

Giving three ratings instead of just one can be a good way to get bias out of recruiting and performance review systems. Be specific about what you are looking for, even if the qualities are subjective, and give numerical ratings for each rather than one overall rating.[12]

Career advancement: Don't promote people who bully

Do not promote bullies. It's that simple. Give them feedback, encouragement, goals. If the behavior does not change, fire them. The long-term damage these people cause is not worth any quarterly result they may be delivering. As many leaders have observed, it's better to have a hole than an asshole on your team.

When I worked for a large tech company, I worked with Roy, a particularly prodigious bully, especially of women. One man I worked with commented, "Well, I have never had a problem with Roy myself, but I've never met an executive who is so universally hated by women."

Here are a few of the things I saw. Every interaction was an opportunity for him to make women uncomfortable. His job required frequent trips to Japan. Driving into Tokyo from the airport, he'd point out all the sex hotels along the way. He loved to start what he leeringly called "catfights" between women at the office. Once, he told me that he knew I secretly hated another woman on his team. When I assured him that in fact I liked and respected her, he began bad-mouthing her to me, asking how I could be supportive of someone who'd been promoted over me when she didn't deserve it. When I disagreed again, he became visibly angry. Another time, Roy stood onstage in front of a few thousand people flanked by his direct reports. He looked to his right, looked to his left, then smiled creepily and said, "Ooooh, the ladies dressed up for me today," as if he were a pimp instead of a tech executive.

Even though the company prided itself on being a place where nobody would have to pay the asshole tax, Roy kept on getting promoted.[13] The message they wanted to put out was "Don't be an asshole," but Roy's promotions told a different story: assholes get ahead. People stopped trying to confront his bullying behavior because not only was it working for him, it was getting *rewarded*. Which made more people think that they had to be like Roy to get ahead: abusive and domineering.

As Roy continued to get promoted, his behavior went from bad to worse; he started bullying men as well as women. And that's when the bell rang for Roy. I'd left the company to get away from Roy and joined a competitor. The CEO of that competitor tried to hire one of Roy's lieutenants, a well-respected man. When Roy found out, he called the CEO and said they ought to hire him, not his lieutenant. The CEO was horrified and said no. But word got around about what Roy had done, and that was the beginning of the end for him.

When he was abusing women, that was just dismissed as Roy being Roy. But when it started affecting men, management showed him the door. By the time Roy finally got fired, the company had lost a bunch of its top performers, not "only" women. I hope that by this point in the book I don't have to underscore the obvious lessons here, but— just to be safe—I will. Bullies don't pick on people their own size. At that company, women were safe targets. If management had been paying attention, they'd have improved things both for the women and for the bottom line. They finally got rid of Roy but only after he had cost the company greatly. Roy got fired from his next job too, for bullying, unethical behavior. Correlation is not causation, but bullying and low moral standards often go hand in hand.

BLOVIATING BS IS AN UNRECOGNIZED FORM OF BULLYING

We can all think of typical bullying behavior: finger-pointing, name-calling, and yelling, and ridiculing, threatening, and intimidating others. One particularly insidious form of bullying that gets tolerated all too often is what I call bloviating BS.

Comedian Sarah Cooper has illuminated what bloviating BS looks like and what a disaster it is for good decision-making and justice. You've probably seen her TikTok videos. She also explains how this kind of bloviating BS plays out in the workplace: "When I worked at Google, it was usually a product manager who would come into a meeting, talk in circles, throw around a buzzword or fifty, and walk out looking like a key team player despite the fact that no one was even sure what he'd said."[14]

BIAS   PREJUDICE   LEADERS & BULLYING   ⚡ DISCRIMINATION   HARASSMENT   PHYSICAL VIOLATIONS

We've all seen some form of this in the workplace. Frank Yeary was a senior finance executive at Citigroup who led his firm's early diversity and inclusion efforts. He noticed that though women tended to come to meetings better prepared than men, the men did most of the talking, even speaking over the women if the women tried to get a word in edgewise. This was not only bad for the women's careers, he explained, it was bad for the bank.

In studies of team effectiveness, Carnegie Mellon University professor Anita Woolley has found that "as long as everyone got a chance to talk, the team did well."[15] But if only one person or a small group spoke all the time, the collective intelligence declined. The air time didn't have to be perfectly equal in every meeting, but in aggregate, it had to balance out.[16]

Bloviating BSers are usually from groups who are overrepresented. In a study conducted by John Jerrim and Nikki Shure of the University College London and Phil Parker of Australian Catholic University, researchers asked men and women whether they were experts in 16 distinct math topics, 3 of which were made up. Men were much more likely to claim expertise in these made-up topics than women, as were the rich over the middle class.[17] What's more, the researchers discovered, people were more likely to call BS on those they perceived as their equals than on those they thought had more power than they did. So if you're a leader, you need to make sure you're creating the conditions for people to call BS on you.

Not getting called out on one's BS breeds a problematic overconfidence. This can work in the BSer's favor in situations such as job interviews and grant applications.[18] But it's bad for the success of collaborative efforts, and bad for you as a leader if it means you are hiring the wrong people, listening to the wrong people, promoting the wrong people.

In high school, I participated in Model United Nations, where I learned a lesson that has stood me in good stead for my whole career. Since my school was all girls, Model UN was one of the few opportunities I had to compete with boys. The first three years I was a delegate, I was extremely well prepared, but I never managed to distinguish myself. My senior year, on the other hand, I was too busy applying to college and breaking up with my first boyfriend to prepare properly, and so I had to wing it.

In the past I had spent the first hour of the session assembling my facts and arguments. Now, liberated from any actual knowledge, I was forced to look around instead of rummaging about inside my head, and I noticed something surprising. The delegates who were most vocal had no idea what they were talking about. They were just making things up and hurling insults at one another. Hell, I could do that! It didn't matter that I wasn't prepared; in fact, it was helpful to be unconstrained by reality.

I gave bloviation a try. I hurled some gratuitous insults mixed in with made-up "facts" and big words. I got a lot of laughs. Emboldened, I kept going. By the time the day was over, though, I felt a little ashamed of myself. I didn't go to the awards ceremony, certain someone would call me out for my bad behavior. Instead, I got a phone call. Where was I? I'd won the best delegate award!

For me this was a cautionary tale in several respects. Preparation is not enough; the ability to assert oneself is also critical. But I didn't want to choose between being a studious mouse and a bloviating BS artist: I wanted to have something intelligent to offer and then to have that contribution recognized.

At several points in my career I've watched people make stuff up and get away with it because they project confidence and dismiss or insult anyone who challenges them. Leaders, take note: This approach is far more effective than it should be. It's your job to create consequences for it so bloviating BS doesn't take over your company.

Bloviating BS prevents a team from getting to the best decisions. So it's ineffective. And it's also unjust because it only works for BSers who are in the dominant group. Underrepresented people can rarely get away with bloviating BS. The answer is not to let underrepresented people get away with BS. The answer is to eliminate bloviating BS.

As a leader, it's your job to make sure that everyone feels comfortable participating in meetings online or off and also in the everyday back-and-forth of conversations at work. Here are some things you can do.

BIAS   PREJUDICE   ┌ **LEADERS &**
                   │ **BULLYING** │   ⚡   DISCRIMINATION   HARASSMENT   PHYSICAL VIOLATIONS

Share the research
Help people understand why they need to contribute more, less, or differently, and come up with strategies for altering the pattern of bloviating BS. Share the research that shows why it's important that everyone on a team gets opportunities to contribute to conversation.[19]

Give the quiet ones a voice
Ask what you can do to make the environment more comfortable for the quiet people. Jony Ive, the former chief design officer at Apple, said a leader's job is to "give the quiet ones a voice." How can you do this?

Annie Jean-Baptiste, who is the head of product inclusion at Google and an introvert, had a manager, Seth van der Swaagh, who noticed she was quiet during meetings. He asked her, "How many times have you had an idea and someone else said it, but you were afraid to speak up?" He then asked her, "Is it OK if sometimes I directly ask you in meetings if there are any thoughts you'd like to share?" By creating space that allowed Annie to speak up, he created a virtuous cycle. The more he asked her opinion, the more she spoke; the more she spoke, the more comfortable she became speaking. It was just like building a muscle: her voice got stronger over time. It is also helpful to send out the agenda beforehand so that introverts and others who often need to process information before they are on the spot have time to prepare what they want to say.

Block bloviation
If one person is doing all the talking, gently interrupt that person and say that you'd like to hear from everyone. Simple things can help, such as asking a question and then going around the room and giving everyone a set amount of time to answer. When I taught at Apple University, an experienced professor taught me to body-block people who wouldn't shut up—literally, to walk over to them and stand in front of them. If they still didn't get the hint, the professor added, put your hand in the air in a "pause" gesture and say you'd like to hear from others in the room.

Encourage people to track their air time
There are a number of air-time trackers folks can use to figure out what percentage of the time they spend talking. This is especially

important for virtual meetings, which are even more likely than in-person meetings to be dominated by one person. If Zoom and Google Hangouts and Microsoft Teams and other videoconferencing services offered a private air-time report to folks who spoke more than three times their "air time" in a meeting, it would be a great service to both team effectiveness and inclusivity. Of course, you don't want to get too obsessed with measurement here. There may be a good reason why one person is talking a lot and another not at all in a particular meeting. But it would be useful to ask folks on your team to self-monitor.[20]

Pay attention to body language

Sometimes you may not know enough about a topic to spot a skilled BSer. But chances are others will, and their body language will give it away. Watch how colleagues respond to the person who is hogging the spotlight. Are they rolling their eyes or crossing their arms and saying nothing? Invite them to speak up.

Make sure everyone does their homework

One of the most frustrating things that happens in meetings that have been called to discuss a particular document is that only half the attendees have read it, yet often those who haven't still "contribute" more than those who have. There are two solutions. Tell people not to come to the meeting unless they have read the document in advance. Or give people a "study hall" at the beginning of the meeting to read the document.[21] I like the latter solution because then prep time for meetings is baked into the meeting time, rather than done late at night when folks ought to be asleep.

WHEN DO YOU FIRE SOMEONE?

Don't overpunish for bias. If the consequences of saying something biased are too dire, bias interrupting doesn't work: colleagues don't want to play the heavy, and it becomes too dangerous for people to admit they screwed up. Unless bias is chronic and the person causing

BIAS   PREJUDICE   ⌐LEADERS &
                   [BULLYING]   ⚡ DISCRIMINATION   HARASSMENT   PHYSICAL VIOLATIONS

harm refuses to address the issue, unconscious bias doesn't have to be formally punished. When you are dealing with bias and not prejudice or bullying, it's relatively unlikely that you'll have to fire someone.

There will be some people on your team whose bias is unshakable. Some may continue to impose their prejudices on others. Some may not stop using bullying tactics. Maybe they don't want to learn. Maybe they can't learn. Here we come to one of the most difficult decisions you have to make as a leader: when to fire a person because their attitudes and behaviors are not changing and are dragging a team down and creating a hostile work environment. If you've given people feedback that the way they are speaking to their colleagues is unacceptable, you've taken measures to help them learn, and you've talked to them about how they don't seem to be learning, then you've got a performance issue and it's your job to take action.

In *Radical Candor* I make three suggestions about firing people that apply here:

1. Be fair.
   Give people enough feedback that they've had a fair chance to address the issue.
   Don't make the decision unilaterally—make sure you invite others to question your decision. In the case of bias, this is especially important.
2. Don't wait too long.
   Give people a chance to fix the problem, but not an infinite number of chances.
   Giving too many chances is not fair to the rest of the team.
   And it's not so great for the person who's doing a bad job and failing to get any better, either.
3. Be kind.
   Remember you can still care about a person whom you're firing. Go in thinking about the things you appreciate about the person and give voice to these things; don't give in to the tempting narrative that you are firing the person for being a horrible human being.
   Follow up. This is hard, but if you can email people a month

after you fire them and check in to find out how they are and to offer to make any introductions they might want (as long as they haven't behaved in a way that would make you uncomfortable doing that), it can be enormously helpful both to that person and to alleviating the distress that firing another person causes most managers.[22]

CHEAT SHEET

By acting consciously and with intention, leaders can minimize the ways in which biases skew decision-making and cause us to act irrationally. Leaders can develop a code of conduct that prevents some people from demanding that others conform to their prejudices. When leaders create a culture in which respect for each person's individuality is a norm, all can feel free at work and therefore do their best work. Finally, leaders can create consequences for bullying so that such behavior doesn't ruin the ability to collaborate.

As leaders, we must constantly be encouraging and supporting individuality in all the ways that nourish the possibility of collaboration and creativity while interrupting behaviors that are heedlessly coercive or conformist. See the chart on the next page.

PROBLEM	RESPONSE

BIAS
NOT MEANING IT

**BIAS
INTERRUPTER**

Bias-busting Norms

PREJUDICE
MEANING IT

**CODE OF
CONDUCT**

People Shall Not Impose
Their Prejudices on Others

BULLYING
BEING MEAN

**CLEAR
CONSEQUENCES**

Conversation,
Compensation, and Career

BIAS   PREJUDICE   BULLYING   ⚡ DISCRIMINATION   HARASSMENT   PHYSICAL VIOLATIONS

PART TWO:

Discrimination, Harassment, and Physical Violations

How to Manage Power So It Doesn't Manage You

Power is bad. That is a debatable statement, but I'm going to say it because I believe what Lord Acton said: "Power tends to corrupt and absolute power corrupts absolutely."[1] Powerlessness is also terrible. But the solution to powerlessness is not power. It's agency, accountability, and justice. When managers have too much power, things quickly get even more unfair and inefficient. Bias and prejudice give way to discrimination. Bullying gives way to verbal or psychological harassment. Unchecked power, whether positional power or physical power, paves the way for the full range of physical violations ranging from the creepy hug to the violent assault.

In the absence of mechanisms that hold managers accountable and give all employees a reliable way to report abusive behavior, discrimination and harassment are predictable. If people are allowed to rule by fiat, injustice and inefficiency will thrive. Innovation will suffer. Morale will plummet, and your most talented and hard-to-replace employees will run for the exits. Your most vulnerable employees, who have no easy exit, will stay and suffer and perhaps eventually sue you.

Each of us likes to think that we are good people and no matter what temptations we face, no matter what kind of system we find ourselves in, we will behave like the good people we aspire to be. However, both history and psychological experiments demonstrate that this is often not the case.

A growing body of research suggests that the more power a person has, the more likely their decision-making is to be flawed by bias and prejudice. Research also shows that bias and prejudice rather than rational decision-making often influence how resources are allocated.[2]

Increased power also means increased bullying when the person who has power feels insecure, incapable of controlling things, and not respected. And who doesn't feel insecure, at least some of the time? A survey of 775 corporate workers reported that rude, uncivil behaviors were three times more likely to come from people *above* them in their organizations.[3] Having power while being focused on protecting one's high position promotes bad behavior.

The different ways that power eventually leads to the downfall of the powerful are well explained in Berkeley psychologist Dacher Keltner's *The Power Paradox*. Those in power tend to depersonalize those without power. As people gain power, they often begin to indulge in behaviors likely to make them lose their power.[4]

Not only does power corrupt, it doesn't even work that well in the long run. As author Moisés Naím writes in his book *The End of Power,* "Power no longer buys as much as it did in the past . . . From boardrooms and combat zones to cyberspace, battles for power are as intense as ever, but they are yielding diminishing returns . . . Understanding how power is losing its value—and facing up to the hard challenges this poses—is the key to making sense of one of the most important trends reshaping the world in the twenty-first century."[5]

In a healthy economy with employees who feel confident in their abilities and their future, Naím argues, teamwork outperforms the command-and-control hierarchies of the past. In systems where one person dominates, dissent is squashed, conformity sets in, and the skills and knowledge of all the other people don't get adequately utilized. The result is stagnation.

The strength of your team depends on each individual, and the strength of each individual depends on the team. And unlike wolves, lobsters, or other animals, we don't have to organize into crude dominance hierarchies to get things done. We are human beings with spoken language, books, and supercomputers in our pockets. We can create working environments in which all can be their fullest self and so do their best work—thereby making the whole greater than the sum of its parts.

But for that to happen, enlightened leaders must embrace checks and balances on their own power or risk crushing both the individuals and their team's potential for effective collaboration.

6

A Leader's Role in Preventing Discrimination and Harassment

Apply Checks and Balances; Quantify Bias

'll define *discrimination* as excluding others from opportunities.[1] Discrimination happens when you add power to bias or prejudice. *Harassment* is intimidating others in a way that creates a hostile work environment.[2] Harassment happens when you add power to bias or bullying. This chapter will cover verbal and psychological harassment. Physical harassment and violence will be covered in chapter 8.

It's Hard to Be the Boss

Co-founding my first company gave me a chance to set up a fair and transparent compensation system. This was important to me. That first job I had after college was not the last time I was underpaid. I thought that going to work for a woman might solve the problem, and I joined a start-up with a CEO who was a woman. A few months into that job, I found out I was being paid 30 percent less than my peer, a man. When I asked why, she replied, "You don't have a wife and child to support." I don't want to hold women to a higher standard than men. She paid me less than my peer who was a man for the same reason my other bosses did: because she could. Still, it was a particularly dispiriting moment.

At this new venture, I told myself, *No woman will be underpaid on my watch.* That was where my Institutional Courage began.[3] Unfortunately, that was also where it ended. Leaders who practice Institutional Courage leverage their authority to be proactive in addressing and preventing workplace injustice, including sexism and racism.[4] Institutional Courage is in the best interest of the institution in the long run; its opposite, Institutional Betrayal, seeks to cover up wrongdoing, thereby retraumatizing victims and often destroying the institution in the long run.

Here are just some of the many ways I failed to prevent discrimination and harassment at my own company, despite my determination to create a just working environment.

Alex, one of my VPs, was doing terrible work. I had been clear that if he didn't turn things around, there were going to be consequences. When he still came up short, I let him know he was in danger of being fired. As we talked about how he needed to improve, I asked Alex what I could do or stop doing to help him. Part of my Radical Candor philosophy is encouraging employees to offer clear criticism to their boss.

"You know what the problem here is?" he asked.

"No. Tell me."

"The problem," he exclaimed, punctuating the word by stabbing his index finger toward my chest, "is that you are *the—most— aggressive—woman* I ever met!"

This guy had been a senior leader at a tech company where executives threw chairs at people. Our industry was aggressive. He had to be aggressive to do his job. So his problem couldn't be my aggression. His problem was that I was an aggressive *woman*. And that was *his* problem because my gender wasn't going to change. But it was also my problem because if he bullied me that way, how was he going to treat the women who were not his boss? And how was that kind of behavior going to impact the team's ability to achieve its goals?

It was my job to address the problem, but I had no idea how.

The effective response would have been to sit him down and explain to him why the way he'd spoken to me was so problematic, and that if he treated other women the way he'd just treated me, he'd be out of a job. To use an "it" statement backed up by a code of conduct. But I didn't know about "it" statements then and I hadn't written a code of conduct. I should have been direct—"aggressive," Alex might have said—but also clear that I believed he could improve and that I was willing to help him do so.

Instead, I ignored how he'd just spoken to me and kept the focus on what I'd called him to discuss: his lousy performance. In the moment, my choice felt appropriate: I kept my cool, and I didn't let myself get distracted from the original purpose of the meeting. In retrospect, however, I was simply ignoring his bullying behavior—pretending that nothing had happened. As a person harmed, ignoring the way he talked to me was my right. But now I was a leader, and I wasn't doing my job.

A few days later, after a company all-hands, Alex was sitting on a table that was over the garbage can. Madeline, a young woman on the team, walked up to him with a couple of pizza crusts, clearly wanting to throw them away.

"Excuse me"—she gestured to the garbage can—"I need to—"

"Get in between my legs?"

As a leader, it was my job to tell Alex on the spot that this was not an acceptable way to talk to Madeline and let him know I'd be following up with him in a private, longer conversation. If bias interrupters are important, harassment interrupters are even more important. Instead, I said nothing. Why?

I had been on the receiving end of those kinds of comments my whole life, and I had gotten so used to ignoring them that I barely noticed them. This was the thick skin I'd developed as a person harmed. But, once again, I needed to respond as a leader, in a way that would prevent this kind of BS from happening at my company again.

Madeline was early in her career, and in the midst of the pressure and chaos of our start-up, I was not very approachable. There was also no HR team; we were a small company. If she had wanted to complain about Alex's remark and/or my lack of response, she would have had to approach me or my co-founder, a man. Not surprisingly, she said nothing.

Much later, though, we did a round of layoffs in which she was included. After I laid her off, she told me she felt I had contributed to a hostile working environment for women. My first response was to deny that any such thing could possibly be true. Look at what I'd done to make sure women were paid fairly!

BIAS   PREJUDICE   BULLYING   ⚡   ┌─ **LEADERS &** ─────────────┐   PHYSICAL VIOLATIONS
                                  │ DISCRIMINATION   HARASSMENT │

"Well, that doesn't mean harassment doesn't happen here or that you are paying attention to it," Madeline replied.

Now my denial turned to anger. Though it directly contradicted my philosophy, I defensively asked (OK, shouted) for examples. Why did I respond so aggressively to her but so meekly to Alex? Internalized misogyny, I am afraid. I couldn't see it then, but in retrospect it's pretty clear.

Madeline was not intimidated. She brought up a threatening note that Donny, an employee I'd recently fired for poor performance, had sent to a colleague, Alice. I agreed that the note—which detailed his sexual fantasies about Alice and made it clear that he knew where she lived—had been seriously upsetting. But Donny had sent that note *after* he'd been fired, I reminded her. He hadn't done anything sooner because he knew I wouldn't let him get away with it, I said with great self-righteousness.

To this day I regret the way I responded to Madeline. Madeline was telling me something important and I was refusing to listen. Instead, I was replicating the sort of bad-boss behavior that I'd been determined to avoid—such as raising my voice in a bullying manner when criticized by a woman. If I'd listened to Madeline instead of shutting her down, I might have had the opportunity to reflect on some other leadership failures on my part. These are obvious to me now, but I was in denial about them at the time.

For example, at an office party the previous year, I noticed that Donny was blatantly looking up Alice's skirt as she bent over to play a party game. I caught his eye and started to motion him over to talk to me, but then he leered at me as well, as if to let me know he'd been staring at my butt, too. Then I noticed that a couple of the men on the team also saw what was going on. One of them looked at me as if to say, *Do something!*

I immediately shut the game down, but I didn't confront Donny. Nor did I address it with Alice or the rest of the staff. After he leered at me, I shifted into the "hear no evil, see no evil, say no evil" mode I had used to get by throughout my entire career.

Now, however, I had the authority to create a different sort of workplace. Instead of using that power for good, I was in effect saying, "Move along, folks, there's nothing to see here"—even though everyone *did* notice it and probably talked about it over coffee the next day.

If my employees were taking their cues from me about the kind of company we would become, I was setting a dispiriting example.

Not surprisingly, Madeline was not satisfied after her termination and our subsequent exchange: she made a formal complaint against the company; on the advice of our lawyers, we paid her a small sum, and she signed an NDA. I am deeply ashamed to admit that, but it's the truth.

If I had embraced my role as a leader from the start, both Alex and Donny would have known they couldn't harass women and get away with it. Perhaps this would have prevented their behavior; if not, they would have been fired. I would have been seen as an advocate for the women on my team rather than another leader who didn't care enough about injustice to prevent it. And I wouldn't have made my company legally vulnerable to a lawsuit. Though the lawsuit was the least of the problems. The real problem was that the team wasn't functioning as well as it needed to in order to succeed.

The rest of this chapter will cover in detail the specific things I could have done to build a more just workplace, and to prevent discrimination and harassment from happening at my own company.

But before digging into specific business operations, let's start with two overarching principles: apply checks and balances and proactively quantify bias.

CHECKS AND BALANCES

Every workplace gives managers up and down the org chart authority to make decisions that have profound consequences for those who work for them. Traditionally, managers dole out or withhold resources; they decide who gets hired, fired, or promoted; they determine bonuses, who gets the plum assignments, who gets stuck with the grunt

BIAS PREJUDICE BULLYING ⚡ | DISCRIMINATION HARASSMENT | PHYSICAL VIOLATIONS
LEADERS &

work, and so on. This makes it risky for employees to report harassment or discrimination. When managers make all these decisions unilaterally, they have too much power. They can use this power to harass or bully employees, and there's not much their employees can do about it if they want to keep their jobs. Employees are disempowered.

None of this is inevitable. It happens as a result of the choices we make about management systems and processes. You can bake checks and balances into your organizational design, or you can design a system that creates mini-dictators. If you do the latter, the unchecked power you've given people makes harassment much more likely.

When leaders create checks and balances in their organizational design and in their work processes, they help prevent power from corrupting their teams or themselves. For example, one check on my power could have been a reporting system that Madeline trusted. That would have given her a way to report harassment safely. Another check on my power, and also on Alex's and Donny's, could have been giving promotion decisions to a team rather than to the leader alone. When teams make promotion decisions, it becomes far less likely that "a willingness to put up with harassment" will be one of the promotion criteria—not a great criterion, to put it mildly.

Much has been written about "empowering" employees. People who are underrepresented don't need to be told to speak up or to be "empowered" or to be told to be "more confident."[5] What's needed is to address the pressures that keep us silent. When people who are underrepresented are no longer harassed or discriminated against, the strength and confidence that are already within will shine. My advice to leaders is this: stop *disempowering* employees by giving too much unilateral authority to managers. You're not so much "giving people a voice" as you are putting checks and balances in place so that their boss is not able to punish them for speaking up.

Checks and balances are important for achieving results as well as for protecting employees from harassment. Research shows that cohesive, empowered teams will outperform a collection of individuals on a wide range of tasks.[6] High-functioning teams tend to make better decisions than high-functioning individuals.[7] So when teams replace unilateral authority, better promotion decisions will be made *and* fewer employees will be harassed.

By checks and balances I mean management systems in which leaders are held accountable for doing their jobs well rather than given unilateral power or authority. This means that no one person in an organization, including its CEO, should be able to hire, fire, promote, or pay another person without oversight. Mechanisms that employees trust must be in place for reporting harassment or sexual violence.

These kinds of systems of checks and balances are already in place in many of the world's most successful companies. I'm most familiar with the systems in place in tech, where I worked for most of my career. Management systems that stripped unilateral authority from individual managers and gave it instead to empowered teams were an essential design principle of the processes that SVP of Business Operations Shona Brown put in place at Google.

It was difficult to put the checks and balances in place at first but even harder to keep them in place as the company grew and became more successful. Invariably, leaders chafed at limits. This was especially true of the most successful leaders, who felt they had earned unilateral decision-making rights by delivering results. There is no single magic bullet to defending the checks and balances against successful leaders demanding more control. Executives have to have the same conversation over and over. Executives have to explain their rationale persuasively to managers and other leaders so that they don't quit when they don't get their way. At the same time, it is important *never* to cave to the frequent demands for unilateral authority.

It is also crucial that the most senior executives lead by example: *they* have to lay down their power and submit to the checks and balances as well. Leaders are often shocked at executives willing to do this. It is like the scene in *Hamilton* where King George reacts to the news that George Washington is stepping down. "They say / George Washington's yielding his power and stepping away / 'Zat true? / I wasn't aware that was something a person could do."[8] It requires enormous confidence and vision for leaders to lay down their power and replace it with a fair system that they themselves submit to. But when they do, the result is both justice and success.

LEADERS &
BIAS   PREJUDICE   BULLYING   ⚡ ⌈ DISCRIMINATION   HARASSMENT ⌉   PHYSICAL VIOLATIONS

I know from firsthand experience how hard this can be for managers and their executives. When I first arrived at Google and learned I couldn't just decide on my own whom I was going to hire, I was pissed off. I thought they had hired me because I had earned a reputation for hiring great teams. Shona and her team explained their methodology, and over my years at Google I became a believer.

Checks and balances on power in the workplace do not eliminate abuses, but they are an excellent place to start. Both in principle and in practice, they embody the sort of responsive, accountable, and collaborative just workplace we are seeking to create.

If the teams you have in place are homogeneous, however, checks and balances won't be enough to prevent discrimination and harassment, because those responsible for checking and balancing will share some of your biases. And if you don't take proactive measures, teams will become more homogeneous over time. Even though any managers worth their salt know they shouldn't hire people who are "just like them," they do it anyway.[9] This is bad because it leads to both discrimination—conscious or unconscious—and to poorer decision-making, because homogeneous teams tend to make poorer decisions than their diverse counterparts do.[10]

To move from homogeneity to diversity you need to get proactive about noticing and correcting the ways that bias is affecting your decisions about whom you hire, promote, mentor, and fire, thereby reinforcing your homogeneity. This is what I call quantifying your bias.

QUANTIFY YOUR BIAS

Let's decide in advance what weight to give to the data we have on the candidates' past performance. Otherwise we will give too much weight to our impression from the interviews.

—Daniel Kahneman

If your goal is to create a just workplace, proactively *look for* discrimination—for signs that your organization is systematically discriminating against some people while overpromoting others. Do so with the same energy you'd use to investigate a decrease in profitability, research a competitor, explore a new opportunity, launch a product, or enter a new market to grow your business. Think of discrimination as a virus in your operating system. It will eventually kill your system if you don't proactively identify it and fix it.

Quantify your bias. *Measure* the progress you're making toward creating a more diverse, inclusive organization. Quantifying your bias is about using metrics to alert you to problems that need fixing. Measure not just the lagging indicators (i.e., the ones that tell you you've lost the game after you've lost) but the leading indicators (i.e., the ones that tell you that you may lose if you don't change something) as well. For example, don't only measure what percentage of new hires are people who are underrepresented. Analyze each step in your hiring process and look for ways to improve. Measure the impact of these improvements on representation. Measure what percentage of résumés reviewed were from people who are underrepresented. Look at whether your job descriptions use biased language; change them and notice if more people who are underrepresented begin applying. Measure how many people you interviewed were underrepresented, and ask yourself whether there's bias in the selection process.

Be similarly thorough when measuring your compensation and promotion processes. Your organization will not reflect the *exact* breakdown of the population at large. But if your leadership team is 90 percent men, you're missing some great women candidates and probably not promoting the women you do have at the same rate you're promoting the men. And when the numbers don't look good, the answer is obviously not "hire more women even if they are not qualified," any more than the answer would be to fiddle with your books if your profitability looks bad. It may mean that your criteria for judging who is qualified is off due to biased or prejudiced assumptions. When the lagging indicators look bad, you've got to dig deep, figure out what the leading indicators are, and address them.

The resistance with which this is met from leaders who make a big

BIAS   PREJUDICE   BULLYING   ⚡ | **LEADERS &** ————
| DISCRIMINATION   HARASSMENT | PHYSICAL VIOLATIONS deal of being data driven is almost comical. The same leaders who claim to be obsessed with metrics will object when you point out that while 35 percent of the U.S. population are white men, 68 percent of C-suite positions are held by white men, and 90 percent of Fortune 500 CEOs are white men. Meanwhile, 7.4 percent of the U.S. population are Black women, but 1.4 percent of C-suite positions are held by Black women,[11] and as of the writing of this book no Black women were CEOs in the Fortune 500.[12]

When I assert this is an indication of a bias problem, people often respond with one of two ridiculous statements: (1) "I don't see color! I treat men and women the same." If you refuse to look at these numbers and understand what they mean, then you are in denial about sexism and racism. Or, worse, (2) people respond with an obviously biased if not prejudiced assertion that I am telling them to "lower the bar." In fact this metric is a sure sign the bar is lowered for white men and raised for women and is raised even higher for Black women. My solution is to have one standard—for everyone.

When you do dig into the numbers, spend your energy looking for solutions—not excuses or rationalizations. This is hard because few people like to think of themselves or their organization as discriminatory. So you have to overcome your biases and your desire to believe you are not doing anything wrong. You have to dig into the numbers proactively if you are going to understand what you're doing wrong.

Few leaders are bold enough to do this. Alan Eustace is one who is. When he was SVP of engineering at Google, Eustace did a careful analysis of why there were so few women software engineers. Part of the problem was the lack of women graduating from computer science programs at the universities Google hired from. But Alan did not throw up his hands and say, "It's not my fault, it's a pipeline problem, there's nothing I can do."

Instead, Alan learned from institutions such as Harvey Mudd College, which had worked hard to figure out why so few women were majoring in computer science. The leaders of the computer science department at Harvey Mudd realized that "weed-out" courses early in these programs favored people who'd been hacking code in junior high school—and for a variety of social reasons, more boys than girls code in junior high. The heads of the computer science department did not throw up their hands, either. Instead, they got rid of the weed-out courses; four years later, the college had significantly more women computer science grads.[13] Alan encouraged other universities to follow Harvey Mudd's lead. Four years is a long time to wait for new candidates to graduate, but it's not infinitely long. Solving problems such as this requires patience and persistence from leaders.

APPLY BOTH CHECKS AND BALANCES AND BIAS QUANTIFIERS TO KEY OPERATIONAL PROCESSES

Before describing the ways that leaders can create fairer business processes, I want to return to a basic point. The goal is to create an environment which doesn't put artificial constraints on people that prevent them from achieving their full potential—whatever that might be, whoever they are. When building a team, you want to identify the right people for the right job. The more rational and just the processes you come up with to do that, the less often you hire or promote unqualified people and reject people who are most qualified for the job. Just Work is fairer to the individuals who would otherwise be discriminated against. *And* it is fairer to their colleagues, who do better work when surrounded by more qualified teammates. *And* it is more likely to yield good results. It's not as if you're doing people any big favor by allowing them to do their best work. You want them to do their best work. You benefit as surely as do they from their work. It's just management.

Homogeneous teams usually get worse results than diverse teams.[14] When a working environment makes it difficult for people who are underrepresented to do their best or, even worse, drives them away, results suffer along with justice. The pace of change continues to increase, and the world is becoming ever more interconnected and therefore more diverse; by the time you realize how your bias is hurting you, you may already have missed an opportunity or fallen prey to a market that has shifted.

Just Work is about fairness. It's also about enlightened self-interest.

BIAS PREJUDICE BULLYING ⚡ [**LEADERS &** DISCRIMINATION HARASSMENT] PHYSICAL VIOLATIONS

What follows are specific ideas for how to make your operational processes more fair and more successful: hiring, retention, compensation, performance management, coaching and mentoring, psychological safety measures, exit interviews, NDA's and forced arbitration, and organizational design.

1. HIRING

TO HIRE THE BEST PEOPLE, AVOID DISCRIMINATION

Hiring decisions are among the most important decisions any manager makes. This section will go into great detail on how to create a more just hiring process. But the short story is this: a big part of your decision is based on a person's résumé and a skills assessment. Without too much trouble, you can strip all information about a person's gender, race, religion, sexual orientation, and so forth out of résumés. Stripping this information out minimizes the chances that bias and prejudice are skewing your decisions about whom to interview. And once you've decided whom to interview, you can separate out skills assessment and in-person interviewing. In most cases, you can develop ways to test skills without actually meeting the person—again, removing a huge source of bias and prejudice from skills assessment. That leaves the interview, which should test for "culture add," not "culture fit."[15] If you write down the criteria you are interviewing for ahead of the interview and have a hiring committee of three to five people look at each candidate separately, you can avoid much of the potential bias and prejudice that often unfairly influences the process.

TWO SUCCESS STORIES OF HIRING MORE WOMEN

Christa Quarles at OpenTable

When she was CEO of OpenTable, Christa Quarles made improving gender diversity a priority. She knew it had to start from the top, so she and her team publicly emphasized the importance of hiring women and other underrepresented people, then held their recruiters accountable for delivering. She didn't set a specific target *number* but instead focused on the need to fix the *process*.

The results were remarkable. By the *next* quarter, the share of newly hired women engineers at OpenTable had gone from 14 to 50 percent. They then averaged between 40 and 45 percent for the next four quarters. When I asked her what the secret was, she said, "I was frankly surprised by the speed. But it's like any other business problem. You put effort toward something, you measure it, you get results." Use the same skills you employ to solve other issues that are priorities, and you'll improve the diversity of your hiring, too.

Here are more details about how Christa and her team improved their recruiting to hire more diverse teams:

- *They changed their approach to job descriptions.* Often homogeneity in a workplace culture starts with the way a position is described (e.g., using words like "killer" and "aggressive" that might read as though the company is seeking men not women). OpenTable started using Textio Hire, a software program that helps recruiters write job postings free of unconscious or implicit bias.
- *They filtered personal identifying information out of résumés.* They used Canvas, a product that helped them anonymize/redact gender-identifying info on résumés.[16]
- *They cast a wider net.* Sourcers had to identify at least two women candidates for every job opening.[17] This was important because research shows that when there's only one underrepresented candidate, the chance the person will be hired is statistically tiny because the person becomes the "diversity candidate" instead of simply being the "qualified candidate." The term "diversity candidate" often triggers an unconscious bias: many people who are overrepresented hear instead "less qualified candidate." This assumption is not fair to the candidate and will harm your ability to hire the most qualified person.
- *They included women on hiring panels.* In an organization that

was mostly men, this put a lot of burden on a small number of women to spend more time interviewing. Managers had to be aware of this and accommodate it. Christa would also offer her services to cement key hires as a sign of the importance of closing highly qualified underrepresented candidates.

- *They monitored the numbers.* The recruiting team measured and reported their performance on hiring women every quarter. Measuring the growth in women hires quarter over quarter was more revealing about progress being made than measuring the company's gender diversity overall.
- *They made sure everybody got the message.* Christa and her leadership team spent a lot of time talking about improving diversity. The whole company needed to understand this was an important strategic effort. The leaders were focusing on improving diversity and inclusion in their hiring for two reasons. First, because it was important to have an employee base that mirrored their customer base—women make more reservations at restaurants than men do. Second, because diverse teams have quantifiably higher productivity, innovation, and outcomes relative to homogenous teams.

Scott O'Neil at the Philadelphia 76ers

Scott O'Neil, the CEO of Harris Blitzer Sports & Entertainment (HBSE), which has a portfolio of sports and entertainment teams and companies that includes the NBA's Philadelphia 76ers and the NHL's New Jersey Devils, explained why it was so important to hire women to prominent positions. When Scott assumed the role of CEO in 2013, the 76ers were in a turnaround—losing the majority of their games in what would become an infamous four-year rebuild. Despite this, ticket sales were going up and to the right, thanks to O'Neil's dedication to corporate culture and the development of the largest sales staff in professional sports.

The team's number one salesperson was a woman in her mid-twenties who, in her second year with the organization, told O'Neil she was planning to leave the company because she couldn't imagine a future for herself there. Why? he asked, bewildered. At the time, the front office's senior leadership team had several strong women leaders in prominent roles who were consistently nominated for national industry awards by the organization. It was not for lack of women, the young

woman explained; it was that none of the senior women in the organization were parents. She knew she wanted to have a child, and she
wasn't sure it would be possible to achieve work-life balance at HBSE,
given the rigorous demands of the night and weekend sports industry.

And if there were no women with kids at the top of her company,
how likely was it that she could pull it off when others hadn't?[18] We
all need role models—people who seem to want the same things we
do, and who are getting them and are showing us how to get them,
too.[19] The investments you make early in your career pay off big-time
later on, but it's hard to fully invest in an organization if you fear
you're going to have to abandon it because your job might become in-
compatible with the life you want to lead. Finding a good role model is
harder than it sounds, especially for people who are underrepresented.

O'Neil knew it wasn't enough to talk about how he was an engaged parent, that he left work early to coach his daughters' basketball
teams, that he'd missed important 76ers games to attend the games of
his daughters. Appreciating the work-life balance struggle and juggle,
O'Neil routinely stressed "being present" to working parents in his
organization; he was determined to create a workplace that supported
and celebrated working parents.

That meant the women at HBSE needed to reflect all kinds of
working parents, just like the men—married mothers, single mothers,
Black mothers, Latina mothers, LGBTQ+ mothers. The son of a strong
woman entrepreneur and the father to three teenage girls, O'Neil had
an industrywide reputation for hiring young women executives who
went on to highly coveted management roles in sports and entertainment. And he was determined to approach hiring women with a re-
newed emphasis on diversity. O'Neil had long encouraged an unwritten
rule that one-third of all job candidates needed to be from underrepresented groups; now he was determined to make sure he was interviewing talented working mothers. O'Neil's next hire was a woman who
had taken three years away from the competitive sports and entertainment industry to care for her toddler son and newborn daughter.

"I do not believe in diversity for diversity's sake," O'Neil said. "I

BIAS   PREJUDICE   BULLYING   ⚡ | LEADERS &
DISCRIMINATION   HARASSMENT | PHYSICAL VIOLATIONS

believe in diversity as a competitive advantage. We focus on hiring talented, authentic people and good teammates; it's inspiring to me that so many of them aspire to be exceptional executives in the board-room and exceptional parents at home. Our working parents grind around the clock, but their passion for both their home and work lives is palpable and contagious in the office. As a whole, our women leaders are a force, and our working mothers are some of the most determined executives in our organization."

The mother returning to work blew everyone out of the water with what she accomplished at the company. With her hire and dozens of others like her, O'Neil retained his best salesperson and hundreds of women millennials looking up the ladder for a role model whose story might match their own personal and professional ambitions. HBSE developed a reputation as a great place to work, making recruiting talent easier. In particular, it became known as a place that recruited, developed, and empowered women executives; whereas some organi-zations saw diversity, equity, and inclusion as a struggle, at HBSE they became a welcome inevitability.

HIRING COMMITTEES MAKE BETTER HIRING DECISIONS THAN INDIVIDUALS

If the way you are hiring can be proven to be discriminatory, you're breaking the law. But even if it can't be proven in court, when bias or prejudiced beliefs influence your hiring decisions, you are making lower-quality hiring decisions. Good candidates get overlooked, and mediocre ones who look the part but can't do the job get hired. You wind up with a subpar team.

It's difficult for people to recognize bias in themselves but rela-tively easy for them to recognize it in others. This is part of the reason why hiring teams tend to make better decisions than individuals.[20] One way to take bias out of hiring is to transfer decision-making power from individual managers to small committees. One person tends to cancel out or at least challenge another person's biases. So you get fewer examples of managers who try to hire people who "look like them."

And when there is a committee instead of just one person with unilateral hiring authority, sexual harassment is far less likely to enter the equation. It's far less likely that a whole team of people would take advantage of their hiring power to harass a candidate than that a single individual would. Also, if an individual on a hiring committee did harass a candidate or make a racist, homophobic, anti-Semitic, or otherwise harmful comment, there would be more avenues of reporting access with a committee than if the individual were making the decision unilaterally. The candidate might be able to find a sympathetic ear on the committee or might know someone who knows someone on the committee. If the committee is heterogeneous, the odds that the right thing will happen go way up.

HIRING COMMITTEES ARE NOT A SILVER BULLET

Hiring committees come with some downsides that need to be actively managed. They can become a major time investment for committee members, and that comes at the cost of productivity. Companies will need to be aware of how much time they are asking from interviewers.

When an industry or a company is rife with abuse, unfortunately the abuse gets accepted by groups as well as individuals. For example, Angela, an actor, walked by a table of directors in a Hollywood restaurant. One of them called out to her, "You know, Angela, eventually you are going to have to pick somebody." The meaning was clear. *You are going to have to sleep with one of us if you want a career in the movies.* Everyone laughed. She was horrified. She knew about the proverbial casting couch. But now she was forced to confront the possibility that it was less proverbial and more real than she had imagined. She had not expected that these men, several of whom she had become friendly with, would ever behave that way. This was not a hiring committee, but it may as well have been. This kind of behavior made her decide to pursue a career in TV instead of film. Sexual harassment wasn't quite as inevitable in TV as it was in the movies—although that industry has hardly been above reproach.

LEADERS &

BIAS   PREJUDICE   BULLYING   ⚡ | DISCRIMINATION   HARASSMENT | PHYSICAL VIOLATIONS

HOMOGENEOUS COMMITTEES HIRE HOMOGENEOUS TEAMS

When a hiring committee is homogeneous, there's going to be a problem. On homogeneous teams, people are unlikely to spot their shared biases. They are also more likely to circle the wagons if bad behavior is reported. When a hiring committee is dominated by men, gender bias will often creep into hiring decisions; when it's all white people, racial bias will often creep into hiring decisions; and so on. While unconscious bias training can help, it's not going to solve the problem.

Not only is there a downside risk to homogeneous hiring committees, there is an upside benefit to heterogeneous committees. Heterogeneous committees tend to have better close rates (the percentage of people who accept offers) than homogeneous committees. The hiring team at Qualtrics found this to be consistently true, according to Qualtrics co-founder Jared Smith. Other leaders I've talked to have reported the same thing anecdotally—though I don't have comprehensive data.

If your team is homogeneous, how do you create diverse hiring committees? Many companies try to solve this problem by asking underrepresented people to sit on more than their fair share of hiring committees. Problem solved, right? No. Now people who are underrepresented are spending a lot of hours helping other people fill jobs. People may get appreciated for "corporate citizenship" or told "everyone is *expected* to help with hiring," but in most companies what gets people promoted is delivering results in their core function. So asking people who are underrepresented to do extra hiring-committee work damages their prospects for advancement, creating another kind of unconscious discrimination. This puts the burden for solving the problem on the very people most harmed by the problem.

This is not an impossible double bind, though. Unconscious bias training, combined with a norm of interrupting one another's biases and a disciplined approach to bias quantifiers, can help even homogeneous hiring committees learn to recognize and question their biases. If you have the budget, hire a bias buster to join your hiring-committee meeting. Over time, as you hire a more diverse team, you get a repu-tation for being a great place to work and recruiting becomes easier. You create a virtuous cycle, as Scott O'Neil showed.

QUANTIFY BIAS AT EVERY STEP OF THE PROCESS

Take a look at your new hires every quarter. If the numbers don't re-flect the population where you work or aren't at least moving in that direction, bias or prejudice may be creeping into your hiring process, even if you don't mean for them to, even if you can't imagine such a thing would happen on your watch. Measuring results is more fruitful than measuring intentions. Go back and analyze every step in your hiring process.

Here are some things you should measure proactively.

WHAT IS THE BREAKDOWN OF THE RÉSUMÉS YOUR SOURCERS LOOKED AT?

Look for under- or overrepresentation. Ask yourself what you can do to make sure résumé sourcers are looking beyond traditionally tapped groups. Even if there is an explanation, you can still examine what you might be doing to discourage people who are underrepresented from applying.

For example, is bias baked into your job descriptions? You can use tools such as Textio Hire to identify biased language. Also, make it clear which qualifications are necessary versus which are nice to have; if you list qualifications, women tend to apply to jobs where they meet 100 percent of criteria, but men tend to apply to jobs even if they don't meet all the qualifications listed.

Another thing to beware of: referrals. Many companies rely on employee referrals. This source of candidates rarely improves diversity. As an experiment, I one day decided to notice how long it would take LinkedIn to suggest I connect with one Black person in the "people

BIAS   PREJUDICE   BULLYING   ⚡   **LEADERS &**
                                  | DISCRIMINATION   HARASSMENT | PHYSICAL VIOLATIONS

you may know" suggestion page. I was appalled to find that it took me clicking through eight pages before it suggested I connect with a single Black person—and about three out of four people it served up were men, even though I'm a woman and went to an all-girls high school and have a robust network of women friends and colleagues. It wouldn't be fair to lay all the blame for this on LinkedIn's algorithms, however. Part of the problem is my network—the people I know, the companies where I've worked, the universities I've attended. The algorithm both reflected and *reinforced* that over- and underrepresentation that was a reality of my network. And if I connected mindlessly with whomever LinkedIn served up, the over/underrepresentation problem would worsen rather than improve over time.

If we want to create real diversity, we must consciously interrupt such patterns. Measure the diversity of employee referrals, and if this source of candidates is making your company more homogeneous, then don't rely so heavily on referrals.

WHAT IS THE BREAKDOWN OF RÉSUMÉS PASSED ON FOR INTERVIEWS?

If the percentage of people who are underrepresented who are invited for an interview is lower than the percentage of people who are underrepresented who applied, ask yourself why and what you can do to improve it.

As mentioned above, one strategy is to strip identifying information out of résumés so bias doesn't creep into assessment of résumés. You can use a program such as Canvas or hire interns and ask them to redact with a Sharpie information that identifies a person's gender, race, sexual preference, names, pronouns, and so on. That means getting rid of information about, for example, membership in fraternities or sororities. Some software programs can do this, though many that claim to do this just introduce "algorithmic" bias into your system.[21]

If you take this step and more underrepresented people make it through your screening process, you've not only identified bias in your candidate sourcing system—you've also found a way to interrupt it.

WHAT IS THE BREAKDOWN OF THE PERCENTAGE OF PEOPLE WHO ARE OFFERED JOBS?

If there's yet another drop-off in the percentage of people who are underrepresented, why? Do you make job offers to 20 percent of the men who interview but only 5 percent of the women? What can you do to improve that?

Consider doing three things: (1) develop a skills assessment that doesn't reveal the identity of the candidate; (2) be explicit about what you are interviewing for when you interview; and (3) look for culture add, not culture fit.

(1) **Assess skills, not identity.** Orchestras offer a great example of how well skills assessments that don't reveal the identity of the candidate can work. In 1970, the share of women on the highest-ranked orchestras in the United States was only 6 percent. This metric alone indicated that the orchestras were probably not hiring the best musicians. But the answer was obviously not to hand a woman, any woman, a bassoon or a French horn. The answer was to figure out how to eliminate bias from the selection process.

Auditions behind a curtain were an obvious answer. But they didn't go far enough. The candidates also had to be barefoot because the telltale tap of high-heeled shoes gave away the gender of candidates. After auditioning barefoot behind a curtain became common practice, the percentage of women musicians in orchestras grew to 21 percent in 1993 and just over 50 percent by 2016.[22]

It's impossible to know whether it was unconscious bias or conscious prejudice that kept women out of the top symphony orchestras. It might also be that the women auditioning for these slots were operating under a bias of their own: they may have been experiencing stereotype threat. When people have the power to put their unconscious biases or conscious prejudices into practice, discrimination can become a self-fulfilling prophecy; dissipating those biases and beliefs can create a virtuous cycle.

Furthermore, auditions behind curtains have not done enough to

BIAS   PREJUDICE   BULLYING   ⚡   ┌─ LEADERS & ─────────┐   PHYSICAL VIOLATIONS
                                 │ DISCRIMINATION HARASSMENT │
                                 └───────────────────────────┘

address the issues that keep BIPOC musicians out of orchestras. It's too soon to declare victory here.[23]

(2) **Be explicit.** Here is some advice from Daniel Kahneman about how to avoid bias when interviewing: be explicit about the specific traits you are looking for when you interview someone. Write them down—no more than six. Make sure all interviewers are interviewing for the same traits. Ask each interviewer to rate the candidate for each trait on a scale of one to five. Ask each interviewer to put the rating down for the attribute, together with evidence, before moving on to the next attribute—this avoids halo effects, a bias in which we assume that because people are good at one thing, they are good at everything. Promise yourself you'll hire the candidate whose score is highest, not the one you like the best.[24]

(3) **Look for "culture add."** Often one of the attributes people are looking for in interviews is "culture fit." This is a big mistake that will give biases free rein. Melissa James, CEO of the Tech Connection, recommends that hiring committees look for "culture add," which she defines as "the likelihood that someone will not only reflect the company's values and professional ethics, but also bring an aspect of diverse opinions, experiences, and specialized skill which enhances not just the team, but the overall company culture."[25]

The "cultural fit" screen in interviews—ostensibly designed to make sure the person will work well with others on the team—is too often a giant back door for bias, an unconscious code for "looking for someone who looks like us." It can reinforce tyranny of the majority instead of interrupting it.

WHAT IS THE BREAKDOWN OF PEOPLE WHO ACCEPT YOUR OFFERS?

Do people who are underrepresented tend to reject your job offers? Ask yourself why and what you can do to improve that percentage. If your team is homogeneous, it's going to be more difficult for you. If that's the case, make sure you aren't getting in your own way. Look around. Does your company have a reputation for being a terrible place for people who are underrepresented? Does your office look like a frat house or have other features that might make women feel unwelcome?

It is your job to become aware of these things, even if you'd rather not know. Read the reviews of your company on sites such as Glassdoor and other such services to learn more about your company's reputation. Ask people to rate their candidate experience. But don't hide behind websites and surveys. When someone turns down your offer, take them out to coffee and try to find out why. Keep a tally of the different reasons candidates give you. If you notice trends, do something to address them.

For example, when Scott O'Neil was recruiting a senior woman to work on his team, he sensed during the interview that she wasn't entirely comfortable, but he had no idea why. Rather than ignoring the awkwardness, which was tempting, he asked her about it.

"It's your couch," she replied.

"My couch?" O'Neil asked, bewildered.

"Have you noticed how I've been sitting?"

O'Neil confessed he hadn't, and she pointed out that the couch was designed for seven-foot-tall basketball players. If she wanted to lean against the back of the couch, her legs would stick straight out, Thumbelina-style. O'Neil bought some cushions for his couch. A simple solution, but having the courage and curiosity to investigate the source of the woman's discomfort was far harder. Fortunately, O'Neil had the self-confidence and discipline to do so.

CHALLENGE BIASED COMPARISONS

In his book *The Undoing Project*, Michael Lewis tells the story of Houston Rockets general manager Daryl Morey's attempts to drive bias out of the process of evaluating draft picks. Like almost everyone else in the league, Morey had missed Jeremy Lin, a Chinese American and Harvard grad who was ignored in the NBA draft but went on to become a successful player. Morey had the guts to admit that he passed on Lin because Lin didn't look like a conventional NBA point guard. "He's incredibly athletic," Morey said. "But the reality is that every fucking person, including me, thought he was unathletic. And I can't think of any reason for it other than that he was Asian."[26]

A big part of leadership is having the courage to recognize when your own biases or beliefs have hurt your decision-making, admitting candidly the mistake you made, then taking steps to keep yourself from repeating the mistake. Try to think of someone you didn't hire but should have. Did bias guide your decision? Did you ever pass on an otherwise qualified female candidate because she didn't seem like a good "culture fit" without realizing that maybe your "culture" was the problem? If so, get it off your chest. If someone asks you about it, think about Daryl Morey. Have the guts to say, "I can't think of a reason why we didn't hire her other than that she was a woman."

If you own your biases and confess how they skew your hiring decisions, others on your team will, too. Tell them where you screwed up and ask them to talk about times they have made similar mistakes. The process might be painful, but it's important. Recognizing bias is the first step to changing it. Once most people grasp how they might unconsciously be contributing to a problem, they will be motivated to fix it.

To prevent another Jeremy Lin mistake, Daryl Morey encouraged his scouts to focus on players' skills rather than their skin color. "If you want to compare this player to another player," he told them, "you can only do it if they are a different race." In other words, scouts could no longer compare a white player to another white player, a Black player to another Black player, an Asian American player to another Asian American player.

Not allowing simplistic comparisons is a good rule of thumb in business as well as sports. As entrepreneur Doug Speight wrote, "Pattern recognition is implicit bias turned practice."[27] Yet it happens all the time in business recruiting. After it became clear how much value Sheryl Sandberg added as COO of Facebook, my women colleagues and I started getting calls from recruiters about COO openings that we hadn't gotten before. "You'll be the Sheryl Sandberg of XYZ company," they'd say. On the one hand, these were great jobs, and it was nice, for once, to experience gender bias tilting in our favor. On the other hand, it was sort of a joke. It wasn't being a woman that made Sheryl a great COO. It was being a kick-ass COO. Her gender had nothing to do with it.

How often did those same recruiters call a man and say, "You'll be the Sheryl Sandberg of XYZ company"? How often did they call a woman and say, "You'll be the Larry Page of XYZ company"?

A well-known venture capitalist said of successful entrepreneurs, "They all seem to be white male nerds who've dropped out of Harvard or Stanford, and they absolutely have no social life. When I see that pattern coming in—which was true of Google—it's very easy to decide to invest."[28]

It's shocking that such an intelligent investor could be so unaware of how his biases were skewing his decisions. Venture capital is supposed to be investing in the future, not the past. One of the ways bias limits your leadership skills is that it keeps pushing you to look backward, fighting the last war instead of the one you're in. Or, as Steve Jobs put it, "Benchmarking best practices just gets you to average." It doesn't result in real innovation. It just copies the past—and often the mistakes rather than the successes of the past.

Furthermore, this investor's understanding of the drivers of past successes was obviously flawed. It's absurd to attribute Google's success to Larry and Sergey Brin's whiteness or maleness or introversion or admission to Stanford or departure from Stanford. And so it's irrational to set those attributes as investment criteria—just as it would be absurd to attribute Sheryl's success at Facebook to being a white woman who graduated from Harvard Business School and therefore hire only white women HBS grads as COOs.

Yet it happens *all the time*. I have gotten a lot of recruiting calls because I share those three attributes with Sheryl. Sheryl is the most organized person I've ever met. I am creatively chaotic—definitely not what you want in a COO. These "type-on-type" formulations confirm biases and subtly transmit stereotypes. And bias leads to hiring the wrong people for the wrong jobs.

BIAS   PREJUDICE   BULLYING   ⚡ ┌ LEADERS & ─────── ┐ PHYSICAL VIOLATIONS
                                    │ DISCRIMINATION HARASSMENT │

TAKE A PAGE OUT OF BILLY BEANE'S BOOK

The movie *Moneyball,* which tells the story of how Oakland A's general manager Billy Beane changed the game of baseball by replacing
bias with rational decision-making, perfectly illustrates the perils of
biasthink.[29] In one scene, Beane is meeting with a bunch of scouts to
evaluate minor league prospects. Even though baseball has tons of
statistics to objectively measure performance, Beane notices that his
scouts base their judgments on irrelevant factors such as strong jaw-
lines or how good-looking a player's girlfriend is. None of the scouts
challenge one another's BS because they don't notice it. Finally, Beane
puts his hand up, opening and closing his fingers in a "Blah blah blah,
you're spouting nonsense" gesture. Beane himself had been hyped as
a future superstar more on the basis of his looks and style than on his
performance. Later in the movie, when he meets a statistician who was
using data to improve decision-making, Beane asks him if he would've
drafted him. The statistician says he wouldn't have. Beane, whose major league career was hardly distinguished, agrees with that decision.
In fact, he wishes he *hadn't* been drafted and had taken the full schol-
arship to Stanford he'd been offered. The bias, ostensibly in his favor,
actually hurt him. He *looked* like a better player than he was. When
bias results in a less qualified person getting a job over someone who's
more qualified, it's bad for both people as well as the team. Bias hurts
everyone when it skews decisions.

Moneyball illustrates three important points. One, bias creeps into
everyone's decision-making, often unconsciously. Two, decision makers
habitually make bad calls based on these flawed observations, and all
too often nobody challenges the bias. Three, bias results in suboptimal
decision-making that is usually bad for everyone, even the "beneficiaries."

Let's look at how biased hiring decisions play out in another arena:
politics. According to the fact check in Claudia Rankine's book *Just
Us,*[30] in 2019 white men made up 30 percent of the U.S. population
but 60 percent of U.S. elected officials. White men are overrepresented.
And there's more. White women make up 31 percent of the U.S. population but 27 percent of U.S. elected officials. It's too soon to declare

victory, but white women are damn near proportionally represented as U.S. elected officials! But women of color make up 20 percent of the U.S. population but only 4 percent of U.S. elected officials. Dramatically underrepresented. Men of color make up 19 percent of the U.S. population but just 7 percent of U.S. elected officials. Also dramatically underrepresented.

So as a white woman who cares about gender inequity and underrepresentation, my efforts are best deployed getting women of color elected. And since I care about representation overall, while I'm at it, I need to help men of color get elected, too. Does this mean I am somehow hurting my father, husband, and son, all of whom are white? No, of course not. I love each of them more than I can say. And I believe to my core that we are *all* better off when the right people get the right job.

Like most mothers, I adore my son and want him to fulfill his potential in whatever career he chooses. I don't believe the best way to help him to find work he loves and is good at is to sneak him into roles that other people may be better suited for. More than anything else he would love to play professional baseball. I can't imagine anyone saying that a great way to help him achieve that dream would be to give white major league baseball players an unfair advantage with scouts. Look what happened to Billy Beane. I wouldn't want that to happen to my son in any field, be it baseball or politics or business or farming or teaching or whatever else he sets his heart and mind to do. I think he'll do better and be happier in a world that's fair.

2. RETENTION

It's difficult to get hiring right. But if you don't also focus on retention, it is like pouring water into a leaky bucket. The following sections on compensation, ratings, promotions, coaching and mentoring, and psychological safety hit on some of the most important things you can do to retain the people you've worked so hard to hire.

BIAS   PREJUDICE   BULLYING   ⚡   ┌─ **LEADERS &** ─────────┐ PHYSICAL VIOLATIONS
                                 │ DISCRIMINATION HARASSMENT │
                                 └───────────────────────────┘

In the end, though, building a diverse team does come down to making it a priority. Here is a tale of two teams, both of them at the same company in Hyderabad, India. One team had 50 percent women. The other team had 0 percent women. A leader at the company went to talk to the leaders of both teams to understand what the difference was. The leader of the team with 0 percent women shrugged and said, "It's really hard to hire women in Hyderabad." The leader of the team with 50 percent women didn't have a formula to offer. He shrugged and said, "I just made hiring and retaining women a priority."

The following sections will give you some idea of what, specifically, you can do to make it a priority. There's no Big Answer. It's a lot of small things, more like brushing and flossing, less like a root canal.

3. COMPENSATION

By far the greatest injustice in compensation is the 1 percent problem. My husband and I have both had multiple financial windfalls over our careers, which makes us part of the problem here. We are committed to changing that. American capitalism will have to be reformed if it is to survive, meaning there will need to be a major redistribution of wealth. Serious leaders in finance agree with critics of capitalism on this point.[31] Mostly, this is going to have to be a macroeconomic adjustment, not something one CEO, even an influential one, can pull off. Billionaires who feel they've done their part by avoiding taxes and oversight and then choosing how they give away their money may be generous at some level, but it is not the answer.[32] There's a lot more to say about that, but this is a book about what individuals can do, not a book on macroeconomic policy.

However, suggesting that income inequality is a "macroeconomic issue" does not mean that individual leaders can't do anything about it. If you are in charge of compensation at your company, it's important to make a *conscious decision* to pay everyone fairly and to double-check your work. You don't want your employees wasting time and mental energy doubting their pay is equitable.[33] That would be inefficient *and* unfair. You can review compensation across multiple parameters (gender, race, age, etc.) to proactively identify issues.

Do you serve on a Board of Directors? When you think about fairness, don't just compare your CEO's pay to the pay of other CEOs. Compare the CEO's pay to the pay of your lowest-paid employees. Of course it's OK for the CEO to get more. But how much more? When your CEO and several top execs own private jets and your new employees are living in their cars or can't afford health insurance, you have a problem.[34] Ben and Jerry said nobody at their company would be paid more than 5x the lowest-paid employee. I'd be OK with 10x or even in some cases 100x. But in a number of places where I worked, it was more like 1,000x and occasionally 10,000x. At one point both my husband and I had employees who were living in their cars while the CEOs of our companies were worth billions. That just seems off. I'm not talking communism; I'm talking common human decency.

If you are in charge of compensation, you can pay people who get paid less *more* and people who get paid most *less*. I will never forget listening to a wealthy person complaining that their housekeeper couldn't afford to buy a home or even to start a bank account and blaming the real estate market and the banking system. It never seemed to occur to the person the problem could be solved if they gave the housekeeper a raise. The person could easily afford to do so. An awful lot of leaders today sound like that.

I have worked with several CEOs who, frustrated at their board's unwillingness to create an employee stock-option pool that felt fair, gave up a significant portion of their own equity to their employees. That was good and generous and took their companies a step forward toward Just Work. However, even in these situations, it was still the superrich sharing with the really rich, and then only voluntarily.

Many of the ways in which our economy has "evolved" to be more "efficient" have both heightened inequality and hampered our efforts to confront it. One CEO I worked with tasked me with figuring out how to give equity in the company to the people who cleaned the offices. This work had been outsourced. I was bewildered by the legal and bureaucratic obstacles to offering these workers equity. The system seemed designed to prevent them from getting a financial windfall, even in the face of two competent executives determined to offer one. I started asking around to find out how others had managed this issue. One executive told me about a time when her firm offered a $1,000 cash holiday bonus to all employees. For most people at the company, $1,000 in cash was nice to have but not that big a deal. She suggested the gift would be more meaningful if it was extended to the janitorial staff. Again, this work was outsourced, and there were incredible, insurmountable difficulties to paying these people the same cash bonus the firm offered its own employees. Frustrated, the executive just pulled out her personal checkbook and gave people she saw every day $1,000 each. And got a lot of crap from different quarters for doing so.

In the end, the only solution the CEO and I could come up with was for him to take money out of his personal bank account and hand out cash to individual cleaners on IPO day. And not as much cash as he would've liked to give. Otherwise we'd run into tax and legal issues.

There are two things every leader can do.

PAY ATTENTION TO THE SPREAD

Take a look at the gap between the highest-paid and the lowest-paid people in your organization. Don't let the gap get too big. You can pay yourself and your top executives less; you can pay the lowest-paid employees more. And be aware of empathy bias. You'll be most aware of the gap between your compensation and that of those who work for you. Often that is how executive compensation grows while that of the lowest-paid employees doesn't. CEOs compare their compensation to that of other CEOs and maybe that of their direct reports but rarely look at the gap between their compensation and that of the person working in the mailroom.

DON'T BIFURCATE

Also, don't outsource all the lowest-paid work to spare yourself the discomfort of knowing just how little the lowest-paid people get. For example, consider not outsourcing janitorial work; instead, hire people and treat them like other employees. If all leaders did this, it would at least begin to bridge the gulf between low-paid work and highly paid work.

Gender Pay Gap: Salesforce

Marc Benioff, the CEO of Salesforce, had said all the right things about the importance of retaining and promoting women. But two of his top SVPs, Leyla Seka and Cindy Robbins, were concerned that, despite the boss's good intentions, women at the company were being paid less than men. When they brought this to Benioff's attention, he didn't believe them. "That's not possible," he remembers saying. "We have a great culture. We're a 'best place to work.' We don't play she-nanigans paying people. It's unheard of."

Seka and Robbins kept pressing, finally getting him to agree to do a thorough analysis of compensation across the company. First, though, they wanted a commitment from Benioff that he would promise to fix any disparities they might find. "The one thing we can't do," Robbins said, "is to . . . look under the hood, [notice] a big dollar sign, and shut the hood."[35]

It was a wise move to prepare the CEO. The analysis showed that Salesforce was indeed consistently paying women less than men to do the same job. Benioff was stunned. "It was through the whole com-pany," he said. "Every division, every department, every geography."

Benioff made good on his word. He fixed the problem. And just as significantly, he took measures to keep fixing it when it happened again, which it inevitably did. He asked Seka and Robbins to regularly monitor pay rates to make sure that women didn't fall behind again.

Measuring the pay gap is something you are well served to do every year. Obviously, you must make adjustments if your measurements reveal a problem. If you are a leader, there is a good chance you are paying not only the women but all the people who are underrepre-sented in your organization less than their overrepresented peers—even if you don't intend to. Your intentions don't matter to the underpaid women. The money does.

BIAS   PREJUDICE   BULLYING   ⚡ | **LEADERS &** DISCRIMINATION   HARASSMENT | PHYSICAL VIOLATIONS

Pay Gap at the BBC

In 2017 a powerful lobby in the United Kingdom demanded that the BBC make the salaries of their highest-earning presenters public. The goal was to make sure the public knew how much money the BBC was spending to get top talent. The unintended consequence was clear and public evidence that the women were not paid as much as the men.

With so much pressure on the BBC to reduce their budget and pay top stars less money, they couldn't fix the problem by paying the women more. They could only fix it by reducing the men's salaries. Needless to say, the men resisted this solution. Conversations meant to be private were leaked. One broadcaster said to another, "I could volunteer that I've handed over already more than you f***ing earn, but I'm still left with more than anybody else and that seems to me to be entirely just."[36] Maybe he was just kidding around. But people who make a lot of money usually do think they "deserve" it.

A top BBC editor, Carrie Gracie, resigned. The BBC apologized to her and gave her back pay; she donated the full amount to the Fawcett Society, a charity focused on gender equality and women's rights.[37] Since 2017, the BBC has issued a public gender pay gap report and has committed to fixing the problem. They have indeed reduced the pay gap every year. In 2019 it was 6.7 percent, significantly lower than the national average of 17.9 percent.[38]

The BBC story reveals another way that bias plays out. It's hard not to contrast the man's bravado about how he deserves to be paid more with Carrie Gracie's decision to give her back pay to charity.

Wealthy women, even when they are dramatically underpaid vis-à-vis their men counterparts, face a level of intense scrutiny and resentment that wealthy men simply don't. Activating that resentment is an unintended consequence of revealing a pay gap between wealthy men and women—which is where the biggest pay gaps are. In tech, I know many women who are paid not 10 or 20 percent less than the men who are their peers but multiples less. Ten times less, twenty times less.

It's worth repeating that the pay gap between the wealthy and the poor is a far, far greater injustice than a woman earning $1 million while the men who are her peers get $20 million. Income inequality must be addressed across the board. But it shouldn't be addressed by paying women less than men. Journalist Kara Swisher put it well:

"You don't have to feel sorry for rich people, but if they're gonna be rich, they should be equally rich."[39] It's important to recognize that this prejudice about women and money runs deep.

Justice is not a zero-sum game. Federal laws (e.g., the Equal Pay Act, the Equal Protection Clause, Title IX) apply to people across the wealth spectrum because equity is fundamental to a fair and just society. Economic injustice cannot be addressed by pressuring wealthy women to work for less and give their compensation to charity while assuming wealthy men deserve what they have earned and more.

Pay Gap in the United States

On average, women make 82 cents on the dollar compared to men.[40] And things are more unjust at the intersections of race and gender. Latinas are paid 54 cents for every dollar paid to white, non-Hispanic men, and Black women 62 cents.[41] Over a 40-year career, Black women earn almost a million dollars less than white men.[42] In addition to the wage gap, there's a promotion gap, and numerous "invisible" injustices.[43] We can't solve the pay gap until we resolve those issues as well.

But first let's focus on the pay gap in your organization. There *are* things you can do to begin to close it. You may be imagining all sorts of broader social problems that contribute to this pay gap. Those may indeed be factors, and you may not be able to solve those broader problems. But, unless you believe that white men are superior to others and that's why they're paid more, it's impossible to believe that bias is not a factor here. It's your job to 1) measure the pay gap in your organization and 2) identify the ways that bias or prejudice or bullying contribute to that pay gap. Here are some specific things you can do:

CREATE A FAIR COMPENSATION SYSTEM

It's absolutely crucial not to give managers unilateral authority over salaries, bonuses, stock, or other forms of pay. Instead, develop a compensation system that everyone understands and stick to it. Someone

BIAS   PREJUDICE   BULLYING   ⚡ | LEADERS & DISCRIMINATION   HARASSMENT | PHYSICAL VIOLATIONS

in your organization—the compensation group in HR at a big company, the head of HR at a medium-size company, or you, if you're leading a small company—should come up with salaries or salary ranges for particular jobs and functions. People doing the same job should get job offers with the same salary. If you pay bonuses, people in the same job with the same performance rating should be paid the same amount. Any exceptions should require sign-offs from at least three different executives at the same level. For example, if you are hiring five entry-level engineers at the same time, they should all have similar—ideally, identical—offer letters. If there are big discrepancies, there will be problems. If people who are overrepresented are being paid more than people who are underrepresented or vice versa, there will be even bigger problems.

Doing this will do two things for you. One, it will mean that pay will be more fair, less subject to the bias of individual managers or the demands of employees who feel entitled to make them; two, it will "reduce the return on politics," thereby encouraging people to focus more on innovation and less on pleasing their boss.[44]

CONSIDER STANDARDIZED, TRANSPARENT SALARIES

More and more companies are finding that the simplest way to address pay disparity is to take the mystery out of the process. No negotiation. No secrets. Put a page on your website that outlines different salaries and compensation for different roles. That solution will save you and all your candidates a lot of time and emotional energy.

You might lose some candidates to better competing offers. But the job market tends to be relatively efficient. If you set salaries at the right level, they will not be markedly different from those at other companies. If candidates let a small compensation difference determine which jobs they take, you haven't done a good enough job selling the opportunity. And if there is a big salary difference, try to understand why. Perhaps you need to adjust everyone's salary. Underpaying most of your employees and then having one person who is paid a lot more than everyone else kills morale and generates resentment.

If you need something to haggle over, make it a signing bonus. But publish the signing bonus ranges so that people who are underrepresented will know what they are walking away from if they don't push for one.

QUANTIFY HOW BIAS IMPACTS PAY

MEASURE YOUR PAY GAP

What is the pay gap, if any, between the compensation packages of the underrepresented and the people who are overrepresented in your organization? Cut the data by all categories of underrepresentation—by race, by gender, and so on. If one demographic in your organization is consistently paid less than the others, figure out why. Sometimes there might be a valid reason; for example, an exceptionally high bonus for exceptional performance skews a small data set. But these should be outliers, not norms. And some people who are underrepresented should be getting the exceptional pay as well! If it's *always* people who are overrepresented who are the exceptions, ask additional questions. There's probably an issue you need to get to the bottom of.

You may be reluctant to pull data that could potentially be used against you in a discrimination lawsuit. Certainly you should seek the advice of your legal team before you take any advice in this book. Remember, a lawyer's job is to tell you what the risks are, not to tell you to avoid all risks; you get to decide which risks to take. And remember that if you wind up in a lawsuit, this information is going to come out. You are better off knowing early if there is a problem and starting to address it before you're being sued rather than waiting until you have to react.

ADDRESS NEGOTIATION BIAS

A common reason why women are paid less than men is that they are punished for being "abrasive," "selfish," or "not a team player" if they negotiate too hard. This doesn't mean they are bad negotiators; it means that they are rational actors. If a woman thinks she is going to be penalized for negotiating, why take the risk?

LEADERS &
BIAS   PREJUDICE   BULLYING   ⚡ | DISCRIMINATION   HARASSMENT | PHYSICAL VIOLATIONS

Here you have two biases to address. One is the bias against women who negotiate. Two is the bias that says women are bad negotiators, so it's their fault if they don't get paid more. As a leader you can do two things about this. You and your team can work hard to interrupt this negotiation bias, or you can simply not allow *anyone* to negotiate—set salary bands as discussed above and do not deviate. Make sure that you offer bonuses and promotions as part of a routine process that looks at everyone at the same time.

DON'T REINFORCE MARKET BIAS

Another reason why women are paid less than men is that the market itself is biased. A report on wage inequality in tech from *Hired* magazine shows that "63% of the time, men were offered higher salaries than women for the same role at the same company. Companies were offering women between 4% and a whopping 45% less starting pay for the same job."[45] And that only looks at salary. In some industries, a huge part of compensation is equity, where the data is more opaque.

How can this be? Even if you've done the hard work of eliminating gender pay inequity from your own system, you can still "catch" it from other companies. Imagine that you are interviewing a man and a woman for similar jobs. You are careful to offer them identical compensation packages. But these candidates are also receiving competing offers from other companies, and the man's is better. Do you raise your offer? If so, do you also offer the same salary to the woman? If creating a fair workplace is your goal, the choice is obvious: you do. "But my company can't afford this!" you may think. Ask yourself whether your company can afford to keep systematically paying women less than men. The problems you create may be harder to measure in the short run, but they are still very real. When you pay women less than their colleagues who are men, it's demotivating for them and harms their productivity. It creates resentments that make your teams less cohesive. It introduces the risks of class action lawsuits. And it's just not fair.

4. PERFORMANCE MANAGEMENT

DISCRIMINATION CAN BOOMERANG

Here's a story about the way that people who are underrepresented are held back by what amounted to "unconscious discrimination." I'm not letting anyone off the hook by calling it unconscious. In business results matter, not intentions. But too often when we hear the word "discrimination," we imagine a big "men only" or "whites only" sign. Even when there's not such an explicit intention to exclude or under-estimate, discrimination still happens.

Laura, a managing director at Tarweed Consulting (this is a fictional firm), was one of very few women leaders at her firm. Tarweed offered two services: strategy consulting and technology consulting. Laura was responsible for global sales of technology consulting, a newer offering. Her three peers sold strategy consulting, the more established line of business. Don handled sales in the Americas, Mike in Europe, and Jennifer in Asia. Laura and her three peers were all up for promotion.

The business Laura led had grown quickly and now accounted for just over half the company's revenue. Her business was bigger, more profitable, and faster growing than Don's, Mike's, or Jennifer's. By any objective measure, Laura was crushing it. Don's business was next biggest, then Mike's, then Jennifer's. When promotions came around, Laura should have been first in line. Instead, Don and Mike got promoted. "These ambitious leaders have unlimited potential," gushed the email announcing their promotion. Laura was told she still needed to build a track record of success if she wanted to get promoted. What the hell had she just done?

What happened to Laura is so common that it has a name: the "performance/potential" bias or the "prove it again" bias.[46] Men are more likely to be rewarded for perceived potential, whereas women get promoted purely based on past performance.

BIAS   PREJUDICE   BULLYING ⚡ LEADERS & _____
| DISCRIMINATION HARASSMENT | PHYSICAL VIOLATIONS

Laura knew about this bias, but, still, she didn't think it would happen to her. It wasn't only a sense of injustice that bothered her. That promotion came with a 100 percent pay raise. Laura decided to ask other executives at the company why she'd been passed over. She got a bunch of different answers.

One answer was that sales for technology consulting didn't involve golfing with renowned CEOs. Don and Mike needed the bigger titles to be effective in the ego-addled world in which they traveled. OK, Laura said. It was true that her customers tended to be IT departments, not the vaunted C-suite. But what about Jennifer? She sold into the C-suite. It wasn't as if CEOs in Asia had smaller egos than those in the Americas or Europe. Why didn't she "need" the title? There was no good answer to that question, other than that Asia was a smaller market for the company.

"Well, maybe it would be a bigger market for us if Jennifer had the right title," suggested Laura. She got no response. It was as though she hadn't spoken.

Another executive told Laura that she didn't have as big a "span of control" as Don. Translation: Don had more people reporting to him, even though he ran smaller businesses. That meant she ran a tighter ship, and as a result, her business was more profitable.

Wait, *what*? Don got rewarded for his "span of control" but Laura got punished for building a more profitable business? She should have been rewarded for her efficiency, not punished. That this "span of control" rationale could be taken seriously at a company that considered itself "data driven" and explicitly opposed to empire building was infuriating.

This begged the question: Why was Mike promoted when he had both a smaller team *and* a smaller business than Laura? Jennifer ran a tight ship and had a more profitable business that, while smaller than Don's and Mike's, was growing faster. Should she hire more people and be less profitable to increase her "span of control" and get the promotion next time? Laura wanted to know. "Don't be irrational," she was told.

Laura didn't think the executive she was talking to about "span of control" was *consciously* prejudiced against women. Yet she couldn't get him to engage in further conversation. When she tried to talk about profitability, he looked at her as though she were lacking in basic quantitative skills. What did she not understand about the fact that Don managed more people than she did? Maybe this executive's bias about her analytical skills was more pronounced than she'd thought. She was so frustrated by his willful obliviousness—or was it strategic ignorance?—that she quit talking.[47] What he said seemed so thoroughly unreasonable that she even wondered if she was missing something. That is how gaslighting works.[48] It made Laura question herself when she needed to be questioning the other person.

As she continued to ask around, she got some even more blatantly gendered explanations of why she wasn't promoted. One executive contrasted her so-called shrillness with Don's and Mike's so-called charisma. When she objected to the obvious double standard, he told her not to "play the woman card." Again, her frustration with this kind of irrationality had a silencing effect. By now she felt angry and isolated.

Benedict, a coach who worked with a number of the company's top executives, was the only person willing to admit how unjust and flawed this promotion decision was. He told Laura that when an executive team was so homogeneous (nine of ten were men, nine of ten were white, nobody was gay), bias regularly went unnoticed. Misogynistic comments routinely went uncorrected.

What kind of comments? Laura wanted to know. Benedict said he'd been in a meeting where an executive on the team commented about a director's "tits and ass" when he should have been assessing her technical and leadership skills. Nobody in the room had said a word.

Laura could well imagine that the lone woman on the team did not feel inclined or empowered to serve as the gender censor in a room where she was a minority of one.[49] She had probably buried the obnoxious remark in the back of her mind the same way Laura herself often had throughout her career. Willful compartmentalization. "Did I just hear him say 'tits and ass'? I don't wanna deal with that. Oh, look, there's a squirrel!"

But what about the men? Three had pretty openly problematic attitudes about women.

BIAS PREJUDICE BULLYING ⚡ **LEADERS &** | DISCRIMINATION HARASSMENT | PHYSICAL VIOLATIONS

Still, six of the men on the executive team were actively trying to create a more diverse, inclusive workplace. But she knew from her own experiences that even these men tended to assume that if the woman in the room didn't speak up, a comment—even an egregious one—was OK.

Laura asked Benedict what she should do. He said, "You will never be taken seriously by a team like that. Start looking for opportunities where your skills will be put to full use." While she was glad that at last someone was being candid, it was also depressing. She knew he was right, that she should start looking for other jobs. But she loved her job. She loved the team she'd built. She didn't want to leave.

Then one day Laura was in a meeting with Don and Mike. Don was sitting next to her, and he reached over, pulled some of her curls, watched them bounce back, and grinned as if he'd found a satisfying new fidget toy. Laura glared at him and shook her head no. Then he did it again. "Stop it!" she whispered. "Lighten up," he hissed back.

That was it. Laura tuned out of the meeting and started sending emails to her professional contacts, letting them know that she was looking for a new job.

The discrimination Laura experienced probably wasn't legally actionable. There was no hard proof that Laura had hit a glass ceiling. The company could have found some mix of metrics to "prove" the problem was Laura, not senior leadership's promotion criteria (or lack thereof). And even if she could have won in court, she felt she had much more to gain—both for herself and for other women—by pouring her time and energy into her career. Laura concluded that the ROI of a lawsuit just wasn't there for her. Better to invest her time looking for a job where she could succeed.

(Sometimes these battles are worth fighting, ROI be damned. Consider Lilly Ledbetter, whose pay discrimination suit went all the way to the Supreme Court. She lost there on a legal technicality, but the case was so grossly unjust that Congress later passed legislation, called the Lilly Ledbetter Fair Pay Act of 2009, to close the loophole. Ledbetter's willingness to fight this fight created a more just world for millions of women.)

Within six weeks of the day that Don pulled her hair and told her to lighten up, Laura had an offer to become the CEO of Gilia Consulting, a small but fast-growing competitor to Tarweed. When she gave notice, Laura's boss, rather than congratulate her or express regret for losing her, criticized her for being ambitious. This struck her as strange—not only was he *very* ambitious, he had explicitly praised Don and Mike for this trait when he promoted them.

Ironically, it wasn't ambition that had propelled her out the door—she hadn't been gunning for a CEO title—it was the company's failure to acknowledge her worth. She was worn down by it—and, worse, by not being allowed to accomplish everything she was capable of. The accumulation of the many ways she had been treated unfairly—both big and small, overt and subtle—caused Laura to start looking elsewhere.

Gilia had been struggling with a chaotic, revolving-door approach to management. Under Laura's leadership, the company immediately stabilized and within a few years emerged as Tarweed's most significant competitor. Laura became far better known as a competent executive than Don, Mike, or even the boss who let her walk out the door. Many have since speculated that, had Laura been properly recognized and given more authority at Tarweed, Gilia would have gone out of business.

If Laura's boss at Tarweed had run the numbers and asked himself why he was not promoting the person on his team with the largest, most profitable business, he might have noticed the bias in his decision-making. If he'd promoted Laura, he could probably have retained her. In the end, his bias hurt both him and his company more than it hurt Laura. But it still hurt her career at the time, and it was unjust.

Not every woman has the opportunity to respond to discrimination by getting another job, let alone a better job that gives her a platform to showcase so dramatically what she is capable of. Justice is rarely so poetic or so swift. But it's worth celebrating justice when it happens and learning from it so that we can help it happen more often.

Below are some additional things you can do to avoid ending up in Laura's boss's shoes.

BIAS   PREJUDICE   BULLYING   ⚡   **LEADERS &**
DISCRIMINATION   HARASSMENT   PHYSICAL VIOLATIONS

ANALYZE PROMOTION DATA TO
QUANTIFY YOUR BIAS

The ratio of men to women in the lower ranks who were promoted to first-time manager is very telling: for every 100 men promoted to management, only 72 women were promoted—80 white women, but only 68 Latina women, and only 58 Black women.[50]

What is happening in your organization? Take a look at the numbers and dig in. Perhaps bias doesn't explain 100 percent of the under-representation in your promotions. There may be *some* factors beyond your control. But it's impossible to believe that bias is not a factor at all in these numbers. When you identify the bias revealed in your promotion data, you're much more likely to work on figuring out what to do to improve the situation. Measure what matters, and when your measurements reveal problems, go solve them.

RELY ON A PERFORMANCE MANAGEMENT
SYSTEM NOT UNILATERAL MANAGERIAL
DECISIONS

In most of corporate America, and also in small businesses, managers have had near-dictatorial powers in conducting performance reviews and doling out raises and promotions. If you get on the boss's bad side, you're screwed, even if your results tell a different story. This state of affairs introduces inefficiency and injustice into management decisions.

The solution is to create systems that take performance reviews and decisions about ratings and promotions out of the hands of managers. When checks and balances limit the power of individual bosses to control these processes unilaterally, the results tend to be much more just. You wind up with the right people in the right roles. You get more collaboration between boss and employee and fewer narrow-minded bullies. Having a bully for a boss is an asshole tax nobody should have to pay. A performance review system need not be burdensome and can work well on a team of five people or at a huge company.

How exactly does this work?

Rather than allowing managers to write a unilateral performance review, try instituting a 360 process so that people's performance is assessed by their peers as well as others above and below them in the hierarchy. Create a ratings calibration process that makes sure managers are not easy or hard graders. Create promotion committees that review an employee's work and make promotion decisions. Managers give input to these promotion decisions, but they are not unilateral deciders.

A word of caution: over time such systems can become bloated and time wasting. At one company where I worked, the performance review period began to be known as "perfcrastination" because no other work got done for a couple of weeks. I had a family vacation ruined by a promotion committee run amok. So create your process, but manage it and keep it as simple and streamlined as possible.

QUANTIFY BIAS IN PERFORMANCE MANAGEMENT SYSTEMS

TRACK THE RATE OF PROMOTION FOR PEOPLE WHO ARE UNDERREPRESENTED

Are the people who are underrepresented in your organization getting promoted at a slower rate than the people who are overrepresented? If so, why? Tracking these numbers and investigating discrepancies thoroughly and openly is as uncomfortable as it is crucial.

You want to be fair in both directions when you measure ratings and promotions. For example, at one company I know well, gender equality was measured by a color-coding system. Departments where women's ratings were the same or higher as men's ratings were marked green. Departments where the ratings were higher for men were marked red. The idea was that one wouldn't expect one gender to do better on performance ratings. If men were consistently rated higher than women, it was a flag that some investigation into why was needed.

BIAS PREJUDICE BULLYING ⚡ | LEADERS & DISCRIMINATION HARASSMENT | PHYSICAL VIOLATIONS

It was great that this company had the desire to measure bias. But a man who worked there asked a logical question: Why did the system only highlight departments whose ratings were skewed in favor of men? Why was it considered OK for men to be consistently rated lower than women, when the reverse was viewed as a serious problem? This man felt that *any* gender disparity—toward men, women, or non-binary employees—should be flagged red. Unfortunately, the team that had done the analysis seemed unwilling to grant that the system should be consistent.

The goal must be to ensure ratings are fair.

LINGUISTIC ANALYSIS

If managers are required to give employees written performance reviews or promotion recommendations, the language they use can reveal a lot about their biases. The classic example is the "abrasive" problem already mentioned.

There are simple ways to correct this. You could hire people familiar with how gender bias plays out in performance reviews and ask them to read performance reviews and flag possible bias. Or you could opt for a technical fix: writing your reviews with an augmented writing tool such as Textio to flag the kind of language that may indicate bias. Or you could adapt the Gender Bias Bingo game by having managers read through one another's reviews and look for evidence of the kinds of gender biases that hold women back. When they are found, it's crucial that the manager who wrote the review not be strung up by the thumbs but instead asked to reassess. The point here is not to punish but to learn to identify our biases and correct them.

5. COACHING AND MENTORING

Formal systems such as compensation and ratings are important for an employee's career development. Often, informal mentoring is even more important. Having good mentors can be an enormous boost in a young person's career. But few things are hijacked more by bias than mentorship.

Mentoring people who are underrepresented gets into a gray area that is almost everyone's reality. The only way to build a diverse team is to make sure you and your team are not biased about whom you are mentoring. Make mentoring transparent. Don't build these relationships behind closed doors, at strip clubs, at golf clubs, in your hotel suite, whatever. Have these meetings, no matter whom you're mentoring, in public places.

Evan Cohen, the Americas managing partner at the law firm Clifford Chance, had an experience that is broadly shared among leaders. He was wondering why so few women were becoming partners at his firm and what he could do to change it. He got his answer during an exit interview with an especially promising woman who'd decided to quit the firm. Why, he asked her, was she leaving when she had such a clear path to partnership? She was taken aback by the question. She had no idea anyone saw a big future for her at the firm. The promising men in her class of associates were all mentored by various partners. She had occasionally been mentored as well, but nobody had sat her down and told her she was on track to make partner someday.

Cohen promised himself this would never happen again. He realized that when the mostly men partners chose mentees, they tended to select the associates who reminded them of themselves as young men. He took action and asked all the firm's partners to pick more diverse folks to mentor. He essentially held up a mirror and asked people to look into it: Are you mentoring only people who look like you? Without any quotas or formal mentoring programs, the number of partners who chose to mentor women increased, and the number of women who've made partner has been on the rise ever since. Of the Clifford Chance U.S. lawyers promoted to partner in the last three years, 45 percent were women, and the overall percentage of women partners has more than doubled in six years under Cohen's leadership.

If you're a leader, be intentional about whom you're mentoring and seek out people who are different. If you are a leader of leaders, pay attention to who is being mentored. If women are getting left out, you

LEADERS &
BIAS   PREJUDICE   BULLYING   ⚡ | DISCRIMINATION   HARASSMENT | PHYSICAL VIOLATIONS

have a problem. Unfortunately, it's not one that's so easy to fix. Mentoring is not codified. It's not imposed from above. The best kind of mentoring happens in ad hoc ways—in a shared car back to the office after a meeting, on a coffee break, over lunch when traveling.

DON'T MEET WITH MEN ALONE
IF YOU WON'T MEET WITH WOMEN ALONE

More and more I'm encountering situations where a man I work with will refuse to meet alone with women at work. A variety of beliefs are behind such a policy. Sometimes it's a fear of false accusation. Sometimes it's a strategy to avoid the temptation to stray. Sometimes it's a religious belief. Occasionally it's a woman, not a man, who holds such a religious belief; however, this rarely happens at work because these same beliefs often but not always prohibit the woman from being at work in the first place.

No matter what the reason, there are several problems with anyone's refusal to meet alone with almost half the world's population. One, this policy is discriminatory, especially when the person doing the refusing is in a position of authority. Two, it makes an incorrect assumption that the whole world is straight and cisgender. Sometimes people "stray" with people who are the same gender as they are or with people who are gender fluid.

As a leader, your goal in these situations is to come up with a workable solution for everyone, not to debate the person's religious beliefs or approach to self-control or fear of false accusation. You might tell people, "It is discriminatory, and therefore illegal, to meet alone with men and not with women, or to meet alone with women and not men. If you won't meet one-on-one with women, the only way to avoid discrimination and still hold true to your beliefs is not to meet with men alone, either." Or you could explain it like this: "It is impossible for the women to do their job if you meet with the other men on your team but not with the women. It is also an HR violation and illegal to exclude people on the basis of their gender. An important management responsibility is to have one-on-one meetings with each direct report. If you refuse to have one-on-one meetings with the women who work for you, you will be relieved of your management responsibilities."

If you are a man concerned about false accusations, there are simple, straightforward ways to address this concern rather than refusing to meet with women. One, you can meet with people in public places. You do not need to have one-on-one meetings with anyone behind closed doors. You can leave your door open, you can meet in a conference room, or you can meet at a table in a cafeteria or other public place.

Refusal to meet with one gender but not another is a form of discrimination that your company's code of conduct might cover. It's trickier to apply such a code to mentoring, yet equally important to do so.

Recently, I met a man, a colleague of many years, for lunch. When I returned home, a houseguest gave me a hard time. "Doesn't your husband worry when you have lunch with men?" she asked. My husband and I both found this question absurd. Refusing to meet alone with men would make it nearly impossible for me to do my job. I was the only woman on a board of directors, for example. My editor was a man. Refusing to meet alone with women would be less onerous for my husband since he is a software engineer and 75 percent of the people on his team are men, but it would make things pretty difficult for him, too. Especially when his *boss* was a woman. More important, we trust each other.

As it happened, my colleague and I had met not in a candlelit boîte but at a bustling restaurant in downtown Palo Alto where, between the two of us, we knew half the people eating around us. I had mentored him early in his career. In the intervening years, he had become an enormously successful entrepreneur and was now a mentor to me in turn. These kinds of relationships are an important part of one's professional growth. If I had refused to mentor him because he is a man, or if he'd declined to mentor me because I am a woman, both our lives and careers would have been impoverished.

BIAS   PREJUDICE   BULLYING ⚡ ⌈ **LEADERS &**
| DISCRIMINATION   HARASSMENT ⌉ PHYSICAL VIOLATIONS

DON'T MEET IN STRIP CLUBS

This headline may seem so obvious that it's ridiculous to write it down. But it happens often enough that I'm going to write about it. For example, I once worked for a leader who routinely took the guys at the company out to strip clubs. I don't think he *intended* to exclude women. But his intentions didn't matter. The truth was that while these guys were tossing back drinks and ogling the exotic dancers, they were also having important work-related exchanges and bonding. The boss wasn't aware of how much this combination of sexism and exclusion bothered the women in the office because, unsurprisingly, nobody ever told him. In fact, nobody told me about these excursions either—not until I dragged the details out of Nancy, a woman on my team, after I found her crying in the bathroom.

When I asked Nancy what was wrong, she said the project she'd been working on had been canceled. I'd never seen Nancy complain, let alone cry. I had a feeling there was something she wasn't telling me. So I took her out for a cup of tea—a casual setting is always a good way to elicit feedback from a person clearly reluctant to give it. That's when I got the real story. What she was really upset about was that on one of the boss's lap dance excursions, her male colleagues had learned that her project was being canceled. Not only was it humiliating to get the news secondhand, had she been in the loop earlier she might have been able to fight for a different outcome.

The leader in question made a big deal about being open to feedback, so rather than fuming silently I went to talk to him. All I had to do was say "strip club" and he was appropriately chagrined. I was impressed by the way the leader took responsibility for causing harm. He apologized to all the women who knew about the strip club outings—pretty much all of us. He also acknowledged that it wasn't only women who'd been excluded—it was also the men on the team who had no interest in lap dances. He apologized to them too. Crucially, he talked to all the men who had ever gone to a strip club with him and let them know that this kind of thing had to end, immediately. And it did.

This was an example of Institutional Courage. He listened, honored the truth-teller, apologized, and took responsibility to prevent future harm. When you're open to criticism and willing to confront your mistakes, you can resolve a situation before it metastasizes into something much more dangerous.

6. MEASURE PSYCHOLOGICAL SAFETY

Harvard Business School professor Amy Edmondson has not only defined psychological safety but also come up with an effective way to measure it. She developed a brief survey that gauges employee reactions to seven statements:

- If you make a mistake on this team, it is often held against you.
- Members of this team are able to bring up problems and tough issues.
- People on this team sometimes reject others for being different.
- It is safe to take a risk on this team.
- It is difficult to ask other members of this team for help.
- No one on this team would deliberately act in a way that undermines my efforts.
- Working with members of this team, my unique skills and talents are valued and utilized.[51]

If you break the answers down by gender or any other group of underrepresented employees, this simple series of questions offers a remarkably powerful indication of how people feel about the place they go to work every day. The results will give you a snapshot of your team's microcultures. Share the data with everyone. If the survey indicates that individuals or groups do not feel psychologically safe, work on specific things you can do to improve the situation. Maybe this is a sign you need to put bias busters in place, or maybe it's a sign that

BIAS   PREJUDICE   BULLYING   ⚡ [LEADERS & DISCRIMINATION   HARASSMENT]   PHYSICAL VIOLATIONS people feel harassed or discriminated against. Don't assume. Ask. Act on what you learn. Give the changes some time to have an impact and then measure again to figure out what is working and what isn't.

One of the keys to establishing and maintaining a psychologically safe atmosphere is making sure everybody is comfortable with flagging problems—knowing that they will be listened to and that there will not be reprisals for having done so. If, however, you already *know* that people are feeling unsafe, asking others to flag problems for you may not be the place to start. You may need to flag your own problems, create solutions, and then ask people if you went far enough or too far. In an atmosphere rife with bias, prejudice, or bullying, women might not feel comfortable answering honestly or discussing these sensitive topics—especially if they think you are part of the problem.

7. EXIT INTERVIEWS

Exit interviews can also be useful in providing a qualitative snapshot of your organization. When people whom you wanted to retain quit, you should do everything you can to get them to tell you why. Reassure them that the truth will not "burn bridges," and while you'd love to convince them to stay, that is not the purpose of the meeting. You are there to learn about mistakes that you or your organization made so that they aren't made again.

If you really want to know why that valued employee has quit, get as senior a leader as possible to do the interview. People usually leave managers, not companies. That manager might be the last person who'll hear the unvarnished truth. But the manager's boss? Then the employee might be eager to talk.

This is good management hygiene for all regretted attrition, but it's especially important when it's people who are underrepresented who are quitting. Investigate why the people you've worked hard to recruit and retain don't want to work for you any longer—whether it's mistakes you've made, mistakes others in your organization have made, or problems endemic to your workplace culture. Quantify it. What percentage of people who are underrepresented quit because they have experienced harassment or discrimination at your company?

How many because they've experienced bias, prejudice, or bullying? How does this compare to people who are overrepresented who leave the company? If the data reveals a problem, figure out how to fix it!

8. END NON-DISCLOSURE AGREEMENTS AND FORCED ARBITRATION AT YOUR COMPANY

I have used NDAs, so it may seem hypocritical for me to recommend against them. I understand the appeal—and also why they are a terrible idea.

Do not adopt the practice of requiring all employees to submit to forced arbitration if they get in a dispute with the company. Nor should you require your employees to sign NDAs in the unlikely event that the forced arbitration finds the company at fault and recommends a payout. These practices constitute a blatant attempt to dodge the checks and balances that our legal system puts on employers. Remember that these checks and balances are there to protect the company and its leaders, as well as employees. Covering up discrimination and harassment ensures they will keep happening; and the payout + NDA system invites frivolous lawsuits and suspicion that real problems are not real.

Granted, going to court usually costs more than the payout to the person harmed, and it is also an enormous distraction. As a general rule, it's better for everyone involved not to have to go to court. The best way to avoid going to court is to not cover up problems. That just ensures that these problems will get worse until many people have been harmed and they are so big that you can no longer cover them up. The best way to avoid going to court, then, is to do what you can to prevent discrimination and harassment from the outset; to offer multiple safe ways to report it when it does occur, despite your best efforts; to investigate reports fully and fairly; and to take appropriate action when the reports prove true. If you keep your house in order and can prove you have responsible protocols in place, you are far less vulnerable to lawsuits.

BIAS   PREJUDICE   BULLYING   ⚡ LEADERS & [DISCRIMINATION   HARASSMENT]   PHYSICAL VIOLATIONS

Non-disclosure Agreements (NDAs): *She Said* by Jodi Kantor and Megan Twohey and *Catch and Kill* by Ronan Farrow detail how the truly bad actors have been able to take advantage of NDAs to pursue victim after victim after victim. In *She Said,* actor Rose McGowan, one of the many women Harvey Weinstein preyed upon, explained, "The problem was worse than Weinstein . . . it's not just him, it's an entire machine, supply chain. No oversight, no fear. Each studio does the victim shaming and payouts. Almost everyone has an NDA."[52] This legalistic maneuver is now a standard method used by the powerful to silence the powerless. And it's not just Hollywood, either. It's tech. It's finance. The cover-up perpetuates the crime.

Some leaders explain that an NDA is not a cover-up at all but a way of protecting themselves from false allegations. But when you understand how NDAs are abused, it makes any argument that they protect innocent people from false allegations appear specious and dangerous. Furthermore, they don't protect the company—the opposite is true. If people know there is a chance for them to get a payout with little investigation and no real legal process, it only increases the temptation for an aggrieved party to make a claim. The best way to protect both the real victims of real crimes and also yourself from false allegations is to settle these matters transparently. Nobody should have the right to buy silence from another person.

Forced arbitration: When employees make a complaint, especially about such things as discrimination, harassment, or sexual assault, many companies insist that they sign away their right to resolve the dispute in the justice system before they will discuss a settlement. Often, employees have already signed away that right in the employment contract they signed when they joined the company, agreeing to take any legal claims to private arbitration.

There are a number of problems with forced arbitration, but let's focus on two: it's bad for employees and it's bad for the organizations where they work. Forced arbitration is bad for employees because the private arbitrators are chosen and paid by the organization, and their interest isn't so much in justice but in making sure the company keeps hiring them. Under such conditions, impartial justice is highly unlikely. While forced private arbitration may offer some short-term benefits to an organization—it can avoid the cost and publicity of a lawsuit—in the long run it increases their operating risk. Susan Fowler, who would know because she documented abuses that ultimately caused her former employer, Uber, incalculable harm, explains it like this: "Forcing legal disputes about discrimination, harassment and retaliation to go through secret arbitration proceedings hides the behavior and allows it to become culturally entrenched."[53]

One benefit of forced arbitration, companies argue, is that it protects everyone's privacy. In a lawsuit, any claims made are public, and the name of the person making them must be public as well. This creates some risks for both defendant and plaintiff. Whatever the defendant is accused of having done is now part of the public record, and this can be damaging, whether it's proven true or not. It can also work against the plaintiff. When the plaintiff applies for a new job, the lawsuit may turn up in background searches. Even though it's illegal not to hire people because they've sued a previous employer, many employers quietly decide to pass over a candidate for that reason.[54] That may or may not factor into plaintiffs' decisions about whether to file a suit, but it must be their decision. For a current employer to insist that employees sign a forced arbitration agreement "for their own protection" because future employers may illegally discriminate against them for bringing a lawsuit is simply absurd. It is saying, "If you pursue a case in court, future employers may illegally use this against you, so I am going to make it impossible for you to take me to court—for your own good."

Microsoft ended forced arbitration for sexual harassment cases in 2017.[55] Uber followed suit, followed by Google, then Facebook, and many others.[56] This is a welcome trend. The bad news is that approximately 60 million Americans still work under forced arbitration.[57] You can end forced arbitration at your workplace and leave your corner of the world a little more just.

BIAS   PREJUDICE   BULLYING   ⚡ | **LEADERS &**
 DISCRIMINATION   HARASSMENT | PHYSICAL VIOLATIONS

9. ORGANIZATIONAL DESIGN

What if the CEO misbehaves?

If the company has a board of directors, it is the board's responsibility to address the CEO's misbehavior—it's one of the reasons you have a board of directors in the first place. However, HR is often blamed for not holding the CEO accountable or for mishandling HR violations reports. I'm all for speaking truth to power, but this doesn't seem fair. It's pretty hard to investigate your boss.

For these situations, companies have a compliance function that should have a strong leader. The compliance function should report directly to the audit committee and can go around the CEO if needed. The internal audit function works the same way for the same reasons. If someone needs to report financial wrongdoing or discrimination or harassment, they need to be able to go around the CEO if the CEO is the problem.

This works better in public companies than it does in private ones. Author and board-of-directors-governance expert Dr. Dambisa Moyo explains that public corporations have far greater obligations—from all manner of stakeholders—for transparency and disclosures around forward-leaning social and cultural issues than privately held companies do. For example, issues of gender diversity, pay parity, climate change, and ESG (environmental, social, and governance) factors are all areas where public companies are subject to scrutiny and reporting whereas private institutions generally are not.[58]

The person who leads HR should report directly to the CEO and have a real seat at the table. Too often HR gets "layered" under a COO or has no real influence on the CEO's team. When HR doesn't have a strategic seat at the table, its ability to be effective is compromised, and the organization loses trust and respect for the function. Also, the Chief Human Resources Officer ("CHRO") can be an invaluable partner for the CEO; you want to strengthen that partnership with a direct reporting relationship.

The issue here is that the people who have the most power—the people on the board of directors—are generally best positioned to dodge accountability. This puts HR in a terrible position unless the organizational structure is deliberately designed to limit the power of the CEO, and unless the law holds the board of directors accountable for holding the CEO accountable. The board of directors must hold the CEO accountable and have HR's back.

At too many companies, CEOs appoint board members specifically *not* to challenge their authority, *not* to hold them accountable, as Françoise Brougher reported Ben Silbermann's explanation of how he chose his board at Pinterest.[59] CEOs also hire HR people who will serve them rather than be real partners who can hold them accountable. When this happens, HR investigations can go badly off the rails, as Susan Fowler described in her blog post about how HR responded to her complaints at Uber (see chapter 7).

And then there are all the small businesses that don't have a board of directors. Bars, restaurants, dry cleaners, bodegas, and so on. My own executive-education company has no board of directors. How can small business owners hold themselves accountable? A few things can help. One is to appoint an ombudsperson whom people can go to with complaints. This ombudsperson needs to be someone who carries a lot of sway with the business owner—a mentor—and who is willing to give a personal email address and phone number to all employees. Another idea is to form a complaints committee: two or three employees who are generally trusted by the rank and file because they will not be afraid to bring problems to your attention.

BIAS   PREJUDICE   BULLYING   ⚡ | LEADERS & DISCRIMINATION   HARASSMENT | PHYSICAL VIOLATIONS

CHEAT SHEET

PROBLEM	RESPONSE

DISCRIMINATION

Bias / Prejudice + Power
to exclude

BIAS
QUANTIFIER

Measure what matters to make
the right hiring, pay, promotion,
and mentoring decisions

HARASSMENT

Bullying + Power
to intimidate others

CHECKS AND
BALANCES

No unilateral
decision making

BIAS   PREJUDICE   BULLYING ⚡ **LEADERS &** _____
                               | DISCRIMINATION HARASSMENT | PHYSICAL VIOLATIONS

7

For People Harmed and Upstanders

How to Fight Discrimination and Harassment Without Blowing Up Your Career

Beware of Enterprises That Require New Clothes*

I once had a boss who told me he didn't like the way I dressed. Knowing my fashion sense leaves a lot to be desired and wanting to show I was open to feedback, I went out and bought some new clothes. Still not good enough. Without consulting me, my boss sent a woman on the team out to buy me an outfit; she returned with a pair of supertight jeans, a shirt that slipped off my shoulder and showed my bra, and dainty red slippers that I found as uncomfortable psychologically as they were physically. Finally, there was a blazer, a man's jacket half-heartedly adapted for a woman's body with rolled-up sleeves and a pinched-in waist. I was then handed a jaw-dropping bill for these clothes I had no interest in wearing.

After a few trial runs I refused to wear the revealing shirt. I also retired the tight jeans, which gave me a terrible stomachache, and the slippers, which hurt my feet. As a gesture of compromise, I wore the jacket. But I didn't like it.

I did, however, like my job. The projects were fascinating. I was on a small team with two of my favorite people in the world. So I sucked it up

---

* Henry David Thoreau, *Walden*.

and paid the bill. I rationalized the whole thing, telling an old friend that my boss was trying to be helpful. WTF? She still teases me about that.

A few months later my boss called me into his office and said that I needed to repair my relationship with Jack, a colleague on another team. Apparently my "communication style" had upset him. I asked a few clarifying questions, but my boss had a hard time articulating what, exactly, I'd done wrong. He wondered out loud if this was the competence-likability bias at play. I didn't know what that was, and he explained that research had shown that often the more competent a woman is, the less people like her.[1] I felt briefly hopeful that he might raise this possibility with Jack, might interrupt the bias, until he went on to say that, no, the problem was that I was "objectively" not likable. Ouch!

I was still reeling from this insult when my boss said that Jack had another problem with my behavior. I had a close working relationship with two colleagues on my team, and Jack felt excluded. Jack wasn't on my team, but evidently he wanted to be.

Now I was really confused. Was the "problem" here that I was objectively not likable or that I was too well liked? I *was* close with the colleagues my boss had mentioned. I'd known both for more than a decade. One had recruited me to the company, and I had recruited the other. They were the main reason I hadn't quit after the jeans incident.

"At any rate, all this is making my job harder," my boss concluded. He was tired of hearing about me from Jack. Couldn't I just try to make nice with him? Perhaps I could solicit some fashion advice from him, my boss suggested with an expression I interpreted to mean, "Why aren't you wearing the clothes I went to all the trouble of procuring for you?"

So I had lunch with Jack, who immediately proposed that he take me shopping. He explained that my jeans needed to be tighter and longer, so that my legs would look better and I would appear taller. Jack was gay, so I knew he wasn't hitting on me. I had a hunch that my boss had asked him to give me these pointers, not wanting to do it himself. Furthermore, in spite of what my boss had said, Jack didn't seem to have any malice toward me. I suspected my boss was trying to turn a conflict he was having with Jack into a conflict between Jack and me. I wasn't going to let that happen.

"Look, I recently gave birth to twins. I have the right to keep my postpartum body private. I'm not going to wear tight jeans," I said to

Jack, wanting to move away from the subject of my wardrobe. Instead, I asked for his thoughts on a work project. He was enormously helpful. Once I got him off the topic of my jeans, we bonded.

I told my boss I'd succeeded in building a better relationship with Jack, that there were no issues between us. A month later, though, my boss called me into his office. "I think I've got a solution to your—er, problem," he said.

If he demoted me, then perhaps Jack would feel less threatened and would stop asking to join my team.

Wait, *what*? What was the bogus justification for this proposal? My boss was demoting me because of a likability-competence bias? He was demoting me because it was easier than explaining to Jack why my boss wasn't offering Jack the role he wanted?

Finally, I found my voice. I objected to his "solution" to my "problem." He countered that he had an "objective" rationale for my demotion: my two peers had PhDs, and so did a third he'd recently hired, whereas I did not. I pointed out that I didn't have a PhD when he hired me, either. If that was a job requirement, he should've told me *before* hiring me.

"Well, you've given me a lot to think about," he said, concluding the meeting.

I went back to my office and reached out to two of my mentors. The first one, a well-known Silicon Valley CEO, recommended I begin documenting what was happening in preparation for a legal escalation. My other mentor, also an experienced tech executive, gave me the opposite advice. "Just get another job. Quit quietly. Don't blow up your career."

I took the latter's advice. In retrospect, I regret it. I had a lot of options at the time and thus the "blow up your career" risk was certainly lower than it felt. And even if I did blow up my career, I'd already won the job lottery, and so had my husband. No matter what happened, we were going to be able to put food on the table. If I'm honest with myself, it wasn't safety I was seeking. It was upside. Did I want to stay and fight for justice when I could just walk away from this nonsense and get another, better job? I told myself the fight wouldn't make any sense. I left quietly.

At the time I thought I was taking the wisest course of action, but now I understand the way that systemic injustice silences people with its promises of other, future rewards. I believe in confronting problems head-on, in a way that shows you care enough to help the person creating the problem to fix it. That is Radical Candor. But instead of offering Radical Candor, I made a half-hearted effort to explain my departure. It was clear my boss didn't get it, and I didn't make sure that he did.

As a person harmed, I had every right to choose my battles. However, over time I came to notice that my silence hurt my self-respect and my sense of agency. For my own sake, I wish I had confronted the injustice more forcefully. Worse, my silence left other underrepresented people who were more vulnerable than I was without an ally. For other people's sake, I also wish I had escalated the situation more effectively.

I didn't acknowledge any of that to myself until a few years later, when I was on a panel about women in tech with Sarah Kunst. Sarah and six other women had recently called out venture capitalist Dave McClure for sexual harassment and assault, causing one of the early #MeToo reckonings in tech.[2] Before our talk, I told her the story of my mentor who advised me not to blow up my career. I was planning to pass that advice on to other women.

"Do you know what the problem is?" Sarah asked me. "The problem is that people will listen to you! If you tell people that they will blow up their career if they speak out, everyone will continue to stay silent, and nothing will change. Look at me. Is my career blown up?"

Sarah, who is one of the too-few Black leaders in tech, was kind enough not to point out the obvious: that it would have been a hell of a lot safer for me as a white woman to speak out than it had been for her. She'd had to work harder for success than I had. Yet she had been willing to take the personal risks required to challenge the sexual predation of a rich and powerful man. Not only had she left this world a little more just by doing so, not only had she survived, she had thrived. She went on to become managing director at a venture capital fund in addition to already being a managing editor at *Marie Claire*. She is enormously successful by any measure. I'm not saying that no women have had their careers blown up by confronting sexual harassment or predation. Many have. But it's also true that we often overestimate the risks. We have a negativity bias here. We will be more successful fighting injustice by optimizing for the upside rather than the downside.

Anyone who has been through this kind of thing knows the long list of "reasons" not to confront this kind of behavior from a boss: "It's like tilting at windmills"; "You're sure to lose"; "Your every failure will come under the microscope"; "You'll get a reputation as a troublemaker and not get hired again."

But my biggest silencer was that staying and fighting didn't make good business sense—at least, that was how I saw it at the time. I was confident that I could get another well-compensated job pretty easily, whereas if I went the legal route, which was far more arduous, even if I won I would just end up with a settlement. And I could earn much more money by working than I was likely to be awarded in a settlement. Now I call this "the golden gag of privilege."

If you stood on a street corner and asked 100 people, "Would you rather spend the next two years fighting a lawsuit you'll probably lose or working at a start-up company where you'll have a lot of fun and get stock options that could allow you to retire and leave your children secure?," you would find few heroes willing to walk away from the latter opportunity for a fight in a legal system that feels rigged against you.

In other words, if you take justice out of the equation and just do an ROI calculation, the decision is not difficult. But some decisions can't be made with an ROI. Capitalism is so good at rewarding what we can measure, so bad at rewarding what we value.

There wasn't a good ROI for Sarah in fighting her fight, either. Yet, she decided to follow her values. She is a big part of the reason why I am writing this book now. If we wait for a convenient time to speak out, we'll be waiting forever. If we wait for leaders to confront their own biases, a fair working environment will become even more elusive.

Years later, when Françoise Brougher was fired as COO of Pinterest in the summer of 2020 for what seemed to me like painfully gendered reasons, her predicament[3] felt so familiar to me. Ifeoma Ozoma and Aerica Shimizu Banks went public about racial and gender discrimination they faced at Pinterest just before Françoise did.[4]

Going public was enormously risky and difficult for all three women. In Françoise's case, the rewards for pretending that she was leaving the company voluntarily were significant—not only the payout Pinterest was offering but, more significant, the next big job and all the board seats she was eligible for. If she chose to go public, many of these opportunities might evaporate. Fortunately for the rest of us, she still chose to go public with her story.

Still, the risks Françoise took are very real. Shortly before she published her piece, a recruiter had asked me for names of potential board members. I had recommended Françoise. After Françoise's piece came out, the recruiter dropped me a note: "I think it is great for her to speak up but I do think it will make her candidacy tricky in future."

I replied, "Here is what I would advise companies. You want a board member who will hold the CEO accountable. Françoise will do that, clearly. You also want to show that you care about ending the kind of systemic injustice that has held underrepresented people back. Françoise will do that. And you want someone who understands tech. Nobody understands tech—how to build it, how to deploy it, how to sell it, how to manage it—better than Françoise. This whole 'we don't want to hire people who speak out' BS has got to go . . . Do they want to demonstrate Institutional Courage or Institutional Betrayal?" The response? Radio silence.

I do not blame the recruiter. But I do blame the leaders at the companies for whom the recruiter works. When leaders quietly refuse to hire people who speak out against injustice rather than *competing* to hire them because these are the very people who will help them and their teams Just Work, it perpetuates a workplace injustice.

This chapter is not going to tell you that you "should" do what I myself was unwilling to do. Rather, I'll give you the list of options that I wish had been clearer in my mind when I faced that choice. I'll give you a way to think about the pros and cons that takes into account what you can measure and what you value.

When you are confronting harassment and/or discrimination, or when you are an upstander for someone else who is, you're likely to feel angry and confused. That's legit. Before you decide on tactics and strategy, take some time to find people who have compassion for what you're going through, folks who can help you assess your situation.

Whether you are a person harmed or an upstander, I suggest three preliminary steps:

1. Document
2. Build solidarity
3. Locate the exit nearest you

Once you have oriented yourself and decided to move forward, here are four other escalation choices you may want to consider, depending on your situation:

4. **Talk directly with the person who caused you harm**
5. **Report to HR**
6. **Take legal action**
7. **Tell your story publicly**

If you are an upstander, you probably won't be taking the last two steps, but you may help the person harmed take them.

I will unpack each of these steps below. Before doing so, I want to reiterate that it is not for the purpose of telling you what to do, but rather to leave you feeling that you made your decision with agency, on the best information available. My goal is to leave you feeling supported and a little bit less alone, no matter what you decide to do.

1. DOCUMENT

If you are experiencing or observing discrimination or harassment, especially if it's from someone who is more powerful, you can document it every time it occurs—even if you're thinking you probably won't sue or go to HR. Take a little time each day to jot down what's happening. It doesn't have to be a journal of your feelings if you don't want it to be—or it can be. Make sure the facts are there as clearly as possible. This will do three things for you. One, it will give you perspective, which can remind you that you have agency. Two, it will give you confidence in the truth of what occurred, making you less vulnerable to gaslighting. Three, it will give you options—your documentation will be invaluable should you pursue a lawsuit or go public.

Whenever possible, note the time and place, what was said or done and by whom, and who was present. Don't feel it has to be perfect—this is just a first step. Here's a basic example of what documentation might've looked like for my experience with the tight-jeans boss:

- January 20—boss told me I needed better clothes
- January 22—bought new clothes (receipts _here_)
- January 24—boss presented me with new clothing purchased for me by a colleague; included supertight jeans, revealing shirt, uncomfortable shoes, and a blazer; told me the company would pay (conversation with college roommate about the exchange that night)
- January 27—boss asked me to reimburse the company (photo of check _here_)
- February 14—boss asked me to improve my relationship with Jack; speculated that I was suffering from competence-likability bias but then decided that I was "objectively not likable" (husband will recall my story and my tears that night)[5]
- March 18—boss suggested a demotion might improve my relationship with Jack (talked to my colleague about this)

Another thing to think about when documenting: Which of these facts can be corroborated by others or by some sort of paper trail? For example, snapping a picture of the receipts for the new clothes and storing them in my personal Google Drive folder; keeping a picture of the canceled check I'd made out to the company to pay for the clothes in the same Google Drive folder. Also, after my boss bought me the clothes, I called my college roommate to discuss, so making a note of that was important. Regarding the February 14 meeting, my husband heard the story and would no doubt remember it as it ruined our Valentine's Day dinner.

If someone is sending you offensive texts, emails, pictures, or videos, take screenshots of them and store them in a place you control. *Don't save all this information on a work computer.* Any documents you keep on a work computer, even personal journal entries, belong to your employer. You can email them to a personal email account, save them on your own computer or a thumb drive if you have one, upload them to a Google Drive or Dropbox account (or whatever other technology you use and control). Just be sure that you don't save any confidential or proprietary company information on a personal account, as this can be grounds for immediate termination.

If your work computer doesn't permit any of those things, pull out your phone and start taking pictures. Send them to someone you trust to establish what's called a "contemporaneous record." For example, the mentor who thought I should sue recommended that I send him an email each time these things happened, which I did. You can also establish a contemporaneous record by telling friends or trusted colleagues and then emailing confirmation of your conversation.

2. BUILD SOLIDARITY

Harassment and discrimination can leave you feeling isolated. Yet if you are experiencing these things, you are far from alone. Now more than ever, you can reach out to others who will understand what you're going through.

Throughout the worst experiences of my professional life, my friends were there for me. When I told them what was happening, they could help me distinguish between feedback and gaslighting. They could help me know when I was truly being mistreated versus when I was just having a bad day; when it wasn't me who was off-kilter but my leadership.

My friends didn't just provide emotional support. They armed me with information and introductions. We discussed our salaries openly, and when we found out what our peers who were men were paid, we shared that information as well. Whenever things got so bad that

PEOPLE HARMED, UPSTANDERS &
BIAS   PREJUDICE   BULLYING   ⚡ | DISCRIMINATION   HARASSMENT | PHYSICAL VIOLATIONS

I decided to leave a job, the best introductions have always come from friends, mentors, and former employees.

When you speak out about discrimination or harassment, you're likely to experience a "smackdown." Author Kate Manne puts it into perspective: "Whenever I wrote honestly and forthrightly, I'd get smacked down. I came to recognize that, along with smackdown, there'd be support and solidarity. So thank you, friends and followers."[6]

A good therapist can be an enormous source of strength if you have a health plan that will cover it. But beware. Sometimes a therapist may reflect the very bias that is behind the discrimination or harassment you're experiencing. Don't give the therapist too much authority.

When I've felt most alone, I've also turned to books. Claudia Rankine's *Citizen* helped me find compassion for my own silence. Audre Lorde reminded me that my silence would not protect me. Tina Fey's *Bossypants* made me laugh out loud just when I needed it most. Movies usually punish any woman who defends herself, so if you turn to movies, choose carefully. I found *9 to 5* cathartic and hilarious. There are numerous online professional organizations and women's groups to join such as Lean In circles or Meetup groups. Or you can Google "women's networking groups near me."[7]

YOU DON'T HAVE TO BE POWERFUL
TO MOVE THE NEEDLE

You don't have to be an SVP at Google or the president of your university to begin to address the problem of discrimination in your field.

When she was a sophomore at Colgate University in 2012, Lauren Yeary decided to take a computer science class. She loved the work, but there was one problem. The computer science intro classes had so few women she was often a minority of one. For many women, that was reason enough not to study computer science.

Lauren wasn't going to let social awkwardness chase her away from work she enjoyed and a lucrative profession. Nor was she willing to accept the loneliness of being so outnumbered. She worked hard to recruit other women to major in computer science. She started a computer science club for women (Women in Computer Science, WiCS). By the time she graduated, the student enrollment in the computer science department at Colgate was well over 30 percent women.[8]

Lauren moved the needle on an issue that has consumed millions of hours of impotent hand-wringing and excuses ("it's a pipeline problem and it's not our fault and we can't do anything about it") for the extreme gender imbalances at software companies. And her accomplishment does beg a question of university administrations. Why don't more universities make a conscious, proactive effort to make it more comfortable for women to enter male-dominated majors and for men to enter female-dominated majors?

PEOPLE HARMED: ASK FOR INFORMATION

A big part of building solidarity and finding support is sharing information. I once shared my offer letter with a former colleague who was also considering joining the company. We would be peers, but I was pretty sure that I'd learn he was being paid more than me if I asked. I wanted to know, but I hesitated to look at his letter because I was sure it would piss me off. If I hadn't, I might never have learned that I was, in fact, being offered a roughly comparable compensation package. That knowledge was enormously liberating for me. I was glad I asked and grateful to him for sharing.

UPSTANDERS: SHARE INFORMATION

If you have advantages that others don't, if you're getting paid more than others for reasons that are not fair, don't just sit around feeling guilty. Use your advantages to fix the injustice. For example, when actress Jessica Chastain learned that her costar Octavia Spencer customarily made far less than Jessica did, she famously suggested that they negotiate their next joint feature together—and they did. A woman of color, Spencer had been underpaid for years.[9]

As discussed in chapter 6, such pay differences happen all the time, even when an employer didn't *consciously* set out to pay underrepresented people less. Your underrepresented colleague is getting paid less than you are because they were getting paid less at their previous job. When your underrepresented colleague got hired, perhaps it didn't occur to your boss that by paying a "market rate" this reflected and reinforced that discrimination. Of course, you risk having your salary lowered to your colleague's rather than your colleague's being raised to yours. Your boss may also get angry and defensive. It's important to proceed cautiously.[10]

If talking directly to your boss feels like tilting at windmills, find out if there are collective efforts you can join. If you can get together with a large number of people in your organization or even your industry and share information, your risk of being singled out and punished goes way down, and your chance of having a big impact thanks to collective action goes way up. When you support social movements for pay equity, fundamental progress can be made.

ASK FOR HELP

One of my mentors gave me some invaluable advice early in my career. Asking for help, he explained, is very different from asking for a handout. Asking for help is like asking someone to invest in you. And it's the gift that keeps giving. Once someone has helped you, the person has invested in your success and is likely to help again if you need it. You're not indebted to the person who helped you. You are, however, obligated to pay it forward.

Here is a simple calculus you can do to figure out the best way to ask for help. Look for something *specific* the person can do to help you. Don't ask the person to have coffee or lunch with you—they are busy and 15 minutes is a big ask. Look for things that are relatively easy for the other person to do but have a lot of value to you. A great ratio to keep in mind is low effort for the person / high value to you. But don't limit yourself. Often people will go to a lot of effort to help you. People can be incredibly generous.

What might this kind of help look like when it comes to an underrepresented person who has faced discrimination or harassment?

- Ask a mentor for advice on a specific decision you are making. Think through in advance how to present the decision in the most efficient way. Don't ask the person to do your thinking for you. "I could do A or I could do B. Here are the pros and cons as I understand them. Is there another factor I should be considering?"
- Ask a senior colleague for help getting assigned to a different team or to include you on a high-profile project that will help you on a path to promotion.
- Ask a senior colleague to support your promotion.
- Ask for an introduction to a new job opportunity at a company where you think you'll face less discrimination.
- Tell a senior colleague whom you trust about harassment you've experienced and ask for help in figuring out how to report it in a way that won't harm your career.

FIND A DIFFICULTY ANCHOR

Mekka Okereke, an engineering leader at Google, Tweeted some excellent advice on how to ask for help from someone more senior in the organization to make sure you get proper credit for your work. The key is to ask for help from someone in your organization who is highly respected, known to have high standards, but also objective. Someone who's known to be tough but fair. Explain what you're working on and ask the person to meet occasionally to give you guidance on your projects and the specific roles you're playing. This person will become your "difficulty anchor," who will be able to testify in detail about your contribution. If your peers dismiss your work, assuming that the problem you were solving was easy (it must be easy if an underrepresented person could do it!), your difficulty anchor can objectively disagree and explain why it was a hard problem. This sort of evidence is much more effective coming from your anchor than from you.[11] This is a big ask, not a small one, but many people who are established in their careers enjoy this kind of mentoring.

PEOPLE HARMED, UPSTANDERS &

BIAS PREJUDICE BULLYING ⚡ | DISCRIMINATION HARASSMENT | PHYSICAL VIOLATIONS

3. LOCATE THE EXIT NEAREST YOU

Whether you want to stay or go probably depends on what your exit options are. So locate the exit nearest you. When I finally quit my first job out of college, the finance company described in the introduction, and took another job, several people reached out and asked why I hadn't called them sooner. They had no idea I was looking to change jobs! It hadn't occurred to me that I could call them. It's easy to feel stuck and never realize how many exits, in fact, there are.

If you decide you're going to talk to your boss directly or talk to HR or escalate in some other way, you are well served to think through what might happen. You are about to enter a negotiation of sorts. Before you start a negotiation, make sure you know what your "best alternative to a negotiated agreement" (BATNA) is. If you look around and find several other jobs you could get, then suddenly the threat of being fired is not a big deal. If you look around and realize this job is your only option or your best bet, then that will help you decide how much risk you can take.

At times you may realize that even though your BATNA isn't great, you have to go. All of the work you've done above—documenting what's happened, engaging the support of friends, reaching out for help—will, I hope, leave you feeling a sense of agency.

Be skeptical of received wisdom about not quitting a job until you have another. Alex, a person I care about deeply, once worked in a liquor store for a boss who was disrespectful to the point of harassment. Conventional wisdom was "Don't quit until you get another job." But it can also be hard to interview for a new job when you're angry and demoralized in your current one. Alex quit and started driving for Lyft and made ends meet while recovering from the harassing boss. That isn't possible for everyone, but don't assume you're stuck before giving it careful and creative thought.

Another thing I learned too late in my career: if you take a job and realize after a month or two that there are serious problems you couldn't have known about when interviewing, especially if the problems involve workplace injustice, it's OK to quit. You don't have to wait a year. When you take a job and then quit right away, people are more likely to wonder what's wrong with the company than what's wrong with you. Of course, if you take a job and then quit right away several times in a row, that will reflect badly on you. But if you learn something about a new job or your boss that makes your skin crawl, it is probably better for both your psyche and your résumé to act fast.

But at times you really *are* stuck. Maybe there is only one employer in your area who pays enough to keep you above the poverty line. Family commitments—college tuitions, relatives requiring costly medical care—may have you locked into a high-paying job that would be hard to replicate. And if you truly don't have exit options, that's important to know also, painful as it might be. You may not be able to change the shitty situation you are in, but you still have freedom: freedom to choose how you respond. I recommend two very different kinds of books to read if you find yourself in this situation. For inspiration and perspective, Viktor Frankl's *Man's Search for Meaning*. And for practical advice, Bob Sutton's *The Asshole Survival Guide*.

UPSTANDERS: POINT OUT THE EXITS, MAKE INTRODUCTIONS, OFFER ADVICE

In the introduction to this book I mentioned Emmett, a partner at the financial management firm who helped me find another job. He introduced me to the firm that would give me a job offer with a fair salary, freeing me to get out of a situation where I was experiencing discrimination, harassment, and worse. When I was interviewing for that job, he gave me some great advice. Because I was so severely underpaid, he suggested that I not disclose my salary. Instead, I should tell them what I *expected* to make. Getting a new job that paid me fairly and working with people who treated me respectfully was enormously healing. I am not sure I would've gotten there without his help.

If you are an upstander, take a page out of Emmett's book. When you notice someone experiencing discrimination or harassment, think about how you can help the person make an exit if it becomes necessary. Affirm the person's perspective on what has happened. When you tell the person harmed that you notice the same things the person does, you've just dispelled gaslighting. That in itself is a valuable service. And if you can proactively offer to introduce people to someone who might give them a job, then you dramatically improve their BATNA and give them an opportunity to negotiate from a place of strength. Perhaps there are people you know who might be able to advise or help them in some other way—a lawyer, a coach. You offer a real lifeline when you make these sorts of introductions.

4. TALK DIRECTLY WITH THE PERSON WHO CAUSED HARM

Sometimes it works to just be direct. When Ruchi Sanghvi, the first woman engineer at Facebook, was negotiating her compensation with Mark Zuckerberg after she found out she was paid less than her peers who were men, she said, "Please bring me up to par on . . . compensation. I don't want to have this in the back of my mind while I'm working, nor do you. I only want to be thinking about building stuff!"[12] Ruchi understood intuitively that she would not only be happier but also do better work if she knew she was being fairly paid in comparison with her peers. Receiving proper compensation gave her the freedom to Just Work.

I have mentored countless people frustrated by injustice in their workplace—by the lack of real efforts to recruit more people who are underrepresented, by the visibly slower career growth for people who are underrepresented, by comments reflecting bias and prejudiced beliefs from senior leaders, and by other manifestations of harassment or discrimination. It's clear to me that these folks are ready to bolt.

"Why don't you talk to your boss?" I'll ask. "You've got one foot out the door already. You don't need to be afraid of getting fired. So why not try it?"

"Why bother?"

"Would you rather keep this job or get another one?"

"I'd rather stay."

"But you won't stay if this continues, right?"

"No."

"And nothing will change if you don't say anything. So . . . ?"

For many people, it simply boils down to their reluctance to have an awkward conversation. Your boss is insufficiently invested in you and doesn't care enough to address that problem. Why set oneself up for further disappointment, or even humiliation?

These sorts of direct confrontations are highly personal. You'll have to make your own list of pros and cons, costs and benefits. Here's one I made for myself.[13]

COSTS/RISKS	BENEFITS
Loss of denial: confronting the problem makes it real	But it **is** real—and the only possibility of changing the reality is to confront it.
Time	Waking up at 3:00 A.M. pissed off because I've said nothing also takes time.
Emotional labor: Do I want to put myself through this?	I don't have to do it. But the lack of resolution/being stuck working with someone I can't trust is also emotionally draining. If I confront them, I'll have a greater sense of agency and self-respect. That's a good ROI on my emotional labor.
Possible retribution	This person might fire me if I bring it up or try to hurt my reputation. But I can get another job. And if I remain silent, it ensures this behavior will continue or even get worse for me and for others.
I might feel even more angry than I already do if there's no resolution or a bad response.	If I don't confront this, there's no possibility of resolving the situation or repairing the relationship that will otherwise be marred by lack of trust. That will also make me angry over time, and also erode my sense of agency.
I might get emotional and feel ashamed.	It's OK to get emotional. If they can't deal with my emotions, it's their problem.

5. REPORT TO HR

There are a number of important reasons to report any discrimination or harassment you experience to HR.

First of all, HR *can* be helpful. When HR resolves the issue, you are spared the time and hassle of having to find a new job or take another action.

I have been lucky and have had strong relationships with most of the HR partners I've worked with. Throughout my career they've given me excellent advice and helped me grow professionally. Given my fascination with creating business environments in which colleagues thrive and business prospers, I find HR the most intellectually interesting function at any company. That said, there are sometimes nightmare scenarios in which HR is in the pocket of the very person who's causing you harm. That's happened to me, too. But it is certainly not *always* the case.

Even in the event HR is *not* helpful—if you get a BS response like the one that Susan Fowler described in her blog post about Uber ("he is a high performer, this was his first incident, you are the problem")—it's still important to have reported the incident. For one thing, it is a form of evidence. If you wind up suing your company or going public with your story, creating a record of your complaint and how it was handled or not handled is an essential first step. If your issue is not resolved, that record will be crucial if you decide to take further action. Susan Fowler's blog post about her treatment at Uber would not have been nearly as powerful if she hadn't gone to HR first.

Finally, reporting to HR may help others even if it doesn't help you. One of the things I felt worst about when I walked away from the job with the tight-jeans boss was that other women at the company experienced similarly bizarre, gendered behavior from him. Had I reported my issues before I left, it would have been harder for the company to soft-pedal future complaints. And it wouldn't have taken that much effort on my part—especially after I'd gotten another job and was leaving anyway.

EXIT INTERVIEWS

Your exit interview is a good moment to tell the people at the company exactly why you are leaving. Sure, you don't want to burn bridges. But this is a moment in which you can share some observations that you were hesitant to share while you were still at the company. This is an opportunity to state the facts of what happened, to describe the harassment or discrimination you experienced. It is also an opportunity to help the person you're talking to understand why the work environment was the cause of your departure. You can point out that you have no intention of suing, but that you would like things to be better for those you are leaving behind. Doing so may enormously help the people who are underrepresented at the company.

One risk of giving an honest exit interview is that you may be asked to sign a nondisclosure agreement. Do not allow yourself to be pressured to sign anything you don't want to sign. Be careful with exit documents and releases. I know several people who were so eager to leave they signed and then felt muzzled for years. Remember, you are always free to walk out any door. *You do not have to sign anything.*

6. CONSIDER LEGAL ACTION

Obviously, significant risks are associated with taking legal action, not least the time and emotional energy it can consume. I don't have any data behind this assertion, but it seems to me that getting an outsize payment is about as likely as winning the lottery.

But making a conscious decision about whether you want to sue, and seeking advice from multiple employment lawyers, does not have to be all-consuming. These conversations can help you zero in on how best to protect yourself, what you might want out of a lawsuit, and whether you're likely to get it.

SHOP AROUND FOR A LAWYER

Hiring a lawyer can feel daunting, and it's not uncommon to feel intimidated by lawyers. But a good lawyer can be the dogged ally you wish you'd had all along—full of practical advice, emotional support, and horizon-expanding wisdom. Oftentimes people dealing with workplace abuse issues find consulting with a knowledgeable, compassionate attorney gives them an invaluable plan of action. Numerous legal organizations are out there with resources to help you.[14]

Remember, you are about to hire someone to work for you. You are the boss, not the other way around. The lawyer will give you advice, but you don't have to take it. You get to decide whether you will act on the lawyer's counsel or ignore it.

Don't talk to just one lawyer, talk to several before deciding whom to hire. You don't have to pay for that first conversation any more than an employer has to pay people to interview for a job. Don't be afraid to ask hard, uncomfortable questions. Lawyers are used to that. Look for a lawyer who seems to respect your time and understand what's important to you.

Many lawyers work on contingency, meaning they only get paid if they win a lawsuit or if there is a settlement. Because such lawyers get paid a percentage of a settlement, which often requires that you sign an NDA, they may push you to accept the settlement-and-NDA route. Be aware that some NDAs are so restrictive you're forbidden from discussing what happened to you with anyone—even a therapist or a spouse. If you're not going to be comfortable doing that, make your position clear and make sure that your attorney respects it.[15]

7. TELL YOUR STORY PUBLICLY

RISKS OF TELLING YOUR STORY	BENEFITS OF TELLING YOUR STORY
Painful to re-live	Self-awareness. Writing can be cathartic.[16] Sometimes you find meaning in painful experiences when you write about them.
Writing or telling these stories can be painful, difficult and time-consuming	Living with having been treated unjustly is also painful and time-consuming.
You may be blamed, re-victimized. "Blame the victim."	Silence is also re-victimizing. Often you'll feel more agency if you tell the story and get unjustly blamed.
Risk of retribution	You might find more support than retribution when you tell your story. Often the result is solidarity with others who've been through what you've gone through, support from friends and strangers alike. Knowing that you're helping other people from experiencing discrimination or harassment is gratifying. Often the value of the solidarity outweighs the cost of the retribution. Plus, you can choose your level of exposure to retribution by how and with whom you choose to share your story.
It probably won't make any difference	You might create consequences for the person who harmed you if you tell your story; they'll almost certainly get away with it if you remain silent.

A significant #MeToo reckoning in the tech sector occurred in 2017 when Susan Fowler published a blog post[17] detailing the sex discrimination and harassment she'd experienced at her former company Uber. She had just left Uber and started a new job at Stripe. After going viral and making headlines around the world, Susan's blog post contributed to Travis Kalanick, Uber's founder and CEO, losing his job. His downfall surprised and elated many because leaders who create this kind of toxic workplace are so rarely held to account.

One of the things that made Susan's blog post so effective was how dispassionate and factual it was in describing the systemic gender injustice at the company and management's consistent refusal to acknowledge it. This is how what psychologist Jennifer Freyd calls Institutional Betrayal[18] works: a violation does even more harm when an institution you depend on (1) could have prevented the harm, but didn't, and (2) fails to respond supportively when you report it. It's a classic case of adding insult to injury. Uber's response to Susan's reporting her manager's harassment was to punish her and to protect him. Institutional Betrayal retraumatizes the victim, makes it less likely that people will report problems, ensures there will be more victims in the future, and ultimately does far more harm to the institution than a more courageous response in the first place would have done. It's bad for everyone.

Over many months Susan reported specific instances of sexual harassment and discrimination to Uber's HR department. She continued doing this even after it became clear to her that Uber's HR was part of the problem and not part of the solution. This was strategic. Continuing to report violations and to document lousy responses was part of what made her story so compelling and part of what helped her effect real change at Uber. Putting her complaints on the record was crucial to Susan's ability to document and then communicate how deep the problem of gender injustice at Uber ran.

VICTIMHOOD, VULNERABILITY, AND STORYTELLING

Many people are reluctant to tell their story because our society hasn't traditionally treated victims well. All kinds of false narratives about victims are out there. Let's question them.

Sh*t happens. Sometimes, sh*t happens to you. You may be a victim in a particular situation. That doesn't mean you've been robbed of agency or will always be a victim in the future. Telling your story does not mean you are "playing the victim." As Brené Brown wrote, "Vulnerability is not winning or losing; it's having the courage to show up and be seen when we have no control over the outcome. Vulnerability is not weakness; it's our greatest measure of courage."[19] She also explains the etymology of the word "courage." "It means to tell the story of who you really are with your whole heart."[20] That's why some of the most effective, courageous "you" statements to confront bullying and harassment are "You did this to me. You were wrong to do it."

There's agency in expressing your pain and in choosing the way you respond to your pain. Acknowledging that one has been harmed can be healing. By acknowledging the truth of our experience, we regain some of our agency.

CHEAT SHEET

PROBLEM	RESPONSE

DISCRIMINATION

Bias / Prejudice + Power
to exclude

Document

Build solidarity

Locate exits

Talk directly

Report to HR

Consider legal action

Tell your story

HARASSMENT

Bullying + Power
to intimidate others

PEOPLE HARMED, UPSTANDERS &
BIAS   PREJUDICE   BULLYING ⚡ | DISCRIMINATION   HARASSMENT | PHYSICAL VIOLATIONS

8

Touch

How to Create a Culture of Consent and the Cost of Failing to Do So

I t would be nice, at least from the manager's perspective, to have absolute rules regarding touch in the workplace. No touching. No dating. No affairs. No casual sex. But humans have never been able to follow these sorts of rules. And employee romance is not *always* a bad thing. Before we got married, my husband and I dated while working at the same company. Work is a place where many of us meet our life partners.

While it's impossible to legislate matters of the heart, you can put guardrails in place. Here is a basic articulation of a culture of consent:

> *It is the responsibility of the toucher to be aware of how the other person feels about being touched. If the other person doesn't want to be touched, don't touch. If there's any doubt, don't touch. If you don't know or aren't sure, don't touch. Get to know the person better. Learn how to tell, how to ask. If you're too drunk to know, don't touch. If you can't control yourself when you get that drunk, don't drink, especially at work.*

If you apply this rule to all the different ways that touch can manifest in the office, you'll have more productive relationships in your workplace, and fewer disasters.

This chapter will cover the different ways that touch can go wrong at work, how to try to prevent them from happening, and what to do if they happen despite your best efforts to avoid them.

ALCOHOL IN THE WORKPLACE

Ask ten people to think of a sexual encounter with a work colleague they later regretted. Now ask them if alcohol was involved. I bet you'll find that, nine times out of ten, it was. Perpetrators must still be held accountable for their actions. Blaming alcohol rather than the person is an unacceptable abdication of personal responsibility. But that doesn't mean it makes sense to booze it up on the job.

This section may seem strange to you if you are not familiar with the boozy workplace culture I experienced in finance and in tech. I spent most of my career in Silicon Valley, where there is a great deal of alcohol, and often drugs, in the office. The company chef at one place where I worked routinely made hash brownies. In the middle of another office where I worked was a bar stocked with high-end spirits and fine wine. Another place had regular lunchtime kegs. This kind of behavior, while shocking to some, is routine in many industries around the world.

It would be denial to say that alcohol in the workplace doesn't greatly increase the likelihood of everything from an unwanted, creepy hug to sexual violence. Serving alcohol at work or at work functions is undeniably risky—for the employees and for the company. I don't recommend it. But if you're going to do it anyway, here's how I recommend managing it.

PEOPLE HARMED

If this were a just world, you'd be able to pass out drunk and be safe. The first person who saw you would make sure you were OK, not rape you. If you get drunk, even blackout drunk, this does not give anyone the right to harm you. If you get blackout drunk and are raped, it is the fault of the person who harmed you, full stop.

But even if it's not your fault, you're still the one who gets hurt. So if you love to drink, and/or you work in a culture where drinking to excess is part of how people bond, it's a good idea to think explicitly about how you are going to manage the risks. Here is a cautionary tale and a way to think about managing the risks of drinking.

BE REALISTIC ABOUT YOUR PHYSICAL LIMITS

When I was working at the finance company early in my career, I flew to Ukraine to teach Sergei, the general director of a tank factory, how to write a business plan for U.S. investors. I thought I'd be meeting with Sergei and his deputy, but when I arrived, I walked into a whole roomful of men. Sergei had decided that about 30 people at the plant would benefit from understanding business plans. I was surprised to see them. But not as surprised as they were to see me.

"Sergei told us a big, bad *kapitalist* was coming to town!" one man exclaimed. "But you're just a little girl!"

Unfortunate sexism aside, the day went pretty well. When it was over, that same man said, "Well, we know you can write a *beeznees plan*. Now let's find out if you can drink vodka!"

They told me their tradition was that if you opened a bottle of vodka, you had to finish it. Like everyone else at the table, I had an open bottle of vodka placed next to my water glass. I was going to have to down the whole bottle! The scene in *Indiana Jones* where the woman drinks all the men under the table flashed in my mind and somehow convinced me I could match these men shot for shot. Never

BIAS   PREJUDICE   BULLYING   ⚡ DISCRIMINATION   HARASSMENT   PHYSICAL VIOLATIONS

mind that most of them were three times my weight. We started drinking with the appetizers. One bite of pickle, one shot of vodka.

As the dinner plates were being passed around, I felt that telltale tugging under my chin. I barely had time to think, *I am not the kind of person who would blow chunder at the dinner table*, before—*bam!*—I threw up on the plate of beef stroganoff that had just been set before me. Suddenly the room became still. Just as I thought I'd never recover from the humiliation, Sergei broke the silence by saying, "Shall we dance?"

A band was playing, and Sergei danced me around the restaurant while the waitstaff cleaned up my mess and brought me a new plate of food. Thankfully he wasn't a predator, he was an upstander. A waitress also brought me a small glass of kefir, a thick yogurt drink, to coat my stomach. Undeterred, I finished dinner—and my bottle of vodka.

Trying to match men three times my size shot for shot was a poor decision. That I weighed almost 200 pounds less than Sergei was not a sign of weakness. My weakness was giving in to some sort of macho BS that I had to finish that bottle of vodka. I was lucky that I didn't pay a higher price.

I never again succumbed to pressure to drink like that.

I'm not telling you that you should or shouldn't drink. That's your decision. But whatever you decide to do, understand the risks. You may think you're safe with people you work with, but people you know are statistically more risky than strangers. So it behooves you to plan.

If you go out drinking, go with people you trust and have some explicit agreement to keep an eye on one another. Make sure there's a designated driver who also plays the role of designated decider. That way, there's always a sober person to keep you, or at least deter you, from doing anything you'll regret deeply.

PEOPLE WHO CAUSE HARM

Drinking impairs your judgment, just as it impairs your ability to drive safely. Your friends may be able to take your car keys away, but they can't take your sex drive away. Can you trust yourself not to harm another person when you've been drinking?

Alcohol poses another risk as well. If the person you want to have sex with is drunk, the person may be too impaired to give consent. If you have sex anyway, in most jurisdictions you are committing rape. What's more, you may be too impaired to judge accurately whether the person has given consent or not. But you are still guilty if you push someone to have sex when the person is too drunk to give consent— just as you are still guilty of drunk driving even if your judgment was so impaired by alcohol that you drove despite your intoxication. So make a plan *before* you go out drinking for how you are going to manage all these risks.

If you're under 24, this is especially important. You're more likely to engage in risky behaviors, and that likelihood is more pronounced when you are with peers or friends.[1] Follow the advice of Rob Chesnut, chief ethics officer at Airbnb and author of *Intentional Integrity*. He warns employees before they get to work events where alcohol will be served, "If you wait to think about how much you are going to drink until you're at the party, you're in trouble. Know your limits and decide how many drinks you can have—one or two—before you go. The worst time to think about how much to drink in a work setting is . . . while you're drinking in a work setting."

LEADERS

LIMIT ALCOHOL IN THE OFFICE

Creating a culture of workplace partying is a recipe for everything from awkwardness to disaster. I would recommend not allowing alcohol in the workplace at all. Even workplaces that limit alcohol to special celebrations often find that bad things happen on these occasions.

If you do serve alcohol, remind people to drink responsibly. Don't worry about being the literal buzzkill. Nothing ruins a celebration like a drunk person assaulting a colleague or killing themselves or others in a preventable car accident.

BIAS   PREJUDICE   BULLYING   ⚡   DISCRIMINATION   HARASSMENT | PHYSICAL VIOLATIONS |

Confession: I love to drink. And I don't love to drink just one glass of wine. I love to get drunk. (Or at least I used to. Recently I quit.) I loved the heavy-drinking culture at many of the companies where I've worked. Looking back on it, though, I don't think the fun of those boozy office parties was even remotely worth the harm that was done by them. Low moments have included a rape, a suicide attempt, a marriage destroyed by unwanted sexual advances, and a drunk colleague getting hauled off to jail after punching a cop.

If you want to prevent these sorts of things from happening on your team, it is your job as a leader to calculate the benefits of alcohol as a social lubricant against the risks that too much of it can lead to seriously bad behavior.

Another important thing for leaders to know is that a heavy-drinking culture often creates a hostile work environment for underrepresented people, especially women. Vanessa Kaskiris, who worked in the IT department at Berkeley University, described "a culture where employees would go out drinking every night, which led to hostile treatment of women if they went, and ostracization if they didn't."[2]

Also, let's not forget people who don't drink, for whatever reason. For some, a work culture revolving around alcohol may be uncomfortable or religiously problematic. And if you have a person struggling with alcoholism, such a culture is more than insensitive; it's dangerous.

Leaders can avoid a lot of problems by not serving alcohol or making explicit rules around alcohol at the office. How stringent you make these rules is up to you. Here are some ways I've seen leaders discourage destructive drinking at office events:

- Don't serve alcohol.
- Serve alcohol but make sure people have to give a ticket to get a drink and give everyone only one or two tickets.
- Instruct bartenders to cut people off at two drinks.
- Let people drink as much as they want but issue warnings. You may think that these warnings are simply common sense, but people lose their common sense when they are drunk. So if you are serving alcohol at work, remind your employees of the following:

— Don't drink and drive.

— You are still accountable for the things you do, even when you're too drunk to know what you're doing. You can't read the signs of consent when you're drunk. And "I was too drunk to know what I was doing" is not an excuse for rape any more than it is for drunk driving.

— Getting drunk in the office or at office parties can be career limiting.

— Don't have sex with colleagues who are too drunk to give consent no matter where you are—that is rape.

You probably have better things to do than police your team's drinking. My advice? Keep it simple. Don't serve alcohol in the office.

INNOCENT HUGS VS. "INNOCENT" HUGS AND OTHER LOADED INTERACTIONS

A KICK IN THE PANTS

When one of my employees kicked another in the butt, he considered it a friendly sideswipe gesture. She found it obnoxious. Nobody, including the woman kicked, thought it was a federal case. But she wanted him to knock it off, and it was my job as the boss to make sure he did.

I'll admit that at first I wanted to let it slide. But I knew if I didn't sit down with each of them individually, a small thing could blow up into a huge problem. She had to feel safe, and he had to know not to do that again.

Happily, everything got resolved relatively easily. I told the man he had to apologize. I insisted that first he role-play his apology with me, to make sure he didn't offer the kind of "I'm sorry if you felt uncomfortable but I really didn't do anything wrong" non-apology that would just make things worse. When I talked to the woman, I asked

BIAS   PREJUDICE   BULLYING   ⚡   DISCRIMINATION   HARASSMENT | PHYSICAL VIOLATIONS |

her if she would prefer that he apologize to her directly or if she would rather that I be in the room. She chose the former.

He delivered the apology and promised never to do it again. She accepted the apology, and they worked well together for years after that. It took a couple of hours I could ill afford because I was busy, but I saved myself and the company time, money, and hassle in the long run. Imagine if I hadn't done anything, he'd kicked her again, and she'd sued. I would have failed to act, and she would have had a legitimate case. Rather than investing a couple of hours sorting out the problem, I might have created a 200-hour, expensive problem for myself and my company.

A HAND KISSED

I once was on the receiving end of a different kind of physical violation that also wasn't a federal case but still deserved some attention.

I was working at a large company. My team and I were teaching a leadership class to 500 salespeople. I'd been warned that Frank, the team's leader, had few women working for him and was known to pepper his speech with casually sexist comments.

Sure enough, when Frank introduced my two colleagues (both men), he shook their hands. When he got to me, I stuck my hand out for a shake, but Frank made an absurdly low bow, took my hand in both of his, and kissed it, holding the pose for a painfully long time and leaving the back of my hand damp with his saliva.

I felt singled out, and I believe that was his intention. He was making it clear to me and to everyone else in the room that women were not leaders, they were dance partners. Furthermore, he had no right to slobber on my hand if I didn't want my hand to be slobbered on.

After the meeting I took him aside and told him that his gesture had made me uncomfortable and suggested that in future he not kiss women's hands in a professional context.

"Oh, but surely you don't want me to treat you like a man!" he exclaimed with a mock-tragic expression.

"Yes, I do, actually."

The key point is that his default should have been to greet me in the same way he had the men—with a handshake. (Pre-Covid-19 world.)

This is a good rule of thumb. If you are a man in a professional setting and are inclined to touch a woman in any way, ask yourself, *Would I touch a man in the same way?* If the answer is no, then you are in a danger zone.

Had Frank simply acknowledged that he'd made me uncomfortable and apologized, we could have moved past it without another thought. It wasn't a big deal to me. But he made a big deal of it. He got angry and stomped off, as if it were up to him, not me, to decide how I should feel about his kiss onstage. When I told the VP of HR at our company what had happened, he brushed the whole incident off as if there were nothing he could do about it. This was one of several such incidents that caused me to leave that job.

FOR PEOPLE HARMED

Nobody has the right to touch you in a way that makes you uncomfortable. It's that simple. And yet from a young age we are often taught the opposite.

If you are getting touched in a way that feels creepy or inappropriate, or even if it just bugs you, you have the right to tell the person they have crossed a line and must knock it off. *You* are the *only* arbiter of what sort of touch is OK for you. "I am not a hugger" is a perfectly acceptable thing to say. So is "I would rather fist-bump/ bow/whatever than shake hands." This will be even easier to assert in the post-Covid-19 world. "I am a germophobe" is a more acceptable reason to ask others to keep their distance than it ever was.

If the person is dismissive and defensive and doesn't stop, the person is bullying or even harassing you. Try a "you" statement. "You need to stop trying to hug me." Create a consequence. In the case of Frank the hand kisser, I could have made a face and wiped my slobbered-on hand on my pants, showing how I felt and making him look ridiculous in front of everyone. You can decide if you want to take your complaint to HR or a boss.

Why is it that the simplest and fairest outcome—that if you report an inappropriate touch, your boss just takes the person aside and tells them to knock it off or face consequences—feels like such a long shot? Maybe you're thinking, *Why is it my job to teach people not to behave in obviously obnoxious ways? I want to be left alone to Just Work.*

I'd like to recommend a systematic approach to deciding how to respond. Run through your options described in chapter 7, consider each, and make a conscious decision.

- Document
- Find solidarity
- Figure out where the exits are
- Consider a direct conversation with the person who caused you harm
- Consider talking to HR

Regardless of what you decide, be kind to yourself. If it bothered you, you have a right to be bothered. You weren't imagining it, and you weren't asking for it.

You may be combating a lifetime of people expecting you to let them touch you. Like many people, I was brought up being told I had to hug and kiss relatives, even ones I barely knew, at family gatherings.[3] Indeed, the hand kiss at work was horrible in part because it dredged up memories of a great-great-aunt who used to greet me with a big wet kiss every time I saw her. She was a wealthy matriarch, and if she wanted to lick people, she damn well would. Recently I asked my father why nobody ever asked my great aunt not to lick the family. Like me, he shuddered at the memory of her kisses. "I don't know who would have had the courage to do that," he admitted. The children, if we let them, that's who. Not long after, at a family gathering, I found myself pressuring my daughter to go hug a relative. She said, "I don't want to hug someone I barely know!" She was right. I told her so, insisting she did have to greet the person politely, but she didn't have to be touched.

FOR UPSTANDERS

Five hundred people witnessed Frank drool on my hand after he shook the men's hands onstage. Even if some of them thought that behavior was OK, I'd be willing to bet at least 400 of them thought that it was off. Even more unsettling than his saliva on my hand was that out of 500 people watching this happen, no one said *anything*. If just one person had come up to me and said "Ugh" or "Well, that was awkward!," it would have made a world of difference. If you see something, say something.

FOR PEOPLE WHO CAUSE HARM

If someone doesn't want to be touched, don't touch. It's pretty simple. Read the social cues. If you can't read the social cues, default to no touching.

This is especially true in the post-Covid-19 world. The handshake, that formerly ubiquitous greeting at work, will feel deeply uncomfortable to many. You may feel differently, but you don't have a right to impose your handshake preferences on others. It's also true, though for different reasons, of professional touch between the sexes. If you're about to touch a woman in a way that is different from how you'd touch a man in a professional context, the odds are high that you're about to touch her in a way she won't welcome.

If you're not a mind reader—and who is?—asking out loud is a reasonable thing to do: "Hug, handshake, fist bump, elbow bump, toe tap, or a smile?" Err on the side of caution—a smile from six feet away. I know that can feel strange. But it's even harder for the person you're touching to say, "Don't touch me!" or "I'm a germophobe!" If you are the toucher, you are initiating this contact, so it's your responsibility to deal with the awkwardness. Figuring out how to do this, through words and gestures, in a way that doesn't put too much pressure on the other person will require some effort on your part.

BIAS   PREJUDICE   BULLYING   ⚡   DISCRIMINATION   HARASSMENT   PHYSICAL VIOLATIONS

Once when I stuck my hand out to a man I was meeting with, offering a "nice to meet you" handshake, I noticed he looked extremely uncomfortable. I pulled my hand back and said, "Do you have a cold? I always appreciate it when people don't shake hands when they are sick."

"Actually, I never shake anyone's hand," he said. "My religion forbids me from touching a woman who is not my wife."

"Oh, I see. I am sorry if I put you in an uncomfortable situation."[4]

"No, thank you for giving me a chance to explain. I never know what to say."

"Actually, I wish *nobody* shook hands. Especially during flu season. It just spreads germs. It's really kind of a gross habit."

He laughed, and we talked about how this handshake thing happened to him every single day, usually more than once. Together, we came up with a line he could use quickly: "I'm very glad to see you but I don't shake hands because of a religious belief."

DON'T OVERGENERALIZE

Avoid applying generalizations to specific individuals—otherwise known as stereotyping or essentializing. This muddles your ability to understand things clearly, to respect individuality. You may have heard that Italians are more comfortable touching one another than Americans, but that doesn't mean you can kiss someone on the cheek three times just because the person has an Italian last name.

WHAT ABOUT HUGS?

Is it better to just say, *No hugs*? Many of us long for simple, clear-cut rules: *Here is the line: step over it once, this will happen; step over it twice, that will happen.* But many people, myself certainly included, would recoil from the idea of living in such a cut-and-dried world. There'd be so many exceptions that the rules would quickly become meaningless. What if someone at work gets a phone call and learns that a family member has died? Can you hug the person at that moment? Or if a person is going through a medical crisis and breaks down in tears of pain at work, surely a hug might be in order? Or if someone is just having a crappy day? Do any of us want a book of rules and regulations to govern these sorts of situations? I don't think so.

I propose this instead. Think about times when you've hugged people, when the hug was welcome and when it wasn't, and how they reacted. One person's smile might indicate your hug is welcome. Another's smile might reflect discomfort. If you're not sure what a person's smile means, you can always express sympathy and ask, "I'm so sorry X happened to you—would you like a hug?" If you feel too awkward to even ask the question, that's probably a sign that verbal sympathy would be better. If you're paying attention to the other person and not expecting the person to conform to your preconceived notions of how others "should" act, you'll most likely make the right choices. If you are open to feedback when you get it wrong, you'll learn quickly. If you ignore the feedback and instead insist that everyone should assume you have good intentions so nothing you do could possibly be wrong, you're going to misstep. Admitting to yourself when you've gotten this wrong is hard and takes some courage.

BE AWARE OF YOUR POWER

Henry Kissinger famously said, "Power is the ultimate aphrodisiac." In my experience, what this means is not that powerful people are more sexy than less powerful people. It means they *think* they are sexier. Which they are not.

Studies have shown that power makes people more likely to think about sex, to be sexually attracted to those around them, and to demonstrate disinhibited sexual behavior.[5] But it doesn't mean those feelings are reciprocated by the less powerful people around them. This is a big problem because having power makes people more likely to touch others, whether or not the others want to be touched.[6]

So if you are in a position of authority, remind yourself that every promotion puts you into a higher-risk group for getting in trouble around touch. Whatever you tell your people about being mindful of others goes double for you. Keep in mind that an unwanted hug from a superior will

BIAS   PREJUDICE   BULLYING   ⚡   DISCRIMINATION   HARASSMENT | PHYSICAL VIOLATIONS |

likely kick up a much bigger problem than one between two people with no power over each other—and that it's more likely to happen.

FOR LEADERS

You can help prevent physical violations by creating and enforcing *a culture of consent*. The lessons people learn from relatively minor violations can prevent a serious one. Come up with rules that are clear-cut but also respect that the workplace is an adult setting where good judgment is expected.

OVERCOMMUNICATE YOUR CULTURE OF CONSENT AND CODE OF CONDUCT

For a whole host of reasons it's tempting not to talk about consent at work. One, it can feel embarrassing. Two, it doesn't seem as if it ought to be necessary. Isn't it obvious? No, it's not obvious. Yes, it is embarrassing. Pushing through the discomfort is one of the many things leaders get paid to do. Establishing a culture of consent to avoid "little" violations can help prevent way bigger/worse violations down the road.

MAKE IT SAFE AND EASY TO REPORT VIOLATIONS

No matter how well articulated your culture of consent is, it's not going to prevent violations from happening. You can plaster every available surface of your organization with your policy on consent, and some people will still touch others in a creepy way. Some people will only learn what consent means by getting it wrong. That means as a leader you must do everything in your power to make it as safe and easy as possible for people to report inappropriate touching.

GIVE PEOPLE A CHANCE TO LEARN, BUT NOT TOO MANY CHANCES

If there are multiple complaints of unwanted—or lingering or too-tight—hugs and if the person doesn't seem to be changing behavior despite clear feedback, it is probably time to think about firing that person.

There's no hard-and-fast rule that I believe will be fair in all cases. You and your managers are going to have to investigate and make some hard calls. That's what managers do. They create systems that make it safe for people to speak truth to power. Then they listen to that truth, and to conflicting "truths." They learn the facts. They use their judgment to interpret them. They confront people who need to be confronted. They tell people what's expected of them and help explain to them how to get there. If you have otherwise good employees who are underperforming in one area, you, as a manager, know it's your responsibility to help them raise their game.

Establish a transparent process to ensure fairness—so that one manager is not making a unilateral decision. Just as promotion and hiring decisions are better made by a small team than one individual, so it is with these calls. When managers are on a team that debates important decisions, they are forced to ask others to question their judgment.

Even well-intentioned people will make mistakes. Talk to offenders compassionately but firmly. Communicate that you understand that mistakes are inevitable, and also that you will hold people accountable for their mistakes. Holding people accountable doesn't mean harsh punishment. But it does mean that there must be a shared understanding of the mistake and a clear commitment to not repeating it. If people make a mistake and are called on it, require them to demonstrate active listening so that you know they got it. Ask them to apologize without defensiveness. Help them notice that the person who shared the discomfort with the touch was offering feedback—that they should recognize that as a gift. But also let them know that you'll be paying attention. And if the behavior persists, if they continue to be the object of complaints, or if they retaliate, they will be fired. Because unwanted touching is not so innocent when it happens repeatedly: in addition to potentially being sexual assault, it can be an act of bullying. People will stop bullying behavior only if they know there will be real consequences.

Here's a policy you might put in place:

BIAS   PREJUDICE   BULLYING   ⚡   DISCRIMINATION   HARASSMENT   PHYSICAL VIOLATIONS

You do not have a right to touch anyone ever in any way. You have
a responsibility to be aware of whether the other person wants to
be touched before touching them or the like.

Simple and straightforward, right? Maybe, but you'll get a lot of objections. Here's a quick FAQ:

Q: Don't you think that a world without hugs would be a cold, cold world?
A: I didn't say no hugging. I just said no hugging people who don't want to be hugged.
Q: But how could I possibly know if the person wants to be hugged?
A: Try asking. "Is it OK if I give you a hug?" You may like hugs, but the other person may not. Pay attention to the other person's body language. It's not usually too hard to figure out. If people's arms are crossed, if they look uncomfortable, back off.
Q: This is just too complicated. There should just be a no-hugging rule at work and zero tolerance for any violation.
A: Human behavior has rarely been successfully governed by simple absolute policies like a "no touch" rule. Sometimes a hug at work is really welcome.

REGRETTED SEX IN THE WORKPLACE

What happens when two people who work together have a genuinely consensual hookup and then one or both of them regret it in the morning—or after a week or a month?

Here's an example that was bad for all parties involved. Shortly after I took a job leading a big team, I heard a door slam violently in a nearby conference room. Violently enough that I stopped what I was doing and went over to find out what was going on. When I opened the just-slammed door, I saw a roomful of uncomfortable people.

"Everything OK in here?" I asked.

"Oh, sure, everything's fine," everyone agreed, nodding furiously.

"What was that door slam about? That didn't sound fine." I noticed Bernice, one of the few women in the room, looked pale.

"Oh, no big deal," said several people simultaneously.

"Well, what was the little deal?" I asked.

"Jimmy, he's just going through a hard time."

"Anything I can do to help? Should I talk to him?"

"No, no, no, no, no, no. Really, no big deal."

Turned out that Jimmy and Bernice had hooked up a few times, and then Bernice started dating someone else. Jimmy's heart was broken. "Bernice was the first girlfriend Jimmy ever had," one person on the team told me later. "Or sorta girlfriend. Anyway, she was his first." After the breakup, Jimmy was hurt and angry.

If Bernice opened her mouth in a meeting, Jimmy was apt to interrupt her with a sarcastic comment; and if she persisted, he stormed out of the room, often in tears. I understood that Jimmy was having a rough time, but his behavior was immature and hostile. Most of his fellow team members didn't think about it that way, though. His hurt-puppy act had earned their sympathy and they gave him a pass. But when heartbreak expresses itself in abusive behavior, the situation sometimes becomes violent. It's a red flag.

I had taken that job to build a business, not to be a relationship counselor—or, worse, a breakup counselor. But if I was going to get the team back on track, I was going to have to intervene.

The consensus on the team was that Bernice had to go—either to a different company or to a different part of our company. I had a completely different view. Bernice was handling a difficult situation well; Jimmy was behaving in a way that disrupted the team's efforts. It seemed to me that Bernice was on the wrong end of two different biases: sympathy and gender. Sympathy bias: poor Jimmy and his broken heart.[7] Gender bias: bitchy Bernice, dumping one guy, jumping to another. (Flip the story and Jimmy is a virile stud, Bernice a needy woman unable to get a grip on her emotions.)

Clearly the hookup had been ill-advised for both of them, and it was for the best that they not work together. But as for who should go, I didn't think that Bernice, who was behaving professionally in the

BIAS PREJUDICE BULLYING ⚡ DISCRIMINATION HARASSMENT PHYSICAL VIOLATIONS

wake of a difficult situation, should be the one penalized. If one of them worked for the other, then it should be the boss who found a new team. But they were peers.

I had a couple of conversations with Jimmy, shared some stories of my own experiences with a broken heart and the things that had helped me mend. I asked if a couple of weeks extra vacation might be useful, or if there was anything else I could do to help. But I also told him that if he couldn't handle working alongside Bernice, he was going to have to find another team. It was his behavior that was disruptive, not hers.

Breaking up at work is especially hard—for the two people involved, for the people around them, and for their manager(s). But it's going to happen. So let's talk about how to deal with it in a way that is fair to everyone and minimally disruptive.

PERSON HARMED AND PERSON CAUSING HARM

My first advice about casual hookups with colleagues is the same as drinking in the office: don't do it. If you fall in love, that's something different. It's probably worth risking your job for true love. But a fling with someone you're going to have to keep seeing day after day at work offers so many potential problems that it's best avoided.

Of course, things happen. If you hook up with a colleague, and then one or both of you regret it, first let me say I'm sorry. It's a difficult and painful situation to find yourself in.

But you're not a teenager anymore. You have to act like a grown-up. In the story above, Jimmy's heart had been broken, but he was behaving in a way calculated to make Bernice miserable and to be maximally disruptive to the whole team. That wasn't OK.

Here are some guidelines:

- If you are the manager of the person you got sexually or romantically involved with, or if you are significantly more senior in the organization, you have abused your power. You are the one who should get a different job.
- If the other person no longer wants to be romantically involved and you keep pressuring that person to resume, you are violating

the rule of consent. You are the one who should get a different job.

- If you can't contain your emotions and are disrupting the team, you are the one who should get a different job.
- If you regularly hook up with people in the office, you should take the steps necessary to break this destructive pattern. Now.

UPSTANDER

Nobody wants to be in the middle of someone else's romantic entanglement, especially at work. But pretending problems aren't happening never helps to solve them. Again, if you see something, say something. If you notice one person treating another cruelly or disrespectfully, say something. If you hear folks making biased comments about one of the two people in the romance, say something. If the dynamic is disruptive, say something.

Sometimes a problem arises not between the two people who had a fling but in the rest of the team. The other men now treat the woman as though she is "fair game." They form a sort of "competition pod" around her as though they are fighting for "whose turn" it is next. It becomes uncomfortable for her to come into the office. Needless to say, this is bad behavior. Just because she dated one man on the team does not mean she is interested in any of the other men. If you notice this sort of thing happening, say something.

LEADER

People spend most of their waking hours at their jobs. It's unreasonable to adopt a zero-tolerance approach to relationships at work. But for reasons already discussed, such relationships do need to be managed. You can't have a free-for-all in your office if you want to get sh*t done.

Here are some simple suggestions:

1. *Put in place a "No sex, physical intimacy, or dating in your chain of command" rule.*

BIAS   PREJUDICE   BULLYING   ⚡   DISCRIMINATION   HARASSMENT | PHYSICAL VIOLATIONS |

You can use a euphemism such as *no fraternization* if you must, but make sure people understand what you mean. In other words, bosses who have sex or sexual intimacy with or date their employees—or the employees of their employees—must be terminated.

When people violate this rule, which they inevitably will, the more senior person is the one who must leave a job, not the more junior person. To be just and also to prevent undesirable behavior from powerful people, the rule must protect the less powerful. If executives do not create any penalties for senior leaders who date more junior employees but instead push all the penalties onto the more junior people, at least some of these powerful people will keep having sexual encounters with the less powerful.

The most senior leaders at a company—the direct reports of the CEO and *their* direct reports—should not date or have romantic or physical involvements with *anyone* at the company. The theory behind this policy is that at a certain level of seniority a person has so much authority that sexual advances or relationships risk feeling coercive and/or abusive. That's bad for the person coerced, and it also creates unnecessary financial risk for the company and a dysfunctional dynamic on a team that can make it hard to get sh*t done.

2. *Consider an explicit "No sex or physical intimacy in the workplace" rule.*

You might assume that this is common sense and does not require a rule. Who has sex in the office or on the factory floor, anyway? Quite a few people, as it turns out. I have observed "sex in the office" problems several times throughout my career. Especially if you have a lot of young employees, you may want to consider making this rule explicit and known.

3. *Don't (wink, wink, nudge, nudge) undermine those rules by tacitly encouraging hookups.*

This seems obvious, right? Yet over and over again I've seen leaders encouraging their employees to hook up.

I myself did this inadvertently. Trying to adopt a casual atmosphere,

I turned a conference room into a "team cozy" with couches and beanbag chairs instead of a conference table and chairs. One morning I came into a staff meeting to find a bra and a pair of boxer shorts in the folds of a couch. I got rid of the couches and beanbag chairs. I also told the whole team why I'd done it.

Later, I worked at another company that had a conference room that felt designed for hookups: low lights, lots of fabric with kind of a tentlike feel, no windows, and a nook with a couple of bottles of whiskey in it. I was like a broken record, agitating for the leadership to change that decor. They didn't do it until *after* sexual misconduct occurred there.

    4. *Forgive mistakes, create consequences for patterns.*

If a person on your team repeatedly hooks up with people in the office, there should be real consequences for that person, up to and including being fired.

ABUSE-OF-POWER RELATIONSHIPS IN THE WORKPLACE

Sometimes people at work fall in love. They may move in together or get married or have children or all three. As I wrote at the beginning of this chapter, my husband and I worked at the same company together before and after we got married. It had no impact on our teams or the company or our relationship. We worked on different teams and were more or less at the same level in the hierarchy. I had no power over him; he had no power over me. It was all good.

However, things can go badly wrong when one person in the romance is the boss of the other or considerably more senior in the organization.

Meg was a contracts manager at her company. She started dating her boss's boss's boss. As the relationship got more serious, they decided to have a child together. She got pregnant and everyone knew

BIAS   PREJUDICE   BULLYING   ⚡   DISCRIMINATION   HARASSMENT | PHYSICAL VIOLATIONS |

who the father was. The company had the kind of "No dating in your chain of command" rule described above. But it hadn't mandated that it was the more senior person who should leave. When the relationship became publicly known, management told Meg she should find a new role. Nobody at the company suggested that the man, who was more senior, should be the one to get a different role. To some, this seemed "natural." He was an executive overseeing a specialized department. It wasn't as though he could suddenly become an executive over another function of the company where he didn't have expertise.

But the same was true for her. She also had expertise in that function that didn't translate to another department. And she was in a more vulnerable situation, being earlier in her career. Also, she had recently given birth to their son. When she left her department and tried a new job in a different function that she didn't have expertise in, the combination of a new job and a new baby was difficult. She performed at expectations, whereas she had consistently exceeded expectations before. She felt she wasn't doing her best work, and she felt bad about it. Then, her son had some health issues that required a lot of time away from the office.

The man she was dating, the father of her child, encouraged her to quit. From her perspective, this meant leaving a lot of stock options on the table. She had joined the company early and the company's rise was meteoric, so she was walking away from quite a lot of money. It was a lot of money to her, anyway. To him, it was chump change. He'd made hundreds of millions. She understood that he'd support her and their child so she could focus on her son's health issues. Not long after she quit her job, however, the executive left her and the child, declining to pay child support until she sued him.

This was not a physically abusive relationship, but a relationship in which one person had more power than the other and abused it. It was an abuse-of-power relationship. She was pushed out of a job she loved into one she wasn't trained to do, then encouraged to leave the company. As a result of this relationship, she walked away from stock options that would have helped her raise her son. Her partner lost nothing financially.

When people hear stories like this, they often shrug and say, "It's too bad, but that's just the way things are." The way the "chain of command" rule played out for Meg—that she, the less powerful person, had to change jobs—is a form of abuse that is tolerated at most companies, as it is in society at large. But it certainly doesn't have to be that way. If the rule had been that *he* had to quit, he probably wouldn't have started the relationship in the first place.

Yes, losing him would have hurt the company. But keeping him at the company was also terrible for the company's culture. Think of the message sent to all the less powerful people there: *Leaders can behave as they please, whereas you are disposable.* This company spawned many abusive relationships, and several of them hit the press in a significant way that ultimately caused more damage to the company than his departure would have. Institutional Betrayal harms victims in the short run, and in the long run it harms the institution, often dramatically.

If we are going to create an environment of Just Work, we must change our conception of what happens when rules like this get broken. Otherwise, the rules cease to have any meaning. The result is that the less powerful get harmed, and the more powerful get off scot-free until things become so bad that the company is forced to change.

The good news is that there are signs that the norms are changing around work, power, and sex. The executive who dated Meg eventually left his job after it came out that he had dated multiple women at the company. Before #MeToo, that would have been inconceivable. The bad news is that he had abuse-of-power relationships with several other women before that happened.

PEOPLE HARMED

I'm going to tell two personal stories. I'm telling them because of all the confusion about what constitutes an abusive relationship. Just because you're a strong, independent person doesn't mean you're not in an abusive relationship. And the corollary is also true: just because you are in an abusive relationship doesn't mean you're not a strong, independent person.

I once worked for a man whom I considered not just a boss but a real mentor. After I quit working for him we kept in touch. I had met

BIAS   PREJUDICE   BULLYING   ⚡ DISCRIMINATION   HARASSMENT   PHYSICAL VIOLATIONS

the woman he lived with a couple of times; they were clearly still deeply in love a decade into their relationship. When she died shortly after I quit working for him, he was devastated. He invited me on a boating expedition. As the afternoon wore on, he suddenly reached out to hold my hand in a way that made what he wanted unmistakable. I was shocked he'd been so bold but even more dumbfounded to find myself attracted to him.

Before that moment, I'd been planning to go back and work for him after earning my MBA. Once I allowed him to take my hand, though, I knew that was off the table. I'd learned the hard way about the perils of dating your boss. I wasn't going to make *that* mistake again. If we slept together, I couldn't go back to work for him as planned.

That was the first bit of abuse in the relationship. He didn't intend it, but he also chose not to notice the problem inherent in the logic of the situation: I couldn't take a job I'd intended to take, a job he wanted me to take. This story reveals a dynamic that plays out over and over: a bad power dynamic can introduce abuse into a relationship—even when there is consent.

I am not saying a relationship between two people where there is a power imbalance (age, money, status, etc.) is impossible. But it's only healthy if both parties—particularly the one with more power—acknowledge the situation and take active measures to address it. If you're the less powerful one, the burden shouldn't mostly be on you.

That's not the way my relationship with this man played out. When we bumped into his more famous friends, he would not introduce me. I'd be left standing there like a pet he was slightly ashamed of and hoped nobody would notice.

When he decided he wanted to buy an apartment where we would live together, he gave me no say in where we'd live. I said of one apartment we looked at, "I could never live here." The next day he made an offer on it. He didn't get it, so things didn't come to a head. He wound up buying the apartment I liked best, which he claimed was for me. I knew that was BS, but I didn't pay enough attention to the warning signs. I moved in.

He never once referred to the apartment as "ours." It was his. I just lived there. Sometimes when he had dinner parties, he would ask me to make myself scarce. Once I came home at the appointed hour and I heard the guests were still there. Knowing he'd be angry if I entered the apartment where I supposedly lived, I waited in the building's stairwell for them to leave. When I confronted him, he acted as though I were being ridiculous. Of course, I could've come in. Gaslighting.

Trying to address my feeling of not belonging in the place where I was living, I told him I wanted him to start using the pronoun "we" when it came to important decisions. Thinking he was clever, he spelled out "we" in diamonds and put it on a chain for me. Not amused, I told him he should treat me like a senator—no gifts over $25. He bought me an expensive painting. I returned it to the gallery and asked them to refund him. We got in a fight, and he exclaimed, "I can barely control you!"

"You can't control me," I countered. But as soon as I said the words, I realized that he was, in fact, controlling me, in numerous subtle and not-so-subtle ways.

I knew that I had to leave him to regain my sense of dignity and live the life I wanted, but years passed. Because he wasn't physically abusive, I continually downplayed the ways in which he repeatedly used his wealth and position in the world to put me into degrading, harmful situations.

Even now, I can't fully explain why I was so stuck. But I can identify the things that did help me get unstuck. Help from unexpected sources got me out.

A friend asked me a good question: "Ya seem like the kind of woman who gets what she wants. Why do you feel so helpless in this situation?" When he said that I was the kind of woman who gets what she wants, he said it with real admiration. Too often people criticize women and praise men for getting what they want. This was important: he was reminding me that I had a right to try to get what I wanted. I think behind an awful lot of abuse is an expectation that women "should" not expect to get what we want or need.

I did succeed in getting out—with a little help. One of my bosses asked me an insightful question. He and I were taking the train from DC to

BIAS PREJUDICE BULLYING ⚡ DISCRIMINATION HARASSMENT | PHYSICAL VIOLATIONS |

New York City for a business meeting. When I opened the newspaper, I read that the man I was dating had been invited by a member of the cabinet, probably the most powerful woman in the world at the time, to the holiday party at the White House. Like anyone who finds out the person they are dating is going out with someone else, I felt a gut punch.

My boss knew about my relationship with this man, so he understood at least part of why I looked so upset. Rather than pretending that nothing was wrong, as many in his position would do, he was courageous enough to say he was sorry—and also to ask me a question, quoting Sheryl Crow: "If it makes you happy, then why the hell are you so sad?" This was a great question about that relationship, and it moved me toward the door.

A couple years later, I still hadn't managed to get out of the door, however. When I mentioned to one of my employees that I wanted to get a dog but that the man I was living with wouldn't allow it, my employee insisted that I get the dog anyway: it would be my dog in the office, and he would take the dog home with him at night. This was an extraordinarily generous offer, and I felt more than a little sheepish about it, but I agreed. Naturally, once I got the puppy, I brought her home after work. This was a big part of the reason I finally moved out of that apartment and got my own place. *Still*, the relationship continued, even though we were no longer cohabitating.

After my start-up failed, I bumped into a colleague of mine whom I'd worked with earlier in my career. In our brief conversation, he noticed I was struggling. We didn't know each other that well, but he invited me out for a burger. Over dinner he suggested that perhaps a new job would help me regain my footing and encouraged me to interview for a job at his company. I felt a little awkward—he was offering help, and it felt a little like charity. I remembered my mentor's suggestion about asking for help, though, and I accepted the offer.

Going through that interview process prompted me to call a friend from business school for advice. She had something better than advice. She invited me to come interview for a great job 3,000 miles away from this man. I'm not sure I would have been able to break free without that much distance between us.

Getting out of an abusive relationship is hard. Not everyone has a contact who can offer them a new start in a new place: I recognize that I was both extremely lucky and privileged. But my point is this. Don't hide your situation from others; the more your friends recognize what is going on, the more they will try to help you, and small steps will lead to bigger ones: an office dog translates into a new apartment; a burger results in an interview, which leads to a phone call, which prompts a much bigger move. Accept help when others offer it. Let people who care about you help you *get out*!

The brazenness with which the powerful will abuse their power never ceases to amaze me, but I have gotten more skilled at dealing with it.

Later in my career, after I was happily married with children, a mentor who was a legend in Silicon Valley volunteered to help me out on a project analyzing how the tech industry was evolving. I'd just started a new job. Bringing him on board—a man with one of the most strategic minds in the industry—boosted my credibility enormously.

We met every other week. After several months had passed, he invited me and my family to spend a long weekend with him and his wife at their beach house. Then, two days before we were to arrive, he announced that he was physically attracted to me. That was why he'd been helping me. Some have said I "should" have known, but that's victim-blaming BS. I was caught completely off guard.

I was not even remotely attracted to this man. More important, I loved my husband, and nothing was more important to me than my family. I made this clear to my mentor. He accepted what I said but insisted that it would be awkward if we didn't show up for the weekend—his wife had already bought all the food.

For a moment, I'm ashamed to say, I wavered. I wasn't so worried about the food, but what would I say to my husband? Telling one's spouse you have to cancel plans with another couple because you've been propositioned is not something anyone relishes doing. And there was also my reputation at work. How was I going to tell my new colleagues that the Silicon Valley legend I'd been getting advice from was suddenly off the project? Credibility would turn to scorn pretty quickly there. My mentor knew all this and thought he could persuade me to

BIAS   PREJUDICE   BULLYING   ⚡   DISCRIMINATION   HARASSMENT   [PHYSICAL VIOLATIONS]

pretend nothing had happened so he could enjoy a game of cat and mouse with me at his beach house.

But at this point I could imagine all too clearly what would happen if we went to the beach house. It would be creepy, awkward, and miserable, and I would feel sullied by playing along with this ugly game. Experience had taught me that it was out of the question.

It took me about 12 hours to work up my nerve to tell my husband what had happened. I need not have felt such dread. The first thing he did was to give me a giant hug and say, "I'm so sorry. That is so, so disappointing. I thought he was the exception." Which was exactly how I felt. I had believed that my mentor was the exception to what seemed to be the rule of tech execs who abused their power. My husband and I made up a lame excuse for not going to the beach house for the weekend. I never met with my mentor again.

WHEN YOU ARE THE ABUSER

As hard as it is to recognize it when you are being abused, it may be even harder to recognize it when you're abusing someone else. Especially if you love this person. It may not be your *intention* to abuse your power—it may be the logic of the situation, logic that you may be unaware of because your power or your wealth or your privilege insulates you from facts that seem obvious to people in different circumstances. But ignorance is no excuse. It is your job to be aware of the impact you have on others, especially if you care about those people.

For example, Nina, a friend of mine, asked Stanley, an executive at her company, to endorse her for a promotion. He admired her work and agreed readily. A couple of days later, Stanley asked Nina out on a date. She wasn't in his chain of command, so technically he wasn't violating any HR rules. But given that he was writing in support of her promotion, he did have some power over her. And she simply wasn't interested. After she politely declined, she called me, worried that he would withdraw his support for her promotion.

I knew Stanley reasonably well. I doubt it ever occurred to him that he had put Nina in an awkward position by asking her out. But it *should* have. If he was smart enough to become an executive at a major tech company, he was smart enough to figure out this dynamic. But he didn't because he didn't think through the implications of his actions. In these situations ignorance, willful or not, obliviousness, cluelessness, or bumbling is no excuse.[8] If he'd taken just a moment to think about it—and all overtures of this nature in the workplace deserve that moment—he would have realized this was not the time to ask her out.

A wealthy friend of mine, on the other hand, explicitly acknowledged this sort of power imbalance in his prenuptial agreement: he gave his fiancée a large sum of money, no strings attached. She could leave him for another man even before they got married and she'd still get the money. He never wanted her to feel controlled by his wealth.

Here are a few guidelines to help you avoid becoming the abuser.

1. Don't get romantically involved with people who work for you or with people who are significantly junior to you in an organization. Don't flirt with them, don't allow them to flirt with you, don't ask them out on dates, don't touch them in a sexual or flirty way, at all, ever.
2. If you begin to have romantic feelings for someone who works for you, ask yourself this question: Would you be willing to give up your job to pursue this relationship? If so, by all means, quit your job and ask the person out. If not, exercise the executive function that got you into this role in the first place to manage your own behavior. Do not announce your feelings and then expect the other person to clean up the situation you just created.
3. If you break the above rules and wind up romantically involved with someone who works for you or is junior to you, it's time for *you* to find a new job. Don't expect or allow this person to sacrifice a career for yours. The all-too-common but flawed logic of such situations is that the junior person is the one who changes departments or gives up their job. After all, you have the "bigger" job. But the person's career is just as important to the person as yours is to you. And, the person can *less* afford a career derailment, being the more junior with fewer resources.

BIAS   PREJUDICE   BULLYING   ⚡   DISCRIMINATION   HARASSMENT   [PHYSICAL VIOLATIONS]

LEADERS

When you read the job description for your role, it probably didn't mention that you should prevent abusive romantic relationships from harming your team's productivity. However, if you as a leader don't give some thought to preventing this from happening, it probably will happen.

Here are some preventative steps you can take, and some suggestions for what to do when prevention fails.

1. Lead by example. Don't get romantically involved with the people at your company.
2. Make sure everyone understands the "no sex or dating within a chain of command" rule described above.
3. Enforce the rule. This may mean letting go of some managers who are getting results. It's painful, but you've got to do it if you want to come down on the side of Institutional Courage and not Institutional Betrayal. As I was writing this book in the fall of 2019, the board of directors of McDonald's fired the CEO when it emerged that he'd been sexting with an employee, despite that under his watch the company's share price had doubled.[9]
4. Leaders must disclose past relationships. After it was alleged that the McDonald's CEO did not disclose relationships he was having with three other employees, in addition to the one that got him fired, McDonald's sued him to get back the severance it had paid him.[10] Once a board member of a company I led recommended I hire someone without disclosing that he used to date her. I then discovered this in a way that was awkward for everyone. I wished he'd disclosed this information when he recommended I hire her.
5. Don't create environments in which unequal relationships can thrive. One venture capital firm in Silicon Valley used to host two parties every holiday season: one for the wives and one for the mistresses. (There were no women partners, no gay

partners.) Don't be surprised when your culture goes toxic in a damaging public way if you do things like that.

6. Educate yourself. If you are not sure what constitutes an abusive relationship, here's a simple definition: one person has power over another and uses that power to control or coerce the other to do things the person doesn't want to do.

SEXUAL ASSAULT IN THE WORKPLACE

INSTITUTIONAL BETRAYAL

As #MeToo has revealed, sexual assault happens in the workplace with horrifying frequency. One out of six women is the victim of rape or attempted rape. Twelve percent of sexual assaults occur while the victim is working.[11] Rape at work happens all the time. I once worked at a company where a sham investigation into a rape in the office caused me to quit working there. Since that time, I've given a lot of thought to ways I could have been a better upstander, and also to how leaders can manage this kind of horrible event when it happens on their watch.

As noted by psychologist Jennifer Freyd, "How we respond to disclosures of violence is crucial. A bad response to a sexual violence disclosure often exacerbates the damage . . . A bad response from an institution is Institutional Betrayal."[12] Freyd offers several practical tools for upstanders and leaders to be truly helpful listeners, to investigate the crimes in a way that is fair to everyone.[13]

The response of one company where I worked can only be characterized as Institutional Betrayal. Many factors contributed to this outcome, but I will focus on two: the way that rape myths silence us all and the absence of a culture of consent.

Rape Myths Silence Us All[14]

A moment in the investigation of this rape, which happened in the office at an office party, taught me a lot about why these kinds of

BIAS   PREJUDICE   BULLYING   ⚡   DISCRIMINATION   HARASSMENT   [PHYSICAL VIOLATIONS]

investigations so often go off the rails. I was uncomfortable with the way the investigation had played out. The man who was accused of raping the woman had told me point-blank that he'd had sex with her but that she'd been too drunk to remember clearly what had happened. The lawyer in charge of the investigation knew this. Yet he had not directed the woman doing the investigation to speak with me.

When I raised this point with the lawyer, he implied that I "shouldn't" have spoken with the man in question. Legal gaslighting. Then, the lawyer took me through the details of the case. The woman, it emerged, had not behaved in the way he imagined a rape victim "should" behave. He said, "I can't understand it. Why wouldn't she fight or scream?"

I didn't know then how common it is for victims not to resist when they are being sexually violated. But I didn't need to be an expert not to buy into this rape myth that victims fight off the perpetrator, screaming and yelling as if in a movie scene.[15] I understood *perfectly* why she hadn't fought and screamed.

When I was still in college, I worked at a clothing store for the summer. I'd been riding up a long, empty escalator from the subway platform when I suddenly felt a sharp pain in my vagina and anus. I whirled around to see an old man leering at me. He had crept up behind me and shoved his fingers past my skirt and underwear, penetrating my body. My first instinct was to swing my feet up, kick him in the face, and knock him down that long escalator. I had a right to self-defense.

Or did I?

I imagined this old man rolling down the hard metal stairs, banging his head, getting seriously injured, and me being accused of assault or attempted murder. So I didn't kick him. I wanted to scream, but I didn't know what to scream. If he'd stolen my wallet, I would've known to yell, "Stop, thief!" But what to yell now? I didn't have the words. I just turned around and ran away, hating myself for fleeing when what I wanted to do was to hit back.

It never even *occurred* to me to go to the police. I had no idea that digital penetration is classified as rape in many jurisdictions, including the one I was in. This terrible thing had happened to me and I didn't even know what to call it. And that something so terrible *could* happen, so fast and so unexpectedly, during my morning commute was equally unsettling. When I arrived at work, still deeply shaken, I told a co-worker about my experience.

"That happens on the subway," he said, shrugging. "Get used to it." As if I were stupid to think that I deserved better. In some ways, his dismissal of what happened to me as no big deal was more upsetting than what had happened in the first place. I could dismiss the man who stuck his hand up my skirt as a pervert, and what had happened as an aberration, but what did it mean when a colleague said it was normal and didn't seem to care?

I buried both the incident and my co-worker's casual remark about it in the darkest recesses of my mind. Yet this was the incident that permanently changed my work uniform: It's why, to this day, I wear Levi's 501s. The next time a man, this time a senior tech exec, not a subway rider, tried to grope me, he got a whole lot of nothing, thanks to the impregnable inseam of my Levi's.

I hadn't spoken of it since and I certainly wasn't going to start with the lawyer sitting across the table from me now. So I said nothing, not knowing how to fight my silence about why this rape victim may have remained silent. In retrospect, I sure wish I'd found my voice. Perhaps things would have turned out differently. I will do better next time. As Maya Angelou wrote, "I did then what I knew how to do. Now that I know better, I do better."[16]

ABSENCE OF A CULTURE OF CONSENT

In retrospect, I believe another factor silencing me in that conversation with the lawyer was that I didn't want to confront our not having a shared culture of consent at that company. As #MeToo has laid bare, plenty of powerful men believe they have a "right" to women's bodies. But at the time I had a hard time admitting to myself that was true. It's painful to confront that some men will make a conscious argument that if I am passed-out drunk, for example, they have a right to do whatever they want to my body, and so I had been in denial about this.

BIAS   PREJUDICE   BULLYING   ⚡   DISCRIMINATION   HARASSMENT | PHYSICAL VIOLATIONS |

I tended to chalk mishandling of sexual assault up to "misunderstandings" rather than a fundamental moral disagreement.

Shortly before this conversation with the lawyer, I overheard a conversation in the company hallway. One young man said to another, "Well, she was so drunk. What did she expect?"

This was so egregious that I couldn't ignore it. I jumped into the conversation. "If you have sex with a person who is too drunk to give consent, it is rape."

"No, it is not!" the first one said. His buddy nodded in agreement.

"It *is* rape. You do not have the right to do whatever you want with a woman's body just because she is drunk. I am not going to waste my time arguing with you two," I shot back. "You should know the law if you don't want to find yourselves in prison. Go ask any lawyer if you don't believe me."

This rattled me. I went to talk to Herbert, an executive at the company. Did we need to have consent training at the company? I wondered. How was it that these young men didn't know what rape was? Herbert dismissed this out of hand. I tried to back up and get to a shared understanding of the kind of culture we were trying to build at the company.

"Don't you want this to be the kind of place where a woman could get as drunk as all the men are getting and still be safe?" I asked. "I don't think that's such a high bar: *Don't have sex with a blackout drunk person.*"

"The only problem was that he did it in the office," Herbert replied, angry and defensive. "If he'd taken her home or done it in a restaurant bathroom, it would've been fine."

I felt a crack open beneath my feet in my assumptions about our shared moral universe. Didn't *everyone* believe it was wrong to force yourself on people too drunk to know what they were doing? I realize now that was a naive assumption, one made possible only by denial. It was one thing to argue about how drunk the woman was, or whether the man knew she was that drunk. But it had never occurred to me that the man or anyone else would actually believe it was OK to have sex with a woman who everyone *agreed* was blackout drunk. Shaken, I went home to talk to my husband about it.

He was just as shocked and disgusted as I was: "What is *wrong* with these guys? Don't they have any moral compass?" Luckily, the law in most jurisdictions agrees with my husband and me about right and wrong. Rape is illegal, sex with a person too drunk to give consent is rape, and therefore illegal. As a society, though, establishing a shared morality on the topic of rape is still a long way off. Somehow, I'd never come face-to-face with that before.

It's worth asking why I was so unaware that some men thought this behavior was perfectly OK. Since then I've spoken with several lawyers who specialize in sex crimes. They were astounded that I found this amoral attitude about rape surprising. They were well aware. I had for years refused to notice this. I had refused to notice what I feared I could not fix. Now I know that I am well served to turn that phrase on its head. *I can't fix what I refuse to notice.*

Now that I couldn't avoid noticing, the question for me was, What was my responsibility? I knew that teaching my children to behave ethically and obey the law *was* my responsibility. But was it my responsibility to correct the misogynistic attitudes about rape that were so prevalent I heard them in hallway conversations and arguments with executives? Should I spend more energy explaining to my team the meaning of consent? Should I add consent training to the management training and sales training I was responsible for rolling out?

A giant groan of *NO* rumbled in my gut. I had a big job already. Taking on the added responsibility of deprogramming these men who believed they had a right to women's bodies was NOT part of my job description. But I might have done it anyway if I'd thought I had any chance of success. That was the other problem: I didn't have an ally. There was not a single other executive that I felt I could rely on for help. My boss told me again I was getting a reputation for "being a little obsessed with the woman thing." If there had been even one other senior woman at the company to partner with me on these issues, things might have been different. Part of the reason I felt guilty about leaving was that I knew it would be discouraging for the younger women at the company. But part of the reason I couldn't stay was that there weren't enough women at the company.

I am making it sound as if I were making clear choices, but that

BIAS   PREJUDICE   BULLYING   ⚡   DISCRIMINATION   HARASSMENT   [PHYSICAL VIOLATIONS]

was not how it felt. At the time I was confused as hell. I tried to stay the course for a little while. So many things went wrong at that company; so many aspects of the culture at the company and in the industry and in our society created the conditions for that crime to occur. The company had a "fratty" culture in which bias and even prejudice against women were spoken and any attempts to interrupt these attitudes were silenced. These attitudes, uncorrected, led to discrimination against women. Therefore, there were very few women at the company.

Part of the reason they hired me was to help them clean up this cultural mess. I gave them credit for wanting to fix the problem, and I wanted to help. But I came to see that they considered cleaning it up to be my job, not theirs. And moreover, many there didn't *want* the culture to change. So they were going to fight me instead of thank me for the work I was doing. I stayed for a couple more months, feeling I owed it to the women there. But eventually I realized that the executives would never clean up their mess if they could assign it to me instead. By staying I wasn't protecting the women; I was codependent with the men who fostered the company's misogynistic culture. I would be letting them hide behind my metaphorical skirts. *And* I was setting myself up to be blamed for the situation they had created. I quit.

INSTITUTIONAL COURAGE

I offer suggestions below on preventing and responding to physical violations in the workplace. The goal is to create a culture of consent and to make sure that trusted reporting mechanisms and checks and balances are in place to reinforce that culture. It is possible to respond with Institutional Courage, not Institutional Betrayal.[17]

PEOPLE HARMED

TELL YOUR STORY. LISTEN TO OTHER PEOPLE'S STORIES

The #MeToo Movement was born with a story, and it has unleashed millions more.[18] It began when a 13-year-old girl told activist and community organizer Tarana Burke about being sexually assaulted. Burke, herself a victim of sexual violence, had been unable to respond to the girl's story in the moment. Burke later wished she had simply been able to say, "Me, too." She launched the phrase on MySpace in 2006 to help others find the strength both to *tell* their stories and also to *listen* to the stories of others. Thanks to Burke's brilliant call and the response on social media, countless victims of sexual violence have done exactly that. If you tell your story today, you are more likely to be heard with compassion and solidarity than ever before in history. Doing so may also help other victims and future victims of the person causing harm and pave the way further for other people to tell their stories.

DON'T ALLOW SHAME TO SILENCE YOU

When I got groped on the subway, part of the reason I didn't yell was that I didn't dare shout the words that would accurately describe what he was doing to me. The words "You are digitally penetrating me" do not fall trippingly off the tongue; nor did I feel comfortable yelling, "Get your fingers out of my anus and vagina!" Or even "Why is your hand up my skirt!" Somehow, I felt that describing accurately what was happening was shameful for me but not for him.

Shame is too often used as a silencer. But if we can't use the right words, we can't give the right descriptions, and that allows perpetrators to get away with their crimes. Research shows that when children know and use the correct words for their genitalia, they are less likely to be victimized by pedophiles.[19]

The most satisfying response to being groped I've ever heard comes from author Deborah Copaken. She was on a bus and someone grabbed her butt. The bus was crowded and she couldn't tell who it was, so she reached down, grabbed the man's hand, pulled it away from her body, and shouted, "Whose hand is this?"

Take a page out of Deb's book. She was not ashamed!

This also works preventively as well as reactively. If someone asks

BIAS   PREJUDICE   BULLYING   ⚡ DISCRIMINATION   HARASSMENT   [PHYSICAL VIOLATIONS]

you to do something that makes you feel uncomfortable, tell them exactly and explicitly why you're uncomfortable. I learned this by accident when I was on a train from Moscow to St. Petersburg. I had bought four tickets so that I could have a sleeping compartment to myself and would not have to sleep with three strangers. A man barged in anyway. When he went to the bathroom, I threw his stuff out into the hall and locked the door. He came back pounding on the door and yelling at me. My Russian wasn't good enough to be subtle, so I said, "You are a large man. I am a small woman. It is not safe for small women to sleep with large, strange men." He apologized and found another seat.

I learned an important lesson that night. It is important to be explicit.

FIND THE SUPPORT YOU NEED

I wish I could say rely on the people who love you most. But sometimes the responses from the people closest to you can be hurtful or even retraumatizing.

Still, there are plenty of places to turn. You are not alone, even when those closest to you can't give you the support you need. You can look for a local rape crisis center or support line—they can help connect you with local resources, including counseling. You can chat online with professionals at RAINN (Rape, Abuse & Incest National Network) or call their 24-7 hotline (800-565-HOPE/4673). Tarana Burke's organization, the #MeToo Movement, has some great resources and tool kits.[20] The Callisto Survivor's Guide also offers information and resources for survivors of sexual assault, rape, and professional sexual coercion, as does Option B (optionb.org), a nonprofit that helps people build emotional resilience in the face of difficult or traumatic life events.[21] These are just a handful of the resources out there.

But it's not for me, or for anyone else, to tell you what you should or shouldn't do. It's for us to listen and to offer help and support in the way that you need it. If the people you're turning to aren't giving you what you need, find someone else to turn to.

GIVE YOURSELF A VOICE

Many people find telling their story, either in writing or orally or in an artistic medium, to be enormously helpful in recovering from the trauma of sexual assault. Playwright Eve Ensler's memoir *The Apology* is a moving example of this.[22]

You never know what might happen with your story. But even if your story doesn't go viral, if it helps you heal, it has moved mountains. I wrote a 300-page memoir to help me digest and get out of the abusive relationship described earlier in this chapter. It never saw the light of day and it never will. I wrote it for myself. And writing it helped me get out. That was enough! I like to write, so that worked for me. If you hate to write, find another way to get it out. Sing it. Dance it. Act it. Make a video. Tell it to a friend on a hike or over a meal. Try therapy. Join a support group.

CONSIDER GETTING A MEDICAL EXAMINATION

If you are assaulted, you may want to go to a hospital as soon as possible to get a forensic exam.[23] You may want to reach out to your local rape crisis center to discuss the examination before you go. Rape crisis centers often have advocates who can go with survivors to the hospital. Having an advocate can be important if the medical staff or the police are misleading or treat the survivor poorly. It still happens too often that officials doubt the victim, respond in a way that feels cold or unfeeling, or even tell the victim lies or misinformation. So some people prefer to have an advocate go with them.

After such a traumatic experience, your first instinct may be to take a shower; try to keep in mind that you may be washing away important evidence. But even if you do shower, you can still go to the hospital: there still may be important evidence to gather, and you may have injuries that would benefit from medical attention. It's also a good idea to write down what happened to you and to email what you wrote to yourself or to a trusted friend. Taking these steps doesn't mean you

BIAS PREJUDICE BULLYING ⚡ DISCRIMINATION HARASSMENT PHYSICAL VIOLATIONS

have to report the crime. But if you later decide to do so, the more evidence you have, the better.

CONSIDER REPORTING THE CRIME TO THE POLICE

The downside risks of reporting sexual assault are legion and well documented. Survivors of sexual violence often describe the ways in which reporting the crime can be as traumatic as the event itself. An investigation may be both protracted and invasive. Your attacker's lawyers will use your every action or inaction against you. The odds of a guilty verdict are low. Even if your attacker is found guilty, you may feel that you, also, have been punished by our legal system.

Nevertheless, it's worth considering the upside of going to the authorities: the benefits of reporting are equally real. I will lay them out here, but let me start by saying that you must decide what is best for *you*. There's nothing you "should" do.

"Fear comes from focusing on the costs of speaking up," actor and activist Ashley Judd observed, and "courage comes from focusing on the costs of staying silent."[24] That doesn't mean you are a coward if you decide it's not in your best interest to report an assault. Ashley Judd has resources you might not have. But you don't have to be a famous actor to ask yourself, Does the cost of silence outweigh the cost of speaking up?

Pursuing justice can bring closure. Thirty years ago, a friend of mine was raped in college. She wanted to report the crime, but the university's psychiatrist persuaded her not to. To say that this psychiatrist had a conflict of interest is an understatement. To this day, that my friend didn't report the crime bothers her almost as much as the crime itself.

There are other ways to achieve closure. In a moving op-ed, columnist Michelle Alexander explained how her rapist's apology brought closure, whereas going to the police would have retraumatized her and put her opportunities as a student at Stanford Law School at risk. She says, "Years later, I realized that I was free. I no longer felt fear, anger or resentment toward the man who raped me. Without even realizing it, I had forgiven him. It's difficult to imagine that I would feel the same if he had shown me no care or concern, or if I had been forced to endure a fresh wave of trauma in our court system, or if I had been forced to give birth to a child that I did not choose." She explains why she didn't call the police: "I never once imagined that calling the police could help my situation. It could only make things worse. I envisioned prosecutors, courtrooms and interrogations. I was trying to survive my first year of law school, worried I might fail out, wondering how I would make it through my first round of exams. The last thing I wanted was to become a court case myself."[25]

Our legal system is badly broken, especially for people without financial resources and for anyone who is not white. Yet when people can bring cases to court, they shine a light on its deficiencies, and we all benefit. But an altruistic desire to reform how our legal system handles sexual violence shouldn't be the *only* reason you report—put yourself first.

The costs for victims of bringing these cases to court are enormous. In the end you're going to have to decide based on a determinative factor, that one thing that matters more than anything else. Lucia Evans describes her determinative factor eloquently when she explains her decision to participate in the case against Harvey Weinstein:

> I made this list of all the reasons why I should do it and all the
> reasons why I shouldn't do it. And all the reasons why I shouldn't
> do it—I mean, there were so many reasons—fear for my safety, fear
> for my family, my reputation, my career—everything. All these
> things would just be ruined. And then on the other side, I had
> just written, *"because it feels right."* I didn't really have much else
> to write on that side. It did feel like I could, at the very least,
> hopefully, put him in jail, this person that had assaulted so many
> people and harassed so many people. And I couldn't say no to
> the chance to do that, ultimately. This is the right thing to do.
> I'm going to do it.[26]

BIAS   PREJUDICE   BULLYING   ⚡ DISCRIMINATION   HARASSMENT   ⎡PHYSICAL VIOLATIONS⎤

Evans braved the storm, but ultimately her charges were dropped. Of that infuriating experience, she says, "I also just don't want people to be discouraged from coming forward and doing it. So I would just hope people don't—people, despite all the things I've said about how hard it is, still decide to come forward, because that's literally the only hope that we have."

You probably can't make your decision based on a simple list of pros and cons. But sometimes thinking through such a list can help you get to your determinative factor. Listen to all the arguments people will make to you for and against participating in our flawed criminal justice system, which at times seems more like a criminal injustice system. Then, close your eyes and decide what feels right for *you*.

UPSTANDERS

INTERRUPT

If you witness a sexual encounter in which you question the presence of true consent, call the police and/or interrupt it if your own physical safety is not at risk.

In *Know My Name*, Chanel Miller describes how two young Swedish men rode by on bicycles while she lay unconscious behind a dumpster with her attacker, Brock Turner, on top of her. When the cyclists realized what was going on, they intervened, yelling at him to stop. After Turner fled, they first checked on Miller, then chased after him. "They represented the seers," Miller writes, "the doers, who chose to act and change the story . . . What we needed to raise in others was this instinct. The ability to recognize, in an instant, right from wrong. The clarity of mind to face it rather than ignore it." She describes how the Swedes pinned Turner to the ground and said, "What the fuck are you doing?," and how that inspired her to press charges: "The Swedes had introduced this new voice inside me. I had to teach myself to talk like them. To one day face my attacker and say, 'What the fuck are you doing.'"[27]

LISTEN WITH COMPASSION INSTEAD OF ANGER OR FEAR

At the very least, if you witness or hear about a sexual encounter where there is no consent, don't deny it, minimize it, or lie about it. Don't reflect and reinforce the gaslighting that makes reporting this kind of behavior so difficult.

Here's an example of how sexual harassment often plays out in the workplace and the additional harm that people who fail as upstanders can do.

I once mentioned in a meeting that I was interested in working on an acquisition we were considering in New York City because I was already traveling from California to New York every other weekend for social reasons. One of the executives present, Phil, was known for booking two extra hotel rooms on every business trip because one woman was never enough. After the meeting Phil emailed me because he was flying to New York that very weekend: he could give me a ride on his private jet.

I declined, saying I had to stay home and work that particular weekend. It's always risky to turn down a powerful man you work with, but flying with him on his plane sounded even riskier. And surely, he couldn't object to my working hard? Of course, if I was right about his intentions, he was violating the "No dating in your chain of command" rule. But several of the top executives at that company were breaking that rule. The company was doing well, and the executives there were getting unfathomably rich. Something about making that much money makes most (not all, and the exceptions are to be commended) people believe in their exceptionalism and gives them a sense of being above the rules.[28] And when it was overwhelmingly men becoming the billionaires, it sent an unmistakable message: men were worth more—a *lot* more. They could do what they wanted.

Not long after rebuffing Phil's offer, I found myself at a social event with him. It was the kind of shindig unique to the sudden wealth that was showering down on Silicon Valley at the time. The host had chartered a 727 aircraft specially modified for zero-gravity astronaut training, otherwise known as the Vomit Comet. The plane flew in a parabola. On the way down, passengers experienced 30 seconds of weightlessness. After a few passes, when people got used to the giddy feeling of floating in space, we started playing a game: one person would tuck into a ball and the others would throw that person around the plane. When I was the ball, laughing and having a good time, someone tried to jam two fingers into my anus and vagina. Luckily, I was wearing my Levi's with their impregnable inseam. But I was rattled and pretty sure it was Phil. I knew the other people present well and felt certain none of them would do a thing like that. There was nothing seductive about the grab—it was a violent gesture. Was Phil trying to punish me for turning down the plane ride to New York? What I did know—and found deeply depressing—was that in this environment I could do nothing about it. And I knew that he knew it, too.

For a time, I didn't say anything to anyone. I had stock options that hadn't vested yet. If I could just keep my head down for a couple more years, I might be able to afford to buy a house. Years later, once I'd left the company, I finally told a friend, a former colleague.

"Why didn't you tell me sooner?" was the first thing she said.

Leaders, upstanders, friends, take note. When someone tells you something like this, *never* ask why the person didn't tell you sooner. That question has been asked and answered a thousand times over. In the vast majority of cases, victims don't say something sooner because they are afraid if they speak out about what happened to them, they will be punished. Listen to what happened with compassion, even when it's hard to hear, and an open mind.

Then, she started cross-examining me. "You can't say for sure it was him."

"No, I can't. But here's who else was there." I listed the names. We both knew them well. "Do you really think it was any of them?"

She made a noncommittal noise.

"Come on. I really, seriously doubt any of those men would do a thing like that. And you and I both know Phil *would*."

"It wouldn't hold up in a court."

"I'm not in court. I'm just talking to you."

"Besides, how do you know it wasn't just an accident?"

"Have you ever been grabbed like that? It's an unmistakable gesture. That kind of grab doesn't happen accidentally."

"You can never prove it."

"No, I guess not."

Why was she asking me to prove it? I was talking to her as a friend. I couldn't help but think she was quietly telling me to keep my mouth shut, as if the real danger here was that rumors about *me* might start flying around, not that Phil would keep attacking women at the company.

"Be careful," she warned. "There's a backlash coming."

"Why a backlash? He got away with it! There was nothing I could do. What is he lashing back at?"

Clearly my friend was not an upstander. In some ways this was more upsetting than what Phil had done. I knew Phil was a philandering asshole. But my friend?

Looking back on this exchange now, especially after having written this book, I can better interpret her unhelpful reaction that day. "Why didn't you tell me sooner?" is the sort of remark anxious parents make to a child—unconsciously scolding the child because the misdeeds of the world lie beyond their control. It is blaming and inappropriate but rooted in fear and love. We don't want the people we care about to be hurt. And we like to imagine that if they do the right things they won't be hurt.

Probably also she had some complicated feelings she'd had trouble articulating, feelings I shared but also didn't want to voice. We both had unconsciously adopted strategies to succeed in the cutthroat male-dominated business world by acting more like men ourselves. We pretended that gender didn't matter, but what we were refusing to acknowledge were all the ways, minor and major, that we were being treated as though we were there to serve whatever whim these men had.

My friend had fought her way to the top of our industry. But, as we both knew so well, it was still a man's world, and she was still afraid of losing that hard-won position. The subliminal message my friend sent me boiled down to something like this: *I cannot afford to acknowledge how our industry harms and devalues women. To support you—even in private conversation—I would have to examine the ways I'm complicit in perpetuating this culture.* I'd done a different version of the same thing at my start-up, when I'd mostly dismissed the concerns of Madeline (and then bought her silence) when she tried to warn me that my company had a culture of discrimination and harassment.

I knew why I'd stayed silent at the time. That silence bought me something real. I stayed at the company, my stock vested, and it was worth enough money to buy half a house; my husband, who'd also won the stock option lottery, paid for the other half. But my silence also cost me and the other women I worked with. It also cost the company. Which bothers me, too, because I pride myself on delivering for anyone who puts trust in me.

Furthermore, now that the stock had vested and my husband and I owned our house and I had quit working at that company, why was my friend advising me to stay silent? Of course, there was always more money to be earned, but, really, how much better can you eat? I realized that there wasn't enough wealth in the world to liberate me to speak out. That kind of freedom is not something money can buy. I was going to have to find it within.

Here is another example of the hidden fallout of workplace injustice. Those who wonder why it's important to address this kind of behavior might want to take note: a high-performing senior executive who is positive she was digitally penetrated by an executive at her company and is afraid that reporting might ruin her career at your company is probably not going to be giving you her all and will most likely be thinking more about her exit strategy than your bottom line.

That's the invisible and unmistakable way sexual harassment often works. No one talks about this inappropriate, often criminal, behavior that is extremely difficult to prove. And so it continues and corrodes an organization from the inside out, fueled by an environment of abuse you feel in your bones but can't quite bring to light. Victims think there's no point in speaking out because people who should be standing up for them advise silence. They also know that if they do speak up, leadership is more interested in quiet settlements than public acknowledgment of bad behavior at the company. So perpetrators are permitted to keep seeking out new victims when they should be held accountable. Meanwhile, the people harmed suffer quietly, often for a long time, in any number of ways—emotionally, financially, professionally, and physically. Everyone loses.

LEADERS

Every 92 seconds an American is sexually assaulted.[29] Eight percent of rapes occur while the victim is at work.[30] Which means that if you are an executive, it is not unlikely that you will be forced at some point to lead on this issue.

You may think it's the job of the criminal justice system to deal with sexual assault. But our justice system does not prosecute rape and sexual assault effectively. According to Jess Ladd, the founder of Callisto, a reporting system for sexual assault at universities, "There's a ninety-nine percent chance that a rapist gets away with their crime. There's practically no deterrent to sexual assault in the United States."[31]

If there are incidents of sexual assault in your workplace, it will be up to you to take action. And it's important that you get it right. Few things will destroy morale or divide a team faster than a bungled response to an allegation of sexual misconduct. Furthermore, not responding to workplace sexual harassment can be a violation of Title VII of the Civil Rights Act of 1964.

Educate yourself

Leaders are well served to learn about sexual assault—about how victims respond to it and how perpetrators try to escape responsibility for their actions. To be successful, leaders must do this with the same determination they'd put into facing a competitive threat to their product's sales. This doesn't mean simply forcing your employees to attend a training that might limit the company's liability if the worst happens.

BIAS   PREJUDICE   BULLYING   ⚡   DISCRIMINATION   HARASSMENT   [PHYSICAL VIOLATIONS]

It means working to understand the problem more deeply and learning how other leaders have responded in ways that help victims recover and make it less likely that sexual assault will again happen on your team.[32]

As I look back on the sham investigation that I observed to a rape in the office, I fault myself and the other executives for being unprepared to deal with such a serious situation and for failing to educate ourselves quickly when faced with the unexpected. Neither the company's lawyer nor I knew much about sexual assault. The lawyer imagined it as it's portrayed in the movies. As a result, he didn't know how to respond in a way that was fair to the alleged perpetrator and didn't further traumatize the alleged victim. I knew enough from firsthand experience not to believe the rape myths, but I didn't know enough to know how to confront the lawyer's ignorance.

A victim often reacts with silence or muted emotions. The accused often engages in a behavior pattern called DARVO, an acronym for "deny, attack, reverse victim and offender" (a term coined by Jennifer Freyd and made famous on *South Park*).[33] As Ashley Judd explains, DARVO helped Harvey Weinstein get away with sexual predation for years. This doesn't mean that everyone who DARVOs is guilty. But it's a reminder not to make a decision about innocence or guilt based on your expectations of a person's emotional response.

Learn about sexual misconduct so that you'll know how to recognize and confront it when, and if, it takes place on your watch. Here are a video and four books I recommend you start with:

- "Betrayal and Courage in the Age of #MeToo": This is the title of a panel featuring Jennifer Freyd at a behavioral science symposium at Stanford University.[34] In just over 12 minutes, Freyd summarizes decades of research on the ways organizations can most effectively respond to reports of sexual violence. She explains how handling reports forthrightly, thoroughly, and fairly (an approach she characterizes as Institutional Courage) can help prevent future incidents, allow victims to recover more quickly, and increase the overall trust between employees and leadership. On the other hand, Institutional

Betrayal—engaging in victim blaming, sweeping incidents under the rug, and exhibiting other behaviors we can measure— retraumatizes victims and will harm your organization's reputation in the long run.[35]

- *Know My Name,* by Chanel Miller.[36] This memoir will help you understand not only how a compassionate response to sexual assault can help victims heal but also how forcing victims to relive their assaults through the investigative and legal processes can be as traumatic or even more traumatic than the incident itself.
- *Missoula,* by Jon Krakauer.[37] Krakauer uses the lens of a mishandled rape case at the University of Montana to examine how leaders and society at large fail to prevent and respond to sexual violence. This book shows the terrible human toll Institutional Betrayal takes on both victims and the institution itself. Though set in academia, many of Krakauer's conclusions apply to other workplaces.
- *Not That Bad: Dispatches from Rape Culture,* edited by Roxane Gay. This book brings a variety of different experiences of sexual assault into focus. Many people struggle the most with labeling sexual assault that doesn't fit the typical rape narrative.
- *Redefining Rape,* by Estelle Freedman, is a history of how our understanding of what rape is has evolved over time.

Another thing to be aware of is how different biases may collide when a person is presented with a case of sexual assault. If gender bias or a belief in common rape myths is present, the person may be more skeptical of a report of sexual assault than is justified.[38] When racial bias and body-size bias are also present, the person may be even more dismissive.

Create a culture of consent

Going back to the job where the rape occurred. If everyone in that office had understood the meaning of consent, the incident might not have happened. If you start by setting expectations for shaking hands, hugging, and the like, you can educate about consent without feeling as if you're offering sex education at work. But if dating or hooking up is going on between your employees, don't bury your head in the sand. You'll be well served to talk openly about sexual consent as well.

Build trusted reporting systems

The Sarbanes-Oxley Act requires that publicly held companies maintain a system for employees to report matters that might have a material impact to the audit committee of the board of directors. Most large companies rely on a third-party system that provides an anonymous reporting hotline for this purpose. However, these systems are not designed with sexual misconduct in mind. Leading institutions are investing in systems to improve their access to sexual misconduct data, which helps them manage the risk of undetected sexual misconduct in the workplace.

A number of reporting systems have emerged in just the last several years to meet this market demand. I'm With Them, a nonprofit resource hub about sexual misconduct policies and reporting processes, provides a helpful analysis of the advantages and disadvantages of different systems.[39]

What many of these systems have in common is that they allow people to report incidents anonymously.

Anonymity is important because it offers some protection against the way that victims of sexual assault are often retraumatized when they report the crime. These systems don't automatically punish anyone as a result of an anonymous accusation. They simply trigger an investigation. They also can put victims of the same person together so that if they do decide to report a crime, they can do so together. And they can allow management to notice any pattern of accusations against one person. A pattern of accusations doesn't mean a person automatically gets fired or punished. It simply means that there's more to investigate.

Laurie Girand, president of I'm With Them, explains why being able to report anonymously is so important: "Every person who makes an allegation to any authority is accountable to someone. Many codes of conduct state that falsifying a report can result in termination. Corporations are not courtrooms. Employment is a contract, and many employees serve 'at will,' until the company decides it no longer needs them. Both the alleged perpetrator and the target are entitled to a fair investigation, but the target and allies assume the greater risk in reporting, which is why they are owed anonymity."

A reporting system that operates on the principle of safety in numbers is often the only way to get people to report. In *She Said,* Jodi Kantor and Megan Twohey describe how it took months for even one of Harvey Weinstein's many victims to be willing to go on the record. Finally, two of them, actor Ashley Judd and former Weinstein assistant Laura Madden, bravely agreed to speak up. As they were preparing to go to the press, *Variety* and *The Hollywood Reporter* reported that *The New York Times* was about to expose Harvey Weinstein as a serial sexual abuser, and suddenly, with that news, the dam broke. "For months the reporters had been pursuing women," Kantor and Twohey write of themselves, "aching for them to speak. Now they were coming to Jodi and Megan like a river suddenly flowing in the opposite direction."[40]

Not every serial rapist has two Pulitzer Prize–winning investigative reporters working for months to make it safe for victims to come forward. If you have a repeat offender in your workplace, don't you want to know? That's where anonymous reporting systems can help identify and prosecute repeat offenders in the workplace.

Investigate thoroughly. Don't hide behind sham processes

We were right to order an investigation into the alleged rape in the office. But we failed terribly in not demanding that it be more thorough. It's painful enough for victims to have to recount their trauma to even a sensitive investigator, but it retraumatizes a victim when the investigation is inconclusive and a sham.

BE TRANSPARENT

It's often said that the cover-up is worse than the crime. This is true for several reasons. One, cover-ups are profoundly unjust to the victims. Two, they perpetuate the underlying conditions that allowed the crime

BIAS   PREJUDICE   BULLYING   ⚡   DISCRIMINATION   HARASSMENT   │ PHYSICAL VIOLATIONS │

to happen, making further sexual violence in your workplace more likely to occur. Three, cover-ups often cause more problems for an organization than holding perpetrators accountable would have. That's why it's important to not resort to forced arbitration, payoffs, and NDAs to cover up complaints.

DON'T PASS THE TRASH

Far too often one company fires a person for sexual harassment or even sexual assault in the office and then a competing firm hires that person. How do companies avoid "passing the trash" to one another? Making it public that you fired someone for sexual harassment is legally fraught. Firms have been sued for millions of dollars for doing this. But if you fire someone and haven't disclosed the information, and the press finds out, you're likely to find yourself in a PR nightmare. What's the way out of this catch-22 for leaders?

Tom Schievelbein, a retired CEO of several large corporations, had a practical solution. When there was irrefutable evidence that sexual harassment or assault had occurred in the office, he sent an internal email explaining why the person was no longer at the company. His lawyers tried to talk him out of doing this, but he reminded the lawyers that he was driving the bus; their job was to point out obstacles and to tell him how to get around them but not to tell him where to go or how to get there.

Sending the email around to employees was important for two reasons. One, it sent a strong message: that kind of behavior would have real consequences. Usually many people knew about the behavior, and it was important to demonstrate that action had been taken. Two, it helped with the "passing the trash" problem. Usually when companies hire someone, they do back-channel reference checks. Since a number of people knew what had happened, the reason someone was fired would come out in the interview process.

If you are hiring someone, be rigorous about asking questions about a history of sexual harassment when checking references. And obviously, don't just call the names the applicants supply. If it's a senior hire, don't just talk to people at the person's level. Find out what the person's former employees have to say. This is a good practice to find out what people are really like, what their reputation is, and how they treat the people they oversee—and whether there is a history of sexual harassment or misconduct.

If you have fired someone and another company does a reference check, push yourself to operate higher than the moral standards required by law. The law does not require disclosure of the person's behavior and may in fact punish disclosure. Yet you can do things to make sure sexual predators don't simply get hired by other companies. Investigate ethical and legal disclosures of internal findings regarding sexual violence.

DON'T GIVE UNCHECKED POWER TO MANAGERS

Unchecked power doesn't have to be absolute power for it to allow terrible abuses. In 2017, *The New York Times* published a story about a manager at a Ford auto plant who used his power over who got what shifts to coerce a woman to have sex with him.[41] When she refused his advances, he assigned her a shift that started before her child's day care opened and then threatened to fire her if she showed up late.

Clearly this manager deserved to be fired and prosecuted. But that, in itself, wouldn't solve the problem. The problem was systemic. When managers have unchecked power, some of them are likely to abuse it. Furthermore, when there is only one way to report abuse, it's likely to get back to that manager, who can then punish the person who reported it. Checks and balances make sexual violence less likely to happen and more likely to be reported. The more likely it is to be reported, the more likely you are to detect repeat offenders, making sexual violence even less likely to happen. This is the kind of virtuous cycle we need if we are to minimize sexual violence in the workplace.

COLLECT DATA

If you want to know if people in your organization trust their leadership to do the right thing if they report sexual harassment or assault

BIAS   PREJUDICE   BULLYING   ⚡   DISCRIMINATION   HARASSMENT   [PHYSICAL VIOLATIONS]

in the workplace, conduct an anonymous survey. Psychologists Carly Smith and Jennifer Freyd have designed such a survey and allow companies to use it without charge.[42]

If you launch the survey and discover problems in your organization, you need to address these issues or you'll risk making your employees only feel more cynical and beaten down. Lean on your legal team; consult your top executives. If you can afford it, hire a consultant with expertise in these matters.[43]

Don't Over-Delegate Diversity Equity and Inclusion Work

If you're the leader of a team, don't hire one underrepresented person to do a day job and also fix rape culture at your company. That woman VP you hired to lead finance? It's not her job to prevent sexual assault. It's her job to lead finance. It's *your* job to create a diverse team, equitable management systems, and an inclusive culture.

Let's go back to the company where I worked where the rape occurred. I was hired to grow a billion-dollar business. When I joined, the company was just starting to focus on creating a better working environment for women. It was expected but not said that I would solve that problem, too, without "making a big deal" of it. There was tremendous work to do. It all became much more serious when a crime was committed in the office, revealing a profound immorality about rape shared broadly at the company. I could have done better, but it was just too much to expect of one person. Having a more diverse team would have solved a lot of problems. Men who were real upstanders, real accomplices in helping me to drive change, would have been welcome, too. Expecting a minority of one to do all the work was not reasonable, and it just wasn't going to work.

CHEAT SHEET

PROBLEM	RESPONSE

**CULTURE
OF CONSENT**

If the other person doesn't want
to be touched, don't touch.
If there is any doubt, don't touch.

PHYSICAL VIOLATIONS

Touch + Power,
resulting in everything from the
unwanted hug to violence

**TRUSTED
REPORTING SYSTEMS**

Make it safe to report
anonymously. Build a fair
investigation process.

PART THREE
Systemic Justice and Injustice

Everything that I have written is most minutely connected with what I have lived through, if not personally experienced ... for every man shares the responsibility and the guilt of the society to which he belongs. To live is to war with trolls in heart and soul. To write is to sit in judgment on oneself.

—Henrik Johan Ibsen

At this point in the book, we've dismantled the engine of workplace injustice and laid out all the parts in the driveway.

Now it's time to examine how the engine works when the parts are operating together as a whole system. In daily life we do not usually experience these attitudes and behaviors discretely. They interoperate dynamically, and these dynamics create systemic injustice.

What happens when bias, belief, bullying, harassment, discrimination, and physical violations aren't limited to the occasional bad actor? What happens when they are baked into the systems that govern the workplace, when they skew our hiring, pay, promotion, and firing decisions? What happens when people who work hard *not* to be bad actors harm their colleagues without being aware of it or understanding how the system they are operating in benefits them and hurts others? When this happens, a huge number of people are consciously or unconsciously complicit.

Sometimes these systems are set up quite consciously, as they were in South Africa. After the British Empire fell, white leaders in South Africa set up a commission to study institutionalized racism all over the world. The commission came back with a report of how to repress the majority Black population in South Africa: a set of laws that ran over 3,000 pages and set up a surveillance state meant to keep Black people under total control.[1]

Odds are what is happening in your workplace is not as consciously evil as apartheid was. But don't let that reinforce denial about systemic injustice in your workplace. Results matter more than intentions. The hiring systems, pay systems, promotion systems, and mentorship programs may not be *explicitly* designed to discriminate. Yet they *do* discriminate. The ineffectual reporting systems leaders have instituted may not be explicitly designed to allow repeat offenders to get away with sexual violence in your workplace. That may not be what the leaders *intended* to happen. Yet if that is what *is* happening, and we, whatever role we play, refuse to acknowledge it, then we are part of the problem, not part of the solution.

That is why we need to learn to recognize the dynamics between these different attitudes and behaviors that lead to workplace injustice. These dynamics are not "natural" and not "inevitable," but they do happen all the time. If we are going to interrupt them, we have got to recognize them.

* * *

At some level, Just Work is so very simple. It's about respecting each person's individuality so you can collaborate and get sh*t done. Who doesn't want that? If we weren't so numb to injustice, we'd be shocked that we ever allow it to get in the way of becoming who we want to be and doing what we want to do. And yet we do. All. The. Damn. Time.

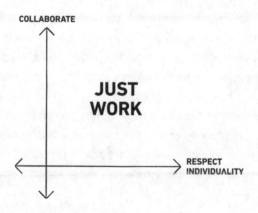

To understand why Just Work is so rare, let's look at what moves us away from collaboration and respect. Partly it's the discrete attitudes and behaviors already discussed. But it's also the dynamics *between* them.

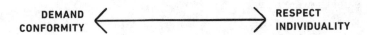

DEMAND CONFORMITY ⟵⟶ **RESPECT INDIVIDUALITY**

The *Conformity Dynamic* drags us away from respecting individuality, usually offering a pretense of being rational, civilized, polite. But this dynamic excludes underrepresented people in a way that is not at all rational and can cause as much or even more harm in the long run as outright violence. The previous chapters have outlined the attitudes and behaviors that cause us to demand conformity: bias, prejudice, and discrimination. They have also outlined what we can do to interrupt each—bias interrupters, codes of conduct, bias quantifiers. The next chapters will illustrate the slippery slope toward conformity, examine how it kills innovation and harms individuals, and provide safety measures to keep your organization off that slippery slope.

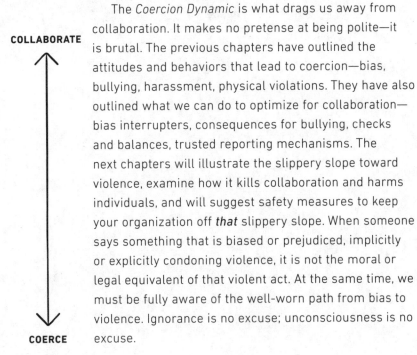

COLLABORATE

COERCE

The *Coercion Dynamic* is what drags us away from collaboration. It makes no pretense at being polite—it is brutal. The previous chapters have outlined the attitudes and behaviors that lead to coercion—bias, bullying, harassment, physical violations. They have also outlined what we can do to optimize for collaboration—bias interrupters, consequences for bullying, checks and balances, trusted reporting mechanisms. The next chapters will illustrate the slippery slope toward violence, examine how it kills collaboration and harms individuals, and will suggest safety measures to keep your organization off *that* slippery slope. When someone says something that is biased or prejudiced, implicitly or explicitly condoning violence, it is not the moral or legal equivalent of that violent act. At the same time, we must be fully aware of the well-worn path from bias to violence. Ignorance is no excuse; unconsciousness is no excuse.

Understanding and recognizing these dynamics, the differences between them, and how they operate together and separately is crucial to our ability to interrupt them before we have created systems that are unjust. Recognizing these dynamics is essential to understand how to replace unjust systems with Just Work.

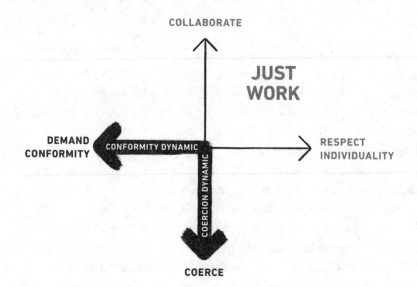

9

Two Bad Dynamics

THE CONFORMITY DYNAMIC

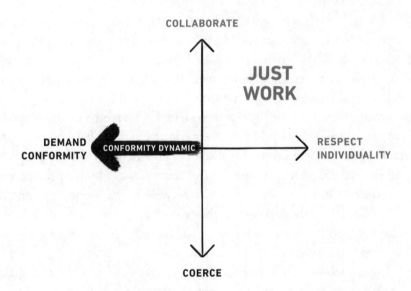

THE SLIPPERY SLOPE TOWARD ABUSE

The Conformity Dynamic implicitly conveys an ancient message: *Be one of us, or make way for us.* And for many underrepresented employees, of course, conforming to that "us" is not desirable or even possible. There are many things about myself I don't want to change, for example, my gender, and others I couldn't change even if I wanted to, for example, my age or the texture of my hair. And when people are excluded from opportunity or subjected to unjust policies because they can't or won't conform with an arbitrary norm, it leaves them vulnerable to abuse, both emotional and physical. The Conformity Dynamic is what some call "polite" racism, "gentlemanly" sexism. This is BS. The fact that it's not overtly violent doesn't mean that it isn't enormously destructive. And yet too often people use the absence of explicit violence in their behavior to deny the harm that their attitudes and behaviors cause. "I'm not racist, it's not like I'm in the KKK," or "I'm not sexist, I would never rape a woman."

Throughout my childhood I experienced a privileged version of the Conformity Dynamic. Far worse things happen to folks, but what happened to me was still destructive and powerful, and it explains this dynamic clearly.

When I was seven years old, my parents were playing tennis at their club as I amused myself by picking wild blackberries along the fence. Suddenly, two men approached the court. I was nervous because I knew the club's rules. Women were not allowed to be members; my mother and I were there as my father's guests. This translated to the following hierarchy for the tennis courts: If two women were playing, a man and a woman could take their court. Once the man and woman started playing, if two men walked up, the men could boot the man and the woman off the court. This, I feared, was about to happen to my parents. But then my mother, who was seven months pregnant, pointed at her belly and said to the two men, "I have a man-child inside of me. So there are two men on the court." The two men accepted this logic and went off to find another court.

I was astonished. My embryonic brother's penis had carried the day in a way that my brilliant, creative, strong adult mother could not have. I was outraged by the obvious injustice of it. At school, we would never have been allowed to invent such ridiculous rules to exclude kids we didn't want to play with. I would have gotten my mouth washed out with soap for saying so, but this was bullshit.

Years later, I would read a passage from Toni Morrison's *Song of Solomon* that captured how I felt about these absurd rules that applied to so much more in our world than the tennis court: "Where do you get the right to decide our lives? I'll tell you where. From that little hog's gut that hangs between your legs. Well, let me tell you something . . . you will need more than that."[1] For the record, my much-loved brother *does* have more than that. But this was the sexist hierarchy that governed our existence.

Growing up, I watched the men around me assume things were theirs for the taking; women, whether at work or at home, had subservient and/or ornamental roles. When I got my first summer job at a bank in Memphis an executive said to me, "Why, I didn't know they let us hire *pretty* girls!" I was eighteen and I had no idea what an "I" statement was or how to respond. So I said nothing. But I decided then and there that I couldn't make my career in my hometown.

But I didn't say anything. I just felt deflated. This kind of erasure wore down all but the toughest women. None of the bank's executives were women. Almost none of my friends' moms worked outside the home. Some of course were happily married, but too many of them were talked over, dismissed, bullied by their husbands and their husbands' friends. Others were cast aside for younger, more decorative counterparts and left without a good way to earn a living. Sometimes, perhaps the worst betrayal, mothers got talked over, dismissed, and bullied by their daughters who were focused on succeeding in a man's world and adopting some of its worst practices.

It's an old story—Simone de Beauvoir's "woman destroyed," or as I like to call her, the Romped-On Woman.[2] No matter what I had to do, I was not going to be romped on. I decided then and there, when picking blackberries at age seven, that I would rather face anything than be kicked off the court for my gender. That childhood decision was what kept me from leaving that first job in finance, where I was facing being frotted in the elevator and groped at dinner. I was prepared to keep dodging such acts rather than retreat home to Memphis, where I would have faced the "I didn't know they let us hire pretty girls" dynamic. I knew exactly where *that* form of discrimination would land me. I was willing to take my chances with harassment if it meant financial freedom.

The Conformity Dynamic is obviously not particular to gender: it plays out wherever bias or prejudice impacts decision-making and leads to discrimination. As a woman I was its victim. But as a white person I was its perpetrator. Too often I hired teams that were all-white. It's not a legitimate excuse to say that I did not intend to discriminate. I failed to actively resist the default of exclusion. By not acknowledging the racism that resulted from the Conformity Dynamic, I reinforced it. By not being antiracist, I did a racist thing: hired all-white teams. And I also at times reinforced the Conformity Dynamic that is sexism. More than once I hired teams that were all men. How could I do such a thing? Denial. Making the Conformity Dynamic undeniably evident so that you won't be in denial and make the same mistakes I did is the work of the rest of this book.

THE COERCION DYNAMIC

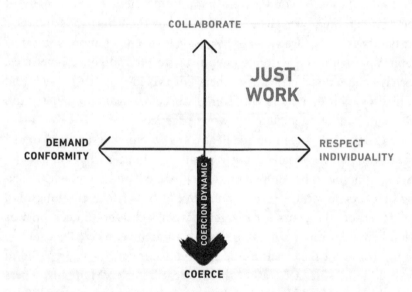

THE SLIPPERY SLOPE TOWARD VIOLENCE

The Coercion Dynamic is an equally ancient, well-worn path that leads from bias to bullying to harassment to violence. When bias gives way to violence—often in a heartbeat—there's nothing innocent about unconscious bias. Chanel Miller went with her sister to a college party ten minutes from home and woke up in the hospital, having been sexually assaulted behind a dumpster by a man she'd never met. George Floyd bought a pack of cigarettes, the clerk called 911 claiming Floyd had used a counterfeit $20 bill, and 17 minutes later he was murdered by police.

Part of the reason why these stories resonate so powerfully is not because they are unusual but because such violent encounters happen so frequently. Violence occurs in the workplace, as we saw in the story in chapter 8. But even when it happens outside the workplace, these experiences come to work with us. We must acknowledge them.

My lived experience of the Coercion Dynamic has also been of a privileged sort. I have rarely had to fear for my physical safety. But here is a story that illuminates why it's vital to recognize it, not to deny it.

I went to a holiday party a few months into a new job. The company's employees were predominantly (over 70 percent) men, so just walking in the door I was a little intimidated. I was greeted by women, mostly naked, dancing in cages. As I did too often in my career, I tried to ignore what was happening around me. Women dancing in cages? Someone's terrible idea of a joke, I reasoned. I tried to ignore how uncomfortable I felt.

I looked around for a familiar face. A colleague, Simon, was headed my way. He handed me a beer. At first, I was glad to see him. Then Simon ruined everything by asking, "Do you know what a Southern girl's mating call is?"

I said I didn't want to know, but Simon told me anyway: "Y'all, I'm so *drunk*."

I didn't feel physically threatened by Simon's rapey joke, exactly, but this brief exchange tripped all my sensors. The context of the party mattered—predominantly men, and a culture that made it possible for someone to think it was OK to hire women to dance in cages as "entertainment." At the very least, Simon was signaling that he was not an upstander. He was letting me know—and not in a nice way—that it would not be wise for me to let my guard down that evening.

If we lived in a world where the Coercion Dynamic did not create a well-worn path from bias to sexual violence, his behavior would have been "only" bullying. A discrete event. But given the world we did live in, he was reflecting and reinforcing rape culture. His behavior was misogynist.

BOTH DYNAMICS ARE SELF-REINFORCING

Let's go back to that first job I had in finance, in the former USSR. Both the Conformity and the Coercion Dynamics were at play there, reinforcing each other. *And* a vicious cycle was at play as well. The way I was being treated reinforced the biases of other people who were not necessarily participating in or aware of what was happening to me.

A decade after we'd left that company, I got together with a colleague from that time, Steve. Over dinner, he and I enjoyed a good laugh about how stressful that period had been: the 80-to-100-hour workweeks, the constant pressure. War stories.

"You always looked like your hair was on fire," he recalled, laughing. "I was kind of worried about you. Those kinds of hours are hard on everyone, especially women."

Was he kidding?! The *hours* had been hard on me? Evidently he thought, *Oh, women can't take these long hours, that's why Kim seemed stressed*. When of course it was not the long hours that had stressed me out.

Steve hadn't been paid less because of his gender; his boss wasn't a bullying ex-boyfriend; his breasts weren't groped by one of the top execs in the company; I was reasonably certain Fred didn't rub his erect penis up against Steve in the elevator. *That* was why Steve was less stressed than I'd been. Not because he was a man but because he wasn't dealing with all the sh*t I was dealing with. I can't blame him for not knowing what was going on with me because I never told him. I barely even admitted it to myself. I'm not telling the story to blame Steve. I'm telling it to show how discrimination and harassment reinforce bias even in those who don't discriminate or harass. Being mistreated had an impact on my behavior, and my behavior reinforced Steve's bias, even though he didn't know what was really going on.

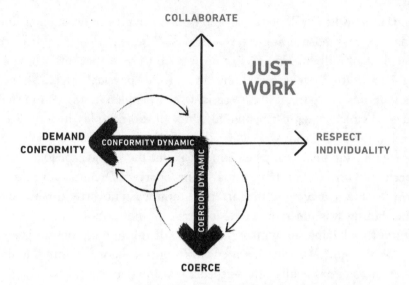

It's surprisingly difficult to interrupt this bias. Even years later, in a friendly conversation, I still couldn't summon up the energy to explain to him how unfair his bias about women and stress was. Why? Fred had died; Steve had gone to his funeral. Steve had loved Fred—which was understandable, since Steve got the mentorship without the frotting. It seemed easier to leave it all alone. That's how the self-reinforcing cycle of workplace injustice rolls.

I'd like to go back and help my younger self speak up and help Steve's younger self listen—and maybe even notice for himself some of what was going on. I hope this book will help the young Kims and the young Steves out there do that for one another and break these vicious cycles. I want to help them learn to collaborate and to respect each other's individuality so they can Just Work, rather than getting sucked into these negative dynamics.

DISCRETE INCIDENTS VS. DYNAMIC INJUSTICE

It's important to understand the difference between a discrete incident of bullying, and bullying that is a part of a dynamic that contributes to systemic injustice. The former is bad but is far less threatening than the latter. When I told my colleague Russ during the podcast recording that he was "born doing the power pose," he experienced a discrete incident of bullying. He was in no way concerned that my behavior, while admittedly bad, posed any threat to his physical safety. My behavior was not part of a pattern in which people like me committed acts of violence against people like him. It did not play into the Coercion Dynamic, that well-worn slippery slope from bias to violence, wasn't misogynist.[3] But when Simon told me the stupid rape joke, I experienced not only bullying but also the Coercion Dynamic, or misogyny. I felt a menacing undercurrent. Simon wasn't overtly threatening me, but he was normalizing a sinister, criminal notion—that people think that having sex with someone too drunk to give consent is just a "party foul." Whether he intended to or not, he was reminding me that I wasn't physically safe—especially if I had a drink.

Let me give another example of bullying that is a discrete incident for one person but plays into the Coercion Dynamic for another. When I was in elementary school one of my teachers told us that any of us who had not been baptized would go to hell. This was painful for me, since my religion, Christian Science, does not practice baptism. I did not believe I was going to go to hell, but I was still upset. I was experiencing bullying from my teacher. The Jewish girls in my class, however, were experiencing something much worse than bullying. Some had grandparents who were Holocaust survivors. For them the violence inherent in the Coercion Dynamic came immediately into play in a traumatic way that it didn't for me. I was experiencing bullying. They were experiencing anti-Semitism. There is a big difference.

If we are going to create the kind of just world we want to live in, we must be willing to be aware of the dynamics that can lead us from bias to discrimination or from bias to violence. Even if we ourselves have never committed an act of violence and don't think of ourselves as the kind of people who ever would, we need to be willing to notice the ways our words can reflect and reinforce patterns of violence. I am sure my Bible studies teacher did not think of herself as a person who would participate in genocide; I know Simon, the guy who told me the stupid "Y'all I'm so drunk" joke, well enough to be sure he did not think of himself as a person who would rape a woman or condone rape. However, both needed to be willing to acknowledge the way their words reflected horrible dynamics in our world if they wanted to show up to others as the kind of people they envisioned themselves to be.

GENDER DYNAMICS: SEXISM VS. MISOGYNY

Sexism describes the Conformity Dynamic as it pertains to gender. Sexism is insidious and also, confusingly, isn't a discrete attitude or behavior, but rather a dynamic between bias, prejudice, and discrimination that leaves women vulnerable to abuse. Misogyny describes the Coercion Dynamic as it pertains to gender. Misogyny is that well-worn dynamic between bias, bullying, harassment, and physical violations that leaves women coerced into roles they would not otherwise choose or even victims of violence.

Moral philosopher Kate Manne explains it like this: "Sexism is bookish; misogyny is combative. Sexism has a theory; misogyny wields a cudgel."[4] In other words, sexism is a concept that shapes prejudices about gender that justify discrimination, while misogyny uses bullying, harassment, and violence to dominate, coerce. Sexism is intellectualized, misogyny is more emotional, physical. Sexism artificially dichotomizes what's "male" and "female" and degrades the "female." Misogyny expects to be dominant and rages, often violently, when it is not.

Why parse the difference between sexism and misogyny, or the Conformity Dynamic and the Coercion Dynamic? The reason is that the difference points to which strategies are the most effective for combating them.

If you are dealing with misogyny in the absence of sexism, you don't need to waste time discussing the person's beliefs because the person has no beliefs. You can focus on creating consequences for the bullying as a way to prevent harassment and violence. When you understand misogyny, you understand why it is so important to address the bullying, to address the "Y'all, I'm so drunk" comments. Such "small" things reflect and reinforce rape culture, and when you know the dynamic at play, you know that silence about these smaller things paves the way for far worse to come.

If you are dealing with sexism in the absence of misogyny, you can focus on creating a clear boundary so one person can't impose their sexist beliefs on others. If the relationship with this person is important enough to justify the effort, you can have a conversation that invites the person to consider a different perspective on these beliefs. Consequences are unlikely to change a person's thinking. Logic and argument might.

It's useful to have words that describe a dynamic and where it leads, so we can differentiate between a discrete behavior and a dangerous dynamic. Having different words for different dynamics is helpful in diagnosing the problem and finding a solution. It's also useful to have a picture in our minds of how the system of workplace injustice works as a whole—its discrete problems, and the dynamics between them.

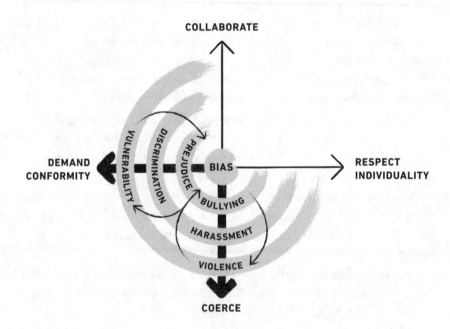

DENIAL

That's a pretty depressing picture and it is tempting to ignore it, deny it, refuse to look at it. When things can and do go badly wrong quickly in a way that is an all-too-familiar dynamic, it is *everyone's* moral imperative to become conscious of and interrupt our biases: none of us can afford to be in denial about the danger of the dynamics at play.

Unfortunately, denial is all too common a response. For example, Black employees at a number of Silicon Valley companies I'm familiar with have complained for years that security often checks their badges but not those of their white peers. This is without a doubt either racial bias or prejudice on the part of the security guards. It also reflects a dynamic of racism. I am white; I worked in tech for decades; no security guard ever checked my badge, anywhere, anytime. And I don't fear experiencing police violence when I get pulled over for not stopping at the red light.

When Cary, a Black employee at a tech company, complained about the badge checking at the company's cafeteria, the mostly white leadership shrugged it off as though it were a form of unconscious bias that they couldn't do much about. Even if the security guards were unaware of the bias that made them stop Cary and other Black employees but not white employees, what was happening was more than a discrete incidence of "unconscious bias." Given the dynamic of bias to violence, racism, that is prevalent for Black people in our society, what was happening went beyond a discrete incident of bias or prejudice.

The executives' job was to eliminate racism in the workplace. Yet, they were in denial that this was racism. Their denial was hard to understand, given that Cary raised this incident in the wake of George Floyd's murder, when her leadership was making noises about being antiracist. Cary tried to explain how being stopped by security guards when her white colleagues were not left her feeling unsafe. She mentioned Breonna Taylor, the Black EMT who was shot in her own home by police.

"I don't know who Breonna Taylor is," said the white executive. If he had followed up this admission of ignorance with "Please tell me," he would have signaled a willingness to listen and learn. But he stated it instead with aggressive finality—as though his ignorance meant that it didn't matter who Breonna Taylor was and excused him from finding out.

What made his response all the more incomprehensible was that Breonna Taylor's name was literally all over the news. And that Cary had sent the executive team an email the day before that had mentioned

Breonna Taylor, reminding executives who she was. Cary's note had explained that brushes with violence outside the office had worn her down and left her emotionally raw. She was deeply shaken by an encounter with an extremely aggressive police officer on her commute home recently. She felt angry, under siege, worried not just for herself but her family—how would her brother handle a situation like that? And even more worrying, how would the cop? It was impossible for her not to bring such experiences in to work.

But the white executives had no empathy, refusing to acknowledge that this badge-checking incident in the cafeteria had anything to do with racism; indeed, when they were confronted by it, each of them in a different way said things that reinforced a "she's an angry Black woman" bias.

The white executive's response was a classic example of denial, if not strategic ignorance. He didn't know who Breonna Taylor was because he didn't want to consider the possibility that what he dismissed as everyday unconscious bias in the company cafeteria was somehow connected to police killings. But given that it *is* connected, and that people all over the United States and even the world were protesting just this sort of systemic racism, the implication that his ignorance granted him some sort of immunity from engaging with the issue was inexcusable.

Tiffani Lee, a partner at the law firm Holland & Knight who leads its firmwide diversity and inclusion efforts, described a step her firm took to prevent this kind of denial from setting in. They found that addressing the problem of racism head-on actually took less effort than pretending it's not happening.

In the wake of George Floyd's murder, the firm held a town hall over Zoom with more than 1,300 people who worked there. Several people told stories about personal experiences they'd had with police brutality. A Black paralegal assistant who'd recently joined the firm described watching one of his relatives be murdered by the police and the resulting trauma suffered by his family. Hosting such a town hall was vital to interrupting the tendency of white employees to distance themselves from the reality of police violence. This violence wasn't happening to "other" people "elsewhere." It was happening to their own colleagues in their own community.

We see denial play out with gender issues as surely as it does with race. The screenwriter Scott Rosenberg had this to say about Harvey Weinstein's decades-long sexual predation: "Let's be perfectly clear about one thing: everybody fucking knew."[5] A few brave people spoke up and were punished or were paid and silenced by an NDA. And so for many years Weinstein's behavior continued. He was a bad actor, but a whole system—legal, corporate, social—enabled him. Everybody knew, but almost nobody said, "Hey, something is not right here."

New York Times columnist David Leonhardt called this kind of response a conspiracy of inaction. He wrote, "Every big case has had something in common . . . People knew. Even if they didn't know the details . . . they knew that something was wrong."[6] People know, but they don't *know,* or they deny or, for whatever reason, the knowing doesn't translate to action.

Leonhardt wrote, "The changes can't be only about policies and organizations. They need to be personal, too. I'm guessing that you get angry when you think about the abuse committed by Weinstein, O'Reilly, Trump . . . about the long-lasting misery they have inflicted on other human beings. I certainly do. The next time I [notice] something that doesn't seem quite right, I'm going to remember that anger."[7] Anger can break through denial and spur us to action.

It's easy to condemn and hard to understand how things could have gotten so bad at the Weinstein Company. But, even if it's not that bad, ask yourself what kind of injustice is happening where you work. If we are going to change the system, we have to look within—and keep looking, even when we aren't proud of what we see. Especially when we aren't proud of what we see. Part of what makes systemic injustice so difficult to recognize is that it is so disturbing that we really, really, *really* do not want to notice the dynamics—even when we know intellectually how bad things get if we don't intervene *before* things have gone to the very worst place.

The horrors that each of these dynamics can lead to are so deeply awful and disturbing that we refuse to notice because it's painful to notice. Let's go back to the story that started this book. None of us wanted to confront that the Soviet bureaucrats who were our business partners were trafficking Bolshoi Ballet dancers. So we didn't confront it. We pretended it was a joke, just "locker room" talk. Though if pressed we all would've admitted this probably wasn't just bluster; the Soviet officials had the power to coerce, and they almost certainly used it. A conspiracy of inaction. I was complicit in my silence.

GETTING PAST DENIAL

As Ibram X. Kendi wrote in *How to Be an Antiracist,* "Denial is the heartbeat of racism, beating across ideologies, races, and nations. It is beating within us."[8] Denial is also the heartbeat of misogyny, anti-Semitism, homophobia, and so many of the dynamics that lead to injustice. We must learn to recognize these dynamics so that we can fight them.

To move past denial, to dismantle the system of racism, we have to practice what Kendi calls antiracism.[9] Nonracism is a passive rejection of extreme racist behaviors such as burning crosses rather than a pro-active effort to look for and eradicate more everyday racist behaviors such as not sitting next to a Black person in a public place or voting for laws that negatively and disproportionately affect Black, Latino or Latina, and Indigenous people.[10]

To break free of our denial so that we can Just Work, it's not enough to want to be just, to intend to be just. We must take actions that are anti-injustice. We must be able to recognize the different ways that systemic injustice manifests itself.

To help, the next chapter will describe three of the most common forms, and give them names. As Kimberlé Crenshaw has said, when we name a problem, we can solve it.[11]

10

Recognizing Different Systems of Injustice

These dynamics combine in different ways to create three different systems of injustice in the workplace. If we know what to call them, it can be easier to identify them and dismantle them.

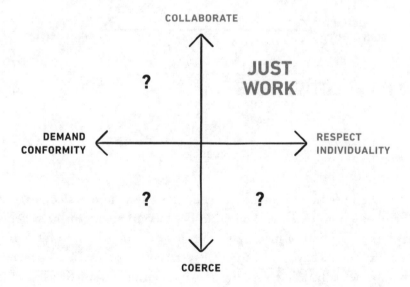

Sometimes you get the Conformity Dynamic without the Coercion Dynamic. I'll call that Oblivious Exclusion. Other times vice versa. I'll call that Self-Righteous Shaming. And sometimes you get both at the same time. I'll call that Brutal Ineffectiveness.

SYSTEM ONE: BRUTAL INEFFECTIVENESS

Brutal Ineffectiveness is what you get when the Coercion Dynamic and the Conformity Dynamic are happening at the same time and reinforcing each other. Sometimes it springs from an evil leader, but it often springs from management systems that fail to hold people accountable for bad behavior or that even *reward* bad behavior. Power dynamics, competition, poorly designed management systems, and office politics can create systemic injustice in ways that may be subtle and insidious at the outset but over time become corrosive, and often even criminal.

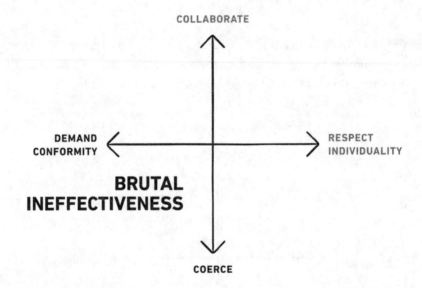

Sometimes leaders intentionally design a system to exclude part of the population. Usually, though, leaders set up management systems with the intention of making it simpler to decide whom to hire, fire, and promote. They intend to create efficient meritocracies. But what they are actually doing is setting up what journalist Kara Swisher calls a "mirror-tocracy"—a workplace that rewards only those who look just like its leader.[1]

And, really, who cares about the leader's intentions? In business, results matter, not intentions. Wall Street would not be at all forgiving of a CEO who said, "Well, I intended to improve profitability. I just can't understand why we are losing money. So let's not measure profitabiity. I am profitability blind. The issue must be a pipeline problem that I can't do anything about, so let's look at this other thing over here." Investors would never say to such a CEO, "Well, you're a good guy with good intentions so we'll buy your stock even though your results are terrible." No. There would be a move to hold the CEO accountable and find someone better able to do the job. We should demand the same good results from leaders who create management systems. If the systems reflect and reinforce the injustice in our society, they need to be changed. If a leader can't figure out how to change the system, the leader must go. But leaders can't change them single-handedly. We all need to play a role.

Here's a story about business processes that created systemic injustice and a leader who refused to take accountability for them, or even to notice what was happening under his watch. It shows how a bad system can reflect and reinforce a bad dynamic, how one dynamic can create the conditions for another, and how difficult (but not impossible) it is to change things once injustice has taken root. It's dark, darker than reality. Nobody in this story behaves well, which happily is not usually the case in real life. I've seen these dynamics play out in almost every company where I've worked, though usually there's been *some* human warmth to redeem the situation. The humanity of people often masks the problems in the system. So I've written a story in which nobody has any real humanity. I've written it this way to lay the dynamics of systemic injustice bare, not because I am as pessimistic about human nature as this story.

Tom, Dick, Harry, and Mary

Tom, Dick, and Harry are senior vice presidents reporting to Adam, the president of a software firm. Adam hates conflict, so the three work hard to appear as one happy, unified team. However, Tom, Dick, and Harry all want the same thing—to succeed Adam. Since only one of them will get his job, they have every incentive to weaken each other. Adam, who hates conflict, has unwittingly created a kind of shark tank. The battle always comes to a head at the end of the year when bonuses and promotions are handed out.

There's one bonus budget, controlled by Adam, allocated among the three SVPs' teams. If Tom's team gets bigger bonuses, then Dick's and Harry's teams get smaller ones. On top of that, this year Adam has decided only three people will be promoted into the VP ranks. Another zero-sum game. If, say, two of Dick's people get promoted, only one from Tom's or Harry's team does. The people who work for Tom, Dick, and Harry are all watching closely. No one wants to be stuck working for the boss who can't deliver a good payday.

Adam doesn't understand this game because he never had to play it. He thinks he is "above politics," and that everyone else should be, too. His father started the company, and there was never any question that one day Adam would be in charge. He has moved through his career in a kind of bubble. He won't tolerate it when Tom, Dick, and Harry fight in the open. Taking no responsibility for the power dynamics inherent in the rules of the game he's created, Adam says that his three SVPs are adults and ought to be able to work out their issues independently. As a result the tensions go underground, and there's a lot of behind-the-scenes maneuvering.

Tom realizes that the best way to attack Dick and Harry is to discredit the people who work for them, and that the easiest targets are the women on his rivals' teams. He goes after the women who work for Dick and Harry with special ferocity. (Everyone reporting to Tom, Dick, or Harry is white—nobody ever wonders why.)

Tom is "only" playing to win. He's not sexist, but if the women on his rivals' teams are vulnerable, he's going to attack them to get a bigger payday for his team. The strategy works. Tom's team gets the lion's share of bonuses and promotions. Some of the best people, including women, on Dick's and Harry's teams move over to Tom's team. They don't know about the behind-the-scenes maneuvering. They just notice that Tom's people tend to do better.

Dick picks up on Tom's game. But Harry is not as political; he still thinks Tom and Dick are his friends. To Harry's dismay, several of the best people on his team defect to Tom and Dick. Even though these defectors are all fond of Harry, they have their bonuses and promotions to consider. Harry gets a reputation for being a weak leader, unable to fight for his people; as more people defect, his results suffer further, and before long he's forced out of the company.

Bonuses and promotions are less reflective of the contributions a person has made than they are of a boss's power to attack the contributions of people on other teams. And it's usually easier to attack the contributions of underrepresented people. So underrepresented people on the team overall get lower ratings and get promoted more slowly. Never having had to play this game himself, Adam truly believes his process is meritocratic.

Tom, meanwhile, is starting to feel like kind of a stud. All the women want to work for him. He thinks it must be that they find him attractive. It never occurs to him it's because he fights hardest and gets the highest ratings for the people who work for him. He starts walking into women's offices, closing the door, and asking intensely personal questions. Or massaging their shoulders. He asks women to go have drinks with him. Once, a few drinks into the evening, he grabs Anika, a woman on his team, and forces her to kiss him. Anika talks to Denise, the HR VP, who knows that she herself will get fired if she brings this to Adam. Denise assures Anika she will give Tom "a stern talking-to." She does, and Tom treats the whole thing like a big joke.

Knowing that Adam hates conflict, none of the women complain to him. They are pissed off that the men in the company tend to get promoted faster, get bigger bonuses, and don't have to put up with Tom's creepy, predatory behavior. No one knows this better than Denise from HR. Finally, she decides she has to talk to Adam. But to protect herself, she doesn't point fingers at any specific men at the company. She knows that if she picks a fight with Tom, Adam will take Tom's side. Instead she simply points out that the women who perform the best consistently leave the company. The same is true of Black and Latino or Latina employees, but one injustice at a time, Denise decides. It doesn't occur to her that she'd have much more leverage if she broadened her perspective. She can't effectively address the problem of gender injustice without considering diversity, equity, and inclusion writ large.

Adam realizes she's right and wonders why he's never noticed it. It's important to him that his company be known as having a good working environment for women. But he has no idea how to solve what he now thinks of as "the woman problem." It never occurs to him that it's not a woman problem but a systemic injustice problem, one he himself created. When he starts the search for Harry's replacement, he tells his recruiters to focus on finding a woman. He figures hiring a woman will solve the woman problem.

Enter Mary, who has an impressive résumé and a history of increasing revenue at every company she's ever worked for. She assumes Adam hired her for this reason. Nobody mentioned to her that Adam expects her to solve "the woman problem."

Mary turns out to be a much sharper corporate game player than Harry was. She figures out the promotion game Tom and Dick are playing and is determined to win. And win she does. The lion's share of bonuses and promotions go to people on her team. Not necessarily because they have done the best work, but because she is even more effective at figuring out who the vulnerable people are on the other teams and undercutting them.

True, a disproportionate number of the most vulnerable people on Tom's and Dick's teams are underrepresented. But Mary hardly notices. Like Tom and Dick, she is focused on winning, not on race or gender. As a result, many of Tom's and Dick's best performers have now maneuvered to work for Mary. She delivers on bonuses and promotions. Many of these women tell Mary about Tom's behavior. She knows she is going to have to be strategic about how she uses it. Like Denise, she knows that going to Adam will backfire.

Meanwhile, Adam is puzzled. Why is Mary not more supportive of the younger women on Tom's and Dick's teams? He doesn't seem to notice how fiercely she pushes for the women on her own team. Nor did it ever bother him when Tom and Dick were attacking the women on each other's teams. But when Mary does the same thing for the same reasons, Adam wonders, "Why do women hate each other?" Feeling woke, he blames her behavior on internalized misogyny, though never to her face.

Tom and Dick realize that Mary is a threat and they unite against her. They joke that they miss having a weakling like Harry to push around. They want Mary gone. Promotion time comes around again. Adam has decided to create a fourth SVP position. If Tom, Dick, or Mary can maneuver one of their people into this new spot, then they will have a valuable ally on the senior management team. The jockeying for position becomes fiercer than ever.

There is an additional wrinkle in the game for Mary. Adam,

through a thousand casual remarks, has made it clear he thinks that one woman in his staff meeting is enough. He can't handle any more "catfights." Tom and Dick, united in their dislike of Mary, get Adam wound up, subtly reminding him of the unspoken reason he hired Mary: to fix "the woman problem," which has only gotten worse. That, of course, was never part of her job description. But they know it was part of Adam's calculation.

This is when things get diabolical: Tom and Dick realize that if they team up to push for Anika, the woman from Tom's team whom he kissed, to get the new SVP slot, that could spell the end of Mary—after all, Adam only wants one woman on the senior management team.

Meanwhile, Mary knows perfectly well that Adam is not looking to have more than one woman on his team. If Anika gets promoted, Mary will likely get fired. The stock options Mary got when she took the job are worth $2 million but are only half-vested. That means getting fired will cost her $1 million. Not surprisingly, she starts questioning Anika's competence fiercely, knowing that if a woman gets the job, Mary will probably be "managed out." That is, Adam will make her life so difficult she'll quit. Or maybe he'll just fire her. So a lot is at stake for Mary. She starts pushing hard for Arnold on her team to be promoted to SVP. Tom and Dick are united and quite nasty in their opposition to Arnold's promotion. Needless to say, it never occurs to Adam to accuse them of "internalized misandry."

Adam takes Mary's opposition to Anika as confirmation of her internalized misogyny, though. He concludes that Mary "is not supportive of other women." As far as Adam is concerned, Mary failed to fix "the woman problem." He doesn't acknowledge to himself or anyone else that he never discussed "the woman problem" with Mary. Also Mary has become a lightning rod for the very kind of conflict Adam finds most distasteful. Both Tom and Dick hate her, and Adam is sick of hearing about it. He starts to wonder why he ever hired her in the first place. How did he miss how unlikable and abrasive she is?

Tom and Dick know Adam has heard enough about how much they hate Mary, so they ask Anika to say bad things to Adam about Mary.

"But I like Mary," Anika objects.

"Well, she doesn't like you," they tell her. "She is fighting your promotion tooth and nail."

"Really? Why would she do that?"

"Go ask Adam," they tell her.

They also decide to find out how far they can push things with Mary herself. They start making overtly sexual comments when they are alone with her. When she lands a big account, they accuse her of sleeping with the customer. Tom drops trou, sits on the copy machine, and leaves Mary a photocopy of his ass and balls.

Finally fed up, Mary tells Adam about the photocopy. She tells him about Tom kissing Anika. This is the last thing Adam wants to deal with. Plus, he's sick of Mary. He finds her abrasive at the best of times, and lately she seems even more short-tempered than usual. So he decides he will just make his life easier. He fires her and gives her a decent severance package, thinking peace will return to his life. He rejects Anika's promotion and promotes Arnold. He's done with having women on his team.

But his life doesn't become more peaceful. Anika quits. She and Mary start a company that competes with Adam's. They create a promotion system that is transparent and fair. Their culture is known for being a bullshit-free zone. Several of the most talented people from Adam's company leave to go work for Mary's company. Over half the women at Adam's company leave. Seven years later, Mary's company is his biggest competitor.

Adam can't or won't notice that Tom, Dick, Harry, and Mary were all just playing by the rules of the game Adam created. It's unfair that Mary can't win in this system. But the answer is deeper than simply trying to help women win in this system. Even if Adam could eliminate the unconscious discrimination from his system, it would still be bad. It would be ineffective even if all at the company were white men who went to Harvard and rowed crew. The system itself is flawed. This is not an environment that encourages senior managers to pull together in the same direction. Adam's intentions may have been good. Maybe he even paid a consultant a lot of money to help set up this system. But instead of allocating bonuses and promotions to the executives who do the best work, his system rewards the ones who work for the biggest bully. This encourages coercion, not collaboration.

* * *

This is what I mean by "Brutal Ineffectiveness." In this story, the Conformity Dynamic was created and reinforced by the way that bonuses and promotions were decided. The Coercion Dynamic was created and reinforced because no checks and balances held the CEO accountable, and the CEO hated conflict so much he refused to hold Tom accountable. It was unfair that Mary wasn't allowed to play by the rules of the system. But the bigger injustice was the system itself, which was broken and in the end created a horrible situation for everyone. It was worst for Mary and all the underrepresented people at the company. But it was a pretty dark place for everyone.

HOW TO REPLACE BRUTAL INEFFECTIVENESS WITH JUST WORK

If your organization is characterized by Brutal Ineffectiveness, here is the checklist of things you need to start working on:

MOVE FROM DEMANDING CONFORMITY TO RESPECTING INDIVIDUALITY

- ☐ Bias interruption is a norm

- ☐ Code of conduct is well understood

- ☐ Bias quantifiers are built into routine business processes

MOVE FROM COERCION TO COLLABORATION

- ☐ There are consequences for bullying

- ☐ Checks and balances are structured

- ☐ Trusted reporting mechanisms are in place

- ☐ Culture of consent is understood

SYSTEM TWO: SELF-RIGHTEOUS SHAMING

The master's tools will never dismantle the master's house.
—Audre Lorde

"Why is such a man alive?" Dmitri said, beside himself with rage. "Tell me, can he be allowed to go on defiling the earth?"
—Fyodor Dostoyevsky, *The Brothers Karamazov*

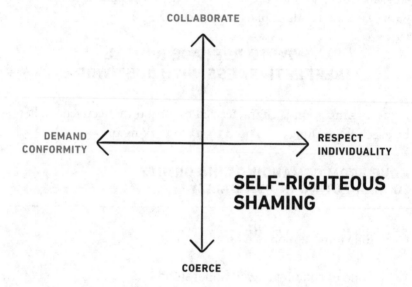

We can—indeed, we must—hold people accountable for unjust attitudes and behaviors, but we should not attempt to *coerce* people into mimicking our own beliefs and ideas, tempting though it may be to try, abhorrent though we may find their prejudices. The problem is threefold. First, it doesn't work. Yes, it may be possible to intimidate people into hiding their prejudiced beliefs, but that doesn't change what they think; it just makes it more likely it will come out in destructive, insidious ways. Second, such bullying tactics violate the very *principle* of collaboration, even when they are employed in the name of morality. They land us in an unjust system I'll call Self-Righteous

Shaming. This brings us to the third problem. This system is unstable. We don't have to respect prejudices that demand conformity; indeed, we must challenge them. But when we disrespect the *people* who hold them, then over time we are demanding conformity—ironically in the name of respecting individuality! We slide from Self-Righteous Shaming over to Brutal Ineffectiveness.

Yet we all too often use shame to attempt to coerce one person or group to respect another person or group. In a July 2020 podcast on accountability and shame, author Brené Brown warned against this kind of coercion:

> Shame is not an effective social justice tool. Shame is a tool of oppression. Shame is a tool of white supremacy. Humiliation, belittling, those are tools of injustice. They're not tools for justice. First, shame corrodes the belief that we can be better and do better. And it's much more likely to be the cause of dangerous and destructive behaviors than the cure. Shame itself is inherently dehumanizing. I go back to Audre Lorde's quote, "The master's tools will never dismantle the master's house" . . . Shame begets shame and violence.[2]

Self-Righteous Shaming exemplifies a decidedly fixed mindset that allows for condemnation but not growth or redemption. The people being shamed are spurred/galvanized to defend themselves rather than to examine their own flawed logic or destructive behavior. The same goes for the other side: the people doing the shaming rarely notice their own flawed logic or coercive tactics.

Shame sometimes comes from the top down—an ultimatum delivered by a boss or manager. Other times, it can rise from the bottom up, as on Twitter, Slack, or an employee intranet. Either way, it makes true collaboration at work impossible. Psychologist Lisa Schievelbein explains, "Shame is problematic in both the painful experience in the moment and its ripple effects on motivation and interpersonal behavior. Research has revealed a propensity to process shame-fueled anger in non-constructive ways, such as direct and indirect aggression, resentment, irritability, blaming others, and indirect expressions of hostility."[3]

Shaming is popular because it is relatively easy—much easier than having a respectful exchange of ideas—and powerful. A minimal effort—a blistering phrase in a public forum, a withering put-down released into the world with the push of a button—with potentially enormous impact. No wonder it has spread like a noxious invasive weed throughout social media.

But it is vital to understand the difference between *feeling shame* and *being shamed*. When we are held accountable for something we have done or said that harms others, we often *feel* shame, even though the person who pointed out the problem is not shaming us, but rather is giving us valuable feedback. When we feel ashamed, we tend to retreat into denial or to go on the attack—perhaps both. Instead we must learn to work through our feelings of shame and get to a place where we recognize what we have done wrong. In her podcast, Brown underscores the importance of being able to make this critical distinction:

> There is a huge difference between being shamed for being a
> racist and feeling shame. It's my job to regulate my emotion,
> move through shame in a productive way, without defensiveness,
> without doubling down, without rationalizing, without demanding
> to be taught, demanding absolution, demanding comfort from
> the person who is holding me accountable, who is often a Black
> person or a person of color. I am responsible for that emotional
> regulation.[4]

Those of us who are committed to rooting out shaming must be equally committed to genuine inquiry: to holding ourselves and one another accountable with respect and courage; to listening better and taking responsibility for regulating our own feelings of shame; and to making these exchanges feel exciting and inspiring rather than punitive and humiliating. Only then can we break free of denial to become the people we want to be and to create the kind of just workplaces where we can build our most creative, productive careers.

BOTTOM-UP SHAMING: THE CONDEMNING MOB

As Bryan Stevenson wrote, "Each of us is more than the worst thing we've ever done."[5] None of us wants our worst moment to be the thing that defines us forever, the thing that goes viral; none of us wants to be mistaken for someone else at our worst moment and then doxed. But this is not a condemnation of all social media. Despite the excesses, videos and social media have been a tremendous force for justice, rather than injustice, for Black Lives Matter and for #MeToo.

When incidents blow up on social media, as they invariably will, for good and for ill, it requires that leaders lead, rather than following online mobs blindly; and that we learn to use these new tools to hold people accountable but not to rush to judgment or to wield shame like a weapon.

Before considering what a condemning mob looks like when it comes to confronting issues of justice and injustice, let's look at one that most people don't have such strong feelings about: bicycle etiquette.

I was working at a company where the "campus" was a bunch of buildings scattered around a California town. My boss's office was a little over a mile from mine—a 6-minute bike ride, or a 23-minute walk. There was no parking, so driving wasn't an option. To make getting around easier, the company had a number of bikes for the employees to share. Often I only had five minutes between meetings to travel between the two buildings, so I was very dependent on the bikes. As luck would have it, my boss's office was at the edge of campus where there were never any bikes. If I followed bike protocol and left the bike I'd ridden over outside the building, someone else would take it and I would be stranded. So I started wheeling it into my meetings to ensure I could be on time for my next one.

Unbeknownst to me, one of my colleagues was also frustrated by the lack of bikes at that building. One day, when he spied me bringing the bike into a conference room, he posted a description of my bike etiquette violation to an email alias that went out to several thousand people and asked what kind of horrible, selfish person would do such a thing. Lots of people piled on. I didn't have time to keep up with the many intranet forums at this company, so I had no idea that I had become a bike-hoarding asshole everyone was pissed at. The next day, when I did it again, he took a picture of me and posted it with the caption "the most UnCool thing." More comments. More moral outrage. More shaming. The company was pretty big, so it took a while for someone to attach my name to the picture, but eventually someone did, and I got a call from a friend alerting me to the brewing scandal.

My colleague had a legitimate point—after all, he worked in that building and was understandably annoyed that there was rarely a bike there when he needed one. Yet, because he had deliberately shamed me, I was initially unable to acknowledge his point of view. Who was this asshole, following me around, taking pictures, violating my privacy, and hurling moral accusations about me on a public intranet? I got so worked up that it became impossible to acknowledge to myself or anyone else that I had in any way contributed to the problem. If this jerk had enough spare time to surreptitiously snap photos of me while I was furiously pedaling between meetings, he should be fired. I couldn't even get to the legitimate question about his behavior. Why hadn't he just approached me directly? If he'd simply pointed out that I was making things difficult for him, I would've said something like "I am really sorry. I can't afford to be late to my next meeting, but I won't do this again. I'll quit relying on the f—d up communal bike system and bring my own bike with a lock to work tomorrow."

Luckily for me, by the time I became aware of what was going on, HR had already taken down the post and privately told the poster that publicly shaming a colleague was not the way to handle these situations. They also alerted me to what had happened and expressed compassion for the harsh way I'd been treated. Perhaps most important, they committed to solving the bike problem. In the meantime, they asked me to quit bringing bikes into meetings. Which I did. But if no one had intervened and I'd met this moral grandstanding with my own counterattack, who knows how many additional friends and strangers would have been pulled into our squabble. What a waste of time and energy.

I was also fortunate that it isn't that hard to shed the label of being a bike hoarder. Bike hoarding is not the kind of label that sticks. But what if I had been shamed not for bike hoarding but for internalized misogyny or racism or homophobia?

Often our intentions in shaming are good: we are trying to defend a vulnerable individual or a group of people who are being disrespected. Or perhaps we have been shamed ourselves, and so it feels fine to dish it out. Or we are just fed up with a broken system that isn't working for us, so we lash out at a person rather than trying to fix the system—as the guy who shamed me for my bicycle behavior did. Or perhaps the people we are shaming are more powerful than we are, so we assume they somehow deserve it or can take it. We forget that we owe common human decency to everyone, regardless of how powerful or powerless the person is.

For all these reasons, we may resort to shaming rather than attempting to figure out what we can do to solve the problem. Doing the same bad thing that's been done to you just fuels a cycle of injustice. Most often, the shaming fails to transform your own situation; sometimes shaming causes you to change roles from the oppressed to the oppressor. You are still in a bad place, or you have become bad—or both. Self-Righteous Shaming is injustice in the name of justice, is vengeance, not repair, and finally—insofar as we know at some level that it won't work—is an act of despair.

Shaming becomes even more dangerous when a group of people are doling out the shame. Given how addictive the rush of shaming others is, and how social media tend to facilitate this kind of communication, condemning mobs are not only ubiquitous online but increasingly common in today's workplaces.

Another thing that makes Self-Righteous Shaming more likely is when there is not just a majority but a supermajority. When the vast majority of people share a point of view, it's likely that they will dismiss the dissenting voice in a way that shames those who disagree.

No matter which side of an issue the condemning mob is on, mob shaming invariably is counterproductive at both a practical and a moral level. These mobs generally derive their tone of moral superiority from the notion that they are upholding some sort of right or tearing down a system that is unjust to some but not to others. This notion of protecting the rights of individuals lands the condemning mob in this quadrant: coercive, yet not demanding conformity.

TECHNIQUES THAT WORK BETTER THAN SHAMING TO CONFRONT INJUSTICE AT WORK

COLLABORATE, DON'T COERCE

In his book *Active Listening,* psychologist Carl Rogers proposed an approach to disagreement that helps us move away from coercive behaviors such as Self-Righteous Shaming and toward a productive, collaborative resolution.[6] The goal is to confirm that both people understand each other. Rather than pro/con, winner/loser debates, Rogerian arguments require both sides to be able to articulate each other's perspective and also to identify the points in one's own argument that can be amended or adjusted. To clarify your thinking, you listen to the other person and argue with yourself. Rhetorical scholars Sonja Foss and Cindy Griffin have developed a similar strategy for disagreement with respect called Invitational Argument.[7] In *Radical Candor,* I suggest switching roles when a debate at work gets too intense. This is a good way to make sure that egos don't get attached to ideas, to make sure that we are listening to each other and respecting each other.

Recall the argument I had with my colleague about being a working mother, described in chapter 2. We didn't necessarily have to agree about "what was best for children" to work well together; but we did have to talk enough about the issue with enough respect for each other as individuals that we could get to a modus operandi. I did not and do not respect his prejudiced belief that mothers of young children must stay home; but more broadly I did and do respect him as a human being. It was possible to work with him, to talk to him, to insist he respect my choices, and to respect his choices.

GET ON AN EQUAL FOOTING

One reason we shame others is that we feel we are up against unfair power dynamics. Molly Ivins pointed out that satire, which she defined as "holding people up to public contempt or ridicule," is the "weapon of the powerless against the powerful."[8]

I do not want to rob the powerless of a weapon against the powerful. If you want to satirize me, to ridicule me in public, I will try to learn what I can from your critique. However, I am not sure this will work as well with your boss as it will with me. I'm not saying don't hold your boss accountable. I am saying you probably have more effective tools than shame at your disposal. If you are a comedian or a journalist, satire may work for you. But if you take this approach with your boss, you may create an enemy unnecessarily. Maybe the person was going to be your enemy no matter what you said. But maybe, just maybe, this person is actually trying, if ineffectively, to be an ally. Few things will turn potential allies into enemies faster than shaming them.

When you can approach people in positions of authority as fellow human beings, it becomes easier to hold them accountable without shaming them *or* fearing them. I have observed throughout my career that the people who are able to treat their bosses and other executives "above" them as equals are most able to challenge them effectively. They don't hesitate to offer criticism when it's merited. They don't hide their opinions. They don't kiss up—*and* they don't treat people who have authority like tyrants to be toppled. In the vast majority of cases, this approach builds trust. You do take a risk—sometimes you'll get into trouble when you confront an authority figure. But in my experience, the risk pays off in the end.

If you feel vulnerable, though, it's hard to get on an equal footing. You may not be comfortable interrupting bias. You may have a hard time trying to create consequences for people who bully you. Even if there is a system of checks and balances or a reporting system, you may be reluctant to escalate for fear of consequences. What can you do to take a more active stance so that you can confront injustice in a way that is more effective than writing off others as useless, worthless human beings?

Maria Konnikova, a psychologist and author of *The Biggest Bluff*, explains what she learned about taking an active stance in life and at work by playing poker. She learned how to act as though she had a strong hand even when she didn't.

There's a false sense of security in passivity. You think that you can't get into too much trouble—but really, every passive decision leads to a slow but steady loss of chips. And chances are, if I'm choosing those lines at the table, there are deeper issues at play. Who knows how many proverbial chips a default passivity has cost me throughout my life? How many times I've walked away from situations because of someone else's show of strength, when I really shouldn't have? How many times I've passively stayed in a situation, eventually letting it get the better of me, instead of actively taking control and turning things around? Hanging back only seems like an easy solution . . . It isn't a pleasant realization, but it is an important one. Now that I [notice] it, perhaps I can start working through it.[9]

Figure out how to practice ignoring power dynamics so that you can treat others as your equals at a human level. Games are useful because the feedback is more immediate and less messy. You can try chess or improv techniques. Or just practice a different approach with a safe group. One woman I worked with held a spaghetti dinner in which all came with a story about something obnoxious their boss had said to them. Then they would all practice what they "could have said." The stories were outrageous, and often the different approaches people came up with were as funny as they were confidence boosting.

DON'T PILE ON

If you notice an online mob forming on a Slack channel or an employee intranet at work, don't pile on. Check in with the targets to get their perspective, even if what they did does seem pretty terrible. A beautiful example of this sort of intervention is in *Rising Out of Hatred,* a book about how Derek Black left white nationalism, as described in chapter 2.[10]

When you see a clip of someone doing something shameful that is widely shared on Twitter, try to pause and think about a moment when you did something you were later ashamed of. Try to use it as an opportunity to learn how you might do better rather than as an opportunity to say, *Look how horrible that person is! I sure am glad I'm not that bad.*

TOP-DOWN SHAMING: ZERO TOLERANCE

The power of a condemning mob is bottom up. It lies less in the status of its members than in its sheer size. Weak leaders fear this kind of mob and seek to avoid its wrath at all costs; strong leaders seek to learn from it and are able to guide it to a more productive outcome.

One way leaders seek to avoid provoking the mob is to adopt a zero-tolerance company policy—that is, "One strike and you're out"—in a top-down bid to stamp out unwanted behavior. Admittedly, this approach is tempting. It allows a leader to signal strong, virtuous opposition to problematic attitudes and bad behavior. It also promises to cut through ambiguity and avoid the time, energy, and cost of due process. Unfortunately, it doesn't work and it is unfair.

Zero tolerance seeks to avoid the problem. A better goal is to *fix the problem*. Which means first acknowledging this can be a hard, messy process—one that involves tolerating mistakes and learning to distinguish between those that can be gently corrected and those that merit consequences. It also means conducting a due process that protects people harmed without being unjust to people accused.

Yes, your job as a leader is to take a strong stand against injustice in the workplace. Your job is *not* to shame people who don't have as much power as you do in order to make yourself look good. This behavior is known as virtue signaling and is merely another form of bullying. Instead it is your responsibility to create a *genuinely* respectful working environment in which everyone can make mistakes, be held accountable for them, and learn a more effective way of collaborating with their teammates. Fighting prejudice and bullying with more bullying won't achieve that goal.

Also, any policy's promise to cut through ambiguity is a false promise. Many leaders hope that zero tolerance will allow them to avoid confronting messy situations or making complicated judgment calls. But confronting messy situations and making complicated judgment calls is an integral part of creating a respectful work environment. Sometimes as a leader you'll make the wrong call; ideally, you'll have the opportunity to learn from it and grow as a leader. *Extend that same opportunity to the folks on your team.*

Zero tolerance, in short, brings with it serious unintended consequences. It neither protects the vulnerable nor persuades the people causing harm to change their behavior.

If a company deems some behaviors fireable offenses, it is a leader's job to make sure that everyone knows what they are. But no matter how clear the line is, a fair process is necessary to figure out which side of the line a specific incident falls on. These situations are volatile and complicated, and it's easy for emotion to take over from rational adjudication. Remember: slowing down and looking at all the ambiguities and complexities is not the same as siding with the alleged transgressor, no matter how vehemently the mob is demanding someone's head.

I knew one organization where a neuro-atypical employee tweeted, "I like trans women so much more than real women." Without understanding the implications of what he was saying, he wrote something that was insulting to both cisgender and trans women. Some leaders at the company called for his dismissal in the name of zero tolerance. Luckily, the leader of the organization persuaded them that education was in order in this case.

Many companies have started firing people whose social media posts get massively condemned, whereupon people blame the social media platforms for getting them fired. But Twitter didn't fire these people. Their bosses did. Often even the people who did the shaming are horrified to learn the target has been fired; they wanted the behavior to change but didn't necessarily want the person to be fired.

So if you are a boss, think through what kinds of things you'd fire someone for saying in public. Make this policy clear, part of your code of conduct. And then when people say or do things that explode on social media and are horrifying in ways that aren't necessarily covered in your code of conduct, ask yourself a couple of questions: *Is this blowing up on the internet because that one person is so horrible? Or because what they did is bad and yet happens all the time in private?* If it's a thing that is "bad and yet happens all the time," that means you have other employees who are probably doing the same thing. Maybe you've done the same thing. The right thing to do in these cases is not to point fingers at the employee and say, "You are awful and no longer deserve to work with us," but instead, "This behavior is awful, many of us nevertheless engage in it, and it needs to stop. Let's learn from this, and change." Ask yourself, is firing that person (zero tolerance) the best way to make the behavior stop? Or will it simply frighten your team and breed resentment and fear? Or could this be an opportunity to educate everyone, and prove that you care more about creating a more equitable workplace than you do about avoiding a PR problem? Don't simply fire people because you fear the social media mob will come after you if you don't. Show some leadership.

I understand the allure of zero tolerance. I have succumbed to the temptation of its easy answers myself and watched leaders I admire fall into the same trap.

I was coaching a CEO, Andrew, who wanted to stamp out the "brogrammer" culture at his company. He was especially concerned about his engineering team, which was 90 percent men and had a hyperaggressive, elbows-out culture. His employees liked to say that that was just the way things were. But it wasn't that way for the few women on the team; when they played the game the way the men did, they'd be dismissed as "abrasive" or "bitchy"—especially by the most aggressive men. And when the women were *not* superaggressive, they'd be told in performance reviews that they were "too nice" or lacked "executive presence," and that's why they weren't being promoted. Needless to say, the women on the team felt caught in a double bind.

Many women had complained to Andrew about the company's culture, and he'd talked to the men on his team about it. But as more time passed and nothing changed, he started to get angry. At a meeting with his top managers, he finally lost it. A model of self-righteous indignation, he pounded his fist on the table. "I will not tolerate this behavior!" he shouted. If he continued hearing the same complaints, he warned, the consequences would be swift and severe.

I was glad that he cared so much, but I felt a familiar ache in the pit in my stomach. When I first became a CEO, I'd done the same thing. I'd tried to punish people for sexist attitudes and behaviors, and it just didn't work. It was kind of like trying to house-train a dog by rubbing its nose in poop. Fearful and ashamed, the dog is now likely to poop behind the couch next time, where it still stinks but is harder to find. Much better to make the offenders (usually smarter than a dog) conscious of the bias and explain why it's a problem without shaming them, giving them an opportunity to self-correct.

The overarching point is that leaders must be able to articulate a principled approach and to consider violations case by case rather than simply coming up with absolute rules and then applying them without any willingness to look at the specifics of a particular situation.

Sometimes the Self-Righteous Shaming from the boss springs from a different, more defensive place. For example, Rick once said to one of his employees who was heating up her lunch in the microwave at work, "Are you really going to eat that whole thing?" When she became visibly upset, he told her, "Don't be so sensitive!" He was shaming her for pointing out his mistake.

This wasn't the first time he'd made this kind of bullying comment to her and then tried to make her feel ashamed for being upset. Indeed, he had a reputation for gratuitous insults. Recently, she'd confronted him with several of her colleagues. His response had been, "You are a bunch of snowflakes. Your whole generation just doesn't know how to take a joke." So this time she went to his boss.

Rick's boss explained to him, "You do not improve the dynamic on your team by telling people how they should feel, or shaming them for how they do feel. Either you care about figuring out how to work well with your team or you don't. If you don't, you won't be effective here and you'll get fired."

WHAT WORKS BETTER THAN ZERO TOLERANCE FOR LEADERS?

CREATE A CULTURE OF COLLABORATION: TEACH FOLKS TO "INVITE IN," NOT "CALL OUT"

Even if you are being shamed, use the moment to learn what you can from the poorly delivered feedback. When criticism is directed at you as a leader, don't criticize the criticism; learn from it. If people on your team are shaming one another, though, it's important to teach them a better way to communicate.

Diversity consultant the Reverend Dr. Jamie Washington offers excellent advice in his talk "Woke Olympics: Navigating a Culture of Social Justice Arrogance in the Context of Higher Education."[11] He explains the difference between "calling out" and "inviting in." He offers suggestions for how educators and leaders can prevent Self-Righteous Shaming from destroying the culture in their classrooms or on their teams. He describes the role of leaders in creating a learning environment: inviting people to consider one another's experiences and thoughts rather than getting locked in a vicious cycle of "convicting, converting, and convincing."[12]

Inviting in takes a lot more time than shaming others or hurling an insult. Admittedly, having a difficult conversation won't give you the quick-hit rush that condemning another person wholesale often provides. It's hard work. But, unlike shaming, this work creates a more just environment. You get more out of it than you put into it.

This is especially important in an era of remote work and communication tools that allow us to broadcast harsh judgments from behind the safety of a screen. But it's your job as a leader to minimize the impact of moral grandstanding.

ALLOW YOURSELF TO BE HELD ACCOUNTABLE

When you are held accountable for having done something wrong, it's natural to feel shame. Remember: that doesn't mean you are *being* shamed. It means you *feel* ashamed. There's a big difference.

But even when the condemning mob is shaming you, treat it like feedback: there may be an underlying issue you need to address. Even if the person or the mob didn't do such a great job holding you accountable, listen anyway—and try to understand the human need behind the attack. You can learn from harshly delivered feedback as well as from humanely delivered critiques.

Sometimes your job as a leader is to serve as the emotional shock absorber for your team. Other times you will find yourself functioning as a projection screen for everyone's unresolved authority issues. This is deeply uncomfortable. But it's part of your job. But there may *also* be times when you have courteously and clearly been told what you or your company are doing wrong and it makes you feel terrible. Because you feel terrible, you may instinctively go on the counterattack. You have the power to go on the counterattack. You can probably get away with it in the short term. Don't give in to that temptation. If you can learn to expect these moments and to lay your power down so you can learn, you'll be more successful in the long run.

Try not to let shame hijack your brain. That said, sometimes you are going to fail. Shame triggers your "fight-or-flight" lizard brain and shuts down your prefrontal cortex. Moving through it is easier said than done. But remember: when you are a leader, it's your job to allow others to hold you accountable as much as it is to hold them accountable.

DON'T CRITICIZE THE CRITICISM

Maybe you feel ashamed but you were not shamed. Maybe you were shamed. Either way, some criticism is being leveled at you. If you are the boss, this is not your moment to criticize the criticism. This is your moment to listen, to get curious, to try to understand what you're being told with as little defensiveness as you can humanly muster.

LAY YOUR POWER DOWN

Even if you've done all the right things—built norms for interrupting bias, created consequences for bullying, established checks and balances, and put in place anonymous reporting systems—people on your team may still fear retaliation if they give you feedback on something unjust that you've done. When that's the case, they're more likely to resort to shaming you. This can be especially painful when you've gone to great lengths to help people feel safe. What more do you have to do to earn trust?? Here you've done all this work and *still* you're being attacked in a way that is making it hard to get sh*t done! It's tempting to use your power to crush the mob.

Brené Brown calls this "armoring up." Here are the unproductive steps that a lot of leaders go through when they feel shame or are being shamed:

- *I am not enough.*
- *They will use it against me.*
- *No way am I going to be honest about this.*
- *Screw them.*
- *This is actually their problem, they're . . .*
- *In fact, I'm better than them!*

She explains that the path from "I'm not enough" to "I'm better than" is incredibly short—indeed, feeling superior is the exact same standing-still position of pain and shame.[13]

If you are a leader, use your executive function to guide yourself out of shame to a more productive place. Take accountability and take action to make things right. Don't ask people less powerful than you to make you feel better.

MANAGE ONLINE COMMUNICATION

Given how addictive the rush of shaming others is, and how often public online communication media play a role in bringing out the mob, leaders may want to ban anonymous commenting. When flame wars start, you may have to tell people when their communication is counterproductive. This is difficult because you will invariably be accused of censorship. But your job as a leader is to get sh*t done, fast and fair. Self-Righteous Shaming between team members gets in the way of that.

DO WE HAVE TO TOLERATE INTOLERANCE? NO

But we have to combat it in a way that doesn't create a new in-group and a new out-group, thereby compounding the very problem we are trying to correct. The touchstone is always collaboration. Intolerance fragments the team. How can that fragmentation best be healed? Fighting prejudice by creating a new kind of prejudice is not effective, either practically or morally.

Psychologist Gordon Allport warns of the pitfall of shaming and essentializing in his 1958 book *The Nature of Prejudice:* "A student in Massachusetts, an avowed apostle of tolerance—so he thought— wrote, 'The Negro question will never be solved until those dumb white Southerners get something through their ivory skulls.' The student's positive values were idealistic. But ironically enough, his militant 'tolerance' brought about a prejudiced condemnation of a portion of the population which he perceived as a threat to his tolerance-value."[14]

Racism in the South was real and needed to be addressed. But in essentializing all Southerners, the student in Massachusetts was personifying racism and locating it elsewhere, outside himself, outside his region. Shaming someone else is often a form of denial about one's own issues. The student referred to "the Negro question" when he should have used the word "racism." *Racism* was the problem, not Black people. By essentializing Southerners, he failed to notice his own racism. He also failed to support the people of both races in the South who were fighting for racial justice.

Too many of us make the mistake that student in Massachusetts made—not only about racism but about all forms of intolerance. Attacking men and masculinity does not serve the cause of feminism; it just reinforces another sort of damaging prejudice. And asserting that religious intolerance is a big problem in Ireland or Israel or India and labeling all a country's citizens as bigots harms champions of religious freedom in that country and makes religious bigotry harder to recognize at home.

Sometimes when white people engage in antiracism they unconsciously frame it through "superiority" that reflects the underlying attitudes of white supremacy culture.[15] When mob shaming adopts an Orwellian notion of "pure" thought and "pure" speech, and when the punishments for saying the wrong thing become too draconian, it starts the swift slide into Brutal Ineffectiveness.[16]

It's important to be able to distinguish between the truly bad actors and the people who made a mistake they can learn from. When people are allowed to admit they made a mistake, then they don't have to protect the truly bad actors in order to protect their own potential missteps. But if the punishment for having said the wrong thing or even done the wrong thing is too severe, then people won't admit it when they have screwed up, and they will be afraid to acknowledge far worse behavior in others for fear of being lumped in the same category. Yes, it's important to understand the dynamic that leads from bias to violence. But, no, we can't treat everyone who says a biased thing the same way we'd treat a person who commits violence.

HOW TO BECOME LESS SELF-RIGHTEOUS AND MOVE TOWARD JUST WORK

If your workplace is characterized by Self-Righteous Shaming, the good news is, you're already part of the way through your Just Work checklist. You're struggling with one bad dynamic but not two. The bad news is that if you don't continue to work your way down the checklist, not only will bad things happen, but the good work you've already done will likely get undone. Self-Righteous Shaming is unstable, as its bullying leads quickly toward discrimination and abuse.

RESPECT INDIVIDUALITY: YOU'VE MADE SOME GOOD PROGRESS (BUT IF YOU ALLOW SHAME TO RUN ITS COURSE, THIS WILL BE CORRUPTED)

- ☑ Bias interruption is a norm

- ☑ Code of conduct is well understood

- ☑ Bias quantifiers are built into routine business processes

MOVE FROM COERCION TO COLLABORATION: YOU'VE GOT SOME WORK TO DO

- ☐ There are consequences for bullying

- ☐ Checks and balances are structured

- ☐ Trusted reporting mechanisms are in place

- ☐ Culture of consent is understood

You may think you don't need to create consequences for bully-ing because you don't hire "that kind of person." Problem is, you are kidding yourself. We *all* have the capacity for bullying because it works. When there aren't consequences for bullying, you are ensuring more, not less, of it. You may think you hire good leaders who can be "trusted." But power corrupts, and sometimes it corrupts the best of us. You may think that you don't need trusted reporting mechanisms because "those sorts of things" wouldn't happen in your organization. They happen *everywhere,* and there's no way to recognize what "sort" of person bullies, harasses, commits violence. That is why repeat of-fenders get away with their crimes for *years*. You may think that a culture of consent is common sense and doesn't need to be made ex-plicit. #MeToo has demonstrated that we do need explicit rules around consent and to enforce those rules, in the office and everywhere. The frequency of police violence reminds us that we need stronger rules of engagement, to hold the police accountable for violating those rules.

Make sure your bias interruptions do not become weaponized. Re-mind people to show compassion for one another when pointing out bias. Any time a bias interruption takes the form of an attack on the other person's morality, it's an anvil being used to pull out a screw: the wrong tool for the job, and it will cause ancillary damage. If that happens, invite the moral grandstander to consider whether the tactic is effective or fair. Do it in private—and don't let it stand. Make sure there are consequences for bullying. Rather than trying to assert your power with zero tolerance, limit it with checks and balances. This will prevent people from abusing their authority and harassing people with less power; it will also ensure that no single leader can implement the kind of zero tolerance that creates intolerance in the name of tolerance. And, finally, put trusted reporting systems in place, so that people suffering from violence or trauma can register a complaint and know that it will be investigated fairly and they will not be retraumatized. Ensure that everyone understands what a culture of consent means, and that its norms are upheld.

Moving toward Just Work requires leadership, but leaders can't do it alone. If you are a person harmed or an upstander, make sure that you understand what your options are for making your voice heard. Even if your leaders have not taken all the advice in this book, or any of the advice in this book, *you* can. Review the things you can do to interrupt bias. You can create a consequence for bullying and also create a system of checks and balances by looking for the exits and quitting if possible. Even without good checks and balances or a reporting system you trust, you still have options: finding another job, talking to HR, taking legal action, or telling your story. Your voice and your actions matter. Without them, it's too easy for others to retreat into denial.

OBLIVIOUS EXCLUSION

Oblivious Exclusion is by far the most common manifestation of workplace injustice. It's the least dramatic and hardest to put your finger on. It's especially easy for the people causing harm to ignore. Things are collegial, pleasant, and civilized—at least if you're on the inside or even close to the inside. Everyone jokes around with each other; they talk about sports and TV and pretend to be interested when Bob brags about what a good chess player his seven-year-old daughter is. There's a generous parental leave policy. But only 1 of the 11 SVPs is a woman, and all of them are white. Nobody wants to think too hard about why this is. They assume it's because women don't want the job. They don't even ask themselves why they are all white. One leader I worked with calls this "false harmony." Another calls it "country club management."

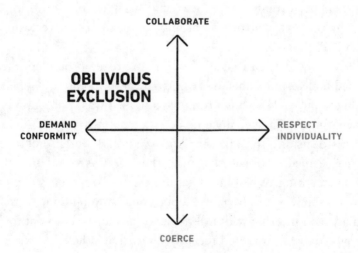

It's also difficult for the people harmed to identify Oblivious Exclusion when it's happening. Brutal Ineffectiveness, that's something you feel. You know something is wrong because you are being harmed in pretty obvious ways. Self-Righteous Shaming slaps you right in the face. But Oblivious Exclusion operates in the shadows. When you try to call it out, the answer is often just "Nothing to see here." It's what I was running away from when the bank executive said, "I didn't know they let us hire pretty girls." Here's a story about what it's like.

Sally's Rise

I was working at a company I'll call Fast Growing Tech Company X. Sally, the only senior woman on the product team, learned that one of her peers had gotten a stock grant worth many multiples of what hers was worth. That was pretty hard to swallow, but she was trying to stay focused on being positive, doing great work, and getting promoted.

Over time, though, she didn't get promoted, despite her many impressive contributions, and she was finding it more and more difficult to stay motivated. She showed me her most recent performance review. Bob, her boss, had written that she was "abrasive" and "not technical" enough, which in Silicon Valley is code for she's hard to work with and not that good at her job. My gender-injustice antennae perked up. By any objective measure, she was far less abrasive than several men who'd been promoted ahead of her recently. And it wasn't at all clear from their performance or educational background or work experience why the men who'd been promoted ahead of her were any more "technical" than she was.

Then Sally learned that Ned was going to be promoted ahead of her. Ned had accomplished less than Sally at the company. When Sally asked why she wasn't being promoted and Ned was, Bob again harped on the "abrasive" issue, since he couldn't point to any results to explain his decision. To Sally, her boss's rationale for promoting Ned over her seemed so obviously unfair that she was wondering if she'd missed something. When I told her no, it's not you, there's real gender bias here, she was visibly relieved. She could stop blaming herself.

In my next meeting with Bob, I mentioned an executive at the company who'd been promoted recently. I mentioned how aggressive this guy could be. "I know," Bob said. "He is a real asshole. But he has to be to get the job done."

I'd set a trap and Bob stepped right into it.

"What about Sally?" I asked. "You told her she wasn't getting promoted because she was too aggressive. Doesn't she have to be just as aggressive as him to get the job done? Aren't you putting her in a kind of catch-22?"

"She just needs to work on her executive presence."

"In my experience that is code for 'She needs to be a man.' She is not a man. But she's damn good at her job."

"I know her team loves her. She's like a mother hen—"

I held up my hand. "Bob, stop right there!"

"What?" he asked, all innocent confusion. But I sensed a glimmer of self-awareness behind this facade.

"Think about what you just said. You would never refer to a man who is loved by his team as a mother hen unless you were trying to insult him." Bob opened his mouth, but I knew what he was going to say so I said it for him. "And you wouldn't refer to him as a father rooster either."

"Oh, come on, Kim, don't be so oversensitive!" Now he was bullying me just a little bit, trying to throw a gender stereotype my way, in hopes I would back off. I wasn't going to, in part because one of my jobs there was to help the executives do a better job hiring and promoting senior women. They were paying me to push them on these issues. So I did.

"You have two problems here," I said, "One is that you don't even notice your own biases—inconsistencies and double standards. That's causing you to skew your decision-making. Two is that if you keep talking that way, calling women mother hens or oversensitive or abrasive, not only will you promote the wrong people, you are going to wind up in hot water."

"Look. I've promoted everyone I'm allowed to promote," Bob said, now defensive. "If I'd promoted Sally ahead of Ned, he would have gone apeshit."

"And if she'd gone apeshit, you'd have dinged her for being hysterical or executive presence or being abrasive or some bullshit. Yet you're rewarding Ned for his bad behavior."

"He would've quit. Sally won't."

"How do you know?"

"She is so loyal."

"And you are going to punish her for her loyalty?! And promote someone who hasn't accomplished as much as she has and hasn't proven his loyalty just because he'll go apeshit if you don't? Isn't that kind of f'ed-up?"

Bob sighed. "Look, I'll promote her if you can get the CEO to give me permission. I've asked, and he shut me down. He doesn't want too many promotions this year. Go talk to him."

The CEO knew Sally's work and agreed she should've been promoted. Even before I brought it up, he called BS on the "too aggressive" feedback for Sally. Prior to this, Kieran Snyder had written an article in *Fortune* about how high-achieving men and women are described in performance reviews; the same attributes are used to justify punishing women and rewarding men. This article had struck a nerve at the company—an email thread about it was 100 conversations deep. The CEO told me that after he'd read the article he'd looked through the recent performance reviews and noticed not a single instance where a man was called "too aggressive," but women frequently were. The CEO mentioned the same superaggressive executive I'd brought up with Bob. "The whole thing is so obvious, it's ridiculous," the CEO said.

He got it. I felt gratified.

"So what are you going to do?" I asked.

His shoulders sagged a little bit as he told me that his first impulse was to order Bob to promote Sally. But that would go against his management philosophy. He couldn't tell his people whom to promote and not promote.

I agreed wholeheartedly with this philosophy. "No, you can't tell Bob how to manage his team. But what if you give him another VP promotion slot?"

"If I give Bob another promotion slot, it still won't go to Sally. He's already decided that Trey is next. And then if we create that extra VP slot for Bob, then everyone else will demand one and we will have too many VPs."

It was one of the most frustrating moments of my career. Here was a CEO who cared about creating an equitable work environment. But telling Bob whom to promote would go against a management philosophy we both shared. Telling people what to do doesn't work. A promotion committee might have helped, but, since all the senior product and engineering leaders were men, it might have just reinforced the bias. I didn't yet know to recommend bias busters or bias quantification to him. Indeed, it was this moment that prompted me to come up with ideas such as the ones outlined in chapter 6, so that the next time I was advising a CEO in this man's shoes I'd know what to recommend.

Sally ended up quitting without even lining up another job first. It was an agonizing decision. She wanted to stay for the sake of the women who worked for and around her. But it seemed futile. Women progressed to a certain level at this company and then their careers stalled. Staying in a situation that would make her bitter or cynical wasn't going to help anyone—Sally or any other woman at the company. Leaving would at least signal to Sally's women colleagues that they didn't have to put up with a culture that treats women unfairly. I told her she was making the right decision. I'd worked with another senior tech exec who'd spent 30 years battling this same kind of BS at her company. I'll never forget the hard edge of bitterness that sometimes turned into depression.

It was a real shame. Sally didn't want to leave. The CEO tried to convince her to stay. As did her team, who loved having her as their boss. It was frustrating for everyone and confounding for many of the company's leaders. They believed they were a meritocracy, denying forcefully the idea that bias was marring their promotion decisions. They couldn't understand why they were not able to retain a great leader such as Sally.

As intended, the women Sally wanted to stand up for got the message. Several of them, discouraged by Sally's shabby treatment, immediately started looking for new jobs. Several years later, I would wind up on calls with senior people who'd left that company. Losing Sally, they'd told me, had not only hurt the company's ability to retain top employees but also to recruit the best candidates to take their places.

A few months later, an even-faster-growing tech company offered Sally a VP-level job. A number of people, both men and women, who'd loved working with Sally followed her to this new company. She did well and quickly became the chief product officer there. That company went on to be one of the most successful in Silicon Valley. Odds are high you have used their product this week, if not within the past few hours. And Ned? He went on to have a perfectly respectable career, but had nothing like Sally's meteoric rise.

In the end, Sally got the last laugh. Some might say she's proof that the system works just fine. Company A didn't value her properly so she picked up and found a job at Company B. But for every success story such as Sally, there are countless other women throughout corporate America whose careers stalled after they were tagged as "abrasive," "not technical enough," or "lacking executive presence." Countless women have been steered into less prestigious roles while men were fast-tracked into running the high-paying profit centers.

To me, Sally's astronomical success is a reflection of how flawed and dysfunctional our system is. In a healthier environment, companies would have better systems in place to retain executives like Sally rather than let them walk out the door because they haven't figured out how to treat underrepresented people fairly.

THE PROBLEM OF SUPERMAJORITIES

Oblivious Exclusion occurs when people in an overrepresented super-majority allow unconscious biases and/or prejudices to impact both day-to-day interactions and also important decisions—hiring, promotion, performance reviews, and the like. Because they value collaboration, they have often put guardrails in place to prevent bullying. Harassment would be met with swift consequences in this kind of environment. But people in the supermajority deny, vehemently, that discrimination is happening.

People in the overrepresented supermajority may well think of themselves as inclusive and collaborative. They do not *intend* to degrade or silence or discriminate against people who are underrepresented. It's more like what happens when a group of hikers passes a lone hiker on a narrow trail. The group doesn't set out to push that solo hiker to the side of the trail, but somehow, unless the group is communicating well and taking active measures to be considerate, chances are good that lone hiker ends up standing in a patch of poison oak as the group passes by, talking and laughing, waving in a friendly way, unaware they've just shoved someone aside.

HOW TO BECOME LESS OBLIVIOUS

If your organization is characterized by Oblivious Exclusion, you're part of the way to Just Work already, but your checklist looks very different than it does for those struggling with Self-Righteous Shaming. You've got to focus on doing the things you need to do to create a culture in which everyone respects individuality.

If you're the leader, the fails here may feel especially discouraging. You have worked hard to avoid the worst kinds of things that happen. You did it because you care. You don't think of yourself as biased or prejudiced. It's hard for you to imagine that your organization is discriminatory. Which is the problem. You are all about good intentions, not hard questions. You are looking at the organization you wish you had, not the one you have. You need help understanding what's really going on around you. It's time to invest in and trust your bias quantifiers and interrupters. Make sure your company's code of conduct is comprehensive and consistently enforced. These actions may not solve every problem, but they will allow you to begin to chart your own course.

RESPECT INDIVIDUALITY: YOU'VE GOT SOME WORK TO DO

- ☐ Bias interruption is a norm

- ☐ Code of conduct is well understood

- ☐ Bias quantifiers are built into routine business processes

COLLABORATE, DON'T COERCE: YOU'VE MADE SOME PROGRESS

- ☑ There are consequences for bullying

- ☑ Checks and balances are structured

- ☑ Trusted reporting mechanisms are in place

- ☑ Culture of consent is understood

11

JUST WORK

A Moment for Optimism

It's inspiring to think about how often throughout history impossible dreams have become expected realities. Monumental shifts in history have, over and over, arisen from the efforts of millions struggling against a common oppressive system. Many couldn't imagine that slavery would ever be abolished after hundreds of years of the institution. Yet it was, thanks to the brave efforts of abolitionists such as Frederick Douglass, Harriet Tubman, and thousands of slaves willing to risk their lives on the Underground Railroad. Some white upstanders and leaders helped out along the way, too.

A decade ago, it seemed impossible that gay people would gain the right to express their love and commitment through marriage. Many who advocated for gay marriage felt it was a long shot, but they pushed for it anyway. Look at the results: what seemed impossible a few short years ago has today become commonplace.

#BlackLivesMatter, LGBTQIA, and #MeToo activists have laid bare the dynamics of injustice and the systems that reinforce them. These systems are present right here, right now, and they harm *all* of us. As Dr. Martin Luther King Jr. wrote in his "Letter from Birmingham Jail" in 1963, "Injustice anywhere is a threat to justice everywhere. We are caught in an inescapable network of mutuality, tied in a single garment of destiny. Whatever affects one directly, affects all indirectly."[1]

When we learn to recognize how the dynamics of bias, prejudice, bullying, discrimination, harassment, and physical violations operate in similar ways for different people, we can unite in interrupting them and make the workplace—and, indeed, the world—more just. This growing understanding of our interconnectedness is reason for optimism. In June 2020, West Dakota and Merrie Cherry, two drag queens in Brooklyn, addressed a painful reality: because Black transgender people are disproportionately the victims of police violence, attending demonstrations against police killings was especially dangerous for them. They discussed how they would feel more safe at a silent rally, like the one the NAACP organized in 1917, when 10,000 people dressed in white marched down Fifth Avenue in New York to demand an end to violence against Black people. The two drag queens decided to organize a silent rally. Two weeks later, 15,000 people wearing white gathered in Brooklyn to assert that Black trans lives matter. The organizers were stunned. They were part of such a small minority. Why did so many people show up? As one person interviewed explained, "If one goes down, we all go down—and I'm not going nowhere."[2]

This broad awareness and unity can lead to fundamental change. However, change will not happen without a conscious, proactive effort—both external and internal. If we are going to achieve Just Work, we are going to have to reform the systems we have created that reinforce injustice. And we are going to have to look within. When we try to blame "other people" for our own shortcomings, when we notice the injustice in others but not in ourselves, we are retreating into denial rather than taking appropriate steps to create justice.

We must also not retreat into denial about the uncomfortable truth that many people are still committed to preserving an unjust status quo, and are working energetically to impose their prejudiced beliefs on others. I ignored that some people believe that rape is morally acceptable until I was forced to confront this sickening notion at work. I would like to imagine that nobody *really* believes that white people are superior to all others. But one of the most painful reckonings of 2016 to 2020 was the extent to which attitudes that too many of us had dismissed as unconscious bias were revealed to be conscious prejudices that were being used to justify discriminatory policies. As they have throughout history, unscrupulous leaders were willing to prey on these prejudices to gain power by exploiting people's fears. Today is no different. If we are to combat injustice, we must take a stand against such cynical manipulations and challenge bias, prejudice, bullying, harassment, discrimination, and physical violations wherever we encounter them.

At the same time, we must always remember in our fight for justice that the way we treat people—even those whose prejudices we reject—*shouldn't contradict our own values*. Trying to coerce others into thinking the way we do will not work, and it will corrupt us. So will pretending we all agree when we do not. Refusing to engage with people with whom we disagree may avoid small short-term arguments, but it will lead to cataclysmic battles or irreconcilable differences if we wait too long.

REDEFINING WHAT IS POSSIBLE

Just Work requires transformational change, and transformational change requires everyone's buy-in. Only an organization-wide agreement that things are bad and likely to get worse will create the conditions for a shared commitment to making them better. It takes the entire community pulling together to build a new workplace. It can't be group against group, rank and file against management.

Be careful with your metaphors here. I like to think of this as a barn raising, a collaborative task undertaken for the common good. Avoid the terminology of warfare or "strong leaders." It's tempting to think of big changes as revolutions. But revolutions too often devour their own and create a new world in which the oppressed become the oppressor. Who wants that?

The goal is to eliminate oppression.

Although the system of Brutal Ineffectiveness is strong, when you look at the attitudes and behaviors that cause workplace injustice and respond to each in the way that most effectively interrupts power dynamics, you replace a vicious cycle with a virtuous cycle of Just Work, which is even stronger.

If you are a leader at this moment in history, you have a real opportunity to create the kind of workplace where people love their work and working together. But you must realize that if people on your team or at your company have suffered for years in an unjust environment, small changes, no matter how well-meaning, will be inadequate. If terrible things have happened, the instinct to bury awareness of them is profound: don't give in to it. Encourage people to tell their stories. Only when you know the details, even if they are painful, can you understand the dimensions of the problem.

Once you get started, you will inevitably get some things wrong and other things right. Don't let getting things wrong stop your progress. The keys to success here are *compassion* for everyone (including yourself), complete *candor* about the problems as you perceive them, and *action*. Things must change, and you can be a part of that change. True, the attitudes and behaviors that cause injustice get managed, not solved—that's why you are a manager. But your efforts to transform your workplace have an enormous payoff, both morally and practically: Just Work. When we design our organizational systems to appeal to the better angels of our nature, there's nothing human beings can't accomplish.

The only way to create an equitable environment is with active participation from everyone. Leaders can't do this alone, but if they have properly laid the groundwork described above, the gratitude and excitement such actions inspire can be contagious. As the fears and resentments and anxieties diminish, teams have much more intellectual and emotional energy for doing what it takes to Just Work.

LOVE AND JOY

In a commencement address to Wellesley's class of 2018, Tracy K. Smith, the 22nd poet laureate of the United States, offered a beautiful reminder that to achieve our ideals, we need to bring love and joy to the work.

> We tend to avoid that word [love] when we talk about politics, about demographics and policy, employing in its place a term like "tolerance." But tolerance is meager. Tolerance means I will make space for you beside me on some kind of imaginary national bus, then slide back over so you don't get too much of what I never stopped thinking is mine . . . Tolerance requires no cognitive shift.

But Love is a radical shift. Love tells me that your needs must be as important to me as mine are; that I can only truly honor and protect myself by honoring and protecting you . . . Love assures me that giving you what you need is a way of ministering to myself, to the Us that you and I together make . . .

In order to embrace Love, I must move past fear, past a fixation on my own claim to power or authority.[3]

We can anticipate the work we must do to create more just workplaces with excitement instead of the deep dread too many people bring to this task. And we can experience this love and joy in small ways, even with people we barely know. In a podcast I recorded recently with Tiffani Lee, a partner at the law firm Holland & Knight who leads its firmwide diversity and inclusion efforts, we talked about how much we love our fathers and also how we can't take the same approach to talking about racism that they did.

She mentioned that her father always told her there are three things people shouldn't talk about at work: race, religion, and politics. Now it was her job to talk about these things at work. I described how my father had advised me, "You are not a racist. Don't admit anything you did was racist!" But I could not live in accordance with my own Radical Candor philosophy if I couldn't admit it when I said or did something racist. I couldn't do right if I refused to notice what I was doing wrong.

So Tiffani and I decided to have a radically candid conversation about race. And you know what? The world did not come crashing down around our shoulders. In fact, we had a great conversation. We laughed a lot. It was a *joyful* conversation. I'm not claiming we changed the world or ended racism with our podcast. But if we all had more conversations like that, we could take one small step as individuals and one giant leap as humanity.

JUST WORK: THE LOOK AND FEEL

Have you ever worked someplace where everything felt more or less right? Where your boss was fair, your colleagues respectful, and the atmosphere conducive to doing your best work? Where there was no bias, prejudice, bullying, discrimination, harassment, physical violations, or at least very little? What was it like? Even if you've never had the experience, dream a little. What *would* it be like? I once had a job at This Company where I felt as if I could Just Work. Let me end with that story—and the lessons I've learned from it.

JUST WORK IS MORE
SUCCESSFUL—AND MORE FUN

In an environment where I felt secure, comfortable, and on an equal footing with my colleagues, I was able to do some of the best work of my life. I brought everything I had to that job. My team and I delivered on my promise to "defy the law of large numbers." We increased our revenue 10x while actually shrinking costs. We built an extremely profitable, fast-growing business. And we had a lot of fun doing it, building relationships that have endured for years. I loved my work and my team; we accomplished a great deal together.

JUSTICE IS BY DESIGN

The work environment at This Company was no accident.[4] This Company had optimized its organizational design to maximize effectiveness and innovation. That design yielded two great benefits: unstoppable business results *and* justice. There were two key principles: Collaborate and Respect Individuality.

COLLABORATE, DON'T COERCE

This Company's leaders believed that in the modern economy, command-and-control management just doesn't work that well. Bureaucracy is inefficient and kills innovation. Their insight was that

COLLABORATE

↑

↓

COERCE

"top-down" leadership, where worker bees are told what to do and how to think, stifles productivity and creativity. As a result, early on, This Company experimented with getting rid of managers altogether. That was a disaster; some hierarchy was necessary. But it didn't have to be a *dominance* hierarchy. This Company built something that *did* work: a *collaboration* hierarchy. There was still an organizational chart with a CEO, VPs, directors, managers, and so on. But in this model leaders at all levels were subject to real checks and balances that were baked into the company's management systems, processes, and organizational design.

The idea was to strip managers of traditional sources of power such as hiring, promotion, and salary decisions. This authority was given instead to teams, which were more likely to make better decisions. No leader at the company, not even the CEO, could hire people without putting them through a hiring process or promote people without putting them through a promotion process. Managers couldn't just pay bonuses or decide salaries unilaterally.

Nobody could coerce employees to do something they didn't want to do. I'll never forget watching an argument between one of the three most senior leaders at the company and a group of engineers working on a project. The executive proposed one approach. The team had a different idea. The executive couldn't convince them, so he suggested taking three or four of the hundreds of engineers working on the project to do a small skunkworks proof of concept for his idea. The team demurred. "If this were an ordinary company, I'd make you all do it my way!" exclaimed the executive. "I just want to try this idea out." The team explained again why the executive's idea wouldn't work and why it would be disruptive to have even three or four people pursuing it. He allowed himself to be overruled. And the team proved that they were right. Their product was a huge success.

This kind of behavior requires a high level of trust going both ways. That's what a good system does: it allows trust to thrive. Across the board, processes at This Company optimized for collaboration and discouraged coercion. When performance reviews came around, managers were rated by their employees as well as vice versa. When people did behave badly at This Company, which happened, they usually got extremely quick and clear feedback from their peers and their manager. And when the person behaving badly was the manager? Even before the manager's boss found out about and corrected this behavior, team members would abandon the manager. This Company made it easy for employees to switch teams without their manager's approval. Having a bully for a boss was an asshole tax that This Company felt nobody should have to pay.

The purpose of the management hierarchy was twofold: one, to ensure accountability; two, to provide a coaching and mentoring service to help employees grow. Managers were held accountable, but they were not given much "control" to get things done. They had to rely on building real relationships with each of their employees and on inspiring or persuading people to get things done.[5] Telling people what to do didn't work at This Company. In fact, using managerial authority to coerce others without allowing them to challenge you was one of the few ways you could get fired. Instead, everyone at This Company was expected to work collaboratively, and ideas came from any and all directions.

If speed is the cheetah's superpower, collaboration is humanity's superpower. When we work together, we use our full capacity to get more done collectively than we could ever dream of accomplishing as individuals. And when one person seeks to dominate others, there's no horror we can't sink to. For collaboration to be successful, therefore, we must design organizations that proactively combat coercive behaviors such as bullying, harassment, and arbitrary, ego-driven, fact-ignoring decision-making.[6]

RESPECT INDIVIDUALITY, DON'T DEMAND CONFORMITY

DEMAND CONFORMITY ⟷ **RESPECT INDIVIDUALITY**

The leaders at This Company also believed that diverse teams are more innovative. Therefore, it was important to respect the individuality of *all* employees. The CEO would exhort employees, "Challenge me! If I'm wrong, I want to know." It wasn't enough for the CEO to respect the individuality of the employees; the employees had to respect one another and him as well. Respecting individuality didn't mean letting people say whatever they wanted about anything. It didn't mean giving one person's ignorance and another's expertise equal weight. It also didn't mean that one had to allow for endless debate and argument. It did mean, though, truly listening to everyone without bias or prejudice. It meant remaining open to different points of view, as well as different and unexpected ways of being.

One of the most visible people at the company often wore large rabbit ears. Nobody objected to this. And nobody dismissed this person's skills because of the unusual choice in headgear. At most companies the employee in rabbit ears would have been ignored or mocked because our brains often automatically censor or dismiss the unexpected. But This Company was disciplined about making sure different points of view got heard and not allowing job titles or sartorial choices to be the filter for what got heard and what didn't. This Company went beyond merely tolerating differences between people. Instead, it took measures to create a culture that was not just open to disagreement and debate but actually made it a *duty* to dissent.

Those early days at This Company showed me that when individuals feel encouraged to bring their whole selves to work—when they feel confident they will be heard rather than shut down if they speak up—they do better work, and they work better together. Productivity increases, innovation flourishes, and things are much more fair. Everyone is happier. It becomes a virtuous cycle.

Admittedly, my own experience felt pretty utopian. I wondered how many other people had experienced Just Work, and I impulsively tweeted, "Did you ever have a job where there was almost no work-place injustice—minimal bias, no prejudice, no bullying, no discrim-ination, no harassment, no sexual assault? If so, will you tell me your story?? DM me!"

I expected the vast majority of the responses to be negative. And some were: "You mean has anyone worked solely for and with ro-bots?" or "Nope. The ACTUAL unicorn in the startup world lol." But 53 percent of the responses—more than half!—were affirma-tive, and my follow-up phone conversations with several of these strangers convinced me that I am not alone. Here are some things people told me:

"I think I work there, I'm very happy at my workplace."

"This is true of my experience with my first employer of
  10 years, as a corporate consultant no less. The key was the
  hiring criteria: smart and nice. This was a culture that really
  valued kindness."

"Got one now . . . I am trusted—that's at the center of it I think.
  To be trusted is so motivating."

"I have a story. It was in Michigan which given current news
  cycle might seem hard to believe but it had it all—transgender
  employees, promotions while pregnant. It was my best tech job
  ever and many of us are still friends."

"I had such an experience. They're ranked as Canada's #1 place
  to work. Learned a lot about how a work environment can be/
  what's possible. Experimentation over perfection. Curiosity
  over assumptions. Kindness over ego."

A PROCESS, NOT A DESTINATION

Here is the key thing to remember about Just Work. It's a process, not a destination. There's no natural stopping point. *You have to keep striving to achieve it*—monthly, weekly, even daily, hourly. Think of your workplace as being at the top of a steep hill. You have a spectacu-lar view, but you have to climb that hill every day to enjoy it. Or think of it as a building. If you hire good engineers and workers, use quality materials, and build a strong foundation, your building will last longer than if you don't. But even a well-made building can quickly become uninhabitable if you don't clean and maintain it. Those are not one-and-done chores but essential responsibilities that remain at the center of your mission every day. And even a beautiful, well-maintained building is a miserable place to be if everyone in it is behaving like an asshole.

Life is change. If you don't revisit and buttress the safeguards in place to make sure that coercion and conformity aren't creeping into the way people work together, then workplace injustice and the inefficiency that accompanies it will take over your culture. The aspects of human nature we are least proud of will always be pulling us away from efforts to collaborate and toward the instinct to coerce; away from respecting individuality and toward demanding conformity.[7] Daily attention is needed to resist these forces and keep your workplace just.

When I began this project, I thought I'd figured it all out and that I was sharing what I'd learned with others. I thought I was writing to help other people—especially young women at the start of their careers. But in fact, I was liberating myself. It took the process of writing this book for me to let go of the ball and chain of denial I'd been dragging behind me my entire life. Throwing it off was a relief like few I've ever known. The rewards of confronting my own silence and telling my stories have been enormous. Eliminating my own fears felt great; if my stories can help you eliminate yours, I'll feel even better.

IT'S SIMPLE, EVEN IF IT'S NOT EASY

When the problems seem insurmountable, return to these two core ideas: First, respect your colleagues for who they are. Don't demand that they conform to some preconceived idea you might have of who they "ought" to be. Second, collaborate with your colleagues. Don't try to dominate or coerce them.

In other words, Just Work!

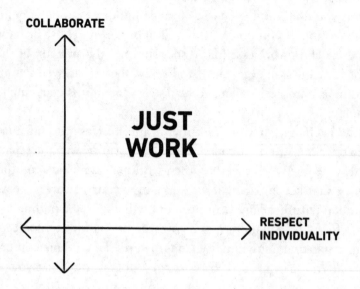

Acknowledgments

Writing a book is an act of collaboration, not a solitary endeavor. The fact that only my name is on the cover of this book reflects a myth that belies the reality. Many people collaborated in writing this book and launching it into the world.

My process is not a linear one, to say the least, and that can be frustrating—at times infuriating, I'm told—to my collaborators. I am deeply grateful to them for sticking with me throughout hundreds of thousands of words written and deleted, and especially for giant changes made after the last minute.

First, my family. My father wins the award for reading this book the most times—he read *six* different drafts. His enthusiasm kept me going when I wondered if I should give up. He gave me a lot to think about for each version, as well as detailed copy edits. As we are going through the final copy edits, my father is battling cancer, and extreme fatigue from his treatments. Yet still he catches more mistakes than anyone. Words cannot express my admiration and gratitude. My mother, my brother, my sister, my husband, and his uncle Jim Ottaway all read this book and their comments and thoughts made it immeasurably better. I could never have managed to write this book without our beloved nanny, Rosy Garcia. And when we were separated from Rosy by quarantine, my husband heroically stepped in to try to fill her shoes and also manage school from home—though we all missed Rosy terribly and were thrilled when she could return. My children helped in so many ways. Their very existence was inspiration to make the world more just. They contributed their common sense, put up with my absences and notable stress levels, and had a lot of good thoughts as to whether the subtitle should be "get it done" or "get sh*t done" or "don't take sh*t, get sh*t done."

Tim Bartlett, the editor (aka the boss) of this book, flew to California and perched on the landing between two rooms to help me begin to create order out of the chaos of my shitty first draft. And then he patiently edited and edited and edited as I wrote and abandoned draft after draft. It kept getting better, and I can promise him that if I could think in a more efficient way I'd do it, but this is the only way I seem to be able to work. Thank you, Tim, for putting up with me! And a huge thanks to the folks at St. Martin's Press who worked with Tim and me to bring this book to life. After reading an early version of the book, Alice Pfeifer sent me one of the most encouraging notes I've ever gotten, just when I needed it most. She kept Tim and me on track and made sure we made it to the finish line, more or less on time. Jennifer Fernandez, Jennifer Simington, and Alan Bradshaw gave this book the copyediting love it badly needed—twice! They improved literally every sentence. Laura Clark's enthusiasm for this project and guidance on how to reach each of its different audiences has always pushed me to clarify my thinking, and to have fun doing it. Gabi Gantz's sense of humor and wisdom keep publicity real—and keeping BS out of PR is indeed a rare and refreshing gift. Danielle Prielipp's drive and organization and spark make marketing fun. Ellis Levine made legal review a pleasure. And deep gratitude goes to my agent, Howard Yoon, who helped me refine the idea for this book when it was still pretty inchoate and who was unafraid to wade into a truly shitty first draft and tell me what was worth thinking more about and what was worth discarding.

I also want to extend my deepest gratitude to the team at Radical Candor: Brandi Neal, Nick Ditmore, Jason Rosoff, Amy Sandler, and Nora Wilcox. Each of them read this book and gave me invaluable insights. They also gave me the greatest gift of all: time. They did all the work of managing the company so I could just write. The candor coaches also read and commented on various drafts of this book, making it better each time. Huge thanks to Melissa Andrada, Becca Barish, Aaron Dimmock, Joe Dunn, Bina Martin, Farrah Mitra, Mike Pugh, and Stephanie Usry.

I think in images but I am no designer and cannot draw worth a damn, so collaboration is essential. Nick Ditmore was my constant companion throughout this book. He drew and redrew every graphic in this book hundreds of times, and each iteration helped me clarify my thinking.

I did not want to be limited by my lived experience here. A number of people offered their expertise and their life experiences to broaden my perspective. First Laura Eldridge, a women's health writer and activist, started talking to me about this project in November 2017. She assigned me reading each week. When I started writing I was woefully ignorant of most of the writers who eventually influenced this book. She read what I wrote each week. When I threw away an 80,000-word draft and started over she didn't seem even a little alarmed. She just kept reading, and we talked every Friday until the last version.

When I first started writing, the head of the wellness program at The Second City, Becca Barish, offered me some Radical Candor: "The way your generation feels about the word 'girl' is the way my generation feels about pronouns. You cannot write this book without taking sexual orientation and gender identity into account." She was correct, and it's hard not to feel ashamed that she had to tell me. But shame is not a productive emotion. Becca, as well as Chris Bartlett, the executive director at William Way LGBT Community Center, both read this book to be my heteronormative bias busters.

Chairman Mom founder Sarah Lacy also offered me some Radical Candor: I was too locked in my perspective as a privileged white woman. But she didn't just offer criticism; she offered help. She did a thorough edit of the book. And, knowing she shares white privilege, she also introduced me to Dr. A. Breeze Harper, co-founder of Critical Diversity Solutions.

Breeze became my bias buster extraordinaire, and also one of my favorite people. For over a year, Breeze read and re-read drafts I sent her, gave me articles and books to read, and was endlessly generous and fun to work with as she helped me confront problems I'd introduced into my manuscript. Breeze was so helpful that she inspired me to seek out other bias busters as well. I got invaluable insights for this book from Heather Caruso, assistant dean, Equity, Diversity, and Inclusion at UCLA Anderson School of Management, Dr. Jennifer Gomez, psychology professor at Wayne State University, Dr. Allyson Hobbs, professor of history at Stanford University, Annie Jean-Baptiste, head of product inclusion at Google, and Danae Sterental, founder of HereWe and lecturer at Stanford University for courses including Equity by Design. I am so deeply grateful to each of them!

One of the most important goals of this book is to give actionable advice to leaders. I wrote first from my own experience, about things I'd done that worked, and things I wished I'd done. But would other leaders find the advice I was giving helpful? Would they put any of these suggestions into practice? I wanted to make sure I was keeping it real. So, I turned to two of the most brilliant operating leaders I know. Shona Brown, the former SVP of Business Operations at Google, and Jared Smith, co-founder of Qualtrics, were both incredibly generous with their time. Shona read as I wrote, giving me advice every few weeks over the course of the last three years. And Jared devoured a later draft of the book; we spent an hour per chapter going over his comments and having lively conversations.

Because I wrote and rewrote *Just Work* several times, it was invaluable to bring in new editors to read it fresh. Naval Postgraduate School historian Dr. Zach Shore helped me work through some of the early ideas for this book, walking and talking. He also read an early version and was able to cut through a lot of clutter and offer a much cleaner way to think about its structure, as well as smoothing out the language in some rough patches. Will Dana, former managing editor at *Rolling Stone*, provided invaluable insight as he edited two different versions of the manuscript. He pushed me hard as a writer, and I learned so much from him. He was also endlessly patient with me on calls that invariably happened in airport waiting areas.

Then, as we entered quarantine, Alice Traux, a former *New Yorker* editor who had been invaluable to *Radical Candor*, took both me and the manuscript in hand. When I had talked to her about this project early on, it was Alice who flagged my own denial for me. And as she read, Alice attended to every word in every sentence, while at the same time nudging me (always with great kindness) toward several major revelations about myself. I had thought I'd understood my denial, but Alice helped me recognize that I had much further to go. *Just Work* is a much better book and I am a happier person thanks to Alice.

As Alice and I were editing, Dr. Lisa Schievelbein, founding executive director of the Center for Institutional Courage, read with an eye to my citations. Not only does Lisa have a keen eye for both structure and detail within the text, her knowledge of psychological research is encyclopedic. I have rarely seen anyone who knows how to get sh*t done faster and more joyfully than Lisa.

So many other people read and edited this book: Aileen Lee, Allison Kluger, Ann Poletti, Anne Libera, April Underwood, Barbara Chai, Beth Ann Kaminkow, Bethany Crystal, Caroline Reitz, Christine Howard, Christa Quarles, Clea Sarnquist, Dambisa Moyo, Dan Pink, Darren Walker, Deborah Gruenfeld, Diane Chaleff, Elizabeth Kim, Ellen Konar, Ellen Ray, Emily Procter, Esther Dyson, Evan Cohen, Françoise Brougher, Frank Yeary, Heather Caruso, Jane Penner, Jason Li, Jim Collier, Joanna Strober, John Maeda, Jorge Arteaga, Joshua Cohen, Julia Austin, Hope Blackley, Kamini Ramani, Kelly Leonard, Lauren Yeary, Leyla Seka, Lisa Krupicka, Meghan Olivia Warner, Mekka Okereke, Michael Schrage, Moira Paz, Moises Naim, Natalie Ray, Olga Narvskaia, Peter Reinhardt, Ruchi Sanghvi, Russ Laraway, Ryan Smith, Sanjay Khare, Steve Diamond, Sarah Kunst, Scott O'Neil, Sheryl Sandberg, Sukhinder Singh Cassidy, Susan Fowler, Tamar Nisbett, and Tiffani Lee were all generous with their time and radically candid with their praise and criticism. So grateful to each of them!

Thank you to the folks I met on Twitter who shared their stories of Just Work with me: Indu Khosla, Joshua Lewis, Miche Priest, Alexandria Procter, "RunningDin," Andrew Prasatya, Sunder Sarangan, Pierre Babineu, Jen Ross, Brandon Belvin, Maulik, Mika Bludell, Betty Carroll, and Tuli Skaist.

How could I incorporate comments from so many people? Google Documents was built for just that. It may seem silly to mention the people who made the tool I used to write this book. But specifically, I want to thank Alan Warren and Jude Flannery. When Alan and Jude and I worked together at Juice Software, we talked a lot about collaboration and document-centric chat. We didn't manage to make this idea a reality at Juice, but then Google hired us and they made it happen there. Though they have both left, the Google Docs team just keeps making the product better. This is a little object lesson in the miracle that is human collaboration. A spark of an idea flares and sputters out, only to be reignited in a different context, and then someone else carries the torch forward.

While we are on the topic of infrastructure, my husband, Andy, also gets some more credit. He came up with the idea of the she-shed in the backyard. Writing a book about gender injustice in one's bedroom is not ideal. Many thanks to Mike Turkington and Alex Cordrey for building me a room of my own, so necessary for a writer.

That is almost 2,000 words of thanks and I know I've forgotten people whom I care about. To whomever that is, blame my faulty brain, but know that I love you and I thank you.

Notes

INTRODUCTION

1   For one of the most accessible explanations of what privilege means, watch this two-minute video: https://twitter.com/bbcbitesize/status/1290969898517254145?s=19. Claudia Rankine's book *Just Us: An American Conversation* (Graywolf Press, 2020) has a fact check on page 26 on the origin of the phrase "white privilege," which is usually attributed to Peggy McIntosh. For a thorough discussion of the term's use prior to McIntosh, see Jacob Bennett, "White Privilege: A History of the Concept" (master's thesis, Georgia State University, 2012), https://Scholarworks.gsu.edu/history_theses/54. P. McIntosh, *White Privilege and Male Privilege: A Personal Account of Coming to See Correspondences Through Work in Women's Studies* (Wellesley, MA: Wellesley College, Center for Research on Women, 1988).

2   When I tell a story in the first person, I'm describing something that happened to me. When I tell a story in the third person, it's either a composite of things I've seen firsthand told abstractly for clarity and efficiency, or it's a story that someone I know told me. Except when I use a first and last name, all names in this book have been changed. I am not naming names because I want to focus on what we can learn from what happened and how we can apply the lessons to create more just workplaces everywhere. Also, I chose names that are common in the United States and do not reflect the cultural diversity of our country or our world. This is because when I chose a different set of names it prompted others to start guessing who was who and to read the wrong things into certain stories. I considered making all the names consistently Russian or Botswanan, but these choices were distracting for American readers.

3   Per Kate Abramson, "The term 'gaslighting' comes from the movie *Gaslight*, in which Gregory deliberately tries to make his spouse Paula lose her mind by manipulating her, her friends, and her physical environment." K. Abramson, "Turning up the lights on gaslighting," *Philosophical Perspectives* 28 (2014): 1–30.

4   K. Manne, *Down Girl: The Logic of Misogyny* (Oxford: Oxford University Press, 2018).

5   To those who haven't been in my situation, and even to those who have, my response may seem inexplicable. Yet repressing awareness of what is happening is a common psychological response to being betrayed by someone you trust. Psychologist Jennifer Freyd writes about this beautifully in her book *Betrayal Blindness*.

6   "Frot" is short for "frotteurism": to rub one's penis up against an unconsenting person. I thought what happened was unusual, shocking. But it turns out it's common enough that there is a word for it. Also known as the Princeton rub, it often refers to two men, not a man and a woman.

7   An excellent analysis of why can be found in Elsa Barkley Brown, "What has happened here: The politics of difference in women's history and feminist politics," *Feminist Studies* 18(2) (Summer 1992): 295–312.

8   When a person is underrepresented along more than one dimension, it's called intersectionality. Intersectionality is a way of understanding how different aspects of a person's social and political identities might combine to create unique modes of discrimination. It aims to broaden the agenda of the first waves of feminism, which largely focused on the experiences of white, middle-class women. K. C. Williams, "Mapping the margins: Intersectionality, identity politics, and violence against women of color," in *The Public Nature of Private Violence,* ed. M. A. Fineman and R. Mykitiuk (Abingdon, UK: Routledge, 1994), 93–118. To understand intersectionality, watch Kimberlé Crenshaw's TED Talk on the interconnectedness of race and gender (and many other axes of identity and oppression): https://www.ted.com/talks/kimberle_crenshaw_the_urgency_of_intersectionality?language=en.

9   Author Annie Jean-Baptiste outlines 12 dimensions along which people tend to be over- or underrepresented: age, race, ability, culture, socioeconomic status, religion, geography, sexual orientation, gender, education, ethnicity, and language. *Building for Everyone* (Hoboken, NJ: Wiley, 2020).

10   "Delivering through diversity," January 2018, https://www.mckinsey.com/~/media/mckinsey/business%20functions/organization/our%20insights/delivering%20through%20diversity/delivering-through-diversity_full-report.ashx.

11   A. Swanson, "The industries where personal connections matter the most in getting a job," *Wasington Post,* March 20, 2015, https://www.washingtonpost.com/news/wonk/wp/2015/03/20/the-industries-where-personal-connections-matter-the-most-in-getting-a-job/.

12   D. Rock and H. Grant, "Why diverse teams are smarter," *Harvard Business Review,* November 4, 2016, https://hbr.org/2016/11/why-diverse-teams-are-smarter.

13   "Diversity wins: How inclusion matters," May 2020, https://www.mckinsey.com/featured-insights/diversity-and-inclusion/diversity-wins-how-inclusion-matters.

14   K. Holmes, *Mismatch: How Inclusion Shapes Design (Simplicity: Design, Technology, Business, Life)* (Cambridge, MA: MIT Press, 2018). I've adopted the three principles of inclusive design described by the author Kat Holmes for this book: (1) *Recognize exclusion.* New opportunities that were easy or automatic for me may be impossible for others. Only when I recognize the way my privilege harms others can I lay it down. I don't want to be like those assholes who were born on third base and think they hit a triple. (2) *Learn from everyone.* I've sought out the perspectives of a wide range of people to make sure that this book is helpful for as many people as possible. (3) *Solve for one, extend to many.* The attitudes and behaviors that harmed me as a woman in the workplace are related, but not identical, to those that have caused injustice more broadly.

15   For a deeper analysis of how Black women are often robbed of their anger, see *Eloquent Rage: A Black Feminist Discovers Her Superpower* by Brittney Cooper.

16   "Women in the Workplace," Lean In online report, 2020, https://womenintheworkplace.com/.

17   L. Buchanan, Q. Bui, and J. K. Patel, "Black Lives Matter may be the largest movement in U.S. history," *New York Times,* July 3, 2020, https://www.nytimes.com/interactive/2020/07/03/us/george-floyd-protests-crowd-size.html.

18   As Kimberlé Crenshaw said in her TED talk, "where there's no name for a problem, you can't see a problem, and when you can't see a problem, you pretty much can't solve it." https://www.ted.com/talks/kimberle_crenshaw_the_urgency_of_intersectionality/transcript?language=en#t-521044.

PART ONE: THE ROOT CAUSES OF WORKPLACE INJUSTICE

1   Philosopher John Rawls defines justice as basic fairness. J. Rawls, *Justice as Fairness: A Restatement,* 2nd ed. (Cambridge, MA: Belknap Press of Harvard University Press, 2001).

2   For a rich exploration of bias, see Jennifer Eberhardt, *Biased: Uncovering the Hidden Prejudice That Shapes What We See, Think, and Do* (New York: Penguin Books, 2019).

3   Nobel Prize–winning psychologist Daniel Kahneman calls this the Thinking, Fast part of our minds. D. Kahneman, *Thinking, Fast and Slow* (New York: Farrar, Straus and Giroux, 2011).

4   Psychologist Gordon Allport described prejudice as "an attitude of favor or disfavor . . . related to an overgeneralized (and therefore erroneous) belief . . . The belief system has a way of slithering around to justify the more permanent attitude. The process is one of rationalization of the accommodation of beliefs to attitudes." G. W. Allport, *The Nature of Prejudice* (New York: Doubleday, 1958).

5   "What's the difference between conflict and bullying?," PACER, retrieved May 31, 2020, https://www.pacer.org/bullying/resources/questions-answered/conflict -vs-bullying.asp.

1: ROLES AND RESPONSIBILITIES

1   J. Freyd and P. Birrell, *Blind to Betrayal: Why We Fool Ourselves We Aren't Being Fooled* (Hoboken, NJ: Wiley, 2013).

2   M. Gomez, "Waitress discusses taking down man who groped her: 'We deal with a lot,'" *New York Times,* July 22, 2018, https://www.nytimes.com/2018/07/22/us /savannah-waitress-video.html.

2: FOR PEOPLE HARMED

1   C. Rankine, *Citizen: An American Lyric* (London: Penguin Books, 2015).

2   N. St. Fleur, "In the world of global gestures, the fist bump stands alone," NPR, July 19, 2014, https://www.npr.org/sections/goatsandsoda/2014/07/19/331809186 /in-the-world-of-global-gestures-the-fist-bump-stands-alone.

3   Research by the United Nations Development Programme indicates the global prevalence of gender bias: 91 percent of men and 86 percent of women exhibit one or more clear biases against gender equality in areas such as politics, economics, education, intimate-partner violence, and women's reproductive rights. Human Development Reports, retrieved May 31, 2020, http://hdr.undp.org/en/GSNI.

4   J. C. Williams and M. Multhaup, "For women and minorities to get ahead, managers must assign work fairly," *Harvard Business Review,* May 4, 2018, https://hbr.org/2018/03/for-women-and-minorities-to-get-ahead-managers-must -assign-work-fairly.

5   V. Jordan and A. Gordon-Reed, *Vernon Can Read! A Memoir* (New York: PublicAffairs, 2009).

6   R. Solnit, *Men Explain Things to Me* (Chicago: Haymarket Books, 2014).

7   Rankine, *Citizen.*

8   Always, "Always #LikeAGirl," YouTube, June 26, 2014, https://www.youtube .com/watch?v=XjJQBjWYDTs; and Disney Australia and New Zealand, "Planes clip—Disney—Head start clip," YouTube, July 30, 2013, https://www.youtube .com/watch?v=KM11r8MWYS8.

9   Asking the question will usually prompt an embarrassed "Oh, yes, of course." It is a little risky because it might prompt the response "Oh, but women are so much better at taking notes." Now you are out of bias and into prejudiced territory, and you want to use an "it" statement not an "I" statement, for instance, "It is someone else's turn" (read next section). Or the person might say something

bullying (read subsequent section), at which point you want a more dominant "you" statement: "You take the notes."

10 E. Crockett, "The amazing tool that women in the White House used to fight gender bias," *Vox*, September 14, 2016, https://www.vox.com/2016/9/14/12914370/White-house-obama-women-gender-bias-amplification.

11 J. Mayden (@jasonmayden), #curbsideministries (Instagram hashtag), https://www.instagram.com/explore/tags/curbsideministries/?hl=en.

12 J. Mayden (@jasonmayden), "Are you an accomplice or an ally?" (Instagram video), September 14, 2019, https://www.instagram.com/jasonmayden/tv/B2Z9z IQHwlV/?hl=nb.

13 D. J. Travis, J. Thorpe-Moscon, and C. McCluney, "Report: Emotional tax: How black women and men pay more at work and how leaders can take action," Catalyst, October 11, 2016, https://www.catalyst.org/research/emotional-tax-how -black-women-and-men-pay-more-at-work-and-how-leaders-can-take-action/.

14 Elaine Blair, Review of *Good and Mad* by Rebecca Traister and *Rage Becomes Her* by Soraya Chemaly, *New York Times*, September 27, 2018, https://www.nytimes .com/2018/09/27/books/review/rebecca-traister-good-and-mad-soraya-chemaly -rage-becomes-her.html.

15 E. Saslow, *Rising Out of Hatred: The Awakening of a Former White Nationalist* (New York: Knopf Doubleday, 2018).

16 Aspen Institute, *The Legacy of Justice Scalia with Justice Ruth Bader Ginsburg,* YouTube, August 4, 2017, https://www.youtube.com/watch?v=auYGdE28KIQ.

17 L. R. Goldberg, "The structure of phenotypic personality traits," *American Psychologist* 48(1) (1993): 26–34.

18 C. A. Murray and the Institute of Economic Affairs, *The Emerging British Underclass* (London: Institute of Economic Affairs, 1990).

19 G. Barbot de Villeneuve and R. L. Lawrence, *The Story of the Beauty and the Beast: The Original Classic French Fairytale* (United Kingdom: CreateSpace Independent Publishing Platform, 2014).

20 J. Mangold et al., *Walk the Line* (film) (Beverly Hills, CA: 20th Century Fox Home Entertainment, 2006).

21 Don't read this book: J. B. Peterson, *12 Rules for Life: An Antidote to Chaos.* Though some of the advice is good, you can get it elsewhere without choking on the misogyny. For example, "For stand up straight with your shoulders back" there's Amy Cuddy. For "Compare yourself to who you were yesterday, not to who someone else is today" there's Carol Dweck's *Mindset.* For thoughts on the dangers of different totalitarian systems like Fascism and Communism, there's *Hitler and Stalin* by Alan Bullock.

22 To understand what objectification means, read Martha Nussbaum and Rae Langton. Nussbaum identifies seven common manifestations of objectification: (1) treating people as tools for one's own purposes; (2) treating people as though they have no autonomy or right to it; (3) treating people as though they have no agency; (4) treating people as though they are interchangeable with other similar people or with tools; (5) not respecting a person's boundaries (i.e., touching a pregnant woman's stomach or the hair of a person of a different race); (6) treating people as though they can be owned, bought, or sold; (7) treating people as though they don't have feelings or as though their feelings don't matter. Langton adds three more: (8) treating people as though they are nothing more than a body part; (9) focusing exclusively on how a person looks; (10) treating people as though they can't or shouldn't speak. My business school interaction was mostly 8 and 9. Cheat sheet: E. Papadak, "Feminist perspectives on objectification," in *Stanford Encyclopedia of Philosophy Archive*, ed. Edward N. Zalta, Summer 2020 ed., https://plato.stanford.edu/archives/sum2020/entries/feminism-objectification/.

For deeper reading: M. C. Nussbaum, "Objectification," *Philosophy & Public Affairs* 24(4) (1995): 249–91; and R. Langton, *Sexual Solipsism: Philosophical Essays on Pornography and Objectification* (Oxford: Oxford University Press, 2013).

23 TED Talk, "Your body language may shape who you are," Amy Cuddy, YouTube, October 1, 2012, https://www.youtube.com/watch?v=Ks-_Mh1QhMc. There's been a lot of controversy surrounding this talk: K. Elsesser, "Power posing is back: Amy Cuddy successfully refutes criticism," *Forbes*, April 4, 2018, https://www.forbes.com/sites/kimelsesser/2018/04/03/power -posing-is-back-amy-cuddy-successfully-refutes-criticism/#17741a703b8e.

24 "What's the difference between conflict and bullying?," retrieved May 31, 2020, PACER, https://www.pacer.org/bullying/resources/questions-answered/conflict -vs-bullying.asp.

25 L. West, *Shrill* (New York: Hachette Books, 2017).

26 B. Brown, *Daring Greatly: How the Courage to Be Vulnerable Transforms the Way We Live, Love, Parent, and Lead* (New York: Gotham Books, 2012).

27 A. Wigglesworth, "Community organizer who trains police on bias injured by rubber bullet during protest," *Los Angeles Times*, June 6, 2020, https://www.latimes .com/california/story/2020-06-06/community-organizer-shot-by-rubber-bullet -during-protest.

28 For the formal psychological terms for these rationalization: J. M. Grohol, "15 common defense mechanisms," Psych Central, June 3, 2019, https://psychcentral.com/lib/15-common-defense-mechanisms/.

29 Denial.

30 Compartmentalization.

31 K. Manne, *Down Girl: The Logic of Misogyny* (Oxford: Oxford University Press, 2018).

32 Minimization.

33 Compartmentalization.

34 Intellectualization.

35 Intellectualization.

36 Management Leadership for Tomorrow, "Authenticity: Who You Are Is Non-Negotiable," Caroline Wanga, YouTube, April 29, 2020, https://www.youtube .com/watch?v=HAIiqOG4KBU.

37 T. Morrison, "A humanist view," May 30, 1975, https://www.mackenzian.com/wp -content/uploads/2014/07/Transcript_PortlandState_TMorrison.pdf.

38 A clear, funny, and painful explanation of how this works is in H. Gadsby (dir.), *Nanette,* Netflix, 2018, https://www.netflix.com/title/80233611.

39 From a conversation with Anne Libera, the author of *Funnier* (Evanston, IL: Northwestern University Press, forthcoming).

40 West, *Shrill.*

41 TEDx Talks, "I've lived as a man & a woman—here's what I learned, | Paula Stone Williams | TEDxMileHigh," YouTube, December 19, 2017, https://www.youtube .com/watch?v=lrYx7HaUlMY.

3: FOR OBSERVERS

1 Here is how Buber explained it (M. Buber and W. Kaufmann, *I and Thou* [New York: Charles Scribner's Sons, 1970]):

> When I confront a human being as my You and speak the basic word I-You to him, then he is no thing among things nor does he consist of things.
>
> He is no longer He or She, limited by other Hes and Shes, a dot in the world grid of space and time, nor a condition that can be experienced and described, a loose bundle of named qualities. Neighborless and seamless, he is You and

fills the firmament. Not as if there were nothing but he; but everything else lives in *his* light.

Even as a melody is not composed of tones, nor a verse of words, nor a statue of lines—one must pull and tear to turn a unity into a multiplicity—so it is with the human being to whom I say You. I can abstract from him graciousness; I have to do this again and again; but immediately he is no longer You.

2 "Bystander Resources," Hollaback!, retrieved June 3, 2020, https://www .ihollaback.org/bystander-resources/.

3 The term "moral grandstanding" was coined by the philosophers Brandon Warmke and Justin Tosi. S. B. Kaufman, "Are you a moral grandstander?," *Scientific American*, October 28, 2019, https://blogs.scientificamerican.com/beautiful-minds /are-you-a-moral-grandstander/.

4 J. Haidt and T. Rose-Stockwell, "The dark psychology of social networks," December 2019, *Atlantic*, https://amp.theatlantic.com/amp/article/600763/.

5 B. Resnick, "Moral grandstanding is making an argument just to boost your status. It's everywhere," *Vox*, November 27, 2019, https://www.vox.com/science -and-health/2019/11/27/20983814/moral-grandstanding-psychology.

6 B. M. Tappin and R. T. McKay, "The illusion of moral superiority," *Social Psychological and Personality Science* 8(6) (2017): 623–31.

7 D. Fosha, *The Transforming Power of Affect: A Model for Accelerated Change* (New York: Basic Books, 2000).

8 T. Morris, "(Un)learning Hollywood's civil rights movement: A scholar's critique," *Journal of African American Studies* 22(4) (2018): 407–19.

9 T. Cole, "The white-savior industrial complex," *Atlantic*, January 11, 2013, https://www.theatlantic.com/international/archive/2012/03/the -White-savior-industrial-complex/254843/.

10 K. Swisher, "Yes, Uber board member David Bonderman said women talk too much at an all-hands meeting about sexism at Uber," *Vox*, June 13, 2017, https://www.vox.com/2017/6/13/15795612/uber -board-member-david-bonderman-women-talk-too-much-sexism.

11 M. Isaac, *Super Pumped: The Battle for Uber* (New York: W. W. Norton, 2019).

12 K. Schwab, "John Maeda's new design problem: Tech's utter lack of diversity," August 19, 2016, *Fast Company*, https://www.fastcompany.com/3062981/john -maedas-next-design-problem-the-tech-industrys-utter-lack-of-diversity.

4: FOR PEOPLE WHO CAUSE HARM

1 D. Kahneman, *Thinking, Fast and Slow* (New York: Farrar, Straus and Giroux, 2011).

2 If you're a man working in an organization that is predominantly men or if you're white working in an organization that is predominantly white, and your whole team is reading this book together, be conscious of the possibility that a large number of people may be asking a small number of people to do them this favor and that it can start to feel overwhelming. You can also ask a man on the team, one who's more likely to notice gender bias than you are, or a white person on the team, one who's more likely to notice racial bias than you are. The same rationale applies for other kinds of biases.

3 In Dweck's words: "Believing that your qualities are carved in stone—the *fixed mindset*—creates an urgency to prove yourself over and over. If you have only a certain amount of intelligence, a certain personality, a certain moral character . . . it simply wouldn't do to look or feel deficient in these most basic characteristics." C. S. Dweck, *Mindset: The New Psychology of Success* (New York: Random House, 2006).

4   M. B. Eddy, *Science and Health: With Key to the Scriptures* (Boston: Christian Science Publishing Society, for the Trustees under the will of Mary Baker G. Eddy, 1930).

5   S. Malovany-Chevallier, C. Borde, and S. de Beauvoir, *The Second Sex* (New York: Knopf Doubleday, 2012).

6   Kahneman, *Thinking, Fast and Slow*.

7   Ibid.

8   There are two important problems to consider with dichotomize and degrade sexism. One is that it degrades women. Another is that it often erases Black women, Indigenous women, and other women of color. "Black women historians have largely refrained from an analysis of gender along the lines of the male/female dichotomy so prevalent among white feminists": Evelyn Brooks Higginbotham, "African-American Women's History and the Metalanguage of Race," *Signs* 17(2) (Winter 1992): 251–74.

9   S. Iñiguez, *In an Ideal Business: How the Ideas of 10 Female Philosophers Bring Value into the Workplace* (Berlin: Springer Nature, 2020).

10 G. Stulp, A. P. Buunk, T. V. Pollet, D. Nettle, and S. Verhulst, "Are human mating preferences with respect to height reflected in actual pairings?," *PLoS One* 8(1) (2013).

11 T. Rose, *The End of Average: How We Succeed in a World That Values Sameness* (New York: HarperCollins, 2016).

12 K. Elsesser, "Power posing is back: Amy Cuddy successfully refutes criticism," *Forbes*, April 4, 2018, https://www.forbes.com/sites/kimelsesser/2018/04/03/power -posing-is-back-amy-cuddy-successfully-refutes-criticism/#17741a703b8e.

13 A. Flower Horne, "How 'good intent' undermines diversity and inclusion," *The Bias*, September 21, 2017, https://thebias.com/2017/09/26/how -good-intent-undermines-diversity-and-inclusion/.

14 R. Ewing, "'That's crazy': Why you might want to rethink that word in your vocabulary," Penn Medicine News, September 27, 2018, https://www .pennmedicine.org/news/news-blog/2018/september/that-crazy-why-you-might -want-to-rethink-that-word-in-your-vocabulary.

15 Here we are at "the Bathroom Problem" again: J. Halberstam, *Female Masculinity* (Durham, NC: Duke University Press, 1998).

16 L. West, *Shrill* (New York: Hachette Books, 2017).

17 B. Mulligan, "Everything I hate about Justin Caldbeck's statement," Medium, September 8, 2017, https://medium.com/@mulligan/everything -i-hate-about-justin-caldbecks-statement-11b6c9cea07e.

18 R. J. DiAngelo, *White Fragility: Why It's So Hard for White People to Talk About Racism* (Boston: Beacon Press, 2018).

5: FOR LEADERS

1   B. Walsh, S. Jamison, and C. Walsh, *The Score Takes Care of Itself: My Philosophy of Leadership* (New York: Penguin, 2009).

2   C. Steele, *Whistling Vivaldi and Other Clues to How Stereotypes Affect Us* (New York: W. W. Norton, 2010).

3   F. Fontana, "The reasons women don't get the feedback they need," *Wall Street Journal*, October 12, 2019, https://www.wsj.com/articles/the-reasons -women-dont-get-the-feedback-they-need-11570872601; and S. Correll and C. Simard, "Research: Vague feedback is holding women back," *Harvard Business Review*, April 29, 2016, https://hbr.org/2016/04/research -vague-feedback-is-holding-women-back?mod=article_inline.

4   S. Levin, "Sexual harassment training may have reverse effect, research suggests," *Guardian*, May 2, 2016, https://www.theguardian.com/us-news/2016/may/02 /sexual-harassment-training-failing-women.

5   M. M. Duguid and M. C. Thomas-Hunt, "Condoning stereotyping? How awareness of stereotyping prevalence impacts expression of stereotypes," *Journal of Applied Psychology* 100(2) (2015): 343.

6   D. Kahneman, *Thinking, Fast and Slow* (New York: Farrar, Straus and Giroux, 2011).

7   J. Mayden (@jasonmayden), #curbsideministries (Instagram hashtag), https://www.instagram.com/explore/tags/curbsideministries/?hl=en.

8   Despite its roots in Viola Spolin's techniques, in 2020 The Second City, along with hundreds of other theater and arts institutions, had a reckoning with its own systemic racism and biases following the publication of open letters from its BIPOC (Black, Indigenous, people of color), Latino/a, and APIMEDA (Asian, Pacific Islander, Middle Eastern, Desi American) alumni. Second City leaders responded, "We are prepared to tear it all down and begin again," and held town halls to collect feedback before enacting an overhaul of its culture and company. As of this writing, The Second City has committed to making fundamental changes across the organization. When systemic injustice is present, as it is almost everywhere, the system needs to be overhauled. More in chapter 11.

9   Workplace Bullying Institute, *2017 Workplace Bullying Institute U.S. Workplace Bullying Survey,* 2017, https://workplacebullying.org/multi/pdf/2017/2017-WBI-US-Survey.pdf.

10   B. Sutton, "How to survive a jerk at work," *Wall Street Journal,* August 10, 2017, https://www.wsj.com/articles/how-to-survive-a-jerk-at-work-1502373529.

11   R. O'Donnell, "How Atlassian got rid of the 'brilliant jerk': A Q&A with Bek Chee, global head of talent," HR Dive, July 24, 2019, https://www.hrdive.com/news/how-atlassian-got-rid-of-the-brilliant-jerk-a-qa-with-bek-chee-global/559168/.

12   Kahneman, *Thinking, Fast and Slow.*

13   R. I. Sutton, *The No Asshole Rule: Building a Civilized Workplace and Surviving One That Isn't* (New York: Grand Central Publishing, 2007).

14   S. Cooper, "Comedian Sarah Cooper on how her Trump parodies came to be," *In Style,* July 10, 2020, https://www.instyle.com/news/sarah-cooper-essay-trump-impressions.

15   A. W. Woolley, C. F. Chabris, A. Pentland, N. Hashmi, and T. W. Malone, "Evidence for a collective intelligence factor in the performance of human groups," *Science* 330 (6004) (2010): 686–88.

16   C. Duhigg, *Smarter Faster Better: The Transformative Power of Real Productivity* (New York: Random House, 2016).

17   C. Ingraham, "Rich guys are most likely to have no idea what they're talking about, study suggests," *Washington Post,* April 26, 2019, https://www.washingtonpost.com/business/2019/04/26/rich-guys-are-most-likely-have-no-idea-what-theyre-talking-about-study-finds/?arc404=true.

18   J. Jerrim, P. Parker, and N. Shure, "Bullshitters. Who are they and what do we know about their lives?," ISA Institute of Labor Economics, April 2019, https://www.iza.org/publications/dp/12282/bullshitters-who-are-they-and-what-do-we-know-about-their-lives.

19   Woolley et al., "Evidence for a collective intelligence factor," 686–88; C. Duhigg, "What Google learned from its quest to build the perfect team," *New York Times,* February 25, 2016, https://www.nytimes.com/2016/02/28/magazine/what-google-learned-from-its-quest-to-build-the-perfect-team.html; and Duhigg, *Smarter Faster Better.*

20   There are a number of tools, and no doubt new ones will be developed after this book is published. Some current ones are www.gong.io and www.macro.io/.

21   R. Umoh, "Why Jeff Bezos makes Amazon execs read 6-page memos at the start of each meeting," CNBC, April 23, 2018, https://www.cnbc.com/2018/04/23/what-jeff-bezos-learned-from-requiring-6-page-memos-at-amazon.html.

22 K. Scott, *Radical Candor: Be a Kick-Ass Boss Without Losing Your Humanity,* rev. updated ed. (New York: St. Martin's Press, 2019).

PART TWO: CAUTION—POWER IMBALANCE

1 J. Dalberg, Lord Acton, *Acton-Creighton Correspondence,* 1887, Online Library of Liberty, https://oll.libertyfund.org/titles/acton-acton-creighton-correspondence.
2 D. Keltner, D. H. Gruenfeld, and C. Anderson, "Power, approach, and inhibition," *Psychological Review* 110(2) (2003).
3 C. M. Pearson, L. M. Andersson, and C. L. Porath, "Workplace incivility," in *Counterproductive Work Behavior: Investigations of Actors and Targets,* ed. S. Fox and P. E. Spector (Washington, D.C.: American Psychological Association, 2005), 177–200.
4 D. Keltner, *The Power Paradox: How We Gain and Lose Influence* (New York: Penguin, 2016).
5 M. Naim, *The End of Power: From Boardrooms to Battlefields and Churches to States, Why Being in Charge Isn't What It Used to Be* (New York: Basic Books, 2014).

6: A LEADER'S ROLE IN PREVENTING DISCRIMINATION AND VERBAL HARASSMENT

1 This book is not going to go into detail about legal definitions. I recommend the Equal Employment Opportunity Commission (EEOC) website for detailed information. The laws are well thought out and clear, even if they aren't always enforced. The legal definition of sex-based discrimination can be found here: "Sex-Based Discrimination," U.S. Equal Employment Opportunity Commission, retrieved May 31, 2020, https://www.eeoc.gov/sex-based-discrimination.
2 Many folks don't know that overheard communication can constitute harassment. In other words, if two people enjoy telling each other dirty jokes at work, and a third person can't help but overhear them, this can be considered harassment of the third person. The legal definition of harassment can be found here: "Harassment," U.S. Equal Employment Opportunity Commission, retrieved May 31, 2020, https://www.eeoc.gov/harassment.
3 Remember, Institutional Courage is a commitment by leadership to lead with integrity when addressing the institution's shortcomings. Courageous leaders reject the temptation to optimize for the institution's short-term financial interest; instead, they prioritize the respect and fair treatment of those who depend on the institution, particularly the most vulnerable, and in so doing invest in the institution's long-term success. J. J. Freyd and L. Schievelbein, "What is Institutional Courage," Center for Institutional Courage, May 5, 2020, https://www.institutionalcourage.org/.
4 J. M. Gómez and J. J. Freyd, "Institutional betrayal makes violence more toxic," *Register-Guard,* August 22, 2014, https://www.registerguard.com/article/20140822/OPINION/308229834.
5 I use the terms "underrepresented" and "overrepresented" rather than "minority" and "majority" throughout this book. Common usage for what I mean is "minority," but this word is inaccurate in most cases. For example, women are not a statistical minority. Yet in the workplace we tend to think of women as minorities. So women are an underrepresented majority in the workplace. White men are 30 percent of the U.S. population but in many workplaces are a majority. Therefore, white men are an overrepresented minority in industries such as tech and finance and in the leadership of companies across a wide range of industries. Conservatives are underrepresented in academia. An alternative commonly used in academic literature is the word "minoritized." I. E. Smith, "Minority vs. minoritized,"

Odyssey, October 17, 2019, https://www.theodysseyonline.com/minority-vs
-minoritize. Author Annie Jean-Baptiste outlines 12 dimensions along which people
tend to be over- or underrepresented: age, race, ability, culture, socioeconomic
status, religion, geography, sexual orientation, gender, education, ethnicity,
language. My experiences of underrepresentation mostly center around gender, but
I have tried to broaden the frame of this book beyond my lived experiences.

6   B. Sutton, "Teams as a double-edged sword," Bob Sutton Work Matters, October
15, 2006, https://bobsutton.typepad.com/my_weblog/2006/10/teams_as_a_doub
.html.

7   Many, especially those tired of working on bad teams, have pointed out that
dysfunctional teams make worse decisions than high-functioning teams. It is true
that high-functioning individuals make better decisions than lousy teams. But if the
high-functioning individual is the boss of the team, it's that person's job to build
a high-functioning team. So the low-functioning team is the boss's fault. Maybe
the boss in this case was a high-functioning individual contributor but is a low-
functioning boss. The solution is *not* to give that person more power. The solution
is to return that person to an individual-contributor role.

8   L. Miranda, *Hamilton: An American Musical* (New York: Atlantic Records, 2015),
MP3.

9   For a fantastic review of the academic literature that shows this over and over, read
the section "The preference for and prevalence of social homogeneity," in D. H.
Gruenfeld and L. Z. Tiedens, "Organizational preferences and their consequences,"
in *Handbook of Social Psychology,* ed. S. T. Fiske, D. T. Gilbert, and G. Lindzey
(Hoboken, NJ: John Wiley & Sons, 2010), 1252–87.

10 S. Beilock, "How diverse teams produce better outcomes," *Forbes,* April 4, 2019,
https://www.forbes.com/sites/sianbeilock/2019/04/04/how-diversity-leads-to
-better-outcomes/; D. Rock and H. Grant, "Why diverse teams are smarter,"
Harvard Business Review, November 4, 2016, https://hbr.org/2016/11/why
-diverse-teams-are-smarter; and E. Larson, "New research: Diversity + inclusion
= better decision making at work," *Forbes,* September 21, 2017, https://www
.forbes.com/sites/eriklarson/2017/09/21/new-research-diversity-inclusion-better
-decision-making-at-work/#7520fff14cbf.

11 "The state of Black women in corporate America, 2020," Lean In online report,
https://leanin.org/research/state-of-black-women-in-corporate-america/section
-1-representation.

12 D. Davis, "One of the only 4 Black Fortune 500 CEOs just stepped down—here
are the 3 that remain," *Business Insider,* July 21, 2020, https://www.businessinsider
.com/there-are-four-black-fortune-500-ceos-here-they-are-2020.

13 W. Kaufman, "How one college is closing the computer science gender gap," NPR,
May 1, 2013, https://www.npr.org/sections/alltechconsidered/2013/05/01/178810710
/How-One-College-Is-Closing-The-Tech-Gender-Gap.

14 For a macro (company/industry-level) perspective: S. L. Brown, K. M. Eisenhardt,
and S. I. Brown, *Competing on the Edge: Strategy as Structured Chaos*
(Cambridge, MA: Harvard Business School Press, 1998). For a micro (team-
level) perspective: R. Sutton and H. Rao, *Scaling Up Excellence: Getting to More
Without Settling for Less* (New York: Crown Business, 2014); D. Walsh, "Three
ways to lead more effective teams," Insights by Stanford Business, September 13,
2018, https://www.gsb.stanford.edu/insights/three-ways-lead-more-effective-teams;
A. Reynolds and D. Lewis, "The two traits of the best problem-solving teams,"
Harvard Business Review, April 2, 2018, https://hbr.org/2018/04/the-two-traits
-of-the-best-problem-solving-teams; D. Walsh, "What climbing expeditions tell
us about teamwork," Insights by Stanford Business, May 29, 2019, https://www

.gsb.stanford.edu/insights/what-climbing-expeditions-tell-us-about-teamwork; L. L. Thompson, *Making the Team: A Guide for Managers* (Upper Saddle River, NJ: Pearson Prentice Hall, 2004); and J. R. Hackman, *Groups That Work (and Those That Don't): Creating Conditions for Effective Teamwork* (Hoboken, NJ: Wiley, 1990).

15 M. James, "Culture fit vs. culture add: Why one term actually hurts diversity," *OV Blog*, May 9, 2018, https://openviewpartners.com/blog/culture-fit-vs-culture -add.

16 Canvas website, https://gocanvas.io/hire-better. OpenTable incorporated the feature "Candidate De-Identification" to remove any implicit bias by masking candidate profile information.

17 S. K. Johnson, D. R. Hekman, and E. T. Chan, "If there's only one woman in your candidate pool, there's statistically no chance she'll be hired," *Harvard Business Review*, April 26, 2016, https://hbr.org/2016/04/if-theres-only-one-woman-in-your -candidate-pool-theres-statistically-no-chance-shell-be-hired.

18 When women lack champions among senior leadership, they are less likely to seek a CEO career track. V. Fuhrmans, "Where are all the women CEOs?," *Wall Street Journal*, February 6, 2020, https://www.wsj.com/articles/why-so-few-ceos-are -women-you-can-have-a-seat-at-the-table-and-not-be-a-player-11581003276.

19 The data suggests she was not alone. A Boston Consulting Group study shows that when there are more women at the top, more younger women seek promotion. F. Taplett, R. Premo, M. Nekrasova, and M. Becker, "Closing the gender gap in sales leadership," Boston Consulting Group, November 21, 2019, https://www .bcg.com/publications/2019/closing-gender-gap-in-sales-leadership.aspx.

20 E. Larson, "3 best practices for high performance decision-making teams," *Forbes*, March 23, 2017, https://www.forbes.com/sites/eriklarson/2017/03/23/3-best -practices-for-high-performance-decision-making-teams.

21 S. Umoja Noble, *Algorithms of Oppression: How Search Engines Reinforce Racism* (New York: New York University Press, 2018); R. Benjamin, *Race After Technology: Abolitionist Tools for the New Jim Code* (Hoboken, NJ: Wiley, 2019); and C. O'Neil, *Weapons of Math Destruction: How Big Data Increases Inequality and Threatens Democracy* (New York: Crown, 2016).

22 C. Goldin and C. Rouse, "Orchestrating impartiality: The impact of 'blind' auditions on female musicians," *American Economic Review* 90(4) (2000): 715–41.

23 I am not sure I agree with the author's recommendation here to end blind auditions, but he makes points worth considering: A. Tommasini, "To make orchestras more diverse, end blind auditions," *New York Times*, July 16, 2020, https://www.nytimes.com/2020/07/16/arts/music/blind-auditions-orchestras-race .html.

24 D. Kahneman, *Thinking, Fast and Slow* (New York: Farrar, Straus and Giroux, 2011), 232.

25 James, "Culture fit vs. culture add."

26 M. Lewis, *The Undoing Project: A Friendship That Changed the World* (London: Penguin Books, 2017).

27 D. Speight, "Pattern recognition is the new insider trading," *Medium*, May 4, 2017, https://medium.com/village-capital/pattern-recognition-is-the-new -insider-trading-f051f49a00df.

28 D. Alba, "It'd be crazy if VC firms didn't fix their gender problem," *Wired*, May 21, 2015, https://www.wired.com/2015/05/ellen-pao-trial/.

29 B. Miller et al., *Moneyball* (film) (Culver City, CA: Sony Pictures Home Entertainment, 2012).

30 C. Rankine, *Just Us: An American Conversation* (Minneapolis: Graywolf Press, 2020), 20.

31 Bridgewater, "How the economic machine works," https://www.bridgewater.com/research-and-insights/how-the-economic-machine-works.

32 See *Just Giving: Why Philanthropy Is Failing Democracy and How It Can Do Better* by Rob Reich and *Winners Take All* by Anand Giridharadas.

33 J. M. Grohol, "How do you use your limited time & brain cycles?," Psych Central, July 8, 2018, https://psychcentral.com/blog/how-do-you-use-your-limited-time-brain-cycles/.

34 I'm not just choosing this example at random. I was working at one of Silicon Valley's hottest start-ups, and an employee was evicted from his apartment and was looking at living in his car because he couldn't find an apartment he could afford. My husband, working at one of the world's most admired tech firms, had an employee who lived in a truck in the company's parking lot.

35 L. Stahl, "Leading by example to close the gender pay gap," *60 Minutes*, April 15, 2018, https://www.cbsnews.com/news/salesforce-ceo-marc-benioff-leading-by-example-to-close-the-gender-pay-gap/.

36 P. Revoir, "John Humphrys and Jon Sopel slammed by bosses for joking about the gender pay gap," *The Sun*, January 11, 2018, https://www.thesun.co.uk/tvandshowbiz/5322720/bbc-gender-pay-gap-jokes-john-humphrys-jon-sopel/.

37 "Timeline: How the BBC gender pay story has unfolded," BBC News, June 29, 2018, https://www.bbc.com/news/entertainment-arts-42833551.

38 "BBC gender pay gap report 2019," BBC, retrieved June 9, 2020, http://downloads.bbc.co.uk/aboutthebbc/reports/reports/gender-pay-gap-2019.pdf.

39 K. Swisher, "Here I am to talk gender exclusion," pscp.tv, https://www.pscp.tv/w/1OdKrWeDwwvGX.

40 American Association of University Women, "The simple truth about the gender pay gap," Fall 2019 update, https://www.aauw.org/app/uploads/2020/02/Simple-Truth-Update-2019_v2-002.pdf.

41 National Partnership for Women and Families, "Quantifying America's gender wage gap by race/ethnicity," Fact Sheet, March 2020, https://www.nationalpartnership.org/our-work/resources/economic-justice/fair-pay/quantifying-americas-gender-wage-gap.pdf.

42 National Women's Law Center, "Wage gap costs Black women a staggering $946,120 over a 40-year career, NWLC new analysis shows," press release, August 22, 2019, https://nwlc.org/press-releases/the-wage-gap-costs-black-women-a-staggering-946120-over-a-40-year-career-nwlc-new-analysis-shows/.

43 M. DiTrolio, "Today, Black Women's Equal Pay Day, illustrates just how much Black women are undervalued and underpaid," *Marie Claire,* August 13, 2020, https://www.marieclaire.com/career-advice/a33588879/black-women-equal-pay-day-statistics/.

44 Safi Bahcall, *Loonshots* (New York: St. Martin's Press, 2019), 222.

45 T. Tarr, "By the numbers: What pay inequality looks like for women in tech," *Forbes*, April 4, 2018, https://www.forbes.com/sites/tanyatarr/2018/04/04/by-the-numbers-what-pay-inequality-looks-like-for-women-in-tech/#75a3511960b1.

46 Gender Bias Learning Project, retrieved June 9, 2020, https://genderbiasbingo.com/about-us/#.XuAVg_IpDs1.

47 J. W. Wieland, "Responsibility for strategic ignorance," *Synthese* 194(11) (2017): 4477–97; A. Bailey, "Phi 363: Race, gender, and the epistemologies of ignorance," 2014, Illinois State University, https://cdn.ymaws.com/www.apaonline.org/resource/resmgr/Inclusiveness_Syllabi/epistemologiesofignorance_ba.pdf; S. Sullivan and N. Tuana, *Race and Epistemologies of Ignorance* (Albany: State

University of New York Press, 2007); and L. McGoey, *The Unknowers: How Strategic Ignorance Rules the World* (London: Zed Books, 2019).

48 K. Abramson, "Turning up the lights on gaslighting," *Philosophical Perspectives* 28 (2014): 1–30.

49 Research backs up these anecdotal observations. Much more gains are made when two or more women are on the board/senior levels: M. Torchia, A. Calabrò, and M. Huse, "Women directors on corporate boards: From tokenism to critical mass," *Journal of Business Ethics* 102 (2011): 299–317.

50 J. Huang et al., McKinsey & Company, "Women in the Workplace 2019," October 15, 2019, https://www.mckinsey.com/featured-insights/gender-equality/women -in-the-workplace-2019.

51 A. C. Edmondson, *The Fearless Organization: Creating Psychological Safety in the Workplace for Learning, Innovation, and Growth* (Hoboken, NJ: Wiley, 2018).

52 M. Twohey and J. Kantor, *She Said: Breaking the Sexual Harassment Story That Helped Ignite a Movement* (New York: Penguin, 2019).

53 S. Fowler, "I wrote the Uber memo. This is how to end sexual harassment," *New York Times*, April 12, 2018, https://www.nytimes.com/2018/04/12/opinion/metoo -susan-fowler-forced-arbitration.html.

54 L. Guerin, "I'm not getting hired because I filed a lawsuit against my previous employer; is this retaliation?," Employment Law Firms, https://www .employmentlawfirms.com/resources/im-not-getting-hired-because-i-filed-a -lawsuit-against-m.

55 S. Cooney, "Microsoft won't make women settle sexual harassment cases privately anymore. Here's why that matters," *Time*, December 19, 2017, retrieved June 9, 2020, https://time.com/5071726/microsoft-sexual-harassment-forced-arbitration/.

56 D. Wakabayashi, "Uber eliminates forced arbitration for sexual misconduct claims," *New York Times*, May 15, 2018, https://www.nytimes.com/2018/05/15 /technology/uber-sex-misconduct.html; M. D. Dickey, "Google ends forced arbitration for employees," *TechCrunch*, February 21, 2019, https://techcrunch .com/2019/02/21/google-ends-forced-arbitration-for-employees/; and K. Wagner, "Facebook followed Uber and Google and is ending forced arbitration for sexual harassment cases," *Vox*, November 9, 2018, https://www.vox .com/2018/11/9/18081520/facebook-forced-arbitration-change-sexual -harassment-uber-google.

57 Fowler, "I wrote the Uber memo."

58 D. Moyo, *Tiger by the Tail* (London: Little, Brown Book Group, forthcoming, 2021).

59 F. Brougher, "The Pinterest paradox: Cupcakes and toxicity," Digital Diplomacy, August 11, 2020, https://medium.com/@francoise_93266/the-pinterest-paradox -cupcakes-and-toxicity-57ed6bd76960.

7: FOR PEOPLE HARMED AND UPSTANDERS

1 C. Cooper, "For women leaders, likability and success hardly go hand-in-hand," *Harvard Business Review*, April 30, 2013, https://hbr.org/2013/04/for-women -leaders-likability-a; P. Agarwal, "Not very likeable: Here is how bias is affecting women leaders," *Forbes*, October 23, 2018, https://www.forbes.com/sites/ pragyaagarwaleurope/2018/10/23/not-very-likeable-here-is-how-bias-is-affecting -women-leaders/#284fb888295f; and M. Cooper, "For women leaders, body language matters," Clayman Institute for Gender Research, November 15, 2010, https://gender.stanford.edu/news-publications/gender-news/women-leaders-body -language-matters.

2   O. Solon and S. Levin, "Top Silicon Valley investor resigns as allegation of sexual assault emerges," *Guardian*, July 3, 2017, https://www.theguardian.com/technology/2017/jul/03/silicon-valley-dave-mcclure-resigns-sexual-assault.

3   F. Brougher, "The Pinterest paradox: Cupcakes and toxicity," Digital Diplomacy, August 11, 2020, https://medium.com/@francoise_93266/the-pinterest-paradox-cupcakes-and-toxicity-57ed6bd76960.

4   K. Schwab, "Discrimination charges at Pinterest reveal a hidden Silicon Valley hiring problem," Fast Company, https://www.fastcompany.com/90523292/discrimination-charges-at-pinterest-reveal-a-hidden-silicon-valley-hiring-problem.

5   Yes, this did happen on Valentine's Day in real life. You can't make this stuff up.

6   K. Manne, Twitter post, August 13, 2020, https://twitter.com/kate_manne/status/1293917612733353985.

7   Lean In circles, retrieved June 21, 2020, https://leanin.org/circles; and Meetup, "Women's Social," retrieved June 21, 2020, https://www.meetup.com/topics/women/.

8   "Computer Science at Colgate University," retrieved June 21, 2020, https://www.collegefactual.com/colleges/colgate-university/academic-life/academic-majors/computer-information-sciences/computer-science/computer-science/. Here is how the numbers changed over time: 2013 (the year before Lauren founded WiCS): 1 female major, 14 male majors; 2016 (year after Lauren graduated): 11 female majors, 20 male majors. And the trend of roughly 30 percent female concentrators continues: 2017: 9 female majors, 24 male majors; 2018: 16 female majors, 31 male majors.

9   L. Respers France, "How Jessica Chastain got Octavia Spencer five times the pay," CNN, January 26, 2018, https://www.cnn.com/2018/01/26/entertainment/octavia-spencer-jessica-chastain-pay/index.html.

10 J. Bennett, "I'll share my salary information if you share yours," *New York Times*, January 9, 2020, https://www.nytimes.com/2020/01/09/style/women-salary-transparency.html.

11 There's much more to be said about this. I recommend reading the whole Twitter thread, which can be found here: Twitter, https://twitter.com/mekkaokereke/status/1027552459873378304?lang=en or by doing a Google search for "mekka okereke difficulty anchor twitter."

12 C. Thompson, *Coders: The Making of a New Tribe and the Remaking of the World* (New York: Penguin, 2020).

13 Remember the strategic defenses for silence in chapter 3? This chart illustrates one way to reason through them.

14 American Civil Liberties Union, retrieved June 21, 2020, https://www.aclu.org/know-your-rights/; MALDEF (Mexican American Legal Defense and Educational Fund), retrieved June 21, 2020, https://www.maldef.org/; NAACP Legal Defense and Educational Fund, retrieved June 21, 2020, https://www.naacpldf.org/about-us; National Center for Lesbian Rights, retrieved June 21, 2020, http://www.nclrights.org/forms/national-lgbt-legal-aid-forum/; National Immigration Law Center, retrieved June 21, 2020, https://www.nilc.org/; and NWLC Time's Up Legal Defense Fund, retrieved June 21, 2020, https://nwlc.org/times-up-legal-defense-fund/.

15 Most of the top law firms take on unpaid, or pro bono, work. Many retired lawyers take on pro bono cases. Search terms such as "legal aid near me" or "pro bono lawyers" on Google for leads.

16 Pennebaker, J. W. "Writing about emotional experiences as a therapeutic process." *Psychological Science* 8(3) (1997): 162–66.

17 S. Fowler, "I wrote the Uber memo. This is how to end sexual harassment," *New York Times*, April 12, 2018, https://www.nytimes.com/2018/04/12/opinion/metoo-susan-fowler-forced-arbitration.html.

18 J. J. Freyd and L. J. Schievelbein, "The Call to Courage," Center for Institutional Courage, May 5, 2020, https://www.institutionalcourage.org/the-call-to-courage.

19 B. Brown, *Rising Strong* (New York: Spiegel & Grau, 2015).

20 TED Talk, "The Power of Vulnerability | Brené Brown," YouTube, June 2010, https://www.ted.com/talks/brene_brown_the_power, _of_vulnerability#t-535103.

8: TOUCH

1   T. Willoughby, M. Good, P. J. Adachi, C. Hamza, and R. Tavernier, "Examining the link between adolescent brain development and risk taking from a social-developmental perspective," repr., *Brain and Cognition* 89 (2014): 70–78.

2   S. Lacy, "The bear's lair: The untold story of gender discrimination inside UC Berkeley's IT department," *Pando*, February 23, 2018, https://pando.com/2018/02/23/bears-lair-untold-story-systemic-gender-discrimination-inside-uc-berkeleys-it-department/.

3   Girl Scouts, "Reminder: She doesn't owe anyone a hug. Not even at the holidays," retrieved June 21, 2020, https://www.girlscouts.org/en/raising-girls/happy-and-healthy/happy/what-is-consent.html.

4   You may be wondering why I feel so strongly that it is wrong to refuse to meet with one gender but not such a big deal to shake hands with one gender. In fact, I believe that if he didn't shake women's hands, it would only be fair if he didn't shake men's hands either. But in this case the "don't touch if the person doesn't want to be touched" principle seemed more salient. I was initiating the touch, so it was my job to back off in a way that made him feel comfortable. Also, refusing to meet one-on-one disadvantages the people you're not meeting with more than refusing to shake their hand. However, if we'd been onstage and he refused to shake my hand but shook the hands of the men, that would have been problematic, though not as disgusting as having my hand slobbered on.

5   J. A. Bargh, P. Raymond, J. B. Pryor, and F. Strack, "Attractiveness of the underling: An automatic power → sex association and its consequences for sexual harassment and aggression," *Journal of Personality and Social Psychology* 68(5) (1995): 768–81.

6   D. Keltner, D. H. Gruenfeld, and C. Anderson, "Power, approach, and inhibition," *Psychological Review* 110(2) (2003).

7   R. F. Baumeister and S. R. Wotman, *Breaking Hearts: The Two Sides of Unrequited Love* (New York: Guilford Press, 1994).

8   L. Loofbourow, "The myth of the male bumbler," *The Week*, November 15, 2017, https://theweek.com/articles/737056/myth-male-bumbler.

9   D. Yaffe-Bellany, "McDonald's fires C.E.O. Steve Easterbrook after relationship with employee," *New York Times*, November 3, 2019, https://www.nytimes.com/2019/11/03/business/mcdonalds-ceo-fired-steve-easterbrook.html; and H. Haddon, "McDonald's fires CEO Steve Easterbrook over relationship with employee," *Wall Street Journal*, November 4, 2019, https://www.wsj.com/articles/mcdonalds-fires-ceo-steve-easterbrook-over-relationship-with-employee-11572816660.

10 D. Enrich and R. Abrams, "McDonald's sues former C.E.O., accusing him of lying and fraud," *New York Times*, August 10, 2020, https://www.nytimes.com/2020/08/10/business/mcdonalds-ceo-steve-easterbrook.html.

11 I got this statistic here: RAINN, "Scope of the problem: Statistics," https://www.rainn.org/statistics/scope-problem/. RAINN cites Department of Justice, Office of Justice Programs, Bureau of Justice Statistics, "Female victims of sexual violence, 1994–2010," 2013.

12 J. J. Freyd, "Be a good listener," University of Oregon, retrieved June 21, 2020, https://dynamic.uoregon.edu/jjf/disclosure/goodlistener.html.

13 J. J. Freyd, "Complete meeting guide: How to talk about sexual harassment,"

Lean In, retrieved June 21, 2020, https://leanin.org/meeting-guides/how-to-talk -about-sexual-harassment.

14 For a searing account of how women who are sexually assaulted are then silenced in ways both brutal and subtle by everyone around them, including the institutions they are part of and even the people who love them most, read *Notes on a Silencing* by Lacy Crawford.

15 M. R. Burt, "Cultural myths and supports for rape," *Journal of Personality and Social Psychology* 38(2) (1980): 217–30.

16 M. Angelou, "I did then what I knew how to do. Now that I know better, I do better," Good Reads, retrieved June 21, 2020, https://www.goodreads.com/quotes /9821-i-did-then-what-i-knew-how-to-do-now.

17 J. J. Freyd and L. J. Schievelbein, "The Call to Courage," Center for Institutional Courage, May 5, 2020, https://www.institutionalcourage.org/the-call-to-courage.

18 "MeToo Movement: The inception," Me Too, retrieved June 21, 2020, https:// metoomvmt.org.

19 J. Sanders, "8 reasons NOT to call your child's genitals 'pet' names," *HuffPost*, January 9, 2017, https://www.huffpost.com/entry/8-reasons-not-to-call-your -childs-genitals-pet-names_b_58743186e4b0eb9e49bfbec3?guccounter=1.

20 MeToo, retrieved June 22, 2020, https://metoomvmt.org/resources/.

21 "The Callisto survivor's guide," retrieved June 22, 2020, Callisto, https:// mycallisto.org/assets/docs/survivors-guide.pdf; and "Option B: Surviving abuse and sexual assault," Option B, retrieved June 22, 2020, https://optionb.org/category /abuse-and-sexual-assault.

22 E. Ensler, *The Apology* (New York: Bloomsbury, 2019).

23 You can read more about what this means and how to prepare and what to avoid doing before you have the exam here: "RAINN: What is a sexual assault forensic exam?," retrieved June 22, 2020, RAINN, https://www.rainn.org/articles/rape-kit.

24 Ted Talk, "#MeToo with Ashley Judd, Ronan Farrow, and Tarana Burke | Adam Grant," YouTube, April 2018, https://www.ted.com/talks/worklife_with_adam _grant_metoo_with_ashley_judd_ronan_farrow_and_tarana_burke?language=en.

25 M. Alexander, "My rapist apologized," *New York Times*, May 23, 2019, https:// www.nytimes.com/2019/05/23/opinion/abortion-legislation-rape.html.

26 L. Garrison, producer, "The Harvey Weinstein case, part 1" (audio podcast), *New York Times*, January 9, 2020, https://www.nytimes.com/2020/01/09 /podcasts/the-daily/harvey-weinstein-trial.html?showTranscript=1.

27 C. Miller, *Know My Name* (New York: Penguin, 2019).

28 M. Lipton, *Mean Men: The Perversion of America's Self-Made Man* (United States: Voussoir Press, 2017).

29 "Victims of sexual violence: Statistics," RAINN, retrieved June 22, 2020, https:// www.rainn.org/statistics/victims-sexual-violence.

30 R. E. Morgan and B. A. Oudekerk, "Criminal victimization, 2018," U.S. Department of Justice, September 2019, https://www.bjs.gov/content/pub/pdf/cv18.pdf.

31 Ted Talk, "The Reporting System That Sexual Assault Survivors Want | Jessica Ladd," YouTube, February 2016, https://www.ted.com/talks/jessica _ladd_the_reporting_system_that_sexual_assault_survivors_want#t-124098.

32 J. J. Freyd and A. M. Smidt, "So you want to address sexual harassment and assault in your organization? *Training* is not enough; *education* is necessary," *Journal of Trauma & Dissociation* 20(5) 2019: 489–94.

33 J. J. Freyd, "What is DARVO?," University of Oregon, retrieved June 22, 2020, https://dynamic.uoregon.edu/jjf/defineDARVO.html; and T. Parker and M. Stone, directors, *It's Called DARVO* (video file), 2019, https://southpark.cc.com/clips /gfwbrf/its-called-darvo.

34 CASBS Symposium, *Betrayal and Courage in the Age of #MeToo* (video file), 2019, https://www.youtube.com/watch?v=dRxyVMzyTG0.

35 C. P. Smith and J. J. Freyd, "Institutional Betrayal Questionnaire (IBQ)" and "Institutional Betrayal and Support Questionnaire (IBSQ)," University of Oregon, retrieved June 22, 2020, https://dynamic.uoregon.edu/jjf/institutionalbetrayal/ibq .html#ibsq.

36 Miller, *Know My Name.*

37 J. Krakauer, *Missoula: Rape and the Justice System in a College Town* (New York: Knopf Doubleday, 2015).

38 M. R. Burt, "Cultural myths and supports for rape," *Journal of Personality and Social Psychology* 38(2) (1980): 217–30.

39 L. Girand, "Ten competing sexual misconduct reporting 'solutions': Who benefits?," I'm With Them, 2019, https://www.imwiththem.org/perspectives /ten-competing-sexual-misconduct-reporting-solutions-who-benefits.

40 M. Twohey and J. Kantor, *She Said: Breaking the Sexual Harassment Story That Helped Ignite a Movement* (New York: Penguin, 2019).

41 S. Chira and C. Einhorn, "How tough is it to change a culture of harassment? Ask women at Ford," *New York Times*, December 19, 2017, https://www.nytimes .com/interactive/2017/12/19/us/ford-chicago-sexual-harassment.html.

42 Smith and Freyd, "Institutional Betrayal Questionnaire."

43 Many great consultants work in sexual violence prevention. The team I know best and admire enormously is that at the Center for Institutional Courage: Freyd and Schievelbein, "Call to Courage."

PART THREE: SYSTEMIC JUSTICE AND INJUSTICE

1 T. Noah, *Born a Crime* (New York: Random House, 2016), 19.

9: TWO BAD DYNAMICS

1 T. Morrison, *Song of Solomon* (New York: Knopf Doubleday, 2007).

2 S. de Beauvoir, *The Woman Destroyed* (New York: Pantheon, 1987).

3 It also wasn't an example of "misandry," the word that describes the theoretical opposite of misogyny, because Russ was not in reality on a slippery slope from my biased notions of men to physical violence. Such a dynamic is theoretically possible—a fictional imagining of what it might be like can be found in Naomi Alderman's novel *The Power.* Of course, men get raped by other men and also by women in the real world; for example, in prisons where women guards have enough power over prisoners to coerce them to have sex (see C. Friedersdorf, "The understudied female sexual predator," *Atlantic*, November 28, 2016, https:// www.theatlantic.com/science/archive/2016/11/the-understudied-female-sexual -predator/503492/). It is just as bad when a woman coerces a man to have sex as when a man coerces a woman to have sex. But 90 percent of adult victims of rape are women (see Department of Justice, Office of Justice Programs, Bureau of Justice Statistics, "Sexual Assault of Young Children as Reported to Law Enforcement," 2000, https://www.rainn.org/statistics/victims-sexual-violence). When a woman is raped, it is both an individual trauma and a collective trauma, part of a dynamic that happens over and over. Rape and domestic violence are not part of a dynamic that informs the way the majority of men navigate the world because it does not happen to them as often as it does to women.

4 K. Manne, *Down Girl: The Logic of Misogyny* (Oxford: Oxford University Press, 2018).

5 M. Fleming, "'Beautiful Girls' scribe Scott Rosenberg on a complicated legacy with Harvey Weinstein," *Deadline*, October 16, 2017, https://deadline.com/2017/10

/scott-rosenberg-harvey-weinstein-miramax-beautiful-girls-guilt-over-sexual-assault
-allegations-1202189525/.
6   D. Leonhardt, "The conspiracy of inaction on sexual abuse and harassment,"
    New York Times, November 5, 2017, https://www.nytimes.com/2017/11/05
    /opinion/sexual-harassment-weinstein-horace-mann.html.
7   Ibid.
8   I. X. Kendi, *How to Be an Antiracist* (New York: Random House, 2019).
9   Ibid.
10 L. King, "Black history as antiracist and non-racist," in *But I Don't See Color*
    (Rotterdam: SensePublishers, 2016), 63–79; J. Olsson, "Detour spotting for
    white antiracists," 1997, Racial Equity Tools, https://www.racialequitytools
    .org/resourcefiles/olson.pdf; and G. Hodson, "Being antiracist, not non-racist,"
    Psychology Today, January 20, 2016, https://www.psychologytoday.com/us/blog
    /without-prejudice/201601/being-anti-racist-not-non-racist.
11 Ted Talk, "The urgency of intersectionality | Kimberlé Crenshaw," TEDWomen2016,
    https://www.ted.com/talks/kimberle_crenshaw_the_urgency_of_intersectionality
    ?language=en.

10: RECOGNIZING DIFFERENT SYSTEMS OF INJUSTICE

1   K. Swisher, "Hitting the glass ceiling, suddenly, at Pinterest," *New York Times*,
    August 14, 2020, https://www.nytimes.com/2020/08/14/opinion/pinterest
    -discrimination-women.html.
2   B. Brown, "Brené on shame and accountability," Unlocking Us podcast, https://
    brenebrown.com/podcast/brene-on-shame-and-accountability/.
3   L. J. Schievelbein, "The relationship of shame-proneness to depression, self-
    compassion, and childhood maltreatment in a residential treatment population"
    (PhD diss., PGSP-Stanford PsyD Consortium, 2017, ProQuest Dissertations
    Publishing, publication no. 102'46945); and J. P. Tangney and R. L. Dearing, *Shame
    and Guilt* (New York: Guilford Press, 2002).
4   Brown, "Brené on shame and accountability."
5   B. Stevenson, *Just Mercy: A Story of Justice and Redemption* (New York: Spiegel
    & Grau, 2014), 290.
6   C. Rogers and R. E. Farson, *Active Listening* (Chicago: Industrial Relations Center,
    University of Chicago, 1957).
7   S. Foss and C. Griffin, "Beyond persuasion: A proposal for an invitational
    rhetoric," *Communication Monographs* 62(1) (1995): 2–18, https://doi.org
    /10.1080/03637759509376345.
8   Ibid., 179.
9   Interview with Stephen Dubner on his podcast: https://freakonomics.com/podcast
    /konnikova-biggest-bluff/.
10 E. Saslow, *Rising Out of Hatred: The Awakening of a Former White Nationalist*
    (New York: Knopf Doubleday, 2018).
11 NCORE Webinar Series, "Woke Olympics: Navigating a Culture of Social Justice
    Arrogance in the Context of Higher Education," YouTube, September 26, 2019,
    https://www.youtube.com/watch?v=0B_qPHYJsDY.
12 You can watch it here: Ibid.
13 Brown, "Brené on shame and accountability."
14 G. W. Allport, *The Nature of Prejudice*, 25th anniversary ed. (New York:
    Doubleday, 1958), 26.
15 M. W. Hughey, "The (dis)similarities of White racial identities: The conceptual
    framework of 'hegemonic Whiteness,'" *Ethnic and Racial Studies* 33(8) (2010):
    1289–309.
16 Allport, *The Nature of Prejudice*, 57.

11: JUST WORK

1 M. L. King, Jr., *Letter from Birmingham Jail* (San Francisco: Harper San Francisco, 1994).

2 A. Patil, "How a march for Black trans lives became a huge event," *New York Times*, June 15, 2020, https://www.nytimes.com/2020/06/15/nyregion/brooklyn -Black-trans-parade.html.

3 T. K. Smith, Wellesley's 140th Commencement Address, June 1, 2018, https:// www.wellesley.edu/events/commencement/archives/2018/commencementaddress.

4 And it wasn't just for everyone, nor did the justice last forever. But for a brief and shining moment I did get a glimpse of what it could be like, and it seems worth sharing that glimpse.

5 There is a lot more to say about how this worked and what caused it to stop working as well. I wrote more in chapter 6 about what, specifically, leaders can do to create just working environments. I believe two things made it stop working. One was the equity pay structure. It turned out that equity got distributed in an inequitable way. And the equity at This Company turned out to be more valuable than anyone expected. So the compensation system caused people to optimize for their compensation rather than for their collaborative work. Furthermore, some executives were simply corrupted by the huge sums of money they were making and began to behave as though they believed they had a right to abuse others. The second was that This Company optimized more for preventing coercion and did not focus as much as it needed to on getting proactive in preventing unconscious discrimination.

6 Point of clarification for readers who are engineers. When I talk about coercion, I mean the dictionary definition: the practice of compelling another party to act in an involuntary manner by use of threats or force. Coercion may involve inflicting physical pain/injury or psychological harm to enhance the credibility of a threat. I do not mean it in the sense of the word as used by the C/C++ or other programming languages in which "coercion" refers to a technique used to change the type interpretation of a variable. For example, the compiler will treat a character as an integer. It's OK to coerce your compiler to do what you want it to do. It is not OK to coerce another human being.

7 D. H. Gruenfeld and L. Z. Tiedens, "Organizational preferences and their consequences," in *Handbook of Social Psychology*, ed. S. T. Fiske, D. T. Gilbert, and G. Lindzey (Hoboken, NJ: John Wiley & Sons, 2010), 1252–87.

Index